GRANT'S CAMPAIGNS OF 1864 AND 1865

THE WILDERNESS AND
COLD HARBOR

GRANT'S CAMPAIGNS
OF
1864 AND 1865

THE WILDERNESS AND COLD HARBOR
(*May 3—June 3, 1864*)

BY

C. F. ATKINSON
Lieutenant, 1st Battalion City of London (Royal Fusiliers)

The Naval & Military Press Ltd

Published by

The Naval & Military Press Ltd
Unit 5 Riverside, Brambleside
Bellbrook Industrial Estate
Uckfield, East Sussex
TN22 1QQ England

Tel: +44 (0)1825 749494

www.naval-military-press.com
www.nmarchive.com

In reprinting in facsimile from the original, any imperfections are inevitably reproduced and the quality may fall short of modern type and cartographic standards.

PREFACE

The title of this work sufficiently explains its scope. It is an attempt to describe the field operations of the principal Union army, directed by Lieutenant-General Grant, from May 3 to June 3, 1864. The operations of other armies within the same theatre of war are dealt with in so far as Grant influenced them, and as they influenced the action of the main army, but no attempt has been made to study them in detail. The general title, "Grant's Campaigns of 1864 and 1865", expresses the Author's hope of an opportunity, at some future time, of describing the later phases of the struggle, in which the Army of the Potomac becomes the pivot of manœuvre for other armies, and of studying Grant as the director of a war of masses.

It will be noticed that Lee and Lee's army are, in these pages, specifically "the enemy". It does not seem desirable to attempt to study the operations of both sides at once. The rival armies even in the American Civil War differ so far in the characteristics of the leaders, the men they lead, and the people they represent, that to oscillate between the two camps is, unless one is fortified by a very thorough and exhaustive preliminary study of each separately, to understand neither. Confederate movements are therefore introduced only in so far as they are necessary to explain the Federal operations.

The chief authorities for the Federal operations in Virginia during May, 1864, are:—

Official Records of the Union and Confederate Armies, Series I., vol. xxxvi., parts 1, 2, and 3 (serial numbers 67, 68, and 69).

Personal Memoirs of U. S. Grant, vol. ii.

The Virginia Campaign of 1864-5 (Campaigns of the Civil War), by Major-General A. A. Humphreys, Chief-of-Staff of the Army of the Potomac, and later Commander of the II. Corps.

Papers of the Military Historical Society of Massachusetts, vol. iv. (The Wilderness and Cold Harbor), including contributions by Major-General Barlow, Colonel Lyman, Colonel Livermore, etc.

Battles and Leaders of the Civil War, vol. iv. Papers by General Grant, General Sigel, General Webb, General MacMahon, General W. F. Smith, etc., etc.

Campaigning with Grant, by Brigadier-General Horace Porter, of Grant's Staff.

Military History of U. S. Grant, vol. ii., by Brigadier-General Adam Badeau, Grant's military secretary.

Atlas accompanying the Official Records. These are, for the most part, field sketches made at the time to elucidate reports and dispatches, and to correct or to amplify the maps in use.

Detailed surveys made by Brevet Brig.-Gen. Michler in 1867.

As to the use made of these, I may say that I have consulted principally the field orders and correspondence of the Union commanders; secondly, Humphreys' work: thirdly, the official reports; and, for the rest, the additional evidence contained in the other volumes in the above list.

A word or two is to be said as to the sketch-maps accompanying the text. The topography is taken from the large scale plans prepared for the War Department by Brigadier-General N. Michler in 1867. On Michler's maps the whole of the works, Union and Confederate, then found in existence, and the abatis and "slashings", are shown in great detail. But on each field the works grew up by degrees: very often half of them were abandoned at the time the other half were constructed, and trees shown as abatis and slashing were upstanding on the 8th, the 10th, and the 12th of May. I have, therefore, tried to reconstruct the existing conditions in each case, a difficult and conjectural work, for mistakes in which, as for mistakes in the text, the surviving veterans who know the ground and the facts will, I venture to hope, call me to account. There is this much in favour of these maps, that no other account of the Wilderness Campaign with which I am acquainted does, as a matter of fact, attempt to give the information.

PREFACE

I have to thank the authorities of this Institution for their courtesy in affording me special facilities in respect of the books and maps in the library.

C. F. A.

ROYAL UNITED SERVICE
INSTITUTION, S.W.,
September, 1908.

CONTENTS

CHAPTER		PAGE
I.	Introductory	1
II.	Lieutenant-General Grant and the Plan of Operations for 1864	18
III.	The Soldiers and Officers of the Civil War	30
IV.	The Army of the Potomac	54
V.	The Strategy of the Virginian Campaigns	70
VI.	On the Rapidan	87
VII.	The 4th of May	112
VIII.	Battle of the Wilderness (1st Day, May 5)	128
IX.	Battle of the Wilderness (2nd Day, May 6)	165
X.	The 7th of May	208
XI.	The Night March to Spottsylvania and the Encounter Battle of May 8	227
XII.	Spottsylvania, Battle of May 10	246
XIII.	Spottsylvania, Battle of May 12	275
XVI.	Later Operations around Spottsylvania—The Richmond Raid	306
XV.	The Manœuvre of May 21	327
XVI.	North Anna, May 23-25	346
XVII.	The Minor Armies—The Army of the James—The Shenandoah Valley Campaign	362

CONTENTS

CHAPTER		PAGE
XVIII.	The Passage of the Pamunkey, May 26–27	391
XIX.	Totopotomoy Creek, May 28–30	407
XX.	Extending to Cold Harbor, May 31–June 2	422
XXI.	Cold Harbor, June 3	443

APPENDIX

Abbreviated Ordre de Bataille of the Army of the Potomac and of the Army of Northern Virginia ... 464

LIST OF MAPS

    I. Virginia
   II. Spottsylvania County
  III. Environs of Richmond

SKETCH MAPS

      I. The United States, 1861–5
     II. Railroad Communications in Virginia
    III. Positions on May 2, 1864
    IV. Positions Morning of May 5
     V. The Wilderness—Warren's Attack
    VI. The Wilderness—Positions at Nightfall, May 5
   VII. The Wilderness—Hancock's Attack, May 6
  VIII. The Wilderness, 11 a.m. to 2 p.m., May 6
    IX. The Wilderness—Reconstruction of the Union Right Wing at Nightfall, May 6
     X. The Encounter Battle of May 8
    XI. Spottsylvania, Battle of May 10
   XII. Upton's Attack on the Salient, May 10
  XIII. Hancock's Attack on the Salient, May 12
   XIV. Spottsylvania, Battle of May 12
    XV. Spottsylvania, Operations of May 14–21
   XVI. North Anna: Manœuvres of May 21 and 22
 XVII. North Anna, May 23, 24, and 25
XVIII. Operations in South-West Virginia
   XIX. Totopotomoy, Nightfall, May 30
   XX. Totopotomoy and Cold Harbor, June 1
   XXI. Cold Harbor, June 3

All maps at end of text.

THE WILDERNESS AND COLD HARBOR

CHAPTER I

INTRODUCTORY

At various dates between December 1860 and May 1861, eleven southern States of the Union passed "Acts of Secession" wherein, acting as the independent sovereign States they conceived themselves to be, they withdrew from the treaty obligations called the Constitution of the United States.

It is unnecessary to defend or to attack the theory upon which these States acted. The natural result of such a theory was that the States seceded, *i.e.* denounced the treaty, when their interests no longer coincided with those of their allies. The time and place of this step was, of course, a matter of expediency only, and on that ground, while it was still a debated political question, the secession movement was opposed by many of the best men of the South. But it occurred to very few to dispute the validity of an Act of Secession when once it was passed by the voice of the majority. To use a well-known phrase, the South was "solid" on the question of what were called States' Rights. Even on the question of slavery —which more than any other divided the South from the North—it would have been impossible to secure the practical unanimity of public opinion which alone enabled the Confederacy, poor and friendless as it remained to the end, to continue the struggle until the last glimmer of hope was gone, long after her commerce was ruined, the flower of the population killed and wounded, and the land made desolate.

The eleven sovereign States, then, decided to withdraw from the alliance, and in so doing they carried with them, of right, the loyal support and devotion of every citizen. The "States' Rights" idea was not merely a theory of constitutional lawyers. Of such the North possessed as many as the South, if not more. It was the weapon every Southerner had been taught to use, the weapon whereby to enforce his own political desires and to resist the enforcement of political desires contrary to his own, and the South, after threatening to use it, and finding threats unavailing, drew it in earnest.

The political crisis which called the weapon into employment turned upon the question of negro slavery. Discussion of the rights and wrongs of this does not fall within the province of a monograph on one campaign of the great Civil War. It was not the question at issue between the two sections.

But without it, the main question, the question of secession, could never have arisen, for it was inextricably interwoven with the whole commercial and social system of the South, and it was generally —perhaps too generally—understood that once the Northern States obtained the upper hand in the Federal councils, their first step would be to interfere with this, the most important of the domestic institutions of the South. Against such a contingency they held their weapon, the so-called right of secession, ready for use. Once the struggle had broken out, it is difficult and also immaterial to distinguish the contest for the institutions protected by the weapon and the contest for the weapon itself, at any rate, so far as concerns the motive forces of the South.*

In the North, on the other hand, there was no urgent need for political weapons to protect domestic institutions. Slavery had long since disappeared, by the mere fact that the North was principally a manufacturing, and not, like the South, an agricultural community. Nothing had as yet occurred to force the Northern population to make a critical investigation of the precise meaning of the Constitution, and its economic and social conditions, widely different from those in the South, naturally produced a different political outlook. Free intercommunication, industrial activity, and the absence of a caste of landed gentry, had as their main result homogeneity, and a Northern statesman, in the first days of the secession movement, defined the political faith of the Northern States—the faith

* In the North, slavery was not directly attacked by the government that controlled the armies until nearly two years had elapsed since the first shot.

which, not less than the faith of the seceding States, was able to move mountains — in one sentence, "I am not a Michigander, I am a citizen of the United States". On this issue—that the United States was, and should remain, one single nation—the North fought through four years of trial to final victory. Slavery, whether intolerable to the enlightenment of the age or not, was the one great power for disunion, and, by force of circumstances, the war against disunion eventually absorbed in itself the war against slavery.

Minor issues, such as the fiscal question between the manufacturing and protectionist North and the cotton-exporting, free trade South, it is not necessary to take into account. Such questions always arise and can generally be adjusted, but from the first it was evident that the larger questions were beyond adjustment and compromise.

There was no basis of an understanding. The South and North did not quarrel and fight over the same things, and when this is the case neither party can grasp, to use a common phrase, what the other is "driving at". Such is commonly the course of a quarrel between man and man. Transferring it to the national plane and admitting that the questions on which each encounters a stubborn and (from his point of view) stupid resistance, are precisely those to which he himself holds as to life itself, we may admit also the impossibility of compromise. It is not merely that naked force alone can decide. There are cases which, because force alone can decide them, are left undecided. "Secession" was not one of these. Each party was roused to the pitch of voluntarily using naked force, and of continuing to use it until the last opposition is crushed.

The moment for the secession of the Southern States came when their representatives ceased to have a sufficiently powerful voice in direction of the common destinies of the allied States. The inauguration of President Lincoln, the embodiment of the Northern spirit and idea, took place on March 4, 1861, and preliminary preparations having been in progress for some time, the Southern States individually left the Union and at once associated themselves as the "Confederate States of America". They chose as their President Jefferson Davis, lately a member of the Cabinet at Washington, and the foremost advocate of States' Rights. He was a soldier by education, had served as a colonel of Mississippi troops in the Mexican War, and had declined promotion to the rank of a general officer because the commission emanated from the President of the United States and not from the Governor of Mississippi. The capital was, provisionally, Montgomery in Alabama, and the government was organized upon the model of that from which they had just seceded—formally, that is, for the spirit was very different.

Trouble soon arose. The Union possessed military posts, forts, and customs houses within the seceded area, and the ground upon which these were built had been leased by the various states to the Federal government for purposes common to all the states constituting the Union.

These purposes ceased when the States chiefly affected withdrew from the bond of alliance, and they naturally sought to resume possession of their own territory. Most of these resumptions were effected peacefully, for it was useless for a post, say of fifty garrison gunners, to defy several thousand State militia, but in Pensacola harbour, Fort Pickens, in Charleston harbour, Fort Sumter, and in Hampton Roads, Fortress Monroe, to mention the principal instances, were strong enough to justify resistance should attack be attempted. The position of the Union officers in these forts was delicate in the extreme, torn as they were between their duty to the national flag, their fears of rashly provoking a civil war, and their personal views on the question of conscience at issue. But their suspense was ended when, on April 12, 1861, the batteries of the South Carolina militia, directed by a general officer of the new Confederate States Army, opened fire on Sumter.

The fort resisted long enough to satisfy the requirements of honour, and to provoke an instant outbreak of Union sentiment in the North. President Lincoln called for volunteers from the various States, and the situation being thus clearly defined as one of war, the "border" States refused to supply their contingents to the Federal army, seceded, and joined the Confederacy. Maryland, Missouri, and Kentucky were reclaimed for the Union, after more or less serious fighting, in the summer of 1861. Richmond became the capital, and Virginia and Tennessee became members--

INTRODUCTORY

Virginia practically the leading member—of the new nation it was sought to establish in the South.

The general character of the first year's operations was, in the West, conquest or securing of territory, and in the East a first unsuccessful attempt to respond to the cry of the Federal newspapers and people, "On to Richmond!" Missouri was secured for the Union by the prompt action of Captain (a few weeks later Major-General) Nathaniel Lyon. Kentucky made a feeble attempt at neutrality before she surrendered to her Northern destiny. Maryland was subdued, in so far as disunion sentiment prevailed and called for suppression, with no more serious fighting than a street riot in Baltimore, in which some Massachusetts militia were roughly handled by the mob. Thus in a few months from the fall of Fort Sumter the frontier between the Union states and the would-be Confederacy was drawn definitively along the Potomac and the southern edges of Kentucky and Missouri.* The N.W. part of Virginia, which was Northern in character and Union in sentiment, was overrun by Ohio and Indiana troops under Major-General McClellan, and soon afterwards became a State under the name of West Virginia.

It was in north-eastern Virginia that the main campaign was fought to the issue of a great battle. Unready as they were for campaigning, the Northern generals were quickly forced by

* The Union occupation of Kentucky was not, however, quite effective until the fall of Fort Donelson in February, 1862.

public opinion to take the offensive, with the result that their raw troops were defeated and practically routed in the first battle of Bull Run (July 21). After this nothing of importance took place in Virginia until each side had spent the winter and spring in welding the young and untrained volunteer troops into organized and disciplined brigades, divisions, and corps. In the West, by the time the Federal army in Virginia moved for the second time towards Richmond, Major-General U. S. Grant had forced the surrender of a large Confederate garrison at Fort Donelson (Kentucky), and, with the aid of Buell's army from the middle Ohio, had defeated the Confederate Western army in the bloody battle of Shiloh (April 6–7). Major-General Pope at the same time cleared south-eastern Missouri, and under great difficulties cut off and captured the garrison of New Madrid and Island No. 10 on the Mississippi, after which the Union forces, under the supreme direction of Major-General Halleck, converged on Corinth, Mississippi, of which, in May, they compelled the evacuation.

This practically closed the Federal offensive in the West for the time being, for General Braxton Bragg, the new commander-in-chief of the Confederates, then suddenly transferred the centre of gravity to Chattanooga and the upper Tennessee, using the Memphis and Charleston Railroad. Thenceforward the Tennessee and Mississippi campaigns are separate events, with little or no inter-relation, until late in 1863.

INTRODUCTORY

In the East, the Army of the Potomac, finely disciplined by McClellan and magnificently equipped, struck, not directly at Joseph Johnston's (soon to be Lee's) Confederate army near Manassas Junction, but at Richmond, being transported by sea to the Virginian peninsula, and there, after a somewhat dilatory siege, capturing Yorktown. From Yorktown McClellan made slow progress amidst great difficulties of climate and ground in this, the "Tidewater", section of Virginia. Johnston's army had of course long since come back to Richmond, and a very severe but indecisive battle was fought at Seven Pines (or Fair Oaks), a few miles east of Richmond, on May 30 and June 1. Johnston was wounded on the first day, and after the battle General Robert Edward Lee became commanding general of the Army of Northern Virginia.

From one reason or another, however, McClellan's assault on Richmond, carefully—his critics said over-carefully—planned, was never delivered. In the Valley of Virginia,[*] Stonewall Jackson had conducted a brilliant aggressive campaign which had inflicted heavy blows on detachments of Federal troops, and drawn to the Valley many more, for whom McClellan was, rightly or wrongly, clamouring to make sure of his enterprise against Lee and Richmond. Having successfully eluded the converging columns of his enemies, Jackson next secretly withdrew from the Valley to join Lee in a blow against McClellan.

[*] Or Shenandoah Valley. The "Valley of Virginia" included more than the actual basin of the Shenandoah.

10 CAMPAIGNS OF 1864 AND 1865

This led to the battle of Gaines's Mill, in which a corps (the V.) of McClellan's army, was after a magnificent defence driven off its ground, and McClellan's line of supply to White House, his centre of operations on the Pamunkey river, cut. Thus pressed, McClellan fought his way with success to a new centre of operations on the James, but the strain of these days exhausted his capacities for aggression, and Lee turned his attention elsewhither.

During the "Seven Days", as McClellan's fighting march to the James was called, another Federal army, in middle Virginia, made up of the forces that had been lately engaged in "trapping Jackson", and commanded by Pope, had begun to advance towards Gordonsville. A fresh campaign followed, marked by complete accord[*] between Jackson and Lee, and complete disaccord between McClellan, Pope, and the new general-in-chief at Washington, Halleck. The result of this was the second battle of Bull Run, in which Pope's motley[†] army and such of McClellan's troops as were involved in the catastrophe were hustled with heavy losses into the defences of Washington itself.

Lee's success gave the impetus for a general forward move of the Confederates all along the

---

[*] In the Seven Days this had by no means been the case.

[†] Pope's own army consisted of the I. Corps, formerly of the Army of the Potomac, of which McClellan had been more or less robbed, and two corps made up from the West Virginia and Valley troops that had fought Jackson. He had also the greater part of the Army of the Potomac, which was now withdrawn piecemeal from the James, and the IX. Corps under Burnside, drawn in from the N. Carolina coast.

line. In the West, Grant, now commanding since Halleck's promotion, was hard put to it to defend his conquests. In the centre Bragg's army advanced to the borders of Indiana and Ohio, and after an indecisive battle with Buell's Union army at Perryville, Kentucky, withdrew with spoils of war and Kentuckian recruits for the Confederate armies. In the East, Lee, using the Valley as his centre of operations, invaded Maryland, in the hope of terrorizing Pennsylvania and gaining over the Marylanders, many of whom were well affected to the Confederate cause. But McClellan, hastily reorganizing the disheartened troops in Washington, led them out, cautiously as usual, to fight Lee, and actually compelled his great antagonist to leave Maryland, after inflicting on him losses that he could ill spare in the bloody battle of the Antietam or Sharpsburg.

All along the line, then, the Confederate offensive had come to an end. The Southern armies had nowhere been decisively defeated, but they had to fall back, and in the same act the Federal offensive was renewed.

McClellan and Buell, magnificent organizers and disciplinarians, but over-cautious generals and dangerous politicians—so at any rate they were considered at Washington—were at this point removed, and replaced respectively by Burnside and Rosecrans. The former was a brave corps commander, as we shall see, but of all the generals who commanded in succession the much-enduring Army of the Potomac, he was the least successful. He flung his troops in vain against Lee's entrenchments at Fredericksburg, and gave place to Hooker, a brilliant subordinate, given to criticizing his superiors. Rosecrans was a soldier of great ability and restless energy, and he signalized his assumption of the command in Tennessee by fighting a two days' battle at Stone's River (Murfreesboro), as the result of which Bragg retired southward. Grant, further west, was confronted with enormous difficulties and hampered by a political subordinate. His objective was Vicksburg on the Mississippi, a newly created fortress which, with Port Hudson lower down, long divided the Union forces, both military and naval, which lay above and below the forbidden reach of the great river. His first attempt, made about the same time as Rosecrans' and Burnside's forward moves, was a complete failure, and many voices clamoured for his removal from the command. He had indeed won no startling success since Donelson, for at Shiloh, it was thought by many if not most people, he was only saved by the timely arrival of Buell, and his then subordinate Rosecrans was locally in command, and received all the credit for stopping the Confederate counter-attack at Corinth in October, 1862. But somehow he was not removed, for much was forgiven at Washington to a general who showed "energy".

The year 1863 opened with a second advance on Vicksburg, this time persisted in with the utmost tenacity until after many months the solution of the problem was found. The end was reached only by the heroic measure of forcing

INTRODUCTORY

the warships and transports past the Vicksburg batteries, marching the troops for days together through the low swamps of the right bank of the Mississippi, opening up through bayoux and creeks a new water-line of supply with the North, and then at immense risk and trouble creating a new centre of operations *below* Vicksburg, from which Grant, still greatly daring, fought his way across country until he had the enemy strictly invested at Vicksburg by land and water. His opponent was not equal to dealing with the situation, and Vicksburg fell on the 4th of July—a day on which the Northern people celebrated a double victory—with 37,000 prisoners. With the fall soon afterwards of Port Hudson, which General Banks and a force from New Orleans was besieging, the Mississippi was cleared from St. Louis to the sea, and the Confederacy to all intents and purposes cut in two.*

In the centre Rosecrans had, after all, proved as hard to move as Buell, and on the plea that it was wrong to fight two decisive battles at once, had delayed his advance until the fate of Vicksburg was decided. He then manœuvred Bragg out

---

* The western half (Arkansas, part of Louisiana and Texas), under the military command of General Kirby Smith and Lieutenant-General Taylor, certainly repulsed a good many partial expeditions of the Union troops, the most important of which was Banks's Red River expedition (1863-1864). After the war the Confederate leaders took great and justifiable pride in the success of their efforts to make this western half self-supporting in men, food, and even munitions of war. But this very fact shows how completely the West was lost by the fall of Vicksburg. A young nation struggling for independence does not from choice organize its various parts so as to make each self-supporting and self-sufficing.

of several successive positions, and in the end, by a complicated and dangerous manœuvre in the mountains on the Georgia border, caused the Confederate general to evacuate Chattanooga.

Meanwhile the Army of the Potomac had not been idle. As soon as the Virginian campaigning season opened, Hooker, Burnside's successor, put his army round Lee's left flank, and entered that same Wilderness which gives its name to the battle and the campaign of 1864. But though the initial movement was daring and successful, the rest of the campaign was marked by over-caution and over-hesitation, qualities that Lee and Jackson were well able to inspire in their opponents. The battle of Chancellorsville (May 2–5) was fought by Lee with 60,000 men against Hooker's 100,000, and it was won by the superior skill which enabled Lee to use every man of his command twice over, whereas Hooker only succeeded in putting into action three-fifths of his whole army. Stonewall Jackson received a mortal wound from the rifles of his own men in this battle. After a month's rest, while Rosecrans lay inactive and Grant was just beginning his final advance on Vicksburg—in fact at the crisis of the whole war—Lee once more " went North " by way of the Valley. Hooker, fettered by his instructions and by the Government's distrust of his capacity, did what he could, and then resigned his command into the hands of Major-General George Gordon Meade, the fifth and last commander of the Army of the Potomac. This was on June 28. On July 1 the battle of

INTRODUCTORY

Gettysburg opened, and on July 4 Lee retreated, having been repulsed with the loss of a quarter of his whole army. Whatever might be said of Antietam, Gettysburg was undoubtedly a splendid Federal victory, and after such blows as Fredericksburg and Chancellorsville, the news of Gettysburg and of Vicksburg, received on the same day, raised the hopes of the patient North to the highest pitch.

Meade, however, was distrustful of his own powers. He had served in the Army of the Potomac from the first and had appreciated his opponents on many a sad occasion. His own army had suffered severely, as was only to be expected, and the original three-years' men had almost completed their term of service. At different times he had to furnish troops to other armies and to aid in enforcing the "Draft" or conscription acts in the cities of the North. Lee was somewhat similarly situated, and both sides being depleted, neither attempted a fresh decisive trial of strength. There was fighting indeed between Meade and Lee in the autumn of 1863, but it was unprofitable to both parties.

Thus Meade's achievement faded by degrees from the public notice, which now centred upon events round Chattanooga.

A distinguished Confederate, General D. H. Hill, gave it as his opinion after the war, that the armies of the North and the South were at their best at Gettysburg and Chickamauga. The latter battle was fought between Rosecrans and Bragg on September 19–20, for the possession of

Chattanooga, and was a Confederate victory as complete in its way as Second Bull Run or Chancellorsville. Bragg was aided by a detachment of Lee's army under Longstreet, which seems to have behaved in the battle as if it were there to show Bragg's men how fighting was understood in Virginia.

The retirement of Rosecrans into Chattanooga was followed by the establishment of a blockade of that place. Rosecrans was sacrificed to the cry for successful commanders, and Thomas took his place. Grant was appointed to the supreme command in the West, and brought over his own forces, now under Sherman, to Chattanooga, whither also Hooker brought two corps of the Army of the Potomac from the East. To this imposing concentration resistance, with the forces at Bragg's disposal, was practically hopeless, for Longstreet was now detached in East Tennessee,[*] facing a new Federal corps (called by the old name of the IX.) under another ex-commander of the Army of the Potomac, Burnside. The ruin of Bragg's army in the battle of Chattanooga (November 23-25, 1863), which was mainly the work of subordinates, set the seal upon Grant's reputation. It was only natural and right that this should be the case. The Union cause in the West, more gravely imperilled than ever before, required, not tactical skill, nor strategical foresight, but moral strength.

[*] This was a strongly Union district, like West Virginia, and its effective occupation was always ardently desired by Lincoln and his advisers.

At Chattanooga it was Grant's mere presence* that redressed the balance.

---

* Grant's quietness in battle may be illustrated by an anecdote of the battle of the Wilderness. During the second day he sat at the foot of a tree and whittled sticks. "Whittling" was the manner of killing time most favoured in the Western States. The intense strain of waiting, which tells hardest on a commander-in-chief, produces an eager, almost uncontrollable longing to do something. Hence we find commanders attending personally to the laying of a gun, or riding in a charge, according to their temperaments, but scarcely ever "letting things alone". Moltke was another general of great *sang-froid*. At the crisis of the battle of Königgrätz, Bismarck relates, he offered Moltke his cigar-case, and judged by the care with which Moltke chose the cigar that all was going well.

CHAPTER II

LIEUTENANT-GENERAL GRANT AND THE PLAN OF OPERATIONS FOR 1864

Such had been the general course of the war, up to the point at which preparations began for the Wilderness campaign, and for the corresponding campaign of the Western armies towards Atlanta.

To direct these and the minor campaigns, Grant was appointed as commander of the "Armies of the United States" in March, 1864. At the same time the rank of lieutenant-general * was revived for him.

It remains to summarize the general military situation at this moment.

With few exceptions every port and inlet on the Confederate seaboard from Norfolk to Galveston was more or less effectively blockaded, and thus the Confederacy, even apart from the loss of ground in the West and centre, was becoming poorer day by day. Cotton was not an article of food. It had to be exported, and meat, clothing, munitions of

* It had previously been held only by Washington. Scott was brevet, not substantive, lieutenant-general. After the Civil War Grant was made full general, and was followed in that rank, in succession, by Sherman and Sheridan. Since Sheridan's death in 1887 no officer of the United States Army has been appointed full general, though since 1898 the title of lieutenant-general has become fairly common.

war imported in return for it, in the face of the overwhelming naval strength of the enemy. Not many months after the battle of the Wilderness home-grown meat was practically exhausted in the South, and the fighting men had to be content with little more than half and quarter rations issued irregularly when here and there steamers managed to run the blockade. As for munitions of war, the Confederates looked chiefly to the enemy's killed, wounded, and prisoners to furnish their needs, and often had to obtain even the bare necessities of existence by a bayonet charge.

The Confederacy was not only miserably poor in material resources of all kinds, from food to rifled guns. It was equally hard pressed for men. Exact figures are not ascertainable, but 500,000 at the outside may be assumed as the total number of men wearing Confederate uniforms and carrying arms under the orders of Confederate officers in January, 1864. About the same time the Union forces numbered some 870,000.*

Authorities differ as to whether Lee's men, when they stood to arms afresh in the spring of 1864, did so with the feelings of men determined to die in the last ditch, or with confidence in ultimate victory. But from whatever source their moral was derived it was if anything of finer temper than in 1862,

* Both sides put forth extraordinary efforts. The North put in to the field 1,700,000 three years' men (counting three one year's men, and two who enlisted in 1864 and thus did not complete their three years' term, as one three years' man each) out of a military population, according to the census of 1861, of 4,600,000. The South, on a similar basis of calculation, furnished 900,000 men out of a military population of 1,065,000 (Dodge, *Bird's Eye View of Our Civil War*, p. 322).

when Europe was ready to take up arms on behalf of the South and independence was in sight. Now the weaker power's only hope lay in wearing out the patience of the stronger. Probably few reflecting men in the Confederate ranks in 1864 thought of ending the war as the object of a battle, but all were determined to fight again and again until the enemy ended it. The destruction of the Confederacy was the object of the North, and the destruction of the war spirit in the Union States and the Union Government that of the South. With the latter, therefore, all fighting was subject to the condition of being able to fight again another day. The expenditure of the last effort on the battlefield to force a decision one way or the other, the correct procedure for Grant, was out of the question for Lee. It is pathetic to read in Lee's messages to his Government the ever-recurring phrase, "By God's blessing our casualties are small". Not false humanitarianism, but hard necessity, imposed this economy.

The military policy of the United States government, as soon as it came into the strong hands of Grant, was divested of details and minor purposes. The Confederacy was almost too poor to exist; that poverty must be increased until the breaking point was reached. It had, by the skill of its generals, made up for numerical inferiority by shifting the centre of gravity from time to time so as to oppose weight to weight at the momentarily critical point.*

---

* Dodge's remark that "at the point of fighting contact, in these fifty battles, the forces were within two per cent. of being equal," which is intended to confute the sneer that Federal troops fought worse than

PLAN OF OPERATIONS FOR 1864

Grant's reply was to press the attack simultaneously at all points and thus to prevent one Confederate army reinforcing another, and incidentally to force the Richmond authorities to the suicidal course of refusing reinforcements when implored by Georgia, or Alabama, or Virginia to aid them in their need. More, he proposed to attack continuously day after day, so as to leave the Confederates no time to recuperate, and no opportunity to furlough their men for work in the fields and the workshops of the interior. But above all, the spirit of resistance being as high and determined as ever, the way to break it down was by annihilating it, "attrition" being the name given by Grant to the process conducing to this end. No prisoners were to be exchanged, for ten thousand men were more precious to the South than twice that number to the North, and the Northern prisoners in the South aided their cause in a measure by the mere fact that they had to be fed out of the dwindling resources of their captors. Battles were the most effective method of killing, wounding, and capturing Confederate soldiers, and Grant proposed to concentrate the whole strength of the Union armies on this end of fighting great battles—to destroy the enemy's armies at whatever cost, and few generals in history have interpreted that well-worn phrase so sternly and so literally as Grant. "I determined", he says, "first, to use the greatest number of troops practicable against the armed force of the enemy,

Confederate, seems to me to afford a most convincing proof of the general strategical and tactical skill of the Southern leaders.—(*Bird's Eye View of Our Civil War*, p. 119.)

preventing him from using the same force at different seasons against first one and then another of our armies, and the possibility of repose for refitting and producing necessary supplies. . . . Second, to hammer continuously against the armed force of the enemy and his resources until, by mere attrition, if in no other way, there should be nothing left to him but an equal submission with the loyal section of our common country to the constitution and laws of the land".

"These views", he continues, "have been kept constantly in mind, and orders given and campaigns made to carry them out. Whether they might have been better in conception or execution is for the people, who mourn the loss of friends fallen and who have to pay the pecuniary cost, to say. All I can say is, that what I have done has been done conscientiously to the best of my ability and in what I conceived to be for the best interests of the whole country".

"In war everything is simple, but the simple is difficult", says Clausewitz in an oft-quoted phrase. Grant's ends were simple enough, but the difficulties of all sorts which beset him, even before he took the field, had already beset and overwhelmed his three predecessors in the post of generalissimo.

The political pressure which a general operating within six or seven marches of Washington had to fear was so notorious that Sherman wrote to Grant, six weeks before the battle of the Wilderness: "For God's sake and your country's sake, come out of Washington". But it was for that very reason that Grant elected to stay in the East. Where the best army and the best general of the Confederacy lay ready to oppose him and where political pressure was strongest, and in its well-meaning unwisdom most dangerous, there was the greatest need for the generalissimo to exercise his skill and his authority.

The concentration of effort purposed by Grant, simple and obvious as it seems, had proved too much for his predecessors.* Department commanders in subordinate theatres of war were loth to part with their troops, sometimes on personal grounds, sometimes because they were apt to over-estimate the significance of their departments in the general scheme of the war. Grant's will prevailed, however. In New England the local commander was a veteran who had been a major-general when Grant was a subaltern, yet the new generalissimo reduced his command to 1800 men before the spring campaign opened. "Economy of force" was not a chapter heading in the course of military art then taught at West Point, but it was a practical man's solution of an actual problem.

The enemy had two field armies, Lee's on the Rapidan in Virginia, and Joseph Johnston's

* With the Confederates concentration was hardly a virtue, for after the field armies had been made up to a respectable strength, there was but little surplus left over. Even so, the Richmond government was not free from blame in this matter. Coast defence proved a severe drain on the scanty resources of the Confederacy, just as coast inroads employed at least 40,000 more Federal soldiers than were strictly necessary for the mere maintenance of occupied points. Grant freely expressed his contempt for the supposed 80,000 Confederate soldiers west of the Mississippi, 40,000 of whom, *simply because no one interfered with them*, were quite useless and unavailable for active service.

(lately Bragg's) on the Georgia-Tennessee border Against these two Meade's and Sherman's armies, reinforced to what Grant considered the utmost useful strength, were to be employed. Their centres of operations were respectively Richmond and Atlanta, and the only considerable field forces of the Union remaining over were to be employed, directly or indirectly, immediately or ultimately, against these places. The grand strategy of their employment is summarized in one of Grant's own terse phrases: "I regarded the Army of the Potomac as the centre, and all west to Memphis as the right wing". This right wing effected an immense left wheel which brought the corps on the outer flank from Vicksburg, *via* Atlanta and Charleston, to the northern edge of North Carolina, directly in Lee's rear. The centre and weak left wing fixed Lee's army, and thus acted as the pivot of the whole wheel, scarcely moving itself but holding its opponent with an unshakeable grip until the far-flung right wing closed upon the rear and ended the Confederacy.

Minor armies were retained only to keep in check, with the bare minimum of force, the isolated Confederates of the extreme West, and to maintain the blockade of the Southern coast by holding the various ports already captured. The forces destined for the occupation of the Shenandoah Valley, and of the Mobile-Macon territory,* were not so much minor armies as detachments told off to the less important parts of the line of battle. Their

* To be carried out by troops recalled from a useless Trans-Mississippian expedition under Banks.

movements were connected with and dependent upon the movements of the main field armies.

Grant watched over the movements of one and all, even when himself in front of the enemy in Virginia. He was generalissimo and also *de facto* commander of the army which opposed Lee, an arrangement which, neither good nor bad in itself, was imposed on him by circumstances. Its disadvantages *vis-à-vis* the executive commander of the Army of the Potomac will appear in the sequel. Its possible disadvantages *vis-à-vis* the other army commanders, such as a misappreciation of the local conditions and situation, were minimized by his wise forbearance and his willingness to trust the " man on the spot ". Only at one moment of grave importance did he interfere directly and authoritatively in the movements of a distant subordinate.

It is, of course, with Grant the local commander in Virginia and not with Grant the generalissimo that we are here chiefly concerned. But it must be borne in mind that, when his headquarters were within cannon-shot of Lee's line of battle, he was still and always the bearer of the supreme responsibility for the conduct of the whole war — of operations against Richmond or Lee or a bridge on the Virginia and Tennessee Railroad, of Sherman's advance into Georgia and of Banks' wanderings on the Mississippi.

It is interesting to sketch, however briefly, Grant's military character. He was a " West Pointer " and a veteran of the Mexican War, like hundreds of others on either side. But he had left the "old army" under a cloud, and in particular he was freely and generally accused of intemperance. Intemperance, however, is not always a test of incapacity—witness Marshal Saxe and Marshal Luxembourg, the only French generals who have defeated British infantry in pitched battles in the open field. Lincoln's reply to those who sought to influence him against Grant as a drunkard was to ask his informants to supply him with the name of General Grant's favourite whisky, so that he could send a barrel to each of his other generals.* The truth of the matter appears to have been that Grant was physically so constituted that "very little upset him", as the phrase is.

For several years preceding the war, he had almost failed to earn a living, and was regarded by his neighbours in Galena, Illinois, as a broken man. It was perhaps in these hard experiences that he learned to keep silence and to bide his time. His plainness and quietness was a new thing in the headquarters camps of Virginia after the brilliance of McClellan, the courtliness of Burnside, and the gaiety of Hooker. General Meade opened the Wilderness campaign by unfurling a gorgeous headquarters flag of magenta and gold and silver, which drew from Grant the remark, "Is Imperial Caesar about here?"† At Appomattox Court

---

* Charles XII. of Sweden, austere as was his private life, rebuffed one of his officers who accused General Stenbock of drunkenness more brusquely: "General Stenbock drunk is more capable of giving orders than you sober". An English parallel is the well-known story of George II. who, when warned that James Wolfe was a "madman", replied, "I wish he would bite the other generals".

† This flag, by the way, disappeared after the North Anna, and was supplanted by a small national flag.

House the general-in-chief of the United States armies received Lee's surrender dressed in a soldier's blouse with the three stars of a lieutenant-general alone indicating that its wearer was an officer. His sword had been left far behind in a headquarters wagon, as he explained apologetically to his great opponent.

Grant's was, in fact, a simple, quiet, unostentatious and lovable character, which was entirely under the control of a tremendous will power. This will power required the stimulus of circumstances to bring it into action. The stimulus once applied, he "made up his mind", in the full sense of this misused phrase. Action with him had its springs in the mind, and was translated from the thought to the deed by all the force of a dominant personality.

If to this will power be added the concentrated common sense resulting from the experience of many arduous campaigns and battles, the gradual development of more and more strength in proportion as the burdens of responsibility increased, it is easy to see that having, by tenacity of purpose, disentangled in his mind the essentials from the non-essentials, Grant would use the whole force of his being to realize them in fact. Modern French philosophers class human mentalities, other than those of mere savages, into the "diffluent" and the "plastic". In the former, man seeks to create an ideal beyond the facts; in the latter, he seeks to shape facts in accordance with the ideal. Grant had little or nothing of the diffluent mentality. His was the plastic, in its nakedest form, and he possessed the natural force which makes the attempt to shape facts successful. It is thus that we may account for his simple faith in success which Sherman, who was no blasphemer, likened to nothing less than the faith of a Christian in his Saviour.

It is obvious from the definition that the diffluent mentality tends to speculation, the plastic to action. " He fights " was Lincoln's answer to one of the many distrustful deputations which asked him to remove Grant. Other generals fought, from time to time, but in Grant alone had the President found a general whose habit of mind was to fight. Lincoln was the representative of the Northern people in character and temperament. Stanton, the Secretary of War, of whom it has been said that "nothing justified his retention in the Cabinet but his magnificent, unfaltering courage", was the incarnation of the particular phase of the Northern temperament called the " war spirit ", and Lincoln and Stanton are not always to be condemned as blundering civilians because they strove to infuse more energy into the conduct of the war. They found the true leader at last by a costly process of trial and error, and they deserved to find him. It was the same with the troops, the volunteers who had come forward " for the war " and meant to end it. They too, like Grant, were expressions of the need of the race, cells in the structure of the nation called into this specialized form of activity by the special circumstances of the time—leucocytes in the biologist's terminology, patriots as the common tongue calls them. " I was", says Grant on the last page of his memoirs, looking backwards from his death-bed, "no matter whether deservedly so or not, the representative of the Union side in the controversy". He was the representative not merely of the war party in Lincoln's cabinet, but of the "need of the race" that was at the time most urgent. That, when the special need that he could meet was passed, he became, as general and President, nothing more than a distinguished and conscientious public servant, is a phenomenon perfectly in accordance with the laws of nature. But in respect of the particular need called the Civil War, Grant is nothing less than heroic.

CHAPTER III

THE SOLDIERS AND OFFICERS OF THE CIVIL WAR

THE Northern armies were recruited first of all from volunteers for three months' service belonging to the militia of the various States ; then, and for the greater part of the war, from men who voluntarily enlisted in new organizations " for three years or for the war." and finally from conscripts obtained by the " Draft ". which came into force towards the end of 1863. It is the second of these classes that is understood when we speak of the American volunteer. The first disappeared, with its gay militia uniforms and its expensive field equipments, after the rout of First Bull Run. The third class contained but few desirable elements, but during the period which we are studying, the good troops were sufficiently strong and numerous to overawe and even to make good soldiers of these unpromising recruits.

The South enforced conscription acts earlier and more ruthlessly in proportion as their need of men was more pressing, and thereby drew into the net, along with the usual proportion of *mauvais sujets*, all the men who, in the ordinary course, would have formed the second, third.

THE SOLDIERS AND OFFICERS

and subsequent contingents of volunteers.* But with this more or less important difference, the Southern and Northern troops may be considered as members of the same race and nation in whom different aptitudes had, in view of different circumstances of life and industry, come to the front in each section.

Many points, of course, the soldiers of both sides had in common. Chief of these is the dogged determination which is supposed by every Anglo-Saxon, and allowed by modern scientists of other races, to be the birthright of the race. "They fought", says an admiring Federal soldier of his opponents, "yes, they fought like men of purely American blood". Even before the armies had become hardened by discipline and experience they stood up to severe losses at Bull Run and to still more severe losses at Shiloh, and this in spite of certain by-products of their individualist spirit which, it is generally admitted, impaired their purely military efficiency.

By contrasting the endurance displayed at Shiloh with that of men of the same race and time in the "bushwacking" fights in Missouri, we may obtain some idea of the part played by the *casus belli* itself in stimulating into activity the racial quality of perseverance. The brave and active Lyon, and other Union commanders in Missouri

---

* Men who had volunteered for three years were held with the colours at the expiry of their term, under the conscription laws. The minimum age was eighteen, but youths of sixteen formed part of the local militia or "reserves" of the various states. Thus a cadet corps from the Virginia Military Institute fought in line with veterans at New Market (May 15), and stormed a Federal battery with the bayonet.

"dispersed" the enemy, but at Shiloh the vanquished were no more "dispersed" than is usually the case when regular troops have been defeated in battle. At Bull Run there was a rout, unquestionably, but there is always a rout at the last, when all powers of resistance are exhausted, and good troops are differentiated from bad, as a rule, by the simple comparison of the losses each can endure before (not *without*) breaking. Men of a border State, with diverse ties of blood and sympathy exerting equal forces of attraction in opposite directions, were almost in equilibrium. They attempted conscientiously, even eagerly, to kill their enemies and be killed, but the breaking strain came very early in the day's battle. At Shiloh the men on each side had outgrown their sympathy for certain parts of the other's political ideal. The lines had been drawn definitely; the quarrel, though differently read by the opposing sections, was plain and simple from the point of view of each, and "fighting it out" having become the predominant need of the moment, the qualities of character necessary to satisfy the need, and the individual members of the race possessing these qualities in the greatest degree, were—by the laws of nature—evoked from inactivity or non-specialized employment. Of the stimulus itself, nothing more need be said than this, that it is idle to attempt to explain it by examination of the legal soundness, or even the abstract justice, of the position taken up by either side. Such tremendous elemental forces are set in motion only in response to the call of a vital need.

THE SOLDIERS AND OFFICERS

The volunteers were, however, ordinary citizens before and after the war. They were not "leucocytes", dormant in peace, active and purposeful only in war, in the same sense as are, say, the officers of a modern European army. They came, of course, from those men in whose personalities the function of self-devotion was strongest, but they stood out from the rest only in that degree; they possessed the ordinary home ties, business ties, hopes and aspirations.

The volunteer was an American like the rest, and though actuated "for the war" by the force of an instinct which was stronger in him than in his fellows, he took with him into the field the other national characteristics in which he had his share. He was imaginative and highly individualized—hence he could respond to the directing influence (when it accorded with his instincts) even without the physical encouragement of being in a long closed line of bayonets. He possessed keen wits, self-reliance, and adaptability, for these qualities had been developed at the expense of others, not only in his own and his ancestors' struggles to reclaim and colonize hills, swamps, mountains, and forests, but also in the competition for work and for trade in the great industrial cities that had sprung up in the twenty or thirty years preceding the war. All this made him a good "individual fighter". An individual he was from the first, before he donned the blue or grey blouse of a soldier; he was a fighter because "extraordinary circumstances cause to vibrate certain brain-cells that are ordinarily unused ".*

So much needs little explanation, but how the most highly individualized nation in the world came to submit itself to a discipline as rigorous as any of which we have record in modern times, it is more difficult to say.

"Discipline, that is the officers", is a saying that has a great vogue in Europe. Defensible as this may be from many points of view, it has relatively little basis of truth when applied to the American armies of 1861–65. The officers themselves were, like the men, ordinary citizens actuated by unsuspected instincts. They did their duty and led their men bravely, but they never possessed, in virtue of their office, the magical, almost hypnotic, ascendancy over them which tradition and daily experience gives the professional officer of the old-world armies. Even a general, in the early days of the war, could not wear his cocked hat without exciting a titter in the ranks.

It is precisely this difficulty of reconciling individual free-will and racial compulsion that gives to the American Civil War its value as an object lesson in military psychology.

First of all, under the compulsion of the racial need, they tended always to fighting, and to following most devotedly the brigadiers and colonels who fought the men hardest. "We knew the fighting generals and respected them", says the American volunteer already quoted; † and such men as

* Gustave le Bon.
+ Frank Wilkeson, *The Soldier in Battle*.

THE SOLDIERS AND OFFICERS

Hancock and Barlow on the one side, Gordon and Early on the other, found their commands, whether brigades, divisions, or corps, intensely susceptible to their personal leadership.

Generally speaking, susceptibility to the impulse of command is characteristic of regular and professional troops more than of armed nations and volunteers; and the next question is, how did the other generals, who were not heaven-born leaders in action, manage to command their men? Many, of course, failed to do so. Some were scoffed at by their rank and file as political nominees, "shoulder-strapped office-holders". Some were nothing worse than inadequate for the situations of responsibility in which events had placed them—had risen step by step, and in the end found their level by proving unable to remain above it. But the great majority managed to sustain with credit posts which in Europe are normally held by selected officers of thirty years' service.

Unaided by years of habituation and by the professional spirit, then, an ordinarily strong personality did actually exercise the art of command. There was always laxity as regards non-essentials; the formal discipline was of the kind best called "free and easy", but this was and is the special characteristic even of regulars in the United States, and must not be regarded, then, as the volunteer's *quid pro quo* in return for submissiveness under control.

The true explanation seems to lie in this, that the same impulse which drove the men (as the instruments of the public weal) to fight, disposed them at the same time to self-sacrifice. Self-sacrifice is, in fact, the particular aptitude of the patriot, the leucocyte of the material body transferred to the moral and mental plane and literally glorified. The instinct of patriotism in this sense—*i.e.* the impulse to fight and to suffer—is obviously a thing apart from the reasoning faculty.

"Go it, Molly", said a Confederate soldier, as a hare fled before the advance of the enemy's skirmishers; "and I'd go with you except for my character!" In the latter part of the war there was every (literally every) temptation for the men of Lee's army to disperse to their homes,* but the last ditch was reached before desertion on a large scale became at all prevalent. Desertion is rightly and almost universally regarded as the touchstone in this matter. A man deserts when he has "had enough", but the only "enough" for the vast majority of American volunteers was the actual or virtual end of the war. Short of that, nothing except the grossest incompetence of the officers could bring the fatal temptations of reason effectively to bear on the patriotic instincts.

Their discipline was one which the instincts of the mass imposed on its individual members. It was, therefore, more potent in battle than in "bushwacking", on however large a scale the

---

* See Major Stiles' *Four Years under Marse Robert*. The most cruel of such temptations was the cry of the starving women, which was, in the last extremity, often coupled with the threat, if the husband did not return, the wife would find other means of support than those afforded by a ruined farm. Lieut.-General D. H. Hill endorsed an application for leave with the words, "Respectfully forwarded, approved. If the men are not given leave occasionally, the next generation in the South will consist of skulkers and cowards".

latter might be. Only by reference to this can we understand the significance of so strange an event as the battle of Kenesaw, where Sherman, after "tapping" and outflanking the enemy's lines for several weeks, suddenly changed his tactics and flung his troops in brigade and division columns against an entrenched position on the mountain side. The moral difference between attacking a position and fighting a battle will appear on many days, and explain many incidents of the Wilderness Campaign.

The general effect of drill and daily discipline is to attune the collective will of troops to the suggestion or impulse of a leader of average powers of command. It was so in the War of Secession as in other wars. The initial and obvious disadvantages of extreme individuality in the men was compensated for by their readiness to set aside personal considerations. Given that the instinct of the mass imposed discipline on the individuals composing it, and that the troops were thoroughly and strictly drilled,* it is easy to see that the sum total of the instincts, old and new, of the rank and file was such as to bring the art of command within the limits of an ordinary capacity. The instincts that the occasion called for predominated, new instincts were acquired on the drill-ground, old and new alike predisposing the men to discipline and resolute obedience, and so long as the officers did not run counter to the instincts † of their men, their men obeyed them,

* We are speaking here of the volunteers of 1861–1863.

† The *reasoned judgments* of the rank and file often differed widely from those of their superiors.

and followed them up to and over the enemy's entrenchments. As the officers themselves, like the men, represented the "war spirit", the instincts of both usually tended to the common end.

Besides these instincts the American soldier possessed a critical habit of mind which experience in several campaigns gradually sharpened. Probably no army in history was as hard to please as the Army of the Potomac. The Army of Northern Virginia was far more docile. Rough as some of its elements were, and turbulent as life in Alabama or Louisiana or Tennessee was apt to be, there was in the South an aristocracy* born to lead, and the habit of deference to social superiors almost insensibly merged into the habit of obedience to the officers—uncritical obedience because based on the traditions and habits of many generations. Where the upper classes served in the ranks on either side they made excellent soldiers, as the upper classes seem to do in all countries. But in the South the middle and lower (white) classes looked up to the upper class more or less as a caste, while in the democratic North the sturdy middle and working classes were apt to take the attitude of—

"I care for nobody, no, not I".

This is of more importance when we come to examine, not the common ground, but the

---

* The Northern wits, and especially Russell Lowell, in the *Biglow Papers*, frequently speak of "F.F.", which stands for "First families of the South".

"She's an F.F., the tallest kind, an' prouder 'n th' Grand Turk.
An' never had a relative that done a stroke o' work".

THE SOLDIERS AND OFFICERS 39

differences of the two sections. Meanwhile it is introduced here as a warning against the somewhat misleading absence of criticism in the ranks of the Southern armies. The critical habit of mind was there in both cases, but in the South it was veiled by social conventions, while for obvious reasons it was strongest by far in the men of the manufacturing cities.

Instincts alone being operative in the heat of battle, the rank and file's appreciations of the situation were nearly always strategical in character.*

Grand tactics they criticized also, but not the actual method of fighting. When in contact with the enemy they, for the most part, lost the individual scientific spirit, and became instinctive, unconscious, hypnotized instruments of the decision-seeking "war spirit" which alone obliterated individual differences and made cohesion possible on the basis of common instincts.

We are dealing, of course, with men of three years' war service in the main when we come to the campaign of 1864. In so long an experience battle must have lost such empty terrors as appeal to the excited novice. The real terrors were better appreciated than ever before, perhaps, and it was—except in the case of the very bravest and coolest fighters—only in camp life, in "wrinkles" for marching days, in engineering ingenuity, that experience, working upon the

---

* As an example of this, Wilkeson's book, above mentioned, may be taken. The author gives us his *impressions* of the battlefield—impressions even of the art of fighting, but there is a note of conviction, of logical certainty, in the often erroneous summing up of strategical situations by the rank and file.

natural intelligence of the American private, turned him into what is nowadays called a "handy man". In Grant's and Sherman's constant "hammering" and "tapping" of the enemy's lines in this 1864 campaign, reason doubtless reasserted part of its influence even on the battlefield itself. The pressure of the "war spirit" on each individual skirmisher was strong enough to keep him up to his work. But when it was required to assault a well-defended entrenchment and carry it *coûte que coûte*, neither side makes the least pretence that the task can be achieved by individual reasoning human beings. The individuals are drawn together into the mass as quietly and stealthily as possible. The mysterious night, the feeling of "something in the air", the sound of occasional shots from the sentries, perhaps a few bullets, bring the masses into a state of moral tension. For want of data, the reasoning faculty falls silent. The mass coheres and acts in virtue of its instincts only, and from these instincts a collective will is formed and brought to a high state of tension. The commander gives the signal and the attack is irrecoverably launched in an instant.* Line after line, each carries forward the wreck of its predecessor, and the whole spends its force, successfully or unsuccessfully, but always without reserve.

The racial and national instincts were common to both sides,† but the North and the South differed

---

* Upton and Hancock at Spottsylvania.

† Apart from certain newly acquired foreign elements, *e.g.* the French creoles of Louisiana, and the Irish and German immigrants in the Northern cities.

THE SOLDIERS AND OFFICERS 41

widely in the balance of these instincts. It is no longer seriously claimed that there was any notable difference between the parties in the supremely important instincts of fighting and self-sacrifice. But of the other instincts, those outstanding and predominant in the South were not altogether those which were outstanding and predominant in the North.

The principal and far-reaching difference was that between an agricultural and a commercial community.* The former, men of the fields and the woods, were naturally at home in fields and woods, and by the fortune of war they had not to fight in circumstances of place and climate to which they were unaccustomed. Both were individualized, the one by seclusion, the other by competition, but in different ways. The Southerner's individuality certainly gave him more of the joy of battle, and his greater familiarity with firearms gave him a greater feeling of confidence in action.

His capacity for enduring fatigue and privation was precisely that of the hunter. He lived in counties in which it was half a day's ride to attend the county court house, and his quarrels were consequently settled on the spot as often as not. The vogue of the duel had indeed passed away, but the tradition of the time when every man defended his own was strong. The individual Confederate

---

* The supposition of greater *élan* on the Southern and greater "staying power" on the Northern side, seems to the writer to be merely an attempt to bring the psychical phenomena of the Civil War into line with a purely climatic theory of world history. To take one example only, "Hood's Texans" were steadfast to the end.

was more than a match for the individual Federal, fighting as he did for his own hearth and his own soil, and being, if not a better, at any rate a readier, fighter. The eager proposals made to Lee in 1865 for a disbandment of the over-matched army and a resort to guerrilla warfare, indicate a widespread belief in the capacity of the Confederate as an independent fighting unit.

A guerrilla war in the North, on the other hand, is almost inconceivable. The Southerner was individualized through seclusion and independence and his opponent by the struggle for existence. The Union man's individualism had not prevented him from, but actually directed him towards, concentrating his will-power on the attainment of the objects. Of this concentration, the workshop is a better school than the fields, where man must wait on nature. Concentration of purpose was, in fact, the way or method in which the " vibration of the unused brain cells, in response to an extraordinary stimulus", was effectively communicated to the objective world. But to effect this the passive resistance of other and non-combative instincts had to be overcome—instincts that were less potent in the South, and thus offered less resistance to the play of the patriotic instinct. Intense concentration of purpose, such as the Northerner possessed, was necessary, as a high voltage to force a current through a bad conducting medium, and the fact that he possessed it in a degree which made him, division for division, the fighting equal of his opponent, is the best proof of his right to indicate the line of later evolution.

THE SOLDIERS AND OFFICERS 43

Wholly to the advantage of the Southern soldier was the social system under which he and his ancestors lived. In the North there was no real officer-class, no upper class possessing the birthright of command. Devotion was, in the Union army, devotion to the Cause, not to the persons called to uphold the Cause. Something has already been said as to this, and it is unnecessary to enlarge upon it, except as a foil to the opposite system that prevailed in "Dixie". The individualism of agriculture and landholding brings with it respect of persons, that of commerce and business the reverse. The "Squire" of the English countryside had his counterpart in the Southern States, and the real Confederate army was recruited and officered as was formerly our own Yeomanry. In the Confederate service, every mounted man, in theory at any rate, owned the horse he rode. Slave labour, whether for good or evil, enhanced the position of the squire to that of a territorial magnate—hence the landed planter aristocracy, derided by the North under the initials "F.F.".

The devotion of the Army of Northern Virginia to Lee, the general, was made possible, in spite of the critical spirit common to all Americans, by the social system which produced Lee, the great Virginian landowner. A Sharpsburg or a Gettysburg would have ruined a Federal commander, yet throughout the war Lee's men idolized him. Criticism of Lee was blasphemy. "God bless Marse Robert", said one of his soldiers; "I wish he was Emperor of this country and I was his coachman".

and there is no possibility of doubting that this was the feeling of the entire army.

The conditions under which the American nation lived in the Northern and in the Southern halves of its domain, then, favoured the development in both of individuality, and in each respectively of intelligence and power of concentration, and of skill at arms, hardiness, pugnacity, and subordination to the hereditary leaders. When "unused brain cells" of each section vibrated with equal intensity in response to the vital need of the moment, and evoked the power to fight and to suffer, the methods by which this power found its way to the battlefield differed in each case in so far as other qualities impeded or helped it.*

The moral value of the defensive idea to the South has often been overrated. Had the war been fought on the simple idea of pure aggression and desperate defence of hearth and home, the moral superiority would naturally be on the side of the defender, and with leaders and fighting men of the stamp of Lee and Jackson and the Army of Northern Virginia, the South would have won its independence after Fredericksburg and Chancellorsville. What the South never understood was that the North regarded the war

---

* The physical advantages of the South, such as habituation to outdoor life and skill with the rifle, tended to diminish chiefly because of the greater capacity for variation in the city dwellers. Men from Vermont and Maine fared surprisingly well in the totally unfamiliar Southern climate, and once habituated to the change, they were not slow to pick up so much of fieldcraft and woodcraft as was necessary for their purpose.

THE SOLDIERS AND OFFICERS

as a matter, so to say, of police, that is, undertaken in the interests of internal peace and good order, not of political aggrandizement. Had the North been actuated by any other motive whatsoever, the temptation to make peace after Antietam and Fredericksburg, Corinth and Vicksburg, Perryville and Murfreesboro, had balanced the gains and losses of each side, would have been too strong to be resisted, yet it was precisely at this time that Lincoln's cabinet, which felt the pulse of the Union States accurately enough, issued the emancipation proclamation which brought slavery for the first time into the political quarrel and made it absolutely necessary for both sides to "fight to a finish". It is fair to argue that if the moral superiority of the defenders was not of sufficient effect to unbalance the spirit of the assailant —if, leadership apart, the result of fighting nine men against ten was a drawn game—it was not of decisive influence, but only accessory to other and more telling factors. Further, given that equal, or almost equal, moral on either side and an almost overwhelming material superiority on one, why was the decision so long delayed? Chiefly, of course, owing to the nature of the country fought over, but more still because the balance of the aggressor's strength over that of the defender, great as it was, was consumed in the maintenance of long lines of supply, the garrisoning of occupied hostile ground, and the non-combatant services and the fighting men detached to guard the wagons, etc. The result of it all was that, the motive power being more or less equal and the friction* on the Northern side very much greater, neither party, in the spring of 1864, "knew which could whip", as Grant puts it.

The Union leaders further had to contend against difficulties in their own ranks from which his "opposite number" was practically exempt. If we may believe contemporary accounts as to the quality of the men supplied by the "draft", compulsion, when applied to those who will not on any account volunteer, brings in only the worst and most unsoldierly elements of the population, in war time at any rate. There were a good many compulsory soldiers in Lee's army, it is true, but in the North free enlistment had been maintained far longer than in the South. The successive calls for volunteers had, it would seem, used up all the best fighting elements in the country. Worse still, the autumn of 1863 saw the rise of the profitable, if dishonest and dangerous trade of "bounty-jumping". A man would enlist for one State or corps, and having received bounty money would desert and re-enlist elsewhere, with the consequence that all recruits were treated like convicts, and what with gambling, robbery, stabbing, and drunkenness, a barrack-room became an inferno.†
It was an understood thing that the loyal troops that found the guards and sentries shot the recruits

* A total superiority of two to one generally dwindled away, locally, to one of three to two or even less in favour of the Union army. Only Grant's relentless concentration of effort produced even a five to three superiority.

† Life in a barrack-room at that time has been described vividly by Wilkeson, the Northern volunteer several times referred to above.

THE SOLDIERS AND OFFICERS 47

on the mere suspicion of an attempt to desert. It was the same when by such drastic methods the conscripts, the bounty-jumpers, and the few unfortunate volunteers amongst them had been got to the front. " A gallows and a shooting-ground was provided in each corps, and scarcely a Friday passed that some of these deserters did not suffer the death penalty", says a general officer* of the Army of the Potomac, in describing the winter of 1863-64. Police surveillance followed them even to the battlefield, the rear of the army being "picketed" by provost guards with loaded rifles, though the kidnapped emigrant, or street-loafer, or bounty-jumper had by that time come under the influence of the volunteer, and more or less willingly submitted to his fate. But when the volunteers, *i.e.* the bravest, had been shot down by the thousand, and their places had been taken by recruits of the same stamp as the recruits of the previous winter, or worse, the remaining good soldiers were too few to carry the bad characters with them. " Cold Harbor", says General Hancock's chief-of-staff, " was a mortal blow to the old Second Corps ".

The superior commands on both sides were held by " West Pointers ", graduates of the famous Military Academy and officers of the " old army ". On the whole the senior officers of the United States Army in 1860 belonged to the seceding

---

* Brevet Major-General MacMahon, Chief of Staff VI. Corps, from whose account we find also the true reason for the excessive use of cavalry pickets all round the army, and outside the infantry outposts. " The bounty-jumpers' favourite time for leaving was during their first tour of picket duty ".

States.* Most of the Union generals had not held any higher rank before the war than that of captain, except by brevet.† Several—Grant, Sherman, McClellan, amongst them—had left the army and engaged in civil occupations. Grant never held field rank in the United States Army, even by brevet. He resigned as a captain, and reappeared on the permanent establishment as a major-general (the highest existing rank) when he had captured Vicksburg and more than thirty thousand Confederate soldiers. West Point and the regimental system of the army certainly justified their methods.‡ In frontier posts of fifty men, manœuvres were unheard-of, and field exercises of small bodies were chiefly practised with a view to savage warfare. But it was of far more importance that the junior officers had from the first been subjected to the burdens of effective and responsible command. "During my army service", said a Confederate general, "I learned all about commanding fifty United States dragoons and forgot everything else". He had learned the greater part of a

---

* The 2nd United States Cavalry, a crack regiment, had four field officers (Colonel A. S. Johnston, Lieut.-Colonel R. E. Lee, Major W. J. Hardee, Major G. H. Thomas). The colonel and lieut.-colonel became full generals, and the senior major a lieut.-general in the Confederate army, and the junior major an army commander on the Union side.

† In 1860 Grant was 38, Sherman 40, McClellan 34, Buell 42, Rosecrans 41, Sheridan 29, Warren 30, Hancock 36. Many of the brigadier-generals commanding divisions and brigades were under 30, some under 25, years of age.

‡ There were about 4000 West Point graduates in the army or scattered over the States in 1861. By no means all West Pointers were commissioned in the army. On leaving the Academy, a certain number entered civil life.

THE SOLDIERS AND OFFICERS

general officer's business when he had learned *all* about commanding men! The senior officers, very roughly speaking,* went to the Confederate, and the juniors to the Union army, and Grant himself says that the Confederate leaders were precisely those senior officers whom, as subalterns, he and his comrades had been taught to respect and to admire.

Lee, for instance, was marked out as the future commander of the United States Army, and was actually, while still in the army (Virginia was almost the last State to secede), selected for and offered the command of the Union field army. The habit of command inculcated into captains and subalterns at lonely frontier posts, and in obscure expeditions against the Indians, proved of inestimable value to the Union cause, but a subaltern's habit of deferring instinctively to the authority of the field officers was not easily shaken off when the subaltern found himself opposed to his former chief on the field of battle.

It should be said that the "West Pointer", after the first few months, was entrusted with the higher commands on both sides, irrespective of age and rank in the old service. The class which graduated from West Point in 1853 included MacPherson, Schofield, and Sheridan, all major-generals commanding Union armies in 1864. Hood, who belonged to the same class, was the only Confederate general of the younger generation who rose to a command in chief. Still

* Of course there were notable exceptions. Lieut.-General Winfeld Scott, in 1861 commanding general of the United States Army, who had commanded in the Mexican War, and had been a general officer since 1812, was a Virginian. Thomas was a Virginian also.

younger were some of the brigadiers on the Union side. Wilson and Merritt of the cavalry graduated in 1860, Upton, one of the most finished infantry leaders in the army, in 1861. Custer joined his regiment on the field of Bull Run, and one cavalry division commander, Ranald Mackenzie, did not leave West Point until the Civil War was half over.

"Volunteer" officers, *i.e.* officers straight from civil life, rose here and there to important commands. The Union government, for political reasons, appointed a few of the volunteers to general's rank in the first month of the war, amongst them Butler, of whom we shall see more, and Banks, the captor of Port Hudson.

These proved good administrators, but, it must be confessed, incapable generals. They were not, however, displaced at once, but moved on from one theatre to another, the Government deeming it inadvisable to offend them. The other volunteer generals rose by degrees until they found their level. "Black Jack" Logan commanded an army at the battle of Atlanta. Sickles lost a leg while at the battle of Gettysburg as commander of the III. Corps. Birney was another good and faithful soldier who came from the halls of Congress. Generals Garfield and Hayes were afterwards Presidents of the United States. Blair, a Western politician, and Terry proved capable corps commanders, while, of the juniors, Miles, a brilliant fighting general of the Army of the Potomac, who lived to become commanding general of the armies of the United States, was a young business man

THE SOLDIERS AND OFFICERS 51

who was considered in 1861 of insufficient age to be appointed captain of a volunteer company he had raised. On the other side a Tennessee mountaineer, John B. Gordon, rose to a corps command in Lee's army.

One of the corps commanders opposing Sherman on the Atlanta line (a West Pointer) had resigned a bishopric to become a major-general. Ministers of all denominations are found serving as field officers, chiefly on the staff. In this connection it is well to recall the fact that Lee's army was a deeply religious body of men. There is no need to go into details: it is sufficient to mention that Lee and many of his generals were constant attendants at the camp prayer-meetings conducted by the chaplains, or more often by the private soldiers themselves. Conviction and a sense of duty acting upon men of the same stock produced the same results. There was something of the Cromwellian spirit in Lee's army, as the reader of such books as Stiles' *Four Years under Marse Robert* and Gordon's *Reminiscences* is well aware.

That the Northern soldier was less religious than the Southern must be admitted, and it cannot but add to the moral interest of the war that this is the case, because the driving force that led the soldier to immolate himself on the altar of duty was equally potent on both sides of the Potomac and the Kentucky border, and we are compelled to explain the devotion of the North by reference, not to religion, the individual pact of man with God before witnesses, as religion was understood in Lee's army, still less to the superstitious fanaticism which has led so many causes to victory, but to the law of "agreement to live", which is the sequel of the law of "struggle to live", and is expressed and ensured by the action of those members of society, whether leucocytes in the human body, or kings and soldiers and missionaries (men and women with a *mission*) in the state, set apart for the destruction of the elements antagonistic to the law of agreement. The spirit of the North was intensely modern, and to our own generation it is comforting to find that "the unsuspected brain cells which vibrate under the influence of an extraordinary need" have not entirely atrophied.

Towards the end of 1863 the United States Government began to raise coloured troops. This step was probably the result of the same need for men which produced also the crimp's recruit and the bounty-jumper, though, of course, the most effective way of demonstrating the theory that the black was "a man and a brother" was to put arms in his hands. The Administration had in this matter official and, to some considerable extent, national support, but the colour line was almost as strongly marked in the Northern as in the Southern camps. In the Army of the Potomac, as it stood in May, 1864, there were no black troops, but the IX. Corps, under Burnside, had a coloured division. This was kept out of the fighting line during the campaign we are studying. There was a coloured division serving in the Army of the James, and the two were later consolidated

THE SOLDIERS AND OFFICERS 53

in the XXV. Army Corps, which was composed solely of black troops. As a matter of course the war, as between the white soldier of the South and the negro soldier of the North, was war to the knife. Here it was not a contest for men's rights, or for men's hearths and homes, but a contest which aroused purely racial passions in all their primeval ferocity. The massacre of Fort Pillow, where the Southern cavalry, as their commander reported, dyed the Mississippi with the blood of the negro soldiers, was simply the expression of the prevailing sentiment in a corner of the theatre of war where life was less settled and discipline and self-control held less in honour. The Southerners themselves made use of their negroes, quite in accordance with their tradition, as hewers of wood and drawers of water to the fighting armies; in this capacity they were of immense military value, even though they were never trusted with a firearm. Not only did they raise the crops and look after the white women and children left at home, but they relieved the combatants of practically all the non-combatant work, such as transport and supply, camp fatigues, and above all the construction of fortifications.

CHAPTER IV

THE ARMY OF THE POTOMAC

THE formal organization of the armies of both sides was based on the common archetype, the " old army ".

The regiment (one battalion) was the infantry unit. It was theoretically about 1000 strong, but in practice the veteran corps had dwindled gradually until by 1864 they almost always paraded with less than five hundred rifles. The colonel, the lieutenant-colonel and the major were, in about thirty per cent. of cases, dead or promoted, and the official report of one regiment is signed by a lieutenant. The vicious system of reinforcement, whereby recruits were organized at home in new regiments under new officers and sergeants, instead of being drafted to the front to fill the gaps in the older and well-tried organizations, was largely responsible for this, and in the Wilderness Campaign a " strong " regiment is practically always to be understood as meaning a raw regiment. It has always been suggested that field rank had to be found for the friends of governors and congressmen, but something must be allowed for the necessity of keeping up the war spirit by displaying its strength in the cities of the North.

The infantry brigade consisted of a variable number of regiments, and was theoretically a brigadier-general's command, but more often in practice a colonel's. The division consisted of three or four such brigades, and was commanded by a brigadier-general, more rarely by a major-general. It had no cavalry. Its artillery was lent to it, for the campaign or the battle, from the corps artillery reserve.

The cavalry was organized, in accordance with the system of nomenclature already prevailing in 1861, into companies, battalions, and regiments. Much has been written as to the peculiar characteristics of American cavalry work. For two years after the outbreak of war the Union cavalry was of small account. In 1861 Lieutenant-General Scott had discountenanced the formation of cavalry, chiefly on the ground that the war would be over before the men had learned their drill. In 1862 things had been little better. "Here and there would be found temporary brigades, but too often regiments were attached to army corps and broken up to serve at division and brigade headquarters". A brilliant young cavalry soldier, General Bayard, was killed at the battle of Fredericksburg while *waiting for orders* at the headquarters of the army. Meanwhile the cavalry corps of the Army of Northern Virginia, led by the brilliant "Jeb" Stuart, and under him by men like the younger Lees, Hampton, Rosser, and others, had become the terror of successive

Federal commanders. Born and bred horsemen, and thus at a great advantage when pitted against the inexperienced Northerners, the Confederate squadrons rode everywhere unchallenged, and their moral superiority grew higher and higher until better counsels prevailed in Washington. A cavalry mass in those days was called a "corps organization", and this the Union cavalry received, after many tribulations, early in 1863. At first under Stoneman, then under Pleasonton, and finally, when Grant wanted "the very best man in the army" to relieve Pleasonton, under Sheridan, the Union cavalry gained and kept its self-confidence. The only great cavalry battle of the war, at Brandy Station (June 9, 1863), was indecisive, but in the words of Stuart's own staff officer and biographer, "it made the Federal cavalry". Something of its activity under the restless, fiery Sheridan we shall see in due course. The horsemen on either side fought, on the rare occasions when charging room was available, with the *arme blanche*, but in the great majority of cases by fire action dismounted. The Union cavalry had the special advantage of possessing breech-loading and magazine carbines.* The formal organization was not abnormal. Regiments numbered about 400 sabres, brigades 1500 to 2000, divisions two or three brigades, and the Cavalry Corps three divisions.

The field artillery was armed partly with

---

* The use of breech-loading rifles for infantry was discouraged, particularly in the South, where there were no facilities for the manufacture of special ammunition.

3-inch rifled guns, partly with "Napoleons" (brass smoothbores). The strength of the arm in a corps averaged about ten batteries. The Federal artillery was admittedly superior to the Confederate throughout the war, one cause of this being the somewhat nondescript *matériel* with which the Southern gunners had to content themselves, and another better tactical handling on the part of the senior officers. In the Wilderness Campaign, however, we shall hear little of artillery preparation. Only at a few places here and there—long reaches of a turnpike road through the woods, good positions in an entrenched line for enfilading the hostile attack — does it exercise any appreciable influence on the course of events. This being so, and the encumbrance of long processions of guns and wagons on farm roads being a most serious evil, the artillery was first allowed to stand idle, and afterwards reduced or sent back to the depôt.

The large army reserve of artillery found practically no scope for its potential activity, with the natural consequence that the "Heavy Artillery" regiments were almost invariably used as infantry. Why this branch of artillery was ever raised in any considerable strength it is difficult to see, but the readiness with which these corps found recruits suggests that the bait of garrison duty away from the front was very effective. Once sent up to the front, however, they found themselves charging with the bayonet and losing twenty per cent. of their numbers in the first great battle at which they happened to be present. Their heavy field guns, 20-pounders—"Parrott rifles"—were returned into store or handed over to the siege train.

Battle tactics were practically infantry tactics only. Normally, at any rate, there was no real artillery co-operation. The guns could no longer dash into case-shot range in the Napoleonic fashion, and breach the enemy's line in front of the attacking infantry, for their teams were now, at four or five hundred yards' range, under deadly rifle fire, and their long-range projectiles—common shell with percussion fuzes and even the venerable round shot—were not effective enough materially to assist the attackers.

Thus the infantry had either to do its own preparation before assaulting, which was almost out of the question against a well-armed and well-covered enemy, or to assault without preparation. There were these two alternatives only, fighting behind cover, or charging—in other words, avoiding or forcing an instantaneous decision. The consequent difficulty of "nursing the fight" ruined many a promising scheme, for the decision was brought about, locally, with far greater rapidity than the superior commanders desired, with the result that troops told off for the assault were not in the due formation at the right place and time.

Apart from skirmishers, the normal formation of infantry for attack and defence was two "lines of battle". In defence these were sometimes reduced to one; in attack they were often thickened within the brigade by contracting the front and thus forming a third and perhaps a fourth line. Battalion columns (on double company front) were also used for the charge. Thus the momentum of a blow could be increased at a predetermined point, and a properly organized attack "such as any major-general in the United States Army now knows how to make", had, as a matter of fact, a fair chance of sweeping away at any rate the first line of the enemy. But if more than a partial success was aimed at, if the attack was intended to surge over every brigade of the enemy it met, and not the first line merely, stronger measures were taken. There was a long front to front fight, kept alive by fresh closed bodies from the rear, and in Napoleon's own words, "the breach is made, the equilibrium is broken" by the attack of a large body of troops at a predetermined point, line behind line or column behind column, each rush carrying on the remnant of its predecessor, and none stopping to fire. Upton's attack on the Bloody Angle at Spottsylvania is the model for all time of what a decisive infantry attack should be in spirit.

A corps was always a major-general's * command. It consisted, in the Wilderness Campaign, of three or four infantry divisions and reserve artillery, the average strength being about 28,000 men. These corps were, by universal consent, too large and unwieldy for manœuvring in Central Virginia. On the first day of battle a corps commander found himself compelled to group his

* This was normally the highest rank in the U. S. Army. Only Washington and Scott (brevet, not substantive) had held the rank of lieut.-general before Grant. In the Confederate service, however, the grades of general, lieut.-general, major-general, and brigadier-general, were used in the ordinary signification.

divisions into small corps under his senior generals, and to act himself as an army commander in the modern sense. These large corps were moreover new units. Up to September, 1863, the Army of the Potomac had consisted of seven small handy corps, and, when the XI. and XII. were sent to the West after Chickamauga, of five such corps. These were consolidated in March, 1864, chiefly, it would appear, through questions of rank, seniority, competence, etc., having arisen amongst the senior officers. The I. and III. Corps were selected for extinction, and their divisions distributed to the others, with the worst effect on the moral of the officers and men. Each corps had its distinctive history, traditions, and badges, its charitable societies, its social assemblies, and was in fact a self-contained unit, welded by three years' campaigning. Thus, while in Europe the regiment is the sentimental unit, here *esprit de corps* was stronger within the division and strongest of all within the army corps. Moreover, the introduction of one or two fresh divisions into each of the corps that were retained, entailed throughout the army a redistribution of brigades and regiments.*

Grant, having decided to place his headquarters with the Army of the Potomac, assumed thereby, as a matter of course, the personal direction of operations in Virginia. All his orders, except in a few emergency cases, were issued through Meade, who remained at the head of the Army of the Potomac. That officer did, as a matter

* The badge of the II. Corps was a clover leaf, that of the V. a Maltese cross, and that of the VI. a plain Greek cross.

of fact, give important orders and make important movements on his own responsibilty, but these decisions were more or less similar in character to those which have to be made by the chief-of-staff of a European army in the absence of the commander. Meade's position was in fact that of a chief-of-staff with unusually wide powers. General Grant thought very highly of him, and while keeping in his own hands the actual direction he refrained as much as possible from interfering in the details of Meade's arrangements.

There are few students of the war, however, and especially few amongst those who served in Virginia in 1864, who can adduce serious military reasons in favour of this dual control, which at worst meant a deadlock between the commanding general and the commander of his principal army on the decisive theatre, and at best involved the necessity of information and orders filtering through two headquarter staffs instead of one. Recognizing this, Grant always placed his headquarters close to those of Meade and thus saved orderly work, but even so, and at best, the clerical work was unnecessarily heavy.

Meade himself was an engineer officer, like Humphreys, Warren, Wright, and other capable generals of his army. He had served with the Army of the Potomac from 1862, and had held all grades from colonel to general commanding. He was at this time 49 years of age, at the summit of the powers nature and experience had given him. His own army had considerable confidence in him, if for nothing else, at any rate because he was the only general who had hitherto defeated Lee in the field. He was sensitive to reproach, but entirely subordinate in thought and action, and he exacted, by a fierce manner and biting tongue, the same degree of discipline in his subordinates that he imposed upon himself. Of his own military character it may be said that he was "safe". In the Autumn campaign of 1863 after Gettysburg, he missed one or two opportunities of inflicting serious damage upon Lee's army, chiefly, perhaps, because his own personality was not sufficiently telling to enable him to exact the impossible. But on the other hand, not even Lee could impose upon him, or flurry him, or treat him in any way as he had treated Pope and Burnside and Hooker.* On May 13, fresh from the assault on the Bloody Angle, Grant wrote: "General Meade has more than fulfilled my most sanguine expectations. He and Sherman are the fittest officers for large commands I have come in contact with. If their services can be rewarded by promotion to the rank of major-general in the regular army the honour would be worthily bestowed, and I would feel personally gratified. I would not like to see one of

* The temptation is strong to take, as a criterion of the powers of command (not the skill or capacity) of the various leaders of the Army of the Potomac, the prominence of their immediate subordinates. The corps commanders are least conspicuous for "individuality" under Hooker and McClellan, and most under Pope, Burnside, and Meade. The two first-named failed chiefly in respect of unsteadiness and want of nerve—certainly not in respect of the absence of personal magnetism and command. With Pope and Burnside as commanders-in-chief we need not here concern ourselves. Meade's peculiarity was that he exacted discipline and respect, but not enthusiasm.

these promotions at this time without seeing the other".

The last sentence suggests not merely that Grant had formed a high opinion of Meade. The contrast between the defeats of the Eastern and the victories of the Western Armies of the Union had been obvious on the surface, and few troubled to enquire into the underlying causes. The Army of the Potomac did not take kindly to criticisms from Western officers after its unfortunate experience under Pope, and Grant could hardly have begun his operations in the East worse than by taking the command of the Army of the Potomac out of the experienced and capable hands of one who knew every detail of it. But it was more than a personal matter between Grant and Meade. Rivalry between the East and the West had to be turned into generous co-operation. Concentration of effort was the key-note of Grant's whole plan, and Grant had been promoted from amongst the other major-generals to effect it. Moral as well as material means came within his scope, and he asked, therefore, that Meade and Sherman, his principal subordinates in the East and in the West, should receive together the highest rank, under his own, which it was in the power of the Government to give them.

Humphreys, the Chief-of-Staff, was born in 1810. He was one of the most distinguished engineer officers in the service, and it has been said of him that the Civil War was only a brilliant episode in the life of a savant. Brilliant it unquestionably was, for, with intervals of staff service, he was in command of a brigade, a division, and finally of a corps in all the battles of the Army of the Potomac. His leadership at Fredericksburg was quoted as an example of care in prearrangement and resolution in execution. He had served as chief-of-staff since Gettysburg, in which battle he had commanded the III. Corps after Sickles' disablement. After the war he returned to engineer duty—which in the United States Army comprised civil as well as military engineering—having earned as much fame, if not more, as a chief-of-staff than as a fighting general. General Humphreys was the author of *The Virginia Campaign 1864-65*, the classical work of the period with which it deals, a tersely-worded narrative which requires and repays the closest study. In so far as it represents any but the critical point of view, it is a defence of Meade and the Army of the Potomac against undiscriminating eulogists of Grant, Badeau for example. Other important officers of the headquarters of the Army of the Potomac were Seth Williams, the adjutant-general; Rufus Ingalls, the quartermaster-general, whom Grant, after a short acquaintance, designated in his own mind for an important command with troops; and Hunt, the chief of artillery, who knew his arm as intimately as any soldier then alive, and could handle it in mass to the admiration of friend and foe.

Hancock, the commander of the II. Corps, earned the soubriquet of "The Superb" in the first fight in which he was engaged as a brigadier, and maintained the reputation. He never rose to command an army, being "too necessary to the Army of the Potomac to be allowed to leave it", but it was hoped and believed that he was the next on the line of promotion to the command of that army. Intense pride in his men and his vocation, and the personal magnetism of the born leader were his outstanding military characteristics. He went through most of the Wilderness Campaign with the wound scarcely healed that he had sustained in repelling the last desperate assault of Lee's reserve at Gettysburg, and finally had to leave the front on account of this injury, eighteen months after he had received it. He moved about in a spring cart or ambulance, but the sound of a volley was enough to make him leap up and call for his horse and sword. He was, in fact, like a knight of old, the most fearless and the most chivalrous, the most ardent fighting general of the Army of the Potomac, perhaps of all American soldiers.

Warren, the commander of the V. Corps, was a young engineer officer of the "old army", and had first made his mark as colonel of a regiment of volunteers in 1862. His most conspicuous service had been as chief of engineers at Gettysburg, where he had fixed upon, and gathered troops to hold, what proved to be the key of the Union position. He was a very remarkable man, with a finely tempered intellect, a calculated personal gallantry, and a cultured neatness in habits of thought, dress, and manners. Grant had at first a very high opinion of Warren, and intended, in case of a casualty to Meade, to place him at the head of the Army of the Potomac. How he came to alter this opinion, and the special character of Warren's leadership which led him to do so, will appear in the sequel. There is no particular reason to doubt that Warren would have done better in the command of an army than in that of a corps. His weakness was a far-ranging mind which led him into feeling responsible for the whole army as well as for the V. Corps, and, subconsciously, into resenting his inability as a subordinate to give effect to the best measures to meet the whole military situation as he conceived it.

"Uncle John" Sedgwick, the commander of the VI. Corps, was a wise, experienced, and thoroughly capable leader, beloved by his men and by his superiors. He was not spared by fate long enough to influence very materially the course of Grant's Virginian campaign, but his memory was always with the VI. Corps in its battles and marches, and Grant said, when he heard of Sedgwick's death, "His loss to the army is greater than the loss of a whole division of troops".

Philip Henry Sheridan, the commander of the cavalry corps, was one of the young and brilliant fighting generals of the West. He had been conspicuous at Stone's River and at Chickamauga in rallying beaten troops and bringing them back into action by the sheer force of his gay delight in battle. At Chattanooga he and his division had contributed perhaps more than any other general or corps to the brilliant episode of the storm of Missionary Ridge, whereby Bragg's centre had been broken and scattered to the winds.

The subordinate leaders of divisions and brigades were for the most part those of the best officers of 1861 and 1862 who had survived not merely battle, but the test of leadership in battle. There were, of course, shoulder-strapped office-holders here and there, and there were relatively few outstanding personalities. We have spoken of the average, and apart from those above mentioned, who were all major-generals, it only remains to mention some names that will become prominent in the course of the operations.

Of the "fighting general" so-called, Francis Channing Barlow of the II. Corps was a fine example, and in the same corps served David Birney, a politician who had not proved a failure as a general, Alexander Hays, who though merely a brigadier was the old friend and comrade of the lieutenant-general in Mexico, and A. S. Webb, who afterwards became Meade's chief-of-staff. In the V. Corps served Wadsworth, a grey-haired Congressman who had taken to soldiering as a "volunteer aide-de-camp" in 1861, and Charles Griffin, a field gunner of the old army with the fiery fighting spirit of the days of case-shot attacks, and the motto "guns can go anywhere". In the VI. Corps, Wright, who succeeded Sedgwick, was an engineer officer and a safe and skilful troop leader; Ricketts, like Griffin,* belonged to the field artillery; and the other division commander, Getty, was to show his qualities of leadership on

* These two officers had as captains commanded the two regular batteries that had been shot down by the Confederate infantry at First Bull Run.

the first day of battle. Amongst the juniors the most conspicuous was Emory Upton, a colonel fresh from West Point, who was soon to be promoted brigadier-general on the field of battle.

The cavalry generals under Sheridan were remarkable men in their different ways. With the idea of infusing new spirit into the mounted arm, the President had picked a handful of very junior officers and made them brigadier-generals in 1863, amongst them Wesley Merritt, a well-taught pupil of General Philip St. George Cooke, the recognized cavalry leader in the old army, Wilson, a junior subaltern of engineers, and Custer, a romantic and daring soldier of the frontier type. Gregg, who had been, from brevet second-lieutenant to brigadier-general, a dragoon, and Torbert, an infantryman of repute, were somewhat senior to the others.

Burnside, the commander of the IX. Corps, which was an independent command, was a former commander of the Army of the Potomac, who had come to grief in front of Lee's Fredericksburg lines in December, 1862. He had great and varied experience, a courteous and soldierly bearing, and capacities as a subordinate which he did not show as a commander-in-chief. He was above all loyal to the cause, and ready to sacrifice his personal wishes thereto, even to the extent of serving under Meade, who was his junior and had, in fact, been a division commander in one of the eight corps that had been under Burnside's orders fifteen months before. This trait in his character seems to have made Grant reluctant to take advantage of it, and for some time Burnside's corps was maintained in its original status of an independent army.

Grant's own staff deserves particular notice as being composed, so to speak, of representative Americans. The "chief-of-staff"—really the principal aide-de-camp — Brigadier-General John A. Rawlins, was an Illinois lawyer. He was without experience in the handling of troops, but had served on Grant's staff from 1861 onwards. "He was a man of undoubted ability, of instinctive sympathy with popular feeling, whether in the army or out of it, and of prodigious energy in manner and language. He was passionately patriotic, and would have died for Grant. His intellect, however, was entirely undisciplined and his genius was quick rather than original or profound". Rawlins was, in fact, the incarnation of the Northern "war spirit". Adam Badeau, who wrote these words, was originally a newspaper correspondent, and afterwards Grant's military secretary. He was a lieut.-colonel in April, 1864. He is chiefly remembered for his monumental, if somewhat uncritical work, *The Military History of U. S. Grant*. Lieut.-Colonel Horace Porter, whose book, *Campaigning with Grant*, is also a valuable work, unusually interesting from the personal side, was a young regular officer to whom Grant had taken a great fancy at Chattanooga. Of him, as of Ingalls, it was said that he was "lost" on the staff. Colonels Comstock and Babcock were men of thorough training and wide engineer and staff experience. Lieut.-Colonel F. T. Dent, Grant's classmate and brother-in-law, was typical of the officer of long standing.

CHAPTER V

THE STRATEGY OF THE VIRGINIAN CAMPAIGNS

THE experience of three years' warfare and eight great battles, in the theatre of war lying between Washington and Richmond, naturally cleared the ground for the generals who were called upon to plan the fourth campaign. Though varying indefinitely in details of local and temporary significance, the operations of both sides had, in all essential features, attained simplicity.

The Northern army pivots on Washington, the Southern on Richmond. Each of these two cities is, in Napoleon's phrase, the *centre of operations* for its own army, the peg on which its operations hang. Both are provisionally fortified, both are the principal depôts of arms, supplies, and stores of all kinds, and as a general rule, and short of some special tactical advantage which it was desired to exploit (as at Chancellorsville), each army manœuvred to cut off the other from its centre of operations. This neither army can by any means afford to lose, and the striking radius of each—measured in time, not in space, be it observed—is defined by the resisting power of this all-important centre. Sometimes the centre of operations was given an unnecessary amount of

STRATEGY OF THE CAMPAIGNS 71

protection to the detriment of the field armies, for political considerations stepped in and gave a moral importance to Washington and to Richmond, to which even as centres of operations they were not entitled. Sometimes, on the other hand, the commanders in the field calculated too nicely, and exposed one or other city to a *coup de main*.

The centre of operations, upon which the field army depended, itself depended upon the *base*, that is, roughly, the whole of the country controlled by the Federal or Confederate government outside (and generally, of course, in rear of) the actual scene of operations. Thence were drawn the men for the field army, the money for their maintenance, the supplies accumulated at the centre of operations and at smaller depôts between that place and the army at the front, and the reserves of warlike material. These came to the centre of operations by every available road, railway and water-way; if one were interrupted, the flow of traffic was merely diverted to a fresh line.

The actual configuration of the base-line itself mattered little. Infinitely more important were the available centres of operations, and the directions in which attacks could be delivered from these centres against the hostile field army, its centre of operations or the interior of the base.

Any point inside or on the edge of that base that has safe and easy communication with the heart of the country may be chosen as a centre of operations, provided it fulfils the necessary conditions as to defence and accumulation of men and material. A capital city attracts to itself so great a proportion of the resources of a country, that it is often the most natural and the most satisfactory centre of operations, but it is merely one of many possible centres, and if we eliminate political and sentimental complications by presuming the capital so far protected as to be independent of the field army, the centre of operations may be any other point from which the field army may best strike at the enemy. Thus, in Napoleon's wars of conquest, Paris was merely an important city in the interior. In 1806 the Prussians lay for weeks within striking distance of the road by which Napoleon travelled from Paris to the front, but the Emperor's centre of operations was Bamberg on the upper Main. Further, the centre of operations can not only be chosen in the first instance wherever most convenient, but it can be changed in the course of the operations to suit any change in the strategical situation. Just before the battle of Austerlitz, Napoleon's centre of operations was Vienna, and accordingly the allies marched to cut him off from that place, but he had already prepared another centre of operations in an entirely different direction. The change is merely a matter of good administrative work in the actual process of transferring the accumulated stores. If an army can make its way to any one of half a dozen such points, and the reinforcements and supplies that it needs have been sent thither, it can abandon its original centre of operations with a light heart, and its freedom of manœuvre is immensely enhanced. In this connection, freedom of manœuvre means freedom to change the centre of operations as often as is necessary to give the decisive battle, or even the threat of battle, its fullest effect.

Theory is, of course, subject to countless modifications in practice. One side or both may be compelled, by the weakness of a politically or materially important place, to select and to keep that place as its centre of operations at all costs. Capitals may be unfortified, insufficiently garrisoned, ill supplied, a coast fortress may be vitally necessary for the maintenance of sea power, a mining district, an agricultural county may be indispensable to the whole country. Nevertheless, the Napoleonic principle holds good, as a matter of theory. An army can very rarely afford to lose touch with its centre of operations, but unless the general's hands are tied by circumstances, this centre of operations may be selected in accordance with the contemplated manœuvre, and changed with every change in the military situation.

Now, applying these theories to the Virginia campaigns of 1862–5, we find that the base-line of a Northern army, enjoying undisputed command of the sea, extends from the coast of North Carolina to the Potomac estuary, thence past Washington to the upper Potomac, and finally round again by the West Virginia border to Kentucky. On this base, Washington is incomparably the most important centre of operations, and is chosen as such by the Union commanders even when adequately protected by its own works and garrison, and therefore able to hold its own irrespective of the field army. Of other conceivable centres of operations, Aquia Creek, White House, Belle Plain, Fortress Monroe, City Point, were most used, Frederick and Harper's Ferry far less frequently, while no serious manœuvre was ever carried out from a centre of operations in the bleak hills of West Virginia.

On the other side, the Confederate base-line extends roughly from Weldon in North Carolina, through Petersburg and the outermost fortifications of Richmond to Charlottesville, whence it enters the famous "Valley of Virginia" about Lexington and Staunton. Of the centres of operations along this line, Richmond was, even more than Washington to the Federals, of paramount importance. For one thing, the capital of the Confederacy was, for want of men and material, rarely in a position to defy a serious attack without aid from Lee's army. On the few occasions when Richmond was irrelevant to the political situation—that is, when the Confederacy was at the zenith, and again when it was at the nadir, of its fortunes—Lee showed no hesitation in making use of his unusual freedom by selecting new centres of operations—Lynchburg, Gordonsville, and the Valley.

Such being the respective base lines and the potential centres of operations, experience had shown first of all that a Federal army had a wider choice of centres of operations, and consequently of directions in which to advance, than a Confederate army. The reason is simple. Given that each side maintained an adequate field army, the superior resources of the North enabled Washington to be equipped as a self-supporting garrison—though the Federal authorities could rarely be brought to regard it as such—while those of the South were rarely great enough to provide, over and above the field army, the men and material to put Richmond on an equal footing with the Union capital. Politics required the preservation of these cities, but the cost of preserving Washington could generally have been met without paralysing the action of strategy, while on the James the contrary was the case.

But Lee did from time to time break away from Richmond, and the Federals were almost always free to break away from Washington, provided that the government was not over-solicitous for its safety. Were there in each of these cases any marked tendencies in the selection of new centres of operations?

As a general rule the Federals were inclined to select points at or near the coast, east and southeast of Washington, while Lee, when at liberty, invariably chose points lying to the west or northwest of Richmond. The reasons are obvious enough. Wherever a Federal commander put his back to the sea, and ships could put in to supply him with men and material, the whole resources of the North could be collected to form a new centre of operations. The movement of the army itself by sea* from one centre of operations to another

---

* This was another advantage to the Union side. The manœuvres of either side on land had always to take account, more or less, of the

was purely an administrative matter, and, if proper precautions were taken, must come as a surprise to the enemy on shore. Similarly, Lee's army always found in the Shenandoah Valley at once a granary and a screen to conceal the direction of its manœuvre. Richmond and Washington apart, then, Lee's possible centres of operations lay toward the left of his imaginary battle line, the Federals' towards the left of theirs, so that when Sheridan, in October, 1864, laid waste the beautiful and fertile Valley of Virginia, he was acting precisely as the Confederates would have acted had they collected a fighting fleet on the high seas. The rightmost of the Confederate centres were practically valueless, from a strategical point of view, owing to the all-powerful Federal navy. Similarly, the rightmost of the Federal centres, Romney or the towns of West Virginia, were unfavourable for the full development of their offensive power, being for the most part situated in a barren and mountainous region where the tactical advantage lay with the weaker party and it was impossible to feed a great army. Thus the Union operations towards the Shenandoah Valley were like those of the Confederate navy on the Atlantic coast— disconnected and trivial. In the supreme effort of the Northern people a surplus of force became available for the destruction of Confederate power in the Valley, but Sheridan's campaign, brilliant as it was, was of the nature of a diversion on a large

possibility of the enemy's interference. At sea nothing could interfere with the Federal transports. Thus troops were hurried from City Point to protect Washington in September, 1864, and their arrival was a matter of absolute certainty.

scale, intended to deprive Lee of merely potential, though vitally important, centres of operations.*

The mention of a "diversion" brings us to consider another feature of the strategical problem. One centre of operations leads the army that uses it against the enemy's army. Another against his capital, a third is a "jumping-off place" for the raiding of lines of communication. There remain, therefore, the questions that concern the selection of the objective or objectives of the operations, and the distribution of the forces or potential effort of the belligerent to attain the desired result. This for convenience we may call the "strategy of forces", and as forces are moral as well as material, and are elastic, while geographical lines are immutable, the larger branch of the whole strategical art is also by far the more complicated.

But just as Leonardo's "Monna Lisa" and an organ fugue of Bach are simple facts for the admiration of all, and the details of their structure are susceptible of explanation for the student of painting and music, so in dealing with an example of a great general's creative power, we can at least attempt a statement of the broad general idea and a study of the methods of execution.

The possible objectives of military operations

* Observe, however, that this is only in respect of what may be called the strategy of *directions*; considered as a display of the strategy of *forces*, Sheridan's Valley Campaign severely shook the moral of the enemy, and notably diminished his material forces. It is an excellent example of the interplay of all parts of strategic art. The importance of a merely potential centre of operations compelled Lee to give a favourable target for the strategy of forces, the action of which in turn guaranteed the Federals against a disconcerting change in the enemy's line of operations.

in one theatre of war may be classed as the enemy's field army, his centre of operations and his territory. The attack of each of these objectives is a means to an end—victory or the imposition of our own will on the enemy. Each reacts upon the other; the destruction of the enemy's field army entails the unopposed occupation of the enemy's territory, and the conquest of territory injuriously affects the field army. The first step then is to place the objectives in order of relative importance, and the second to distribute the available force accordingly.

For the North, of course, offensive measures constituted the greater part of the general policy of the war, but in order that political and material losses should not cripple the war-spirit from which this offensive proceeded, it was necessary to take account also of the various counter-attacks that the enemy might undertake.

Of these objectives, the lesson of experience had very definitely placed the enemy's field army first in order of importance, offensively and defensively. From the point of view of the offensive, Lee's army "carried the Confederacy on its bayonets", and the Confederacy could only be destroyed when that army was destroyed. So much was probably recognized by every soldier and every member of Congress. What was less understood was the influence that the enemy's army had on each of the events, great and small, that went to make up the total "war". There had been times at which it was thought that other means besides direct attack could bring about the universally desired overthrow of the enemy's armed forces—the encouragement of a peace party in the South, the occupation of a few counties, or even the seizure of so-called "strategic points". But experience had merged all these subsidiary means of offence in that of the direct attack and defeat of Lee's army in battle.

The attack of the enemy's centre of operations had been the principal if not the exclusive aim of McClellan in the spring of 1862, and the result of his campaign had been to reduce Richmond to the rank of a second-class, and to raise the Army of Northern Virginia to that of a first-class objective. Of itself, and apart from political questions, the centre of operations possessed no intrinsic importance. It was only the depôt of the army in the field. Its destruction might injuriously affect that army, but could not annihilate it. A subsidiary operation implies a main operation to which it is subsidiary. A main operation against a subsidiary objective was a waste, and in view of the possibility and probability of counter-strokes, a dangerous waste, of force. At best it merely changed the *venue* of the battle to a more cramped area of manœuvre, and at worst it exposed the assailant's own centre of operations at the precise moment when his striking radius was extended up to, very likely beyond, its maximum.

The third objective, the enemy's territory, becomes an objective as a consequence of two ideas, the one military, the other political. The military idea is the destruction or sequestration of the enemy's means of resistance, the political idea the acquisition or resumption of effective political control in the occupied districts. As to the latter, no political control is effective in the face of a victorious hostile army; as to the former, the resources of the enemy, which flow to the centre of operations and thence to the field army, come from the whole country and not from a province or two. Then, as soon as territorial losses become so heavy that the enemy is compelled to regain ground, he will do so by means of the same unbeaten field army, and if the territory threatened is not large enough to influence thus seriously the course of the war, it is certainly not a first-class objective. And, in fact, neither side regarded it as such, except in the doubtful cases of Pope's expedition towards Gordonsville in July, 1862, and Lee's invasion of Pennsylvania in June, 1863; in both these cases, it may be observed, the attempt ended in complete failure.*

The resultant axiom is the same, when approached from the standpoint of the defence. Only the field forces of the enemy can counterattack. The values of all other objectives, as such, are to be measured by their relation to the principal objective—the enemy's field army.

All this, from the defensive standpoint, the Union government had fully realized long before

---

* We are here concerned not with war policy, which handles all means, military and other, that will serve its purposes, but with strategy, which deals only with the means in the hands of the army commander. Such operations, therefore, as the rescue of the Union population in East Tennessee, and the use of small or large military forces to assist in establishing the blockade of the Southern coast, do not form part of the question here discussed.

Grant's advent. Confused as they were in respect of the offensive objects to be pursued, the ideas of Lincoln, Halleck, and Stanton were definite enough as to the defensive necessity of holding Lee's army, and of following it up with the Army of the Potomac wherever it went. It had certainly achieved what the Washington authorities had a right to expect of it according to their ideas of strategy. It had neutralized the finest army and the best generals of the Confederacy, confined them to Virginia, and forced them to leave the other armies to succumb before the tremendous resources of the north-western States. But the time for what one Union general calls a "good, wary, damaging, respectable fight" was past. The new feature in Grant's plan of operations was that Lee's army was to be the objective point, not the disturbing factor, in the Union offensive. The Army of the Potomac was to be told off, no longer to play policeman, but to destroy Lee's army.

The principal objective implies the principal effort, and therefore the assignment of the greatest number of troops. The difficulties of assigning the right percentage of the available total to each objective, and still more of unwillingly foregoing one hoped-for result in order more certainly to attain another, vary in practice from the simple case of one European "nation in arms" fighting another for non-territorial objects, to the very complex case of a civil war or rebellion in which political control over the disaffected territory may be almost as important as military success in the field. In these cases what is wanted is, not reasons and arguments, but a dogmatic rule of faith to sustain the executive in giving definite orders to its armies.

This might be stated, in accordance with Grant's practice, as follows:—The greatest number of troops susceptible of useful employment against the principal objective should be so employed. Any secondary objects which it is sought to attain *at the same time* as the principal one, must be assigned to such forces as are left over after the wants of the principal army have been fully provided for. The spirit of this rule admits of no modification, save those imposed by general military policy (to which strategy as "the practical application of the available means to the end" must be subordinate) and by defensive considerations. The offensive then is, in the first place, a blow aimed at the enemy's field army with every available man.

Grant, it may be admitted, fully and unreservedly gave in his adhesion to this article of faith. He gave the Army of the Potomac a five-to-three superiority in numbers, using his last undeployed reserve, the IX. Corps, to that end. At the same time he set on foot and maintained two subsidiary armies in Virginia, and the reasons for his doing so must, however briefly, be investigated.

The number and importance of secondary objectives (meaning here objectives other than Lee's army) had varied with the amount of direct effort applied to the principal objective. In March, 1862, the Valley and Richmond practically took up every man of the Army of the Potomac and more,

STRATEGY OF THE CAMPAIGNS

while Johnston's army was unopposed. From this extreme events gradually brought the Union executive towards the other, and Grant found, on becoming generalissimo, that the Army of the Potomac was confronting Lee, a considerable force under Butler looking towards Richmond, and a smaller force under Sigel towards the Valley. This arrangement he accepted, reinforcing the Army of the Potomac to what he considered the proper strength from other sources, and even drawing in an army corps from the South Carolina seaboard garrisons to support Butler.

The reasons for this were partly those of military policy—the retention of ground regained in the "rebel" States, the maintenance of the coast blockade, and also, it may here be said, the inadvisability of removing an important political personage — and partly those of the defensive branch of his strategy. But these secondary objectives were not considered as such because they would directly help to end the war, but because they would help to beat Lee's army. The loss of Richmond and the breakage of the Virginia and Tennessee Railroad were both results worth aiming at, as they impaired the efficiency of Lee's army at no particular cost to that of the Union—surplus forces only being employed. Where these surplus forces had failed to attain their objective simultaneously with the effort against the main objective, the secondary operations were not persisted in; on the contrary, every available man was ordered in to make good the losses of the Army of the Potomac.

Further, the secondary armies could do their cause good service whether successful or not. Butler could prevent Lee from being reinforced from the Carolinas, Sigel could keep in front of him the Confederates of the Valley and South-western Virginia. Still and ever, the leading idea is to annihilate Lee's army. While Lee's army is at large no town, no territory, however important, can be suffered to become a first-class objective.

It is the same in the defensive. If Lee's army were beaten, a mere police force would suffice for the protection of the North and for the occupation of the ground gained. Hitherto, this had been seen only partially; the Army of the Potomac had waited on Lee's movements closely enough, but when Lee made one of the sudden shifts of the centre of gravity in which his genius rejoiced, his army swept over the small Union defensive garrisons like a wave, while the Army of the Potomac was hardly yet afoot to follow it up. In Virginia mounted guerrilla bands, "partisan rangers", and even wandering cavalry brigades of the Confederate army were always to be feared. But the less the Army of Northern Virginia was able to spare a serious detachment to support them the less effectual their operations, and the "police" garrisons could be calculated at a minimum figure if the commanding general of the Army of the Potomac did not allow Lee to give him the slip. The only way to assure this was by a vigorous and energetic offensive to occupy Lee's undivided attention.

STRATEGY OF THE CAMPAIGNS

This was the service the offensive army could render to the defensive posts—to guarantee them against attack. But the actual forces available for these posts—after all other wants had been provided for—were in excess of the minimum requirements, and even here small field forces were to be got together * to aid in the general offensive against Lee's army by "keeping the ring" for the two principal combatants.

That done, all the main forces were to make their way to the Army of the Potomac. Napoleon counted his concentration incomplete if a single available battalion was absent, and Grant did not disdain to call in a few hundred fur-capped West Virginian troopers to join the magnificent Army of the Potomac.

We can now turn to the special strategy of the duel between the Army of the Potomac and the Army of Northern Virginia. Here there are no complications; the duty of each is to beat the other sufficiently often and sufficiently thoroughly to bring about a peace on terms dictated by the conqueror. Strategy is for them the art of obtaining a battle under the desired conditions. That part of it which deals with what may be called "troop-leading out of sight of the enemy", we defer until the next chapter, and having considered the directions and forces of the offensive above, we may conclude this section with a brief *résumé* in one sentence. Each army manœuvres to cut the

* There were many defensive posts whence no defensive-offensive was possible for want of a target. These could be stripped to the bare minimum to the profit of the defensive-offensive elsewhere, for if there was no force of the enemy to be attacked there was no force to attack.

other off from its centre of operations, so as to fight the battle under conditions laid down by itself, and in the course of its manœuvring chooses successive centres of operations to gain a better direction for its attack, the Union side leftwards towards the sea, the Confederate leftwards towards the Valley.

It is necessary to observe, before we proceed, that neither side was able to begin its offensive campaign from the theoretically best possible centre of operations.

The necessity of keeping in touch, so as to avoid a complete and unexpected shift of the centre of gravity, and the necessity of holding as much ground as possible—in the case of the Federals for political reasons, in that of the Confederates for reasons of supply in addition—had the natural consequence that the armies faced each other on the only line which was equally convenient for both. This line is, broadly speaking, the Orange and Alexandria Railroad. When a battle had decided the immediate issue—Second Bull Run, Chancellorsville, the Wilderness—it was time for the victor to take up a new centre of operations, and not before.

It is not difficult, therefore, to explain the fact that the winter quarters of the Army of the Potomac and the Army of Northern Virginia lay around Culpeper and Orange respectively. Viewed from this standpoint, Grant's "overland" campaign from the Rapidan to the James is so obviously a necessity of the situation as to need none of the apologies that have been made for it.

CHAPTER VI

ON THE RAPIDAN

THE strategic direction of manœuvre, then, for either side being towards its enemy's right flank, and the initial position of the armies being, to all intents and purposes, front to front, the first attempt of either side will be to outflank the enemy, and if possible to get in rear of him before attacking. The topography of Virginia gave a special character to manœuvres to this end, for nearly all the rivers run from north-west to south-east, *i.e.* between the fronts of the two armies. The temptation to assault solid earthworks is one to which at any time only the strongest commanders are liable, and when those earthworks had swift streams, a hundred feet or more broad, in front of them, frontal attack, pure and simple, was absolutely out of the question. Further, as the river valleys ran parallel to the front, the main roads naturally did so too, as a glance at the map of Virginia (Map. I.) shows. The only important road from north to south is the Valley Turnpike, which was as fine a highway for Lee as the sea was for Grant.

Roads there were besides these, of course, and a considerable network of them, but they were unmetalled, and, with a few exceptions, not even "plank" roads, and the "rainy season" in Virginia deserved its name so far that one rainy day sufficed to cast a spell over the moving armies from which they were only released when the ground had had time to dry. Humourists in the Northern army, when asked if they had been "through Virginia", would reply, "Yes, in a number of places!"

The effect on manœuvring power was disastrous, more especially on that of the Federals. They had always more men to feed, for superiority in numbers was the first condition of their offensive movements, and greater difficulty in feeding them on the country, for if superior numbers told and the Confederates fell back, they left behind them little or nothing for the pursuers to eat. Hence, and also because the greater material resources of the Union were freely used to ensure the comfort of the men, Federal commanders were always encumbered with an enormous and unwieldy wagon train.*

To the Federals, who from the nature of the cause for which they were fighting were almost invariably the aggressors, Lee's country as well as Lee's army presented a barrier which must have appeared to each successive general, when confronted with the responsibility of command, practically insurmountable. The army, and still more the Northern people behind the army, were clamorous for a decision; yet how was a speedy decision to

* Numbering at least 6500 vehicles and 31,000 animals, for 156,000 men, even when no cross-country movement was in contemplation. (Jan. 1, 1863, just after Fredericksburg.) A veteran who had served in all the campaigns of the Army of the Potomac records his first experience of "real hunger" in May, 1864!

be obtained when a movement against the enemy entailed weeks of previous preparation and even then depended on the luck of a few fine days? Suppose, however, that it was attempted and the army moved against Lee's right flank and rear, as it did in the present campaign, the first part of the march would probably be on a good eastward road. The aim, too, of the whole manœuvre might be to deliver the attack westward along another good road. But the flank march from one main road to the other by "dirt" roads or mere tracks, and the subsequent deployment of the army for battle, were most delicate operations in the face of an active and alert enemy, who himself disposed of one or more good east and west roads, and covered by a broad river, could afford to ignore a holding attack on his front. Slow forward movements and sudden lateral shifts of the centre of gravity are therefore the main characteristics of manœuvres in Virginia, and both told heavily against the Federals.

Moreover, at any point during such a manœuvre serious fighting might begin at a time and place not desired by the Union superior leading. The prearranged scheme might be abandoned and the encounter battle accepted, or again, time and room might have to be secured by a detachment of the army while the rest executed the original manœuvre. In either case the fighting value of 1000 Federals *vis-à-vis* 1000 Confederates must be the principal factor in the assailant's calculations. In the West, Sherman was able to rely upon any of his battalions to hold its own against an equal, and for a well-ascertained time, against a superior force of the Confederates. In Virginia, however, Lee's army, starting with equal intensity of purpose, improving year by year under leaders who were not readily changed, self-confident because it had known victory, and above all possessing the desperate courage of the weaker side, was man for man distinctly superior to its opponent. Grant attributed this result not to his men, who, it was to be supposed, had improved, *pari passu*, with the enemy, but to the way in which they had been led, and intended to remedy the deficiency. Still, allowing that he succeeded and made any one Federal soldier the equal of any one Confederate, this would only mean equality after all. Superiority had to be sought in the one remaining factor, numbers. And the greater the difference, in point of moral, between the rival armies, the more urgent the necessity for counter-balancing it by an increase in the ratio of material strength. On this ground Grant has been severely criticized for calculating the required material superiority at too low a figure. He undoubtedly underestimated the temper of his new opponent. It must be said, however, that there was nothing in the history of the Army of the Potomac to show that it could not, when properly led, defeat the Army of Northern Virginia with a much less margin of strength in its favour than the two-fifths that Grant gave it.

If we state the criticisms the other way round and accuse him of putting too much bad metal into his sledge-hammer, he could have replied in the same sense, that if one-fifth or more of his army was entirely worthless—which was far from being the case—he would still possess a certain superiority. Above all, he possessed the means of making good his casualties indefinitely.

In the winter of 1863-4, Lee's army, as already stated, lay in quarters around Orange Court House, its outposts watching the whole length of the Rapidan and the Rappahannock from South-West Mountain to Port Royal.

The interior distribution of corps was as follows (Sketch Map 3):—

A. P. Hill's Corps (3rd) held the left of the Rapidan position, around Orange Court House, a few brigades being distributed on the river itself, but the main body massed well to the rear.

Ewell's Corps (2nd) held the right of the Rapidan position, and the "return" along Mine Run, similarly disposed to Hill.

Stuart's Cavalry Corps found detachments for watching the Rapidan beyond both flanks of the army, but the main body was quartered on the lower Rappahannock, south-east of Fredericksburg, where it had at its command the forage and supplies of a district which the military operations had not as yet passed over. There was no scope for the employment of cavalry on the front of the Confederate army.

Headquarters were at Orange Court House.

These corps were estimated by General Humphreys in April to number 55,000. In addition—

Longstreet's Corps (1st), which in the autumn and winter had been employed elsewhere, lay in and about Gordonsville, nearest to the enemy, should he attack the left flank of the Confederates, but far away in the other alternative of an attack on the Mine Run side, which Lee is known to have considered the more probable of the two. It seems indeed as if Lee desired to control the two centres of operations, Richmond and Lynchburg, as long as possible.

Longstreet's two divisions the same estimate gave as 15,000 effectives.

Other forces, not directly in front of the Army of the Potomac, and to be accounted for, as it was hoped, by Butler and Sigel, were—

Breckinridge (Valley), 10,000.

Pickett's division of Longstreet's corps detached in North Carolina or Southern Virginia, 10,000.

Beauregard's army, concentrating in North Carolina from the various garrisons of the south-eastern States, 15,000.

Richmond garrison, 6000.

Of these last, Sigel was, in the general scheme of operations, required to look after 10,000 and Butler 31,000. They were not, therefore, counted in as influencing the situation on the Rapidan on May 1. They were, moreover, more potential than actual armies, as their concentration had scarcely begun when Grant crossed the Rapidan. Pickett's division was, however, reckoned upon from the first as part of its corps, Longstreet's, and was, therefore, counted in and made Lee's total 80,000.

The total "present for duty equipped" with the Army of the Potomac and the IX. Corps on May 1 was—

ON THE RAPIDAN

Army of the Potomac—Army Troops	.	5,684
Cavalry Corps	.	13,287
II. Corps	.	28,333
V. Corps	.	25,663
VI. Corps	.	24,213
	Total	97,180
IX. Corps	Total	22,762
	Grand Total	119,942

This gives the Union army a superiority in the ratio of 3 to 2, which, if the staff estimate of Lee's forces was by ever so little overstated, would prove in fact to be one of 5 to 3.

Strategy is, according to Moltke, the practical adaptation of the available means to attain the object in view. The means was, material superiority, the end, the defeat of Lee's army in battle. The correlation of these was the task before Grant, when he arrived at Meade's headquarters to discuss plans of campaign with that officer.

First of all it was advisable to avoid, as far as possible, country unsuited to the offensive action of masses. The surplus of force remaining over after many hours of equal battle could not act effectively without room in which to act, and in the vicissitudes of wood fighting, the closed reserves were apt to be frittered away in repairing partial failures. Suitable open country for a great battle —not a local "pitching into a part of Lee's forces"[*]—might be found on Lee's left flank towards Orange Court House and Gordonsville,

[*] See Ch. VIII.

on the Mine Run line, or further to the south, west of Spottsylvania Court House.

The decision between these was made in accordance with the strategical, tactical, and administrative requirements of the situation. If a battle could be obtained east of the South-West Mountain, between Gordonsville and Orange, the tactical conditions would be most favourable. But no strategical object would be gained by bringing about the decision on that flank, save the purely negative one that Lee would not be able, in Grant's phrase, to "go North on a raid". From the supply and transport officer's point of view, such an operation was the worst possible.

Washington would have to be the unchangeable centre of operations, and the long vulnerable Orange and Alexandria Railroad would have to be garrisoned and held at all costs as the only line of supply. The sustenance of an army corps for one day weighed 100 to 130 tons; one train derailed and fired by wandering Confederate cavalry or irregulars meant one day's supplies the less at the front. A line of such importance has to be held strongly at every point, as it is equally vulnerable at every point in it and the defenders may have to be numerous enough at any and every point to ward off an attack on that point. Further, the fifteen days' supplies which the army wagon train carried might be exhausted before the decision had been obtained, and in this case the line of supply would have to be extended from railhead to the front and guarded by further detachments from the fighting strength of the army.

The objection to the Gordonsville-Orange movement from a combatant point of view was equally serious. Not only would the strength of the army be frittered away on the line of supply, but the manœuvre involved a forty miles' march, the object of which could not possibly be concealed from the enemy. Lee would have ample time to take up an entrenched position on the Federal line of advance, and the Army of the Potomac would have to fight, not on the hoped-for open battlefield, but in the defiles of the South-West Mountain, with the alternatives of retiring baffled to the Orange and Alexandria Railroad, and of extending the line of supply still further round in full view of the enemy.

The movement by the left towards a battle-ground on Mine Run or towards Craig's Church, met the strategic and administrative conditions perfectly.

To take the latter first, successive centres of operations and successive short lines of supply could be adopted and abandoned at will. Grant actually managed to do without an organized and garrisoned line of supply, from the time he abandoned the Orange and Alexandria Railroad on May 4 to the day on which he arrived before Petersburg. The convoys of men and material passing to and fro between the army and the centre of operations were of course frequent enough, and in a sense regular enough, but each had to take its chance of meeting the enemy like any other body of troops ordered to proceed from one place to another. It was a move under escort across the open—not even " from cover to cover ", as is the case on a fully established line of supply, still less between two long hedges of bayonets.

The strategic reasons for an advance against Lee's right in preference to his left were those that had dictated all other Union operations in Virginia, and neglecting the specious and illusory tactical advantages of the Orange-Gordonsville battle-ground, Grant, and Meade and Humphreys, with whom he held several consultations, were content to aim at a moderately favourable field, such as that between Spottsylvania and Craig's Meeting House, and to keep the recognized strategical advantages of the movement by the left flank. This is an excellent example of the relation between tactics and strategy. Topographical considerations are, after due consideration, relegated to the background, as inconsistent with the strategical situation, and the call is made upon the tactical art to do its best under the conditions as it finds them. Tactics, in fact, might here be regarded as a compensating arrangement to keep the true balance between the strategical requirements of the army and the nation, and the technical claims of the cavalry, artillery, and infantry.

In the present case there was the additional argument in favour of moving by the left flank, that thereby connection or co-operation with Butler was facilitated. An actual concentration of the Army of the Potomac and the Army of the James was not in view, but Butler had been warned of the necessity of co-operation, like all other subordinate commanders, and instructed that all the serious effort of which his army was capable was to be directed against Richmond. Moreover, serious harm would follow should Lee break loose from the Army of the Potomac and turn on Butler. All students of war in those days had read Jomini, and had assimilated the idea of interior and exterior lines.* It was likely that this idea would have some play in the forthcoming operations. The Richmond authorities had followed the Federal example and begun to collect a second field army under General Beauregard for the defence of Southern Virginia. This was in a backward state of concentration in May, as compared with the Army of the James, but between the four field armies, with the addition of a fifth element in the shape of the garrison and defences of Richmond,† there were many strategic possibilities of exploiting the interior line. As events turned out, however, it was the army from Culpeper that, skirting past all the others, finally appeared on the extreme left towards Hicksford, by which time Lee and Beauregard were united, and also Meade and Butler.

* General Beauregard says that, when taking command of the Confederate forces at Petersburg, he placed on the map the positions of his own, Butler's, Lee's, and Meade's armies, and on measuring the distances and *finding that the Confederates were on interior lines*, proceeded to advise Mr. Davis as to a new plan of campaign based on his discovery. (*Battles and Leaders*, iv. 197.)

† Another form of "interior lines" *à la* Jomini is that exemplified, according to him, in the Jena Campaign, viz. interposition between an enemy's army and its centre of operations or base, where a second hostile army might possibly assemble to support the first. In fact, whenever there are two objectives to attack, and we manoeuvre so as to place ourselves in a position to attack either, we are manoeuvring for or on the "interior line".

The use of "interior lines" does not in fact constitute the whole of the strategical art. It might or might not be good strategy for Lee to ignore his old enemy and to turn upon the new. With this question we are not concerned. But from the standpoint of the Union commander it is difficult to see any special advantage in manœuvring so as to gain the interior line between Lee and Beauregard. He desired to fight Lee *à deux*, not to have the choice of fighting either Lee or Beauregard. His attempts to obtain the interior line between Lee and Beauregard, as apart from his manœuvres against Lee's communication with Richmond, were therefore limited to the negative object of preventing the two Confederate generals from uniting to crush Butler. A positive application of the idea—the transfer of the Army of the Potomac to the James—was not contemplated. Such a measure might have one of several undesired results. One might be that Lee would "go North", another would be that he might hurry to interpose between Grant and Richmond, a third that he might retire from Richmond towards his new centre of operations at Lynchburg. Grant's target was Lee's army and not Richmond, and only in case Lee should choose to defend Richmond, and should arrive in time to do so, was it to be hoped that he could be brought to battle. As a matter of fact, the responsible generals at Brandy Station—Grant, Meade, and Humphreys—all preferred fighting Lee on the Rapidan, where there was room and to spare for strategic manœuvres, to fighting him with his back close up to the fortifications of Richmond. In the other cases, given that Lee failed to save or deliberately sacrificed Richmond, the value of which as a political centre had diminished, and transferred all that made it a military centre to Lynchburg, he might have prolonged the war indefinitely on a new and more favourable line of operations.

In the case of the two minor armies, as we shall see, the game of "interior lines" resolved itself inevitably into applications of the eternal rule of economy of forces. Beauregard and Butler were concerned locally and primarily with the defence and attack of Richmond. As factors in the general strategic situation they were not so much armies as reservoirs of fresh troops. Grant's crossing of the James might indeed be called an operation on the interior line on a grand scale, but it was based not on the position, but on the holding power of Warren's covering detachment. "Interior lines" is a convenient technical term, but it is not a self-sufficing theory of strategy.

All these considerations pointed to a movement against Lee's right rear, preparatory to a battle. On this side there were, roughly speaking, two possible battlefields — Mine Run and Craig's Church—at which to aim, and the choice between them was made on tactical grounds. Both entailed the disadvantage of a preliminary march through the most unfavourable spot in Virginia—rightly called The Wilderness. It was therefore obviously good policy for the Federals to keep as far out of Lee's way as possible during their movement through this region.

Every mile covered between Wilderness Tavern and Mine Run brought the Federals nearer to Lee, every mile towards Spottsylvania interposed more of the forest area between Lee and themselves. Further, the line of Mine Run was a well-prepared defensive position, and the further the Army of the Potomac swung out to the southwest before attacking, the less influence Lee's previous arrangements would have on the fate of the battle. Mine Run therefore was ruled out, and the country to the west of Spottsylvania Court House selected as the area in which to seek the first decision.

To gain this chosen battle-ground, it was decided to turn Lee's right wing by crossing the Rapidan below Mine Run and, after a forward march of some miles, swerving to the south-west. General Humphreys prepared two projects for the manœuvre, which was calculated to take two days. The only difference between them was in the routes to be used on the second day. One of these would have diverted the axis of the movement a little more round to the South, so as to meet the case of Lee's falling back towards the North Anna. The other aimed roughly at New Hope Church on the Orange and Fredericksburg Plank Road, and would there presumably meet and overlap the extreme right of Lee's present position. Sufficient evidence to enable the Union generals to decide would, it was hoped, be forthcoming on the evening of the first day.

Practically no criticism has ever been made of the general idea of this scheme. The time allowed for its execution (two days) has, however, been the subject of comment and discussion. It is admitted that the various corps were not by any means overtaxed by the first day's work assigned them. The marches ordered for the two days could, in fact, have been accomplished before going into bivouac on the evening of the first day. The line of the Turnpike was, however, fixed as the limit of the day's march for the infantry. The reason for this early halt was that the trains—the second line transport of the army, with fifteen days' supplies, which Grant says would have reached in single file from the Rapidan to Richmond—could not be got over the river during the first day.* In order not to uncover this interminable procession of wagons, the columns of the fighting troops, which moved between the train and the enemy, had to advance at a relatively slow pace. The Quartermaster-General, Ingalls, was a brave and able soldier, and he had over three thousand rifles and a cavalry division to act as escort, but bearing in mind that he would have to deal with a whole corps of the enemy with the fraction of the escort available at the point attacked, and that the responsible generals considered that it would be unsafe to leave a wide gap between the river and the rear of the combatant column, it is not easy to condemn the early halt on the first day as a mistake.

In one thing, however, the staff, or rather its theory of war, its "doctrine", is certainly open

* As a matter of fact it was 5 P.M. on the second day before they were all across.

to criticism. If the movement had been executed in one day, it could not have been interfered with by the enemy, whose concentration (the time of which could be, and was, calculated by the Union headquarters) must necessarily take up at least the whole of the first day. On the second day it was certain that sooner or later Lee would make his presence felt.

It was hoped that, as in the Mine Run Campaign of the early winter, Lee would not succeed in concentrating to his flank before the Army of the Potomac had passed the danger point and completed its preparatory manœuvre. This was a hope and no more, and General Humphreys says "both (projects) were subject to material modification or entire abandonment, dependent upon the movements of Lee".

This sentence reveals a very serious fault in the "doctrine". So far had Napoleon been forgotten in the wrangle of the theorists, that the best soldiers of the day, Moltke amongst them, had no place in their theory of war for the idea of binding the enemy before manœuvring. The plan proposed was excellent and beyond criticism, except in the one particular that Lee might interfere with its execution. This was foreseen, *but not provided against*. Grant, though he was far from possessing a formal and expressed theory of war—"I never manœuvre!" he is reported to have said just before crossing the Rapidan—saw so deeply into the heart of things that his confidence can only be understood on the ground that he under-estimated Lee's versatility. Pemberton in the Vicksburg campaign and Bragg at Chattanooga had not interfered with the development of his plans, and in so far he was the spoiled child of victory. The officers of the Army of the Potomac, on the other hand, were used to disappointments of this kind, and had courage to meet them. But this very courage predisposed them in a measure to forego their most carefully thought-out schemes at a hint of Lee's intentions.

To a student of Napoleon's strategy, as we know it to-day, the alternatives would have been simple, either to finish the manœuvre in one day, the period during which Lee had to busy himself with his own preparations, or to provide against the certainty of Lee's interference on the second by telling off a force for the special duty of keeping him occupied during the time necessary for the completion of the manœuvre.

The one alternative was deliberately and for doubtless good reasons rejected, but the second was ignored. The one preoccupation of the staff was to accomplish as much of the second day's manœuvre as possible before Lee stopped it.

The movement, as has been said, was expected to take two days, and the battle would begin about midday on the second day. After that, it was admittedly impossible to forecast events.

The first part of the manœuvre to turn Lee's right flank preparatory to a battle was set forth in the following (abbreviated) order issued on the 2nd of May (see Map II. and Sketch Map 3)—

Headquarters Army of the Potomac, May 2, 1864.

1. The Army will move on Wednesday the 4th May, 1864.

2. On the day previous, Tuesday, 3rd May, Major-General Sheridan will move Gregg's cavalry division to the vicinity of Richardsville. It will be accompanied by one half of the canvas pontoon train, the engineer troop with which will repair the road to Ely's Ford as far as practicable without exposing their work to the observation of the enemy.

Guards will be placed . . . so as to prevent any communication with the enemy. The same precaution will be taken . . . wherever it may be considered necessary.

At 2 A.M. on the 4th May, Gregg's division will move to Ely's Ford, cross the Rapidan as soon as the canvas pontoon bridge is laid if the river is not fordable, and as soon as the infantry of the II. Corps is up will move to the vicinity of Piney Branch Church, or in that section, throwing reconnaissances well out . . . towards Spottsylvania C.H., Hamilton's Crossing, and Fredericksburg.

The road past Piney Branch Church, Tod's Tavern, etc., will be kept clear for the passage of the infantry the following day.

The cavalry division will remain in their position to cover the passage of the army trains, and will move with them and cover their left flank.

At midnight on the 3rd May, the 3rd Cavalry Division, with one half the canvas pontoon train, which will join it after dark, will move to Germanna Ford, cross the Rapidan as soon as the bridge is laid, if the river is not fordable, and hold the crossing until the infantry is up; it will then move to Parker's Store or that vicinity, sending out strong reconnaissances on the Orange plank and pike roads, and the Catharpin and Pamunkey roads, until they feel the enemy, and at least as far as Robertson's Tavern, the Hope Church, etc. . . .

All intelligence concerning the enemy will be communicated with promptitude to headquarters and to the nearest infantry troops.

3. Major-General Warren (V. Corps) will send two

divisions at midnight of the 3rd instant to the crossing of Germanna Ford. So much bridge train as may be necessary to bridge the Rapidan, with such artillery as may be required, will accompany these divisions, which will be followed by the remainder of the corps at such hour that the column will cross the Rapidan without delay. Such disposition of the troops and artillery as may be found necessary to cover the bridge will be made by the corps commander, who after crossing will move to the vicinity of the Wilderness Tavern. . . . The corps will move the following day past the head of Catharpin Run, crossing the Orange plank-road at Parker's Store.

4. Major-General Sedgwick (VI. Corps) will move at 4 A.M. on the 4th instant . . . to Germanna Ford, following the V. Corps, and will bivouac on the heights beyond the Rapidan. The canvas pontoon train will be taken up as soon as the VI. Corps has crossed, and will follow immediately in rear of the troops of that corps.

So much of the bridge train of the VI. Corps as may be necessary to bridge the Rapidan at Culpeper Mine Ford will proceed to Richardsville in rear of the reserve artillery, and as soon as it is ascertained that the reserve artillery are crossing, it will move to Culpeper Mine Ford, where the bridge will be established.

The engineers of this bridge train will at once open a road from Culpeper Mine Ford . . . to Richardsville.

5. Major-General Hancock (II. Corps) will send two divisions, with so much of the bridge train as may be necessary to bridge the Rapidan at Ely's Ford, and such artillery as may be required, at midnight of the 3rd instant, to Ely's Ford. The remainder of the corps will follow at such hour that the column will cross the Rapidan without delay.

The canvas pontoon train at this ford will be taken up as soon as the troops of this corps have passed, and will move with it at the head of the trains that accompany the troops. The wooden pontoon bridges will remain.

. . . After crossing the Rapidan the II. Corps will move to the vicinity of . . . Chancellorsville.

6. It is expected that the advance divisions of the V. and II. Corps, with the wooden pontoon trains, will be at the designated points of crossing not later than 6 A.M. of the 4th instant.

7. The reserve artillery will move at 3 A.M. of the 4th instant and follow the II. Corps . . . crossing at Ely's Ford, take the road to Chancellorsville, and halt for the night at Hunting Creek.

8. Great care will be taken by the corps commanders that the roads are promptly repaired wherever needed, not only for temporary wants but for the passage of the troops and trains that follow on the same route.

9. . . . The commanders of the V. and VI. Corps will occupy the roads on the right flank to cover the passage of their corps, and will keep their flankers well out in that direction.

The commanders of the II. Corps and reserve artillery will in a similar manner look out for the left flank.

Wherever practicable, double columns will be used to shorten the columns. Corps commanders will keep in communication . . . and co-operate wherever necessary. Their picket lines will be connected. They will keep the commanding general constantly advised. Headquarters will be on the route of the V. and VI. Corps. It will be established at night between those corps. . . .

10. The infantry will take with them fifty rounds of ammunition upon the person, three days' full rations in the haversacks, three days' bread and small rations in the knapsacks, and three days' beef on the hoof.

Each corps will take with it one half of the intrenching tools, one hospital wagon, and one medium wagon for each brigade, one half of the ambulance trains and the light spring-wagons, and pack animals allowed at the various headquarters.

No other trains or means of transportation than those just specified will accompany the corps, except such wagons as may be necessary for the forage for immediate use for five days. The artillery will have with them the ammunition of the caissons only.

11. (Army trains) will be assembled under the direction of the chief quartermaster in the vicinity of Richardsville, with a view to crossing the . . . bridges at Ely's Ford and Culpeper Mine Ford.

12. A detail of 1000 or 1200 men will be made from each corps as guard for its . . . trains. . . . No other guards whatever for regimental, brigade, division or corps wagons will be allowed. . . .

This guard will be so disposed as to protect the trains on the march and in park. The trains are likewise protected by cavalry on the flank and rear.

13. Major-General Sheridan . . . will direct the First Cavalry Division to call in its pickets and patrols on the right on the morning of the 4th instant, and hold itself ready to move and cover the trains of the army; it will picket and watch the fords of the Rapidan from Rapidan Station to Germanna Ford. On the morning of the 5th the First Cavalry Division will cross the Rapidan at Germanna Ford, and cover the right flank of the trains while crossing the Rapidan and during their movement in rear of the army.

The signal stations on Cedar, Poney, and Stoney Mountains will be maintained as long as practicable.

14. The wooden pontoon train at Germanna and Ely's Fords will remain for the passage of General Burnside's army. That at Culpeper Mine Ford will be taken up . . . as soon as the trains have crossed, and will move with the trains of its corps.

By command of Major-General Meade,
S. WILLIAMS, A.A.G.

One or two remarks on this elaborate and carefully worked-out order before we pass on to its execution. There are many preparatory orders for the second day's work, as, for example, the order to Gregg to keep the Todd's Tavern road free for the passage of infantry, and the naming of the eventual route assigned to the V. Corps. The precautions for the right flank in paragraph 9 are, it is to be noted, tactical, not strategical, and have in view only the local protection of the marching column from surprise. Two out of the three cavalry divisions are directly or indirectly employed for the protection of the army trains, greatly to the disgust of the energetic Sheridan, who had met with and overcome many difficulties in the organization and mounting of his command, in recalling detachments idly employed with infantry headquarters, and in putting an end to unnecessary outpost work.

The tactical features of the proposed crossing present certain points of interest. Warren is ordered to tell off half his corps, with the necessary artillery, to move ahead and to secure the passage at Germanna, and Hancock receives similar instructions in regard to his point of crossing at Ely's Ford. Gregg's and Wilson's cavalry commands are to precede the infantry and to hold the outlets of the bridges until the infantry is up. Germanna, indeed, which was the point at which, if at all, Lee must oppose the crossing of the Rapidan, presents remarkable advantages over other possible points of passage, besides that of being the point where the only available " plank " road crossed the river. Guns a little way down the slope of the bluffs on the north side could command, almost enfilade, the ford at short range, without fear of reverse fire from the Confederate bank, owing to the shape of the ground. There were plenty of depressions in which troops could be massed out of sight preparatory to the crossing, and several fords lower down which gave facilities for crossing and taking in reverse the defenders of the Germanna Ford. Once a crossing was made. the loop of the Rapidan provided a short line of defence for the leading Union troops to cover the passage of the remainder, and a sufficient safe area for the assembly of the whole army. If the enemy was found in unexpectedly large force, Warren's corps alone would be engaged, and Sedgwick could be diverted to another ford, Warren withdrawing at leisure.

It was a well-planned operation that seemed likely to command success, even if seriously opposed by the Confederates. There was reason to hope, however, that nothing more than outpost resistance would be encountered.

Germanna Ford was nine or ten miles east of Lee's right flank on the Rapidan and Mine Run, and even if Lee had been ready to move at once, half a corps (it will be noticed that Warren's advanced guard was precisely of this strength) could be across before Lee's foremost troops could come on the scene. Even then the whole V. Corps would be across long before the Confederate general had enough force on the ground to crush the two advanced Union divisions. Army orders, it will be noticed, laid special stress on the necessity of moving the second half of the corps immediately behind the tail of the advanced guard.

Given, therefore, that Lee did not concentrate on his right in time to throw a whole corps upon Warren's advanced guard within three hours of the alarm, the safe passage of the Union right column was a logistic certainty. Measures were taken to ensure the necessary condition. The start was made at midnight, so that the passage of the river could begin in the early morning of the 4th. The corps commanders were warned to shorten their columns* and to calculate their marching times and depths exactly. The permissible time-length of the right column, given that Grant's intention was not to fight at or near the Rapidan, but to get his army over the obstacle with the least possible delay, was about four hours—one hour for the alarm and the issue of Lee's orders, and three for the march of his leading division to Germanna. The crossing of the cavalry and the advanced guard of the V. Corps would be the actual alarm signal, and for the rest, four hours gives a space equivalent of thirteen miles, or one and a half army corps closely locked up. The logistics of the movement were, in fact, all that the most critical staff officer could desire.

Warren, Sedgwick, and Wilson alone were to cross within striking distance of the enemy. Hancock's corps, the army reserve of artillery, and the army trains were organized as a separate column and sent round by Ely's, and eventually Culpeper, Fords. The cavalry division of Gregg accompanied the left column, not only for reconnaissance and protection, but on account of the reported position of the enemy's cavalry a few miles to the south-east of Chancellorsville.

About midnight, then, on the 3rd/4th of May,

---

* "Doubling" a line or column meant locking up on to it a line or column of other troops, *e.g.* marching two brigades in fours abreast on the same road, or placing one battalion in line three or four paces in rear of another which was also in line.

1864, the army started on the campaign that was to bring it, after eleven months' practically incessant fighting, to the complete and unqualified victory which ended the war and the existence of the Confederate States of America.

CHAPTER VII

THE 4TH OF MAY

Headquarters. — General Grant, with the headquarter staff, left Culpeper after the army had begun its movement and rode to the front, reaching Germanna just before Sedgwick's corps. He took up his quarters for the night in an old house just beyond the river. General Meade and his staff established themselves between the V. and VI. Corps.

Right Column. — (3rd Cavalry Division, V. and VI. Corps.) The 3rd Cavalry Division (Wilson) broke camp at Stevensburg, 1 A.M., 4th, and crossed the Rapidan at Germanna Ford, 3 A.M. to 5 A.M., the advanced guard driving off a small cavalry post of the enemy. After covering the crossing of Warren's leading division (two bridges were laid by the engineers), Wilson moved on to Wilderness Tavern, scouted his front and flanks, and then, on the head of Warren's column appearing, continued the forward movement, by wood roads, to the south-west. A strong patrol was ordered to push out on the Orange Pike to Locust Grove, to drive away the enemy from that place, and to make its way across country to Parker's Store whither the main body of the division was directed. In accordance with his instructions, Wilson halted and bivouacked in position at this place, sending another strong patrol along the Plank Road towards Mine Run. His position here "enabled him to give timely notice of any movement of the enemy from Mine Run". At 2.10 P.M. Wilson sent to the Cavalry Corps headquarters a civilian—"Mr. Sime, a citizen of Great Britain"—whose information was to the effect that yesterday (3rd), at 2 P.M., Longstreet was between Gordonsville and Orange C.H., Ewell and Hill at the latter place. Later, there were reports of an infantry brigade on the lower Mine Run, and of Rodes' division of Ewell's corps approaching from Orange. Wilson reported further that he had only seen a few slight parties of the enemy here and there, and that the enemy's troops were "well down towards Mine Run on all the roads except this" (the Orange Plank). Later still (at 7.40 P.M.), in asking for fresh orders for the 5th (which apparently he never received), he reported that his patrols had been to the Catharpin Road, but had seen little of the enemy and nothing of Gregg's division (left column). Patrols on the Plank Road* skirmished with the enemy's cavalry one mile short of Mine Run; of that on the Pike (Locust Grove) he has no news. As to the latter, Sheridan himself, further to the rear, reports that during the morning's march the scouts thrown out to the right found Confederate infantry pickets at Bartlett's Mill on Mine Run, and a force of cavalry at Locust Grove. There does not seem

* Which he calls the Pike in his later report of operations.

to be any report of Union cavalry ever actually reaching Locust Grove that day, but General Wilson's report (dated, however, June 1) states that the main body at Parker's Store worked up to the Mine Run crossing on both the main roads, and developed only small bodies of cavalry on that stream.

The Cavalry Corps headquarters were established near Wilderness Tavern. Sheridan was, however, far more occupied with Gregg's adventures than with Wilson's, for a heavy force of hostile cavalry was reported near Fredericksburg.

It seems strange that the reconnaissance of the Turnpike and Locust Grove was entrusted to so small a body of men as a strong patrol. Wilson unquestionably executed his orders. He "felt" the enemy, reconnoitred freely on the Pike and Plank Roads, as well as the roads to the south, and took position at or near Parker's Store. But the effect was that the Pike was reconnoitred, *and not held*. No force of the Union army spent the night out on this road, though one of the objects of Wilson's move was to obtain timely notice of *any* movement of the enemy from Mine Run, and the result was that on the following morning Ewell's Confederates came directly upon the V. Corps, without having to clear away any preliminary opposition.

The V. Corps (Warren) left Culpeper about midnight on the 3rd/4th May, and marched through Stevensburg. The head of the column arrived at the ford about six, and at seven followed Wilson's cavalry division over the bridge, moving on

THE 4TH OF MAY

thence by the Germanna Plank Road to Wilderness Tavern, around which the corps bivouacked in line of battle, and, for the most part, behind improvised defences. Griffin's division was, very prudently, sent out some distance on the Pike towards Locust Grove. Dispositions for the night —

Robinson's division along the Germanna Road, towards Flat Run.

Wadsworth's division, Wilderness Tavern, and eastward along the Orange Pike.

Griffin's division holding the road towards Locust Grove about one and a half miles west of Wilderness Tavern.

Crawford's division on Griffin's left rear.

Corps headquarters and reserve artillery, near Wilderness Tavern.

VI. Corps (Sedgwick) left its camps on the Hazel River about 4 A.M. on the 4th, and marched *viâ* Stevensburg to Germanna Ford, crossing there after Warren, and forming up in bivouac about Flat Run. Sedgwick, like Warren, entrenched, and lay along the Germanna Plank Road, facing west, his left in touch with Warren's (Robinson's) right.

Left Column. — (2nd Cavalry Division, II. Corps, Army Reserve Artillery and Army Trains.) The 2nd Cavalry Division (Gregg) broke camp on the afternoon and evening of the 3rd of May and moved *viâ* Richardsville on Ely's Ford. The leading troops forded the river, while the engineers laid a canvas pontoon bridge.

When the infantry came up to the ford Gregg moved on to Chancellorsville, and later, when the head of Hancock's column appeared at that place, the cavalry moved on again, eastward to Aldrich's on the Plank Road. Between this point and Silver's the division went into bivouac during the afternoon, scouting its front towards Piney Branch Church and its left flank towards Fredericksburg. One of the two regiments at Silver's had a brush with forty or fifty of the enemy's troopers about 4 P.M.

Immediately on crossing the Rapidan in the early morning, General Gregg had sent an officer's patrol towards Wilderness Tavern to get in touch with the right column. General Hancock, as we shall see, took the same precaution in the afternoon, ascertaining that the Pike was clear up to Warren's bivouacs. But Wilson, as mentioned above, received no news of Gregg, after the line of the Turnpike was once crossed, during the whole day. Sheridan instructed Gregg, in the afternoon, that on account of the heavy force of hostile cavalry reported at Fredericksburg, he was to spend the night in close touch with Hancock's infantry, and told him that the 1st Cavalry Division (Torbert) would be sent to join him early on the 5th.

The II. Corps (Hancock), which was quartered by divisions in the area Brandy Station-Stevensburg, began to move about 11 P.M. on the 3rd. At Madden's, the initial point, the divisions assembled in one column, and the corps moved thence, *viâ* Richardsville, to Ely's Ford. The

Army Reserve Artillery followed.* At 6.30 A.M. General Hancock reported to headquarters that his column had just begun to cross the bridge, and at 9.50 he was able to say that his leading division was just going into camp about Chancellorsville. The last wagon of the corps crossed the Rapidan at 1.40, and at four in the afternoon, the whole II. Corps being bivouacked in line of battle at and near Chancellorsville, communication was opened between Hancock and Warren *via* the Turnpike. Hancock was informed during the morning that the Reserve Artillery was to close up on him, the trains from Ely's on the Reserve Artillery, those from Culpeper Ford to near Dowdall's (Wilderness Church). Having reported earlier

---

* The Army Reserve of Artillery (3 brigades) resembled the artillery train of European wars of the time of Turenne. Field and position artillery were mingled in the 2nd Brigade, and the 1st Brigade (Heavy Artillery), armed and employed as infantry, guarded the artillery trains, fought in line of battle with the bayonet from time to time, and acted as a trained reserve as well. One of the regiments (1st N. Y. Heavy) found the detachments for a battery of eight 24-pound mortars, which were usefully employed at Spottsylvania on May 12, and at Cold Harbor on June 2-3.

The employment of the reserve artillery is summarized in General H. J. Hunt's report as follows: —

"On the 5th it followed the II. Corps to near the Furnaces, but was ordered back. At daybreak on the 6th, Kitching's brigade of foot artillery with all its available men, including the guards of the trains, etc., went into action with General Wadsworth's division. On the 7th it was employed in throwing up intrenchments. On the same day a battery of the Reserve was ordered to Ely's Ford for the protection of the trains. On the morning of the 8th, Kitching's brigade was ordered to report to Major-General Hancock. General Hancock ordered it back to the Reserve that night and again called for it next day. From this time this brigade was marched to and fro from one corps to another until it was finally, on the breaking up of the Reserve, attached to the V. Corps. On the 16th the Reserve was, by superior orders, broken up".

that there was no rebel infantry on the side of Fredericksburg, but that their cavalry was to hold a review that day at Hamilton's Crossing, he is ordered to clear the road on the 5th to allow Torbert's cavalry division to join Gregg's. He was also informed that there had been a "few shots" towards Robertson's (Locust Grove), and that "some force of the enemy was coming out towards New Verdiersville".

Trains.—The same day as the army moved, the depôts were evacuated towards Washington as far as the Rappahannock. The supplies accompanying the army (which were maintained throughout upon the same scale) were as follows :—

50 rounds of ammunition per man on the person.

    3 days' full rations in the haversack.
    3 days' bread and small ration in the knapsack.
    3 days' meat ration " on the hoof ".
    Total with the troops, 6 days.

1st Line Transport—half of the ammunition wagons, tool wagons, and ambulance wagons, 5 days' forage for mounted troops, with a few miscellaneous vehicles and pack animals — with the troops. 2nd Line Transport — corps parks, 10 days' forage, 10 days' supplies—massed at Richardsville under Brigadier-General Ingalls, Chief Quartermaster, and thence crossed the Rapidan as quickly as possible (Confederate cavalry having come out north of the Rappahannock, near Fredericksburg), by bridges at Ely's and Culpeper Mine Fords.* The total number of vehicles and animals with the army was 4300 wagons (in addition to the artillery and 835 ambulances), 33,991 public and private horses, and 22,528 mules. The number of slaughter cattle is not on record. Torbert's (1st) Cavalry Division guarded this mass of wagons, and watched the Rapidan above Germanna.

All these movements having been accomplished early in the afternoon, there was nothing for the supreme command to do but to await information and, if necessary, to issue new orders for the 5th. The passage of the Rapidan was accomplished, much to Grant's relief. Only Burnside's corps and the last half of the trains had yet to pass, and their arrival was merely a matter of hours.

By 5.30 p.m. Grant and Meade had the following information upon which to base their orders.

The Union signal station at Stony Mountain, watching the enemy, had reported "no important change" at 7.30. The same station at 9.30 read off a Confederate message from Clark's Mountain to General Ewell: "Everything seems to be moving to the right on Germanna and Ely's Fords, leaving cavalry in our front". At 11 another important signal from Clark's Mountain to General Ewell was taken down by the Union signallers: "We are moving. Had I not better move D and D toward New Verdiersville?" After this came at

* The complicated movements of the bridge trains have not been dealt with in the text. In general, it would appear that the directions in army orders were carried out exactly.

intervals orders and questions relative to the enemy's concentration towards Mine Run, and finally Stony Mountain reported to General Grant at 3 p.m.: "Enemy moving infantry and trains towards Old and New Verdiersville. Two brigades gone from this front. Camps on Clark's Mountain breaking up". General Grant drew from the 11 a.m. message, received at 1.15 p.m., the inference that Lee's concentration had scarcely begun, only preliminary movements having been observed.

The cavalry reports, and that of "Mr. Sime, a citizen of Great Britain", have been mentioned. Mr. Sime said, further, that he had not heard of anything indicating Beauregard's arrival.*

On the other flank, a large force of hostile cavalry was reported at or near Fredericksburg.

Summarized, the information as to the enemy's movements which had reached Grant and Meade up to 5 or 5.30 p.m.—*i.e.* information upon which the orders for the 5th were based—was to the effect that the enemy's army had begun to concentrate some time between 11 and 3, that Longstreet was probably well short of Orange C.H., and that Hill and Ewell were moving down towards Verdiersville and Mine Run. According to the cavalry general, the Orange Plank Road was more or less free of the enemy, and this, coupled with the fact that bodies of Ewell's infantry had been located in the direction of the lower Mine Run (that is, roughly, between the Pike and the river Rapidan), led quite

* From North Carolina and Southern Virginia. There was at this time no reliable information except that "he was in Virginia somewhere".

THE 4TH OF MAY

naturally to the supposition that Lee was concentrating in his well-prepared lines at Mine Run. Now, supposing this view correct, in the Autumn campaign of 1863, he had occupied these lines strongly enough for passive defence, even without Longstreet, and the problem was—what would Lee, after providing for the defence of the lines, do with his disposable "mass of manœuvre", as Napoleon used to call it? He might attack, taking as his general line the Orange Plank Road. He might concentrate further to the rear towards the North Anna, covered by Ewell in the lines. He might adopt a third alternative and "go North on a raid", as Grant phrased it, though this was unlikely, for Lee had, in fact, never begun an offensive campaign northward, without previously crippling the Federals in Virginia. The possibility of an attack all along the line, down the Plank Road and the Turnpike as well, seems to have been ignored, or, if discussed at the Union headquarters, as was probably the case, rejected as improbable on the ground that Lee had not the force wherewith to attempt it. Wilson's report was to the effect that there was no considerable force on the Plank Road, but that north of it *all the roads leading down to Mine Run* were filled with the Confederate infantry divisions. This pointed to a defence of localities on that stream, not to the collection of a striking force on the Turnpike. If, then, Lee was going to attack, the indications pointed to Parker's Store as the point of contact,* and this was in no wise less

* Next morning, when Confederate infantry appeared east of Locust

probable because, on the afternoon of the 4th, Wilson had not found any considerable force there, for Hill's corps was further west than Ewell's, and Longstreet's still more distant. There was, in fact, no indication whatever of Lee's purpose, only a strong probability that the Mine Run lines right and left of the Turnpike would be strongly held by Ewell's corps. If Lee chose to fight a defensive battle along the whole line of Mine Run, the original plans of the Lieutenant-General held good. If he proposed to attack along the Orange Plank, the moving wing of the Union Army might require fresh directions after the fight had opened, but that was all. If he was concentrating towards the North Anna to join Beauregard and to strike at Butler, the immediate task of the army under Grant was to attack Lee's rearguard or containing detachment, turning its inner flank and crushing it with a five-to-one numerical superiority. If Lee was "going North", Grant, with freer hands than Hooker had had before Gettysburg, would find his task even easier. There was no apparent reason, in fine, for anything but slight modifications in the initial plan of operations, and Meade's orders for the 5th were merely the codicil of the original order issued from Brandy Station on the 2nd of May.

But both suffered from the defect that they rested on the preconceived idea of turning the right flank of Lee's position and fighting a battle

Grove, Meade, as we shall see, could not account for their presence save by the hypothesis that they were a bold containing force covering Lee's concentration on the North Anna.

somewhere in the neighbourhood of Parker's Store and Shady Grove, on the 5th or 6th of May. Of course, an idea of the enemy's position and probable intentions is the first necessity to a general who is planning a manœuvre, but having formed his plan, his next task is to ensure his own liberty of action to put it into execution, and this equally applies, even strategically, to subordinate generals. Now, the only way to do this is to protect oneself by detachments in every direction from which danger can reasonably be expected—detachments capable, not of fighting battles, but of holding the enemy fully employed during the time required for the decision. Manœuvres can be prearranged in this as in other respects. In the present case, failing the immobilization of the enemy—who at that moment, about noon on the 4th, did not present any target for the action of a fighting advanced guard—a flank guard should have been thrown out in sufficient strength and at a sufficient distance, if the enemy did advance, to delay him as long as required.

But, although it was fairly evident that Ewell's corps was in the immediate neighbourhood of the Orange Pike on the night of the 4th May, and the surmise that he would stand still rested only on a single cavalry report and on Grant's own reading of the military situation in the enemy's camp, no provision was made by the superior command to hold him off during the development of the main decision on the Plank Road. A subordinate commander, as it happened, remedied the deficiency in part, but Meade's orders to Wilson, both for the 4th and for the 5th—each approved by Grant—cost the Union generals their liberty of action and brought it about that the battle of the Wilderness took shape from Lee's acts, not from Grant's. The 3rd Cavalry Division, massed at Parker's Store or Craig's Church, and scouting from the South round to the North-west on a front of ten or twelve miles, was admirably placed to play its part in the development of Grant's scheme. Unfortunately, the event proved that it was equally well placed to assist Lee's purposes.

Meade's orders were as follows:—

May 4, 6 p.m.

1. Major-General Sheridan . . . will move with Gregg's and Torbert's divisions against the enemy's cavalry in the direction of Hamilton's Crossing. General Wilson, with the 3rd Cavalry Division, will move at 5 a.m. to Craig's Meeting House. . . . He will keep out parties on the Orange Court House pike and plank roads, the Catharpin Road, Pamunkey Road, (etc.).

2. Major-General Hancock, II. Corps, will move at 5 a.m. to Shady Grove Church, and extend his right towards the V. Corps at Parker's Store.

3. Major-General Warren, V. Corps, will move at 5 a.m. to Parker's Store . . . and extend his right towards the VI. Corps at Wilderness Tavern.

4. Major-General Sedgwick, VI. Corps, will move to Wilderness Tavern . . . as soon as the road is clear. He will leave a division at Germanna Ford until informed from these headquarters of the arrival of General Burnside's corps.

5. The Reserve Artillery will move to Corbin's Bridge as soon as the road is clear.

6. The trains will be parked near Todd's Tavern.

THE 4TH OF MAY

7. Headquarters will be on the Orange Plank Road, near the V. Corps.

8. After reaching the points designated, the army will be held in readiness to move forward.

9. The commanders of the V. and VI. Corps will keep out detachments on the roads to their right flank. The commander of the II. Corps will do the same on the roads to his front. These flankers and pickets will be thrown well out and held ready to meet the enemy.

S. WILLIAMS, A.A.G.

The only important modification in these orders concerns the cavalry. Sheridan, with two out of his three divisions, is ordered to seek out and to fight the enemy's cavalry. Torbert was still north of the Rapidan; Gregg was now south and east of Chancellorsville at Aldrich's and Silver's. He had been originally ordered to Piney Branch Church, but later, on receipt of information as to the enemy's cavalry round Fredericksburg, he was stopped on the line of the Orange Plank Road. Humphreys states that it was on Sheridan's own suggestion that the move on Fredericksburg and Hamilton's Crossing was ordered for the 5th of May, but, as a matter of fact, he did not move as ordered, holding his hand until the arrival of Torbert's division on the afternoon of the 5th. The truth would seem to be that Sheridan would have preferred to move out at once on the afternoon of the 4th, that Meade, anxious for the safety of his trains, held him back until the following day, and that in consequence Sheridan would not move, now the alarm had been given, until he had two divisions in hand for serious fighting and knew where the enemy was to be found. Had he acted at once on the 4th, the enemy would still have been at Fredericksburg, but after that there was no certainty as to where they would be. To move thither with one division next morning would have been either to meet superior forces, or to deliver a blow in the air while the trains were being raided by Stuart's enterprising troopers. He proposed, therefore, to collect his two divisions and to reconnoitre before committing himself.

General Burnside had to send back all the material and rolling stock on the now abandoned line of supply to Washington, and to collect his scattered corps before he could move to join the Army of the Potomac. Some of his difficulties may be imagined from the IX. Corps correspondence for the 3rd and 4th of May, preserved in the *Official Records*. Grant's orders, however, were precise: "Put your troops in motion as soon as General Augur* relieves you and the trains are south of Bull Run", and again, "Make forced marches until you reach this place. Start your troops now in the rear the moment they can be got off, and require them to make a night march".

It is generally admitted that these young troops of Burnside's command were seriously overtaxed by a forced march of thirty to forty miles, and that their efficiency for battle on the next day (6th) was correspondingly impaired.

"His first division, General Stevenson, had then (1.15 P.M.) arrived at Brandy Station, and his fourth, the coloured division, had marched that morning from Manassas Junction, more than forty

* Commander of the XXII. Corps and Washington district.

miles distant from Germanna Ford. General Stevenson's division crossed the Rapidan at Germanna Ford on the morning of the 5th, and by the night of the 5th, Potter's and Willcox's divisions from Bealeton and Rappahannock Station, had likewise crossed there and advanced some three miles. General Ferrero's division crossed on the morning of the 6th". (Humphreys.)

As generalissimo, Grant received the information that evening that "Sherman, Sigel, and Butler had started according to programme". The combined movement, called the "Anaconda" policy, had begun promptly and punctually. He had already sent word to General Halleck, at army headquarters in Washington, that the crossing of the Rapidan had been effected. "Forty-eight hours now", he continued, "will demonstrate whether the enemy intend giving battle this side of Richmond".

CHAPTER VIII

THE BATTLE OF THE WILDERNESS

(First day, May 5)

THE Army of the Potomac was put in motion on the 5th of May in the same relative order as on the 4th, and in pursuance of the same plan.

V. Corps.—Warren ordered his corps to be ready to move at 5 A.M.* On the march, flankers were to be thrown out well to the right from each division. The first line trains were to leave by the same road as the troops, on their left flank. The head of the column was ordered to move slowly in order that the divisions should be able to keep closely in touch with each other and to prevent straggling. "The necessity for this is paramount and must be kept constantly in mind", ran the order.

The objective of the march was Parker's Store, which was to be reached by the wood road that passes the Chewning house. The order of divisions was, Crawford, Wadsworth, Robinson, Griffin. But Griffin, whose division, it will be remembered, was kept out all night towards Locust Grove on

* At this moment—in preparation for a battle and not before—artillery was first assigned to the several divisional commanders.

the Orange Pike, was ordered to stand fast for the present.

The delicacy of a march, *tête baissée*, across the front of the enemy was obviously not lost upon Warren, who was preoccupied, moreover, with the necessities of maintaining strict order within his own command, and of keeping in touch with Sedgwick, who was to follow him on the same road. He was aware, too, that Wilson's cavalry division would have left Parker's Store by the time the head of the V. Corps arrived. He therefore made his own dispositions for preventing the enemy from interfering with him. More, he notified the leading division of the VI. Corps that Griffin (or at any rate a brigade of his division) would remain out on the Pike until the VI. Corps had reached the vicinity of the Lacy house. Having taken this precaution as to the Pike, Warren next ordered his leading division (Crawford) to have a screen well out to the front and left flank to prevent an enemy on the Plank Road from working round to the rear of the troops moving towards Parker's Store. He, at any rate, had grasped the fact that the presence of a cavalry division on the Plank Road at 5 A.M. on the 5th, and the reconnaissances on the Pike the previous day, afforded no guarantee that the enemy was not in heavy force on either road or both by 8.

Just as the V. Corps began its march, Warren dispatched a note to the Chief-of-Staff, which may serve to throw some light on the peculiarities of its writer's military character. He reported that owing to the negligence of General Griffin the corps had not detailed its proper complement of men to escort the (massed) trains, and proposed to make good the deficiency by sending a battalion from the main body at once. A strict disciplinarian —in this very dispatch he proposes thus early in the campaign to make " a severe example" of an incompetent engineer officer—he was himself far too sensitively conscientious not to try to remedy a fault for which he was partly responsible, even though he had four hundred rifles the fewer in line of battle that day in consequence. But the special point that this note illustrates is the over-wide range of his thoughts and preoccupations. In his care for the whole army he was apt to lose sight of the V. Corps, to sacrifice simplicity and directness to considerations which he should have left superior authority to deal with. Moreover, as he did not possess the full information that a commander-in-chief would have had, his self-imposed anxieties weighed upon him more than they did upon the actual commander. The trains referred to were part of the mass of wagons under General Ingall's care, every corps in the army had contributed to the escort, and a whole cavalry division was detailed for its protection. In fact, whether from a punctilious sense of subordination, or from anxiety for the trains of the whole army, or from both, Warren took upon himself, in a small matter it may be, the functions of his commanding general. However, the same impulse induced him to keep Griffin out on the Pike as flank guard, not of the V. Corps, but of the army, and on this and other occasions there was good

BATTLE OF THE WILDERNESS

ground for his uneasiness, and need for the intelligent initiative of his unresting genius.

VI. Corps.—General Sedgwick fixed the hour of moving off at 6 A.M. to give the V. Corps an hour's start, and maintained the original order of march of divisions — Getty, Wright, Ricketts. Ricketts' division, it will be remembered, was detailed in army orders to remain behind near Germanna Ford until the head of Burnside's corps should arrive—or rather until Ricketts' own report of that event should have filtered through Grant's, Meade's, and Sedgwick's respective staffs.

II. Corps.—Hancock's corps had gone into position overnight, with all the precautions suggested by depressing memories, on the old Chancellorsville battlefield. At 5 A.M. the advance recommenced, Gibbon leading, Birney and Mott following, and Barlow, who had led the march the previous day, staying behind with the first line transport as rearguard. The march was slow —much slower than Warren's, though Warren moved by rides and paths through the Wilderness —and the head of the column had only marched seven miles in four hours when events gave the corps a new direction. It would be absurd to impute this delay to Hancock, who probably had the greatest difficulty in moving at all. Gregg was in front of him at Aldrich's, Torbert hurrying up behind him, and in the immediate vicinity of the camps of the fighting troops, crowded on a short length of one main road, there was the ever-increasing mass of Ingalls' supply parks, the army reserve of artillery, reserve ammunition, etc.

The route * of the corps, which moved with the same precautions as Warren's and Sedgwick's, was the Furnace, Brock Road, Todd's Tavern, and thence by the Catharpin Road towards Corbin's Bridge and its assigned objective, Shady Grove Church.

At 6 A.M. reports came in from the officer commanding Warren's outposts that hostile infantry was deploying for action on both sides of the Orange Pike, and that a dust cloud was visible further to the rear. Warren had, however, no intention of making any change in his positions and movements unless compelled to do so, knowing that his corps was the unit of direction for the whole army and fearing doubtless to check or to give a false direction to the whole manœuvre. The Confederates on the Pike caused him for the present no alarm. Passing on the outpost report to the Chief-of-Staff, he said, "Such demonstrations are to be expected, and show the necessity for keeping well closed and prepared to face towards Mine Run and meet an attack at a moment's notice". This reassurance and statement of general principles, which, by the way, might have come more naturally from the supreme command to Warren than *vice versâ*, may be taken to mean that a "demonstration" by Lee was liable, if despised, to become a real attack. That it was

* In spite of the order to the cavalry to keep the "road by Piney Branch Church, Todd's Tavern, etc.", free for the infantry, we find that Gregg is near Aldrich's on the night of the 4th and the morning of the 5th, and Hancock is thus compelled to turn off and take the Furnace and the Brock Roads instead of the Catharpin.

BATTLE OF THE WILDERNESS

actually and at the moment of writing a pre-arranged "real" attack on the part of the enemy, Warren naturally did not know, and, as there was no serious force of cavalry to engage the enemy far enough out, he was under the necessity of *sending forward* part of Griffin's division to clear up the situation (6.20 A.M.). Griffin now entrenched his position on the Pike—it seems as if, unlike other generals, he had not done so on the previous evening—and detailed an infantry brigade for the reconnaissance. The rest of the V. Corps was, of course, moving in the direction of Parker's Store, though probably one division at least had not as yet moved off.

Before half-past seven the veil had lifted somewhat. Meade himself was with Warren at the Lacy house, and had ordered that officer, at 7.30, to suspend his march, " to concentrate his column on the Pike, and when his troops were in hand to immediately attack any force on his front". Warren thereupon ordered Crawford and Wadsworth to stop and to come into line of battle facing westward, Wadsworth connecting with Griffin's left, and Crawford with Wadsworth's. These orders were received, and a beginning made in their execution by 8 A.M., at which hour Crawford was already nearing Parker's Store. General Robinson's division was halted, and formed up in mass near the Lacy house. All the first line trains were of course sent to the rear. Orders to the same effect were simultaneously sent to the VI. Corps. A message was sent to the II. Corps to halt at Todd's Tavern, and another ordering the second line trains to stop. Meade, like Warren, is still under the impression that the enemy was merely trying to gain time by delaying the movements of the Army of the Potomac,* but his solution differed from Warren's. Warren as a subordinate had only to provide for the execution of his existing orders, but Meade as commander of the army decided to modify the whole scheme, suspending the flanking movement, and to attack whatever force Lee might have on the Turnpike. Two corps being obviously sufficient to make the Confederates pay dearly for their "demonstration", there was no reason to call in Hancock, whose position at Todd's Tavern was favourable for further manœuvre.

Grant, on receiving Meade's report, answered in one of his characteristic notes—

"Headquarters Armies of the U.S., Germanna Ford.
"May 5, 1864, 8.24 A.M.

"Your note giving movement of enemy and your dispositions received. Burnside's advance now crossing the river. I will have Ricketts' division (VI. Corps) relieved and advanced at once, and urge Burnside's crossing. As soon as I can see Burnside I will go forward. If any opportunity presents itself for pitching into a part of Lee's army do so without giving time for dispositions.
"U. S. GRANT, Lieut.-General".

Ricketts' division was accordingly relieved from

* "At nine A.M. General Meade said to Warren, Sedgwick, and others who were standing by, 'They have left a division to fool us here, while they concentrate or prepare a position towards the North Anna, and what I want is to prevent these fellows from getting back to Mine Run'."—Swinton's Journal (*Army of the Potomac*, p. 421). Compare *Official Records*, Serial No. 68, p. 403.

the duty of watching the ford and sent up to join the rest of the VI. Corps. Wright's division, meanwhile, was told off by Sedgwick to assist Warren's attack by moving against the enemy's left flank by a wood road running past Spottswood's* house, towards the Pike. Getty's (less one brigade, Neill's, assigned to Wright) was advanced to Wilderness Tavern.

It is to be observed that Meade's orders to General Warren were to get his corps in hand and then to attack at once. He informed Grant simply that he had ordered Warren to attack at once, and Grant approved with the colloquial and emphatic words: "pitch in without giving time for dispositions". The phrase "at once" had a different significance in the two brains.† To Meade, an immediate attack was not the same thing as a premature attack at a minute's notice with whatever fraction of the available forces was on the spot. To Grant's fighting habit of mind it meant, as he says, "pitching in without giving time for dispositions". This fundamental difference in the two directing minds was in the nature of things inexplicable to either and directly conduced to the failure of the attack, as we shall see.

The situation about eight is easily summarized.

---

* The Spottswood family in the old colonial days owned the once flourishing settlement of Germanna and the neighbouring mines, and gave their name to Spottsylvania county and Spottsylvania Court House.

† On the evening of this day the same tendencies reappear, Grant wishing to make the attack on the 6th at 4.30 A.M., and Meade wishing to have daylight and time to form a connected and controlled assaulting mass.

Hancock was standing fast, Warren and Sedgwick, under Meade's personal command, preparing to attack Ewell. Of the cavalry, Gregg was reconnoitring southward and eastward, Torbert moving up to Chancellorsville, Wilson heading for Craig's Church, with a strong detachment at Parker's Store under Lieut.-Colonel Hammond watching the Plank Road. The army trains were still crossing the Rapidan, the army reserve of artillery was at Chancellorsville, and Burnside's leading division nearing Germanna. Warren had one division (Robinson's), and Sedgwick also one division (Getty's), in reserve, while on either flank Ricketts' division of the VI. Corps and the whole of Hancock's II. Corps were awaiting events and new orders. At this point Grant, leaving a message for Burnside to close up on the VI. Corps as rapidly as possible, hurried to the front, joining Meade near the Lacy house, where the headquarters of both generals remained throughout the battle. Warren's headquarters were close at hand, and Sedgwick was also present.

The original scheme, then, was suspended, practically abandoned. Grant and Meade flung themselves against the first target that offered—how considerable they had no means of knowing, for there was no cavalry with breech-loading carbines to fight a stubborn delaying action in the thickets beyond Locust Grove, and the order to attack was given before Griffin's reconnaissance had gone out. Warren, with his usual grasp of the whole situation, said to himself that the Confederates in front of Griffin represented either a

BATTLE OF THE WILDERNESS 137

diversion or a heavy attack; in the former case, he proposed to keep his troops in hand, in the latter to prepare the attack of the whole V. Corps with considerable care. In this, Warren may with reason be censured for misjudging Meade's intentions. Meade proposed to attack the enemy—whether holding force or main body—as soon as he was ready and Warren's orders were so far definite enough. But if Meade in his official report quotes his own orders correctly, the commander of the V. Corps had every reason to believe that his superiors did not grudge the necessary time for reassembling the corps, and to resent the accusation of dilatoriness that ere long descended upon him.

There was no fighting on the Pike during these preparatory movements. It was on the Plank Road that the next development came. Here, near Parker's Store, Hammond's troopers offered a long and spirited resistance to the enemy's advance and gained four hours of incalculable value for their side, although Crawford, who had thrown out skirmishers to aid them, was peremptorily ordered in by his corps commander to take part in the fight on the Turnpike.

Crawford's report that the enemy was passing up the Plank Road and driving Hammond, when it reached the army staff, introduced a new factor into the situation. It was deducible from the data that the force in front of Hammond was infantry, and not merely cavalry. It was, in a word, clear that two corps of the enemy, or parts of them, were out, Hill's on the Plank Road, Ewell's on the Pike.

This led at once to an entire alteration of the plan of battle. The original scheme and the original hope of bringing off a battle in the open country were given up. Now that Lee showed the heads of two corps in the Wilderness there was nothing for it but to fight him there, and Grant, astonished maybe, but glad at any rate to have found his target, accepted the challenge.

But the difficulties attending so brusque a change of policy in the face of the enemy were not small.

The attack on Ewell, which thus became the main object, had to take into consideration the possibility of interference by Hill, and as a natural consequence the intersection of the Brock and Plank Roads—on which Hammond was being steadily driven back—became a point of capital importance.

At nine,* therefore, the order went forth for Hancock to come in from his position around Todd's Tavern to these cross-roads. More, lest the enemy should be beforehand, Getty's division, the reserve of the VI. Corps, was hurried thither at once.

By this step, imposed upon them by events which they could have controlled, the Union leaders began the dismemberment of the VI.

---

* Hancock acknowledges the receipt of this order from headquarters with the words, "Your dispatch received—hour not given". Only the day before, this very headquarters staff had issued a circular to corps commanders, reminding them that they should note the time on all orders, messages, etc.

BATTLE OF THE WILDERNESS

Corps, and weakened the principal attack on the side of the Pike by one division, if not two,* out of a total of six more or less available.

Warren, meanwhile, was doing his best in the dense woods to form Crawford, Wadsworth, and Griffin into a connected line of battle from Chewning's field to the Orange Pike. Wright, with his own division and Neill's brigade, was beginning to work south-westward along the Spottswood Road, and Ricketts was marching up from Germanna Ford.

So much had Lee achieved by a mere display of force. Had strong bodies of dismounted cavalry —at Locust Grove as well as at Parker's Store— gathered the necessary information as to what was on foot on the two roads by, say, 6 A.M., there would have been no need to abandon either the original scheme or the idea of developing an overwhelming force against Ewell. It was only necessary in the one case to protect the flank of the V. Corps for five or six hours—Griffin, supported by parts of the VI. Corps if necessary, would have amply sufficed for this duty—and, in the other, three divisions of Warren's corps, and two of Sedgwick's, could have been put in at once, secure in the knowledge that Hancock, stopped in good time and heading north instead of south along the Brock Road, could connect with Crawford when and where it suited the commanding general to deal with Hill's corps. Liberty of action, strategically, means time to accomplish a manœuvre without

---

* With the same object of warding off Hill, Crawford's division was, after all, allowed to remain near Chewning's.

interference, and it was precisely in the matter of time that the Federal general's hand was forced.

Warren's attack opened about noon. Warren's own view of the situation was such that he made no particular effort at first to impress the necessity of haste upon his subordinates, who were struggling to form connected lines of battle in the tangled underwood. Meade's order, too, as we know, allowed due time for proper preparations. But Grant was now at the Lacy house, and his temper was roused by what he conceived to be unwillingness in the officers of the Army of the Potomac. One can imagine the Western general fretting with impatience as he watched the trim, smartly dressed commander of the V. Corps riding here and there with his staff, but apparently achieving no results. One can also sympathize with Warren, who knew the ground of old, and felt that he was being hustled by his superiors into a premature attack. Between the two, Meade's irascible temper was soon roused. The sensitive Warren received stinging reproaches, and passed them on to his subordinates. When Griffin sent in word that he was averse to making an attack, unless properly supported, and recommended instead awaiting the enemy's attack behind entrenchments, he answered Griffin's galloper, as that officer[*] says, "as if fear was at the bottom of his errand". It was afterwards a common report in the army that Warren had just had

[*] Colonel W. W. Swan, *Papers of the Mil. Hist. Society of Massachusetts.*

BATTLE OF THE WILDERNESS 141

unpleasant things said to him by General Meade, and that General Meade had just heard the bravery of his army questioned. Griffin, nursing his wrath, would not budge an inch until Warren came up himself.

The attack was made, after all, without proper co-ordination. Griffin's right was only a few score yards north of the Pike, and Wright (VI. Corps), who was to have prolonged the attacking line, failed to appear. Wadsworth was on Griffin's left, and one brigade of the reserve division (Robinson) on the left of Wadsworth. Crawford, who had led the march towards Parker's Store in the early morning, was still near the open ground of Chewning's, facing west towards Mine Run and south towards the Plank Road, but McCandless's brigade of this division was sent to join Wadsworth. Griffin's attack along the Pike was direct and simple, that of Wadsworth in the woods led to many strange happenings.

It is to be observed that the original attack of the V. and VI. Corps on Ewell's corps, as projected by Meade and approved by Grant, before 9 A.M. has dwindled down to an attack by less than three divisions of the V. Corps, and, so far as effect went, none whatever of the VI.

General Ewell, the Confederate commander on the Pike, had all his own corps fairly well up to the front, but was unsupported by other troops. His instructions from Lee were that he should regulate his own advance by the firing on Hill's front, viz. the Orange Plank Road, and not to bring on a general engagement until the still distant corps of

Longstreet should be on the field. Lee himself was with Hill on the Plank Road. Ewell's leading brigade (J. M. Jones, of Edward Johnson's division) had, therefore, contented itself in the early morning with the display of force that had proved so effectual in stopping the whole Federal manœuvre. Seeing, however, that he was about to be attacked in force, Ewell gradually brought up the rest of Johnson's division on Jones' left, and placed two more brigades (of Rodes' division) behind him.

In this order the Confederates were struck, somewhat after noon, by Griffin's advance. The Federals, forcing their way through the thickets on either side of the Pike, almost blundered on to Jones' brigade and swept it away in a few minutes. The Federal field artillery swept the long straight line of the Pike with their fire, Jones' fugitives disordered Rodes' men behind them, and Jones himself, a very gallant officer, was killed as he strove to rally his men. One of the two Rodes brigades was routed immediately afterwards. Ewell deployed more forces across the Pike, and sent forward the rest of Rodes' division to the first line and Gordon's brigade of Early's division to the right of Rodes. The left centre of Johnson's division, north of the Pike, was meanwhile heavily engaged with Ayres' brigade (U.S. regulars), the right of Griffin's line.

But Griffin was unsupported. The troops of the VI. Corps on the Spottswood Road failed to come up in time, and Wadsworth too went astray, as we shall presently see. The brigade of regulars on Griffin's right was checked, then driven back by Johnson's counter-attack on its front and exposed right flank, and Ayres' retreat involved that of Griffin's other brigades. The whole division, after doing all that could be expected of it, routing two brigades of the enemy and forcing him to put more than half his corps into the battle, was driven back until it faced nearly northward, still controlled by its officers, but breathless and in great disorder. Two guns, that Griffin—artilleryman of the old school that he was—had sent in to case-shot range on the Pike, were abandoned.*

Wadsworth, meanwhile, with Dennison's brigade of Robinson's division on his left, had advanced through blind forest to attack the right flank of the original Confederate position on the Pike. His orders were simple—to advance westward, to attack the enemy wherever he might be met, and to keep closed up on the right. This should have resulted in a partial right wheel of the whole line of battle. As things actually turned out, however, Wadsworth's line swung far too much to the right, so that its straggling outer flank came opposite the rightmost brigade of Ewell's reformed line of battle. This was commanded by Gordon, a young Volunteer officer who within six months from this date rose to the command of a corps of the Army of Northern Virginia.

Opportunities do not go by unheeded in the presence of the born general. Gordon struck instantly at the two leftmost of Wadsworth's brigades. A brigade of Rodes' division followed

---

* They remained between the lines during the battle and on the 7th, and were finally abandoned when the VI. Corps set out for Spottsylvania.

Gordon's example, and soon the Federals were huddled in four or five shapeless groups, and drifting rearwards towards the Lacy house. McCandless's brigade arrived after Wadsworth's movement had begun and in attempting to find its way to the front lost its direction, and had the misfortune to fall in with Gordon's victorious regiments. It was, of course, severely handled and lost heavily, especially in prisoners. Baxter's and Cutler's brigades of Wadsworth's division, however, came back in very fair, if not excellent order.

Crawford, now isolated at Chewning's, was drawn back to the main body of the corps, which entrenched itself on a slightly curved line, three-quarters of a mile to a mile in front of the Lacy house, the right being on the Pike and the left just beyond the wood road from Lacy's to Parker's Store. It was now two o'clock, or a little later. Ewell did not attack, but entrenched likewise, Johnson and Rodes on either side of the Pike, Gordon on Rodes' right, and two other brigades of Early's division on Johnson's left.*

Soon it was the turn of the VI. Corps detachment. Advancing with the greatest difficulty along the Spottswood Road it came on the scene of Warren's battle not earlier than three o'clock. Upton's brigade was nearest the Pike, Penrose's and Russell's in the centre, and Neill's (of Getty's division) on his right. In front of Upton the ground was strewn with the killed and wounded of Griffin's division, and the woods had taken fire. The Union troops

* Ramseur's, Johnston's and Hoke's brigades were not present.

BATTLE OF THE WILDERNESS 145

deployed about 300 yards from Johnson's division, which promptly attacked them with two brigades and was as promptly repulsed, one of the brigadiers (Stafford) being killed. Upton then got into touch with Warren's right. Later, Neill, who was suffering somewhat from the enfilade fire of hostile guns posted in a farm clearing to the north-west, was supported by a brigade (Seymour's) of Ricketts' division. The rest of the division replaced Getty as general reserve near the Wilderness Tavern, and was ordered to report to Warren, who had had to use Robinson's division (his own reserve) to replace Griffin's sorely-tried troops in the entrenchments on the Pike.

When this episode was finished, General Griffin, not in the best of tempers after various reprimands from his corps commander, and conceiving himself to have been robbed of his victory and routed through the negligence of Warren and of Wright, rode up to Meade's headquarters and made his complaints in a loud and angry voice. A strange scene followed.* Grant was with Meade, and was buttoning up his coat when Griffin arrived. Looking up in amazement and then in anger, while Rawlins, his own chief staff officer,† furiously asked Griffin the meaning of his

---

* Reported by Colonel Theodore Lyman, A.D.C. to Major-General Meade.

† Brigadier-General John A. Rawlins was chief of the staff of the lieutenant-general in the field, but acted more as senior aide-de-camp than as a general staff officer. At Washington, the chief of the staff of the army, Major-General Halleck, had for some time before Grant's promotion been General-in-Chief of the United States Armies, and now acted as his military representative at the War Department.

conduct, he said to Meade, "Who is this General Gregg? Why don't you put him under arrest?" Meade's nerves, now the crisis of waiting was over, became calmer as others became excited, and soothingly, as if to a child, he replied, "It's Griffin, not Gregg, and it's only his way of talking", at the same time buttoning the lieutenant-general's coat.

This attack is a valuable object-lesson. The difficulties of wood fighting are presented in an extreme form. Movements of co-operating bodies are mistimed, direction is lost, and whole brigades become separated from their friends. Deployments are difficult, artillery almost useless. Orders miscarry, and the influence of the commanders is confined to troops within their own narrow purview.* Attacks and counter-attacks come very often an entire surprise to the troops attacked, and the decision, at the short ranges within which fighting is possible, is arrived at almost instantaneously. Beaten troops cannot retire in good order, but break up and rally in rear if they have spirit left, and victorious troops are almost as disordered. Successes and failures are, therefore, partial only and cause an incessant demand on the reserves for fresh troops, these being frittered away by brigades and regiments. The general effect of all these conditions was that Warren's corps attacked vigorously and disjointedly and was beaten in detail, and that the

Major-General Humphreys was, of course, Chief-of-Staff of the Army of the Potomac.

* Cf. the Prussian 7th Division in the Wood of Maslowed, July 3, 1866.

BATTLE OF THE WILDERNESS

VI. Corps was broken up, almost as soon as a shot was fired, to find local reserves for the other corps. Not even Sedgwick could do anything with three, four, or five detachments buried in the Wilderness as effectively as needles in a bottle of hay, and, regarding the corps as corps and not as depôts for reinforcements, both Warren's and Sedgwick's commands were neutralized by Ewell's one vigorous blow and threat of more.

One, however, of Sedgwick's detachments was destined to win great glory on the 5th of May, 1864. At noon, Colonel Lyman, of Meade's staff, handed the order to General Getty to proceed as quickly as possible to the junction of the Plank and Brock roads. Riding a little ahead of his men, Getty saw Hammond's cavalry, which all this time had been fighting Hill's advanced guard with their magazine carbines, retiring in little knots up the Plank Road, followed by the Confederate skirmish line. A few bullets flew past the staff, and Getty sent back a galloper to bring on his leading regiment at the double. He himself, surrounded by his staff, with his headquarters flag flying overhead, took post directly at the cross-roads, while the Confederate riflemen came nearer and nearer and their fire became more intense. "We must hold this point at all risks", Getty said to his staff officers as they waited in suspense. At last came the leading Union regiment "like greyhounds" down the Brock Road. Only three words of command were given—"halt", "front", and "fire". Dead and wounded Confederates were found in the woods within thirty yards of the cross-roads.

They belonged to Heth's division of Hill's corps, which was closely followed by Wilcox's. Lee himself accompanied Hill to nurse the battle here until Longstreet's arrival.

It was somewhat after eleven o'clock, perhaps three-quarters of an hour before Warren's attack opened, when the cross-roads were thus saved in the nick of time. The Confederates withdrew their skirmishers about eight hundred yards up the Plank Road, and Getty quietly formed his three brigades in line of battle. For the next two hours there was only skirmishing on Getty's front, and an unsuccessful attempt to get into touch with Warren's left (Crawford) towards Chewning's. Hill too was occupied in closing up. Wilcox's division was sent off to the left, through Tapp's field, to connect Heth with Ewell, and his skirmishers came in touch with Crawford's.

The moral of this incident would seem to be that only the four or five hours' resistance of Hammond's small cavalry force saved the Union army from being cut in two by the advance of Hill's corps on the Plank Road, and preserved for their side whatever liberty of action it had not forfeited by the absence of a similar force, equally well commanded, on the other line. And at this moment Sheridan was complaining bitterly that the cavalry was being wasted, in accordance with the idea that he had "taken up" that, on account of the wooded character of the country in which the main battle was being fought, cavalry should fight cavalry

BATTLE OF THE WILDERNESS 149

and infantry infantry! A Napoleonic cavalry brigade would not have checked Ewell or Hill for twenty minutes, it is true, but Sheridan's troopers were armed with breech-loaders and magazine carbines, and accustomed to fight on foot. Not to go far for a classical example, the Union cavalry division under John Buford, had, by just such waiting and skirmishing tactics as Hammond used, made possible the great victory of Gettysburg.

Turning now to the II. Corps, when Hancock, about 9 A.M., received the first order to stand fast, the head of Gibbon's division deployed across the Catharpin Road close to Corbin's Bridge, behind him was Birney, not quite up to Todd's Tavern, and behind Birney was Mott, who had not as yet emerged from the bye-road on to the Brock Road. Barlow was well to the rear with the corps trains between Chancellorsville and the Furnace. From nine to twelve (when the order to come in was received and acted upon) the corps closed up gradually into a position of readiness—Gibbon deployed as before, Birney at Todd's Tavern, Mott on the Brock Road north of him, where the Furnace bye-road comes in, Barlow at and near the Furnace. Mott and Birney had closed up in masses and thrown out skirmishers. The corps artillery had reached the front, and was at Todd's Tavern with Birney. For the march into the Wilderness Birney was turned about and became the new head of the column; Mott allowed Birney to pass him on the Brock Road and then followed, and Gibbon came back to Todd's Tavern, reformed, and followed Mott, Barlow from the Furnace making his way by the bye-road and secondary paths to the tail of the corps, soon to be the left * of its line of battle. That this complicated manœuvre was executed as the corps commander desired seems to indicate that in this corps at any rate staff work was well understood. Hancock himself galloped forward along the Brock Road till he met Getty at the cross-roads: Colonel Morgan, his chief-of-staff, then rode on to Wilderness Tavern to report to Meade.

Birney's infantry arrived at 2 P.M., closely followed by Mott and Gibbon. Getty's men took ground a little to their right to make room for Birney, who formed two lines of battle on the Brock Road, facing west; Mott and Gibbon took up the same formation on Birney's left; Barlow formed the extreme left, thrown somewhat forward on to high ground where all the guns of the command, except one and a half batteries, were massed. The leftmost of Barlow's brigades (Frank's) faced more to the southward across the Brock Road to cover important bye-roads leading towards Chancellorsville. Getty had already begun entrenching before Hancock's arrival, and that officer approved, and ordered his own divisions to do likewise.

* Some of the official reports note the fact that the regiments moved off left in front, which would be natural enough when we consider that the enemy was supposed to be on the right of the column in its projected march to Shady Grove Church. As things turned out, the march was soon deflected northward, and the enemy appeared on the left of the column, necessitating the order, "Change ranks!" The idea of a "front" remained in British infantry drill up to 1902.

BATTLE OF THE WILDERNESS

Hancock's *rôle* was more or less vaguely outlined in the following dispatch—

"The Major-General Commanding directs that you move up the Brock Road to the Orange Court House Plank Road, and report your arrival at that point and be prepared to move out the Plank Road toward Parker's Store.
"A. A. HUMPHREYS,
"Major-General and Chief-of-Staff".

This was received at 11.40 A.M., a few minutes after Getty had seized the cross-roads, and was followed by a second note, sent at noon—

"The enemy's infantry drove our regiment of cavalry from Parker's Store down the Plank Road, and are now moving down it in force. A. P. Hill's corps is part of it. How much not known. General Getty's division has been sent to drive them back, but he may not be able to do so. The Major-General Commanding directs that you move out the Plank Road, and, supporting Getty, drive the enemy beyond Parker's Store and occupy that place and unite with Warren on the right of it.
"A. A. HUMPHREYS.
"Warren now extends from the Pike to within one mile of the Plank Road in the direction of Parker's Store".

At 1.30 Hancock was informed of the result of Warren's attack on the Pike, and notified that Crawford's division, with which he was to connect on nearing Parker's Store, might be drawn in or driven in. He was to attack, however, as previously ordered. "Push out on the Plank Road and connect with Warren".

This order, and the assignment of Ricketts' division to Warren's command—with this was coupled the promise of Getty's as well, as soon as it could be spared—made an intermediate stage in the development of Grant's plan of battle. The first blow had been delivered against Ewell, Hill being held off by Getty. The second, and wholly transient, idea of attacking all along the line by both roads governed all the orders issued about 3 P.M., which were again modified so as definitively to transfer the centre of gravity to Hancock's front. This last decision may be traced in the order to Getty, quoted below, and still more in the order to Warren (4 P.M.) to " make dispositions to attack if practicable" without Getty and with one brigade only instead of two of Ricketts.

In the course of the afternoon, while his corps gradually came up and entrenched the Brock Road, Hancock was, like Warren, though by the comparatively cold medium of correspondence, subjected to pressure from headquarters.

At 2.15 Humphreys notified him of Wadsworth's and Crawford's retirement. This, however, was not to affect the future course of the battle or the order to attack on the Plank Road (see p. 151).

Hancock replied to the earlier dispatches at 2.40: " I am forming my corps on Getty's left and will order an advance as soon as prepared. The ground over which I must pass is a perfect thicket. General Getty says he has not heard of Warren's left"; and to that of 2.15 at 3: " General Getty in conjunction with two of my divisions will make an attack soon as troops can get into position. I shall keep one division on their left and one division in rear of advancing divisions.

BATTLE OF THE WILDERNESS 153

Objective point, Parker's Store". Meanwhile (3.15) another and more peremptory order from Meade: "The Commanding General directs that Getty attack at once and that you support him with your whole corps . . . the attack up the Plank Road must be made at once". Hancock had not yet been able to form his attack, however, and in the end Meade ordered Getty to attack, whether Hancock was ready or not (4. p.m.). Considering that the head of Hancock's corps only arrived on the ground at two, it was not to be expected that the II. Corps would be in hand as a unit at the cross-roads by four. To some officers it seemed as if there were too many troops at the cross-roads already.

Lyman carried the order. He writes: "3.15. Sent with a written order to Getty to attack at once, with or without Hancock! Delivered it at 3.25. Getty very cool—plainly he thought it poor strategy to attack before more of the II. Corps was up, but he ordered an immediate advance".

At a quarter past four Getty's line broke cover and advanced rapidly to the attack. Hancock sent after him Birney, with his own and Mott's divisions, and a section of field artillery * came into action on the Plank Road itself in the midst of the infantry. The enemy (Heth's division) was met within a few hundred yards at the narrowest

---

* Much of the delay in forming the II. Corps was said to be due to the masses of artillery, guns, and vehicles, collected in the narrow Brock Road.

part of the high ground upon which the road runs, and after a few minutes Heth's men and Getty's, standing, lying, or kneeling, were firing into one another at fifty yards' range with the greatest intensity their weapons permitted.

Hancock, " the Superb ", sat quietly on his horse a few score yards in rear of the troops. Two brigades of Gibbon's division, Carroll's and Owen's, fed the fight. Lyman writes of the arrival of Carroll's brigade: " Sprigg Carroll's brigade came along at the double quick, the men all out of breath, and faced to his left. I remember the cool address of the colonel next me: ' Now I don't want any hollering: that's childish. Prime! forward!' Carroll, as full as ever of the *gaudium certaminis*, rode into the sprout growth with his line and soon came back shot through the arm ".

Hill, realizing the seriousness of the attack, had at once called back Wilcox's division. Lee watched the fight from the position of Heth's guns near the widow Tapp's house. Longstreet, and also R. H. Anderson's division of Hill's corps, were still far away from the battlefield. When Wilcox returned his brigades were sent into the fight at once, passing to the front through Heth's wearied regiments. The chief part of the Confederate infantry advanced south of the Plank Road, doubtless for fear of an offensive against their left from Warren's front. As fresh troops were put in on either side the battle swayed to and fro, now far down the Plank Road, now almost to the Union entrenchments on the Brock Road.

Shortly after Getty was ordered forward, and

before he actually moved, Wadsworth's division of the V. Corps, now recovered from its unfortunate experience of the morning, was ordered to move out south-eastward to strike the flank of Hill's line, but once more his move through the woods was slow and difficult, and he encountered only the flank guards of the enemy, which he drove before him until nightfall. He then halted and bivouacked in line of battle, with his left about 800 yards west of the Brock Road.

On Hancock's extreme left, two brigades of Barlow's division, admirably led by their brigadiers, Brooke and Smyth, struck out against the right of Hill's line and drove it back for some distance. By nightfall Hill's two divisions were much distressed and in disorder. So close were the lines of battle, and so dense the forest, that both Federal and Confederate fatigue parties in several cases strayed into the enemy's lines and were made prisoners.

Hancock's own words may be used to summarize this long and bloody contest: "The lines of battle were exceedingly close, and the musketry fire continuous and deadly along the entire line. . . . The battle raged with great severity until 8 P.M.", *i.e.* little less than four hours, "without decided advantage to either party". To such a pitch had enthusiasm and discipline raised the staying power of the American volunteer!

Comment is needless on the haste with which the attack was forced on Hancock by the Union headquarter staff. Doubtless the results of Warren's and Sedgwick's operations were only fairly satisfactory, doubtless there was the menace of Longstreet's arrival ever present in the minds of Grant and Meade. But the order, Getty to attack " with or without Hancock ", is on a different footing. Whether it sprang from a desire on Meade's part to show Grant that the bravery of the army was not to be questioned, from Meade's yielding to pressure from the lieutenant-general, or from a calculated surmise that Hancock's chivalrous nature would not allow him to leave a comrade unsupported, it produced a piecemeal attack. Getty alone moved deliberately, all the others hurried up at the double, formed as best they could, and were flung into the fight, and the result of the day's work of Hancock and Getty and their gallant men was that two divisions of Hill's corps fought four Union divisions for four long hours at close quarters "without decided advantage to either side".

Brigadier-General Alexander Hays, an old comrade of Grant's at West Point and in Mexico, and an officer of distinguished gallantry, was killed at the head of Birney's 2nd Brigade in the fight on the Plank Road.

To return to the Pike. Here, after 4 P.M., when Warren's second attack was practically abandoned and the centre of gravity was transferred once for all to the Plank Road, there was little of importance, at least on the part of the V. Corps. A renewal of the attack was more or less seriously contemplated by headquarters, and a formal order was actually sent to Warren at

BATTLE OF THE WILDERNESS

6 P.M. But that officer was content to watch for signs of a lateral movement of the enemy towards the Plank Road and obeyed the order only with his artillery, which opened fire to assist the VI. Corps, and with Wadsworth,* who, about five, moved southward to assist Hancock in the battle on the Plank Road, as we have seen.

Meade's orders for the right wing to renew the attack were carried out mainly by the right and centre of Wright's command (Wright's division and parts of Ricketts' and Getty's) on the wood road, Warren's artillery co-operating wherever it could find a target. Severe fighting went on between Wright and Early until nightfall, with heavy losses to both sides. Gordon's brigade, which had fought on the extreme right of Ewell's corps in the morning, rejoined the main body of Early's division during this fight. Generals Seymour, of the VI. Corps, and Pegram, of Early's command, were wounded.

When Wilson's cavalry division moved off southward from Parker's Store to the Catharpin Road and Craig's Church in the early morning, he left behind Hammond with 500 men at Parker's Store, with what result we have seen.† The main body duly moved on to Craig's Church. Soon

---

* *Plus* one brigade of Robinson's division.

† Wilson's report says, "Colonel Hammond was joined by Colonel J. B. McIntosh, 3rd Pennsylvania Cavalry", who happened to be proceeding to the front to take up a brigade command. "These two gallant officers with scarcely 500 men, armed with Spencer (magazine) carbines and fighting on foot, by their gallantry and good management resisted the rebel infantry in force for six hours".

after reaching that place, the 1st Brigade encountered hostile cavalry (Rosser's brigade of Hampton's cavalry division), and by a combination of mounted and dismounted work drove it back about two miles. But about noon ammunition ran short, and Wilson called a halt, soon after which the enemy, reinforced, began to press him closely. The 1st Brigade retired on the 2nd, which was just north of Robertson's Run and close to the junction of the Parker's Store road with the Catharpin Road. Wilson had to use his horse artillery and the fifty sabres of his personal escort freely to extricate the rearguard, but at last all was safely over the run. Then, however, Bryan, the brigadier of the 2nd Brigade, informed General Wilson that it was impossible to return to the Orange Plank Road, and that none of his messengers had reached the main army. Thereupon Wilson determined to withdraw by what he significantly calls a " blind road " towards Todd's Tavern. No sooner had he started than the enemy was seen moving down the Catharpin Road in the same direction, and an exciting race followed for the possession of Corbin's Bridge. Most of the Union column got through, Wilson and his staff last of all, but the rearguard regiment was cut off. It broke away to the left, however, and after wandering through the woods rejoined Wilson late in the evening at Todd's Tavern. On arriving at Todd's Tavern about 3 P.M. Wilson was rejoiced to meet Gregg, sent thither by Sheridan to extricate him. General Gregg turned sharply upon Wilson's pursuers and drove them back again beyond Corbin's Bridge,

BATTLE OF THE WILDERNESS 159

after which the two Union divisions encamped on all the roads around Todd's Tavern. One brigade of Wilson's command pushed out on the Brock Road to find and connect with the left of the main army. That this last skirmish was not a mere fusillade may be judged by the fact that Gregg's two advanced regiments lost nearly one hundred men between them.

It remains to consider the interchange of intelligence and orders which brought Gregg's division to the rescue. Sheridan had, as we have seen, made no move towards Hamilton's Crossing, waiting for Torbert and employing Gregg in reconnaissances. By midday it became certain that the enemy's cavalry had left Fredericksburg and was closing in *viâ* Spottsylvania on the main Confederate position. At that hour, Sheridan, already uneasy on Wilson's account, received news from Meade as to events towards Parker's Store, and at once ordered Gregg to Todd's Tavern and Shady Grove Church, remaining himself with Torbert at Chancellorsville in order to protect the trains and, if necessary, to support Gregg. Gregg moved exceedingly promptly, considering that he was at that moment occupied with various reconnaissances, and arrived at Todd's Tavern just as Wilson's leading troops came up.* At 1.15, in addition, Sheridan ordered Custer (of Torbert's division) forward to the Brock Road.

The Union positions on the night of the 5th were thus as follows:—

* Gregg's report shows incidentally that the rear of Hancock's column was not yet clear of Todd's Tavern at 2.45.

Headquarters of the Armies, and of the Army of the Potomac—Near Lacy's house.

V. Corps (Warren) entrenched from the Pike to the Parker's Store wood road, Robinson on the right, Crawford on the left. Of the other two divisions Griffin was in rear of Robinson, re-organizing his shattered command, and Wadsworth (*plus* one brigade from Robinson's division) facing southward towards the Plank Road, and in touch with the left of the enemy's (Hill's) outposts.

VI. Corps (Sedgwick) is dissipated in three detachments. Ricketts and one of his two brigades was acting as general reserve near Lacy's house; Wright, with one of Ricketts' brigades and one of Getty's, in addition to his own division, in the Spotswood Road, connecting with Robinson's right on the Pike, and extending, in a rough curved line, north-westward. Getty (less one brigade) had been exceedingly severely engaged, and was now at the cross-roads under Hancock's command.

II. Corps (Hancock) had all its four divisions, two of which, and half of each of the others, had been heavily engaged, in the Brock Road lines. Getty's division (3 brigades) of the VI. Corps was with him.

IX. Corps (Burnside), after a severe march, and with many of its units in a more or less exhausted state, was across the Rapidan and snatching a few hours' rest by the side of the Germanna Plank Road. It had outposts towards Mine Run, on the right rear of Wright's command. The three white divisions (Stevenson's, Potter's, and Willcox's) were available for the battle of the 6th.

BATTLE OF THE WILDERNESS

Ferrero's negro troops were still beyond the Rapidan.

Cavalry Corps.—Sheridan had most of Torbert's division with the trains, Custer's brigade on the Brock Road, Gregg's and Wilson's divisions at and around Todd's Tavern.

Army details remained at or near Chancellorsville.

Thus ended the first day's battle in the Wilderness. Grant, not less than Meade and Humphreys, who had experienced its thickets in November, had hoped to avoid fighting until the manœuvre planned on the 3rd should have completely developed, and the troops making it should have reached their assigned positions beyond the impenetrable ground. But Lee's army was, after all, his objective point, and when Lee's army showed itself elsewhere than was expected the manœuvre was thrown to the winds. First of all, and with something dangerously akin to impatience, Grant flung his nearest troops on Ewell. Then, after a momentary lapse into purely "linear" tactics, he turned the full weight of his army upon Hill, and directed a second and less important attack upon Ewell from the front of the VI. Corps—if Wright's command can be so styled. In this, faults of execution apart, there is directness and singleness of aim. In the morning Hancock's movement is suspended, and Getty thrown out as a flank guard towards Warren's left to ensure the success of the battle on the Pike. In the afternoon little attention is paid to the doings of his right wing provided that it "keeps the ring" for his left. It is true that Sedgwick was ordered forward, but the move was little more than a rectification of the general line of battle, and Warren's two almost intact divisions stood still, practically in defiance of Meade's order to move. This may have been counted unto Warren for unrighteousness; but had Grant really wished to do more than hold Ewell—which he effectually did—he would have ridden to the front himself and driven his subordinates to obey.

The contrary view is often stated, that Ewell had securely held Warren and Sedgwick. If by this is implied the headquarters of the V. and VI. Corps merely, it is true; but two divisions (Wadsworth and Getty) were actually diverted to Hill, and part of a third (Ricketts) remained available for general service. Thus Ewell's three divisions actually blocked one and a half of Sedgwick's and two and the remnant of a third of Warren's. It had cost Ewell serious fighting and heavy losses to effect this result.

The idea upon which Grant's leadership was based, apart from the premature abandonment of the original scheme, was simple and sound. In execution there was one cardinal mistake.

This was the undue haste with which the attacks were forced on by the superior leading, and especially by Grant himself, with his half-conscious feeling that the Army of the Potomac needed more than a suggestion of truculence to make it fight to the "top of its bent". In the morning on Warren's front and in the afternoon

BATTLE OF THE WILDERNESS 163

on Hancock's alike, its consequence was that divisions and brigades, supposed to be executing massed and simultaneous attacks, fought disjointedly and ineffectively. Griffin, Wadsworth, McCandless of Crawford's division, were beaten in detail. Four divisions under Hancock, one of the best soldiers in either army, attacking in four distinct groups at different times, gained "no decisive advantage" over two divisions of Hill's corps. Much of this was attributed to the character of the ground and the difficulty of movement, but this is in itself the severest criticism of the Union leadership, for the character of the country had been taken into account from the first, by Grant as well as by the staff of the Army of the Potomac. Particularly flagrant was the order to Getty to attack with or without Hancock. At the moment when Lyman delivered it the tail of the II. Corps had not left Todd's Tavern.

As to the forces engaged, it was clear that Lee had put in almost every available man,* presuming that Longstreet and R. H. Anderson had not been present. Grant, on the other hand, had the best part of Robinson's (V.), Crawford's (V.), and Wright's (VI.) divisions, also Ricketts' (VI.), Barlow's (II.), and Gibbon's (II.), as well as Burnside's whole corps, practically intact.

This was satisfactory, viewed in connection with the prospects for the following day, but it cannot but suggest that the leadership was not all that it might have been on the 5th. Grant had given up his original intention in the hope of beating a

* Part of Early's division alone had not been closely engaged.

part of Lee's army, presumably with the whole of his own. As things turned out, he put into action only about seven divisions against five of the enemy, and no two of his seven divisions actually moved to the attack together except Birney's and Mott's in the II. Corps.

The 5th, then, must be adjudged a day of lost opportunities, lost chiefly by the impatience of the Union commander. But this first day of battle had certainly impressed every officer and man in the army with the fact that the command was in strong hands. There was something remorseless even in Grant's mistakes.

CHAPTER IX

BATTLE OF THE WILDERNESS

Second day (6th May, 1864)

"After the close of the battle of the 5th of May, my orders were given for the following morning. We knew Longstreet with 12,000 men was on his way to join Hill's right near the Brock Road, and might arrive during the night. I was anxious that the rebels should not take the initiative in the morning, and therefore ordered Hancock to make an assault at 4.30 o'clock. Meade asked to have the hour changed to six. Deferring to his wishes as far as I was willing, the order was modified and five was fixed as the hour to move.

"Wadsworth, with his division . . . lay in a line perpendicular to that held by Hill, and to the right of Hancock. He was directed to move at the same time and to attack Hill's left. Burnside, who was coming up with two [*] divisions, was directed to get in between Warren and Wadsworth and attack as soon as he could get into position to do so. Sedgwick and Warren were to make attacks on their front, to detain as many of the enemy as they could, and to take advantage of any attempt to reinforce Hill from that quarter.

"Burnside was ordered, if he should succeed in breaking the enemy's centre, to swing round to the left and envelop the right of Lee's army".

---

[*] He actually brought up three, in obedience to Grant's order to "bring Willcox too if there is no enemy in his front".

The above extract from Grant's memoirs indicates the spirit in which the battle of the 6th was prearranged.

Hancock, Burnside and Longstreet are the principal factors. All three, Union and Confederate, are practically predestined, by their positions and by the general military situation, to fight on the side of the Plank Road. Hancock, with six* out of the eleven divisions of the Army of the Potomac, was already on the ground, and Longstreet was known with tolerable certainty to be aiming in the same direction. Burnside, whose corps was now the only force in Grant's hand that was free to manœuvre, was, as a matter of course, to be brought into the contest at the point where the director of operations desired to force the decision.

The character of the forthcoming battle would be determined largely by the position and acts of Longstreet's corps. The orders to Hancock, quoted below, provided against one course that Longstreet might take, that of attacking the extreme left of the II. Corps on the Brock Road. But Grant was not concerned so much with what Longstreet might do in general, as with what he might do to assist Hill, whose two weary divisions presented an exceptionally favourable target for Hancock's attack along the Plank Road. Hill's corps was the positive object of the initial attack, and Longstreet's only a disturbing factor to be provided against. If the latter should, as was thought likely, attempt to help Hill by attacking

* Including Wadsworth.

the extreme Union left, it was only necessary to hold him off, and this case, as we have said, was provided for in Hancock's instructions. But his support would be more effective if it were given directly from the rear by the Plank Road. Again, Longstreet might fill up the gap on Hill's left so as to protect his comrade against envelopment. Added to all this, there was the chance that he had not yet arrived on the field at all.

The last was provided for by the order to attack at 4.30, which Grant, deferring to Meade's wishes *as far as he was willing*, altered to five. The possibility of Longstreet's presence on or north of the Plank Road—*i.e.* in rear of Hill, or between Hill and Ewell—was dealt with in the orders to Wadsworth and Burnside. The former was simply and unreservedly to attack Hill's left, in conjunction with Hancock. Burnside's *rôle* was less exactly defined in his orders (see below), and it is not difficult to suppose that Grant intended to lead the IX. Corps, his principal mobile "mass of manœuvre", in person. But from the quotation above it is clear, at any rate, that the corps was expected, whether it had first to fight its way through Longstreet's corps, or had merely to pass through an open gap between Hill and Ewell, to swing round and to envelop the whole right wing of Lee's army—Hill alone or Hill and Longstreet together.

If the scheme were carried out on these lines, the lieutenant-general would have under his hand nine out of fourteen divisions* available on the

* Omitting Ferrero.

whole field. The other five were by vigorous action to neutralize one-third of the enemy's forces, and given the initial disproportion between the opposing armies, the plan afforded good prospects of obtaining a five-to-three superiority in Grant's favour at the decisive point. If in addition, Hill could be routed before Longstreet made his presence felt, and Longstreet, along with the remnants of Hill's corps, could then be caught in the net by Hancock and Burnside, the victory might be of such magnitude as to end the war in Virginia altogether. Grant was an optimist. He may well have hoped for such a victory, and it is only one more proof of his greatness, that his patient "faith in success" carried him through disappointments that to the ordinary optimist would have been final and irremediable disillusionment.

The preparations for the frontal and local flank attack on Hill, for the defence of the extreme left, and for the holding attacks on Ewell were made, of course, by the commander of the Army of the Potomac, those for the "mass of manœuvre" by the lieutenant-general.

Meade's first step was to call up all the train guards—Sheridan was now definitely charged with the protection of the trains—and all the heavy artillery regiments to join their commands at the front before daylight. "Every man who can shoulder a musket must be in the ranks", each corps being ordered to send a staff officer to fetch in its own detachment. The artillery units were ordered to report to General Hunt, the chief of

BATTLE OF THE WILDERNESS

artillery, at headquarters, and were thus naturally told off to Warren's command.

Hancock received the following order at 10 P.M. :—

"You are required to renew the attack at 4.30 o'clock to-morrow morning, keeping a sharp look-out on your left. Your right will be relieved by an attack made at the same time by General Wadsworth's division and by two divisions of General Burnside's corps. General Getty is under your command ".*

The hour of attack, as already stated, was changed to five. Grant's ruling idea was to get in the first blow. Meade's was to make the attacks simultaneous and by whole units. He represented that the fatigues of the day before, and the density of the thicket, made it difficult to form up rapidly, and that some daylight was necessary for the direction of the battle after it had opened. Grant, therefore, warned perhaps by the experience of the 5th, allowed an extra half-hour. Warren was informed that he would be reinforced by four artillery and one engineer battalion (serving as infantry), and ordered to attack at 4.30 (5) on the Orange Pike, "where you attacked to-day". Sedgwick's instructions were similar.

* Wadsworth was not assigned to Hancock's command until after the first attack, though the projected movement of Burnside's corps would definitely separate him from the rest of the V. Corps. The separation was implicit, moreover, in the instructions to Warren to reclaim one of General Robinson's brigades at present with Wadsworth, as soon as Burnside was in position. During the first attack Wadsworth sent in his prisoners and casualties to Warren's lines. It may be that in order to bridge the gap between Burnside's and Hancock's masses with a screen, Wadsworth was deliberately kept out of Hancock's sphere of influence.

Sheridan's orders were brief, and not very satisfactory to that ardent officer. He was held responsible for the left flank of the army and for the security of the trains.

Each corps commander was advised of the instructions given to the others. There was no general order.

Burnside, as we know, had taken no part whatever in the first day's battle. Stevenson's division had taken over the outpost line west of Germanna Plank Road, between the ford and Flat Run, while the rest of the IX. Corps filed along the Germanna Plank Road behind him. In the afternoon Burnside had been ordered to send one division to Sedgwick if required by that officer, and had told off Potter's division for this purpose while it was crossing during the late afternoon of the 5th. Willcox's division was massed a few hundred yards south of Germanna Ford. Ferrero's (coloured) was still beyond the Rapidan when night fell. In the IX. Corps only 6000 men in Stevenson's and Potter's commands were old soldiers. The rest of the corps was composed wholly of new regiments. Burnside was informed, on the 5th, that his reserve artillery was to be "parked in a safe place". There was far too much artillery at the front already.

The order to Burnside for the 6th ran as follows:—

"Lieut.-General Grant desires that you start your two divisions at 2 A.M. to-morrow, punctually for this place. You will put them in position between the Germanna Plank Road and the road leading from this place (Wilderness Tavern) to

BATTLE OF THE WILDERNESS 171

Parker's Store, so as to close the gap between Warren and Hancock, connecting both. You will move from this position on the enemy beyond at 4.30 A.M., the time at which the Army of the Potomac moves. If you think there is no enemy on Willcox's front, bring him also".

It may be summarized as a preliminary order to get into position, coupled with a general indication of the chief commander's ulterior purpose.

Hancock's task was to attack on the Plank Road at 5 A.M., and to "keep a sharp look-out for his left", where Longstreet might attack by way of a wood road that ran from the Catharpin Road to the Brock Road near Trigg's house. Barlow, the left of Hancock's corps, was already disposed on the 5th in such a way as to cover the approaches, and Gibbon, whom Hancock placed in command on this side, had at his disposal Barlow's division,* and every gun in the II. Corps except a battery and a half at or near the Plank Road, for near Trigg's was the only open ground on the whole front of the corps. Barlow's left brigade faced almost due south across the Brock Road, looking towards Todd's Tavern, and watching the approaches to Chancellorsville, while further to the left rear Sheridan had his cavalry divisions in hand and ready for action. These precautions on Hancock's part of course weakened his frontal attack along the Plank Road, but the necessity for these was inherent in the plan of battle, and there was no reason to suppose, nor

* His own division (Carroll's, Owen's, and Webb's brigades) was used up piecemeal in supporting the attack on the Plank Road.

did the event show, that the remainder of Hancock's corps *plus* Wadsworth's division would be too small a force for the assault on Hill's two exhausted divisions. The rest it was not within Hancock's province to accomplish, but in that of the lieutenant-general, to whom fell the handling of the whole left wing, as one unit, against Lee's right wing.

It will be noted that Hancock assigned Gibbon to command a small improvised army corps of Barlow's strong divisions and the corps artillery. Birney had been in command of a similar improvised army corps (Birney's and Mott's divisions) on the previous day, and the same officer was now placed in command of Hancock's right, consisting of Birney's, Mott's, and Getty's divisions, *plus* the several brigades of Gibbon's and about one battery (effective) of field artillery. Thus early had the three-corps reorganization of the Army of the Potomac broken down.*

---

* General Humphreys expresses himself somewhat strongly on this matter (*The Virginia Campaign of 1864-5*, pp. 3, 4). " The reason given for this reorganization was the reduced strength of nearly all the infantry regiments composing the army; but it caused some dissatisfaction . . . owing to the spirit of rivalry between the several corps, the divisions of a corps, and the brigade of a division ". The merging of the I. and III. Corps in the others had incidentally caused an entire recasting of the division and brigade organization throughout the army. General Humphreys continues : " In a country so heavily wooded . . . five infantry corps of about 15,000 each would have been a more judicious organization, owing to the difficulty of communication between the corps commander and subordinate commanders . . . and the consequent difficulty of prompt and efficient control of extensive lines of battle, especially at critical moments. . . . The nature of the appointment of a corps commander, emanating as it did from the President, conferred a much wider discretion on him than that authorized in a divisional commander, and that discretion was sometimes needed in

In the very early hours of the morning Hancock drew out and formed his troops in the dense woods bordering the Plank Road. Only one brigade (Webb's, of Gibbon's division) was retained in the breastworks of the Brock Road to act as general reserve.

The first shots of the day were fired from the Confederate entrenchments just before five. The Army of the Potomac's initiative was none too soon after all, but fortunately Hancock was ready, and punctually at five gave the order to advance. Birney had his own and Mott's divisions in first line, Getty's and the two detached brigades of Gibbon's (Carroll and Owen) in second. The result of this massed attack, the first of the battle, in which Wadsworth in the thickets on the right duly participated, may be told in Hancock's own

---

the division commander of a corps 25,000 strong. . . . General Hancock's lines were so extended, and his troops on the right were so separated from those on the left owing to the difference in the character of the tasks allotted to each [right offensive, left defensive], that on the second day he assigned General Birney to the command of his right wing and General Gibbon to the command of his left wing, in which commands these officers needed the authority and the discretion of corps commanders". In this connection we may quote Clausewitz's sardonic remark: "There is nothing more unmanageable than an army divided into three parts unless it be one divided into two!"

The corps spirit died hard in the disbanded units. Later, before Petersburg, some heavy artillery (acting as infantry) was posted to a division that had belonged to the III. Corps. After a time, eight or ten months after the III. Corps had ceased to exist, these heavy artillerymen, who had, of course, never belonged to it, were recognized as "Third Corps men as *we* understood the term", and their officers made members of the "Third Corps Benevolent Association". Another remarkable illustration of "Third Corps spirit" is afforded by the fact that at a review at Brandy Station in April the men of the new 4th Division, II. Corps, wore the III. Corps badge on their caps and the II. Corps "clover leaf" on the tails of their blouses.

words. "The enemy's line was broken at all points, and he was driven through the forest suffering severe losses in killed, wounded, and prisoners". With more or less heavy fighting * Hill's corps was trampled down by the weight of the Union attack.

"Hancock was on the Plank Road—radiant", says Lyman. "'Tell General Meade we are driving them beautifully!'" A little further on, perhaps a mile from the cross-roads, Wadsworth's line of battle crashed into the left flank of the retreating Confederates and the pursuit went on. "Hundreds of prisoners were taken", says a staff officer of the VI. Corps. "passed along the line to the Plank Road, and started down it to find the provost guards for themselves. The road was thronged with these prisoners, frightened and anxious to get out of fire", for Hill's guns, and a few Union field-pieces swept the whole length of the road, "wounded men and stretcher bearers all flocking to the rear, with an occasional staff officer forcing his way through the throng". At the front the victorious infantry was rapidly getting out of hand in the woods, though a general line was maintained and the pursuit was kept up with unabated vigour. Wadsworth's men were gradually crowding Hancock's right back to the Plank Road. The gallant remnant of Heth's division and the artillery in Tapp's field held off the oncoming lines in their immediate front. The Union left, gaining ground while the centre and right were checked by the enemy and pressed inwards by Wadsworth's line,

* Authorities differ as to this.

BATTLE OF THE WILDERNESS 175

was echeloned outwards, so far indeed that some of its fire struck the enemy's batteries at Tapp's in reverse.

The ebb soon came. It was the task of Burnside's troops to complete the victory, but they were still far from the scene of action, and Hancock's attack, spending its force not only on Hill's divisions but also on inanimate obstacles—forests, thickets and the marshy heads of streams—came almost to a standstill about a mile east of Parker's Store. It was now, a little after six o'clock, the turn of the Confederates. Longstreet was on the Plank Road and not on the Catharpin, as Hancock had been led to expect. His two divisions, Field and Kershaw commanding, had arrived at Parker's Store at dawn on the 6th, and Anderson, with the absent division of Hill's corps, was close behind them.

Field and Kershaw, approaching by parallel wood-roads, entered the Plank Road almost at the same moment, and thus moved up to the scene of action in two long columns of fours abreast, dividing the mob of Hill's broken troops like a wedge. Kershaw deployed to his right, Field to his left, both at the double. Kershaw struck the left of Birney's command and the fight swayed to and fro for some time, the Union troops utilizing some of Hill's lost entrenchments, until General Kershaw himself led a charge. This forced back the stubborn though disordered Federals till they were no further forward than their centre. Field, on the other side of the Plank Road, encountered

Wadsworth and a few regiments of Birney's command in or near the open ground of Tapp's field. Here was Lee himself with the headquarter staff of the Army of Northern Virginia. Gregg's Texans, fresh from campaigning in Tennessee, broke into cheers when they saw their old commander, and Lee impulsively galloped out to lead them into the fight. But with one accord the men shouted, "Go back, sir; General Lee to the rear", an officer stepped up and turned the bridle of the general's horse, and the brigade raced forward along with the Georgians of Benning's brigade. But both were brought to a standstill by Wadsworth, and, like Heth and Getty on the previous evening, the two lines fired heavily into one another at close quarters.

After one and a half hours of such work in such country the first essential was to reform. On the Union side, the small units of veterans called by their original name of regiments had kept well together, but divisions and brigades were so far mixed up that the senior officers were losing control over their men. Ammunition was failing on both sides. Lee, too, had every reason to call a halt, for Heth's and Wilcox's divisions (Hill), tried sorely enough on the evening before, and now overborne by numbers, were in entire confusion. Thus on the Plank Road there was a lull of about two hours, from about 6.30 to about 8.30.

Between these hours Hancock was busy enough. His first step was to inform headquarters that Longstreet was on the field, his next to bring up his reserve brigade (Webb) to replace the exhausted

BATTLE OF THE WILDERNESS

division of the VI. Corps, which was now commanded by Wheaton, the brave Getty having been seriously wounded in the fight with Longstreet. At 7 A.M. General Hancock received the following from headquarters—

"Your dispatch is received informing the major-general commanding of the presence of Longstreet's force. The only reserve force of the army (one division IX. Corps) is here and will be ordered to your support should it become absolutely necessary. Call for it, therefore, only in case of the last necessity".

Just before this he had ordered Gibbon to send out Barlow to attack the enemy's right. This order, for some obscure reason, was only partially obeyed by the dispatch of one of Barlow's brigades (Frank's) by itself. There was a good route available—the bed of the unfinished railroad—the value of which the Confederates appreciated later in the day, and the consequences of this neglect, as we shall see, were very grave. Out-of-date information and baseless, though persistent, rumours as to Longstreet's supposed movements on the Catharpin Road certainly gave excessive importance, in the eyes of the Union generals, to alarms in this quarter. First, the enemy's cavalry and horse artillery were mistaken for Longstreet's advance. Then, the sound of Sheridan's carbines away towards Todd's Tavern and Piney Branch Church caused further uneasiness, and about eight a body of convalescents belonging to the II. Corps itself and arriving from Chancellorsville to join their units, was taken for hostile infantry, and word was sent to General Hancock to that effect.

The reluctance of headquarters to send away Stevenson's division was largely due to the mistaken idea that Pickett's division of Longstreet's corps, actually detached in North Carolina, was present but not accounted for, and to the fact that R. H. Anderson's division of Hill had also not made itself felt. However, Grant, in rear of the fighting line, was cooler than Gibbon at the most exposed point, and Stevenson was soon dispatched to reinforce Hancock, arriving at the cross-roads about 8 A.M. At the same time Wadsworth was definitely placed under Hancock's orders. Hancock was also informed that two of Burnside's divisions " had advanced nearly to Parker's Store and are ordered to attack to their left ", and about half an hour later, that Sheridan had received orders at eight to " attack Longstreet's flank and rear by the Brock Road ".

These measures—the detachment of Stevenson's division from the original " mass of manœuvre " to act as a reserve to troops already committed to the fight, the assignment of Wadsworth to Hancock's command, the new movements indicated for Burnside and Sheridan—mark the abandonment of the original scheme and the opening of a new phase of the battle, in which the General-in-Chief, having no longer a mass of troops at his own disposal, has to forego the power of manœuvre and to leave the result to the chances of co-operation between the various generals and their respective local reserves. This system, which is roughly the equivalent of that held in honour in Germany to-day, depends for its success on compelling events to conform to

BATTLE OF THE WILDERNESS 179

the preconceived dispositions. It has never proved itself supple enough to enable a commander to exploit or to evade *any* situation, good or bad, that develops in the course of a manœuvre. If events belie it, its bolt is shot. The supreme command has to abdicate its functions, and in the present case, owing to the amazing density of the woods and thickets, there was not even effective co-operation between neighbouring corps commanders to take its place.

Warren and Sedgwick had advanced promptly at five o'clock as ordered, and engaged Ewell. The Confederates had, however, employed the night well in constructing especially strong earthworks, and there seems to have been no particular desire to force the fighting on the part either of Warren or of his superiors. About 5.30, with the forethought that was characteristic of him, Warren, seeing that Burnside was not in position, sent off Colonel Kitching's heavy artillery brigade to Wadsworth. The V. Corps was reported "disposed for the assault", presumably with a view to taking advantage, as ordered by Grant, of any lateral movement from Ewell's lines towards the Plank Road. Obviously in pursuance of the same idea, Meade desired Warren (6 A.M.) to throw out his pickets and skirmishers well to the front—practically a suspension of the order to assault. Then, at 6.25 Warren notified Humphreys that Griffin had pressed close up to the enemy's lines, and that he thought it best not to make the final assault until preparations were made. Sedgwick acted upon the same principle, holding his command—Wright's division, Neill's brigade, Ricketts' division (returned to him from the V. Corps), and Shaler's brigade (newly joined)—in an attitude of readiness. Ferrero's (coloured) division of the IX. Corps was on his right rear, equally inactive, and at the close of the day was sent to escort the trains. At 7.15, indeed, Warren heard of Hancock's success and of Longstreet's arrival, and was ordered to press his attack with the utmost vigour, to spare ammunition,* and to use the bayonet. But only the preliminaries of this assault had been carried into execution when, about 9 A.M., events suddenly took an unfavourable turn and reduced Warren to the position of reservoir for other corps.†

Hancock had called for Webb's brigade about 6.30, and Birney had ordered it to deploy on the right of the Plank Road and to go forward to replace Getty's (Wheaton's) division of the VI. Corps. Now Getty had been crowded, during the first advance, to the south side of the road, and all troops that had been engaged were being rallied and reformed in close order, so that a gap had opened immediately on the right of the Plank

---

* Quite early in the second day's battle want of ammunition began to make itself felt in the Union army. The infantry soldier's cartridge-box was of an unsatisfactory pattern. It contained 40 rounds, 20 of which, in the under side of the box, were always apt to be forgotten or lost, or, in the case of bounty-jumpers and their kind—commonly called "coffee boilers"—got rid of so as to be able to show empty pouches to any suspicious officer or provost guard.

† "I received 18 orders to send reinforcements to other commands on the second day's battle". From a letter of General Warren to the Mil. Hist. Soc. Mass.

BATTLE OF THE WILDERNESS

Road, between the troops that had been fighting under Birney against Kershaw, and those that had engaged Field's division near Tapp's along with the V. Corps troops under Wadsworth. Whether this be the true explanation or not,* it is indisputable that Webb, advancing through the woods to relieve Getty, found, not Getty, but the Confederates, and was very severely handled.

Frank's brigade, Barlow's reply to the order of his corps commander to advance on the left, made its way laboriously to the left of the II. Corps line of battle (Mott's division) not without fighting,† for more or less heavy skirmishing went on throughout the two hours that elapsed between the first and second attacks of Hancock's command. At this moment, then, about eight, Gibbon's command consisted only of three brigades of Barlow's division. Each of the three brigades of Gibbon's, and one of Barlow's were now committed to the fight, as well as the whole of Birney's and Mott's divisions. Getty's division had withdrawn to reorganize and replenish ammunition. Wadsworth's command—Warren apparently had not yet repossessed himself of the brigade of Robinson's division and of the heavy artillery under Kitching—was partly in the woods north of the Plank Road, partly in Tapp's field. Stevenson's division of the IX. Corps was brought up from the cross-roads, and Hancock had

---

* It is offered only as a suggestion, based on Webb's report, *Papers of the Mil. Hist. Soc. Mass.*, etc.

† It is uncertain at what time Frank came up. It was probable that he connected with Mott's left when the second attack was already in progress.

now under his orders, not only his own corps, but divisions from every corps in Grant's army as well.

On the Confederate side Longstreet was skirmishing heavily and gradually taking up Hill's original line, and Hill's two divisions were being reformed near Parker's Store, and filing off to the left to take up a position between Longstreet and Ewell. Anderson's division arrived on the field about 8 A.M.

At 8.50 Hancock's attack re-opened. The Union troops fought as hard as at any other time in this hard-fought day's work, but not in such splendid order as in the first advance. The lines had, as a Federal private expressed it, "been shot into skirmishing order". Webb, steadying his brigade after its misadventure, found himself in the extreme advance of the Union line; some troops of the IX. Corps were close behind him, and Wadsworth, who had rallied and reformed perhaps three thousand effective men of his own, rode over to Webb and took over general command on the north side of the Plank Road. On the other side of the road Birney had his own and Mott's divisions, Carroll's and Owen's brigades of Gibbon, and (probably later) Frank's of Barlow.

Shortly after the attack had begun, Hancock's chief-of-staff, Lieut.-Colonel Morgan, sent word of a Confederate advance on the Brock Road.* Once more doubts of Longstreet's position assailed the Union generals. Eustis's brigade (of the VI. Corps division now commanded by Wheaton) was sent to Barlow, and Stevenson's, the only intact division

* This was, in fact, the Confederate cavalry before mentioned.

BATTLE OF THE WILDERNESS 183

remaining to Hancock, was ordered to detach Colonel Leasure's brigade to follow Eustis's. This, and the mishap to Webb, effectually weakened the second general attack on the Plank Road.*

Of this attack as a matter of tactics little can be said except that sometimes one party gained a little ground, sometimes the other. Longstreet was not content with a passive defensive, but himself attacked again and again on different parts of the line.

It was not long before Wadsworth's right was hard pressed. Webb, almost alone in front of the Union army, was compelled to swing back his right flank, and shortly after nine a heavy Confederate attack broke upon Cutler's brigade of Wadsworth and swept it backwards, whence it had come, to the open ground occupied by the V. Corps. The enemy's skirmish line followed up sharply, and began to spread out in the gap that Burnside was to have filled before the battle opened. Birney was ordered by Hancock to send a force from left to right to re-establish the broken wing. Army headquarters stopped Warren's offensive at 9.30, and an hour later definitely ordered the V. and VI. Corps to suspend their attacks and to improve their entrenchments opposite Ewell.

Towards eleven the firing died down all along Hancock's front.† It was, as usual, the lull before another storm.

* Eustis was, however, returned to Birney on Leasure's arrival. Carroll also appears to have given up one of his regiments, by Hancock's order, to reinforce Barlow.

† General Webb, in *Battles and Leaders*, vol. iv., places at this

Longstreet and Lee had now decided that it was of little use pressing home the frontal attack on the Plank Road—the attack on Warren's left was Hill's affair—and General M. L. Smith, chief engineer of the Army of Northern Virginia, had been sent, about 10 A.M., to find a practicable "jumping-off ground" for an attack on Hancock's left rear. On receipt of Smith's report a mixed force * was collected, and under his guidance it was marched along bye-paths until it reached the bed of the unfinished railway. The four brigades filed along this for a few hundred yards, front-turned so that they faced north, and about eleven moved forward to the attack. The first unit met was Frank's brigade, that Barlow had sent out about 8 A.M. It had been heavily engaged and was almost out of ammunition, and its commander, "a pleasant, talkative man", was not equal to the emergency. The Confederate line swept over it in a few seconds, and struck the left of Mott's division. A swift

time, viz. after nine, the incident of the isolated charge, by Wadsworth's orders, of the 20th Massachusetts, in which that regiment lost its colonel wounded, and Major H. L. Abbott, universally regarded as one of the most promising officers in the army, mortally wounded. But there is no other record of Birney's men having given way—which was the occasion for the charge of the 20th Massachusetts—up to the flank attack, shortly to be described, made by Longstreet from the railroad bed, and Webb couples with his own account one by an officer of Owen's brigade, which refers solely to later events about the time of Wadsworth's receiving a mortal wound. His official report, too, seems to differ as regards the order of these various events, from his paper in *Battles and Leaders*, and I venture, though with some doubts, to place this incident later. A report, written even within a few months, is hardly to be trusted implicitly as to the sequence of events in this amazing struggle.

* Wofford's brigade (Kershaw), G. B. Anderson's (Field), Mahone (R. H. Anderson), Davis's, under Colonel Stone (Heth).

BATTLE OF THE WILDERNESS

change of front to the left failed to save the wearied Union regiments.*

Field's division fiercely resumed the frontal attack, and Birney, who had just detached two brigades to re-establish the right wing, as already mentioned, was too weak to resist. The line of the II. Corps was rolled up from left to right, and fell back, fighting gallantly but in indescribable confusion. Wadsworth, on the right of the Plank Road, flung the 20th Massachusetts (Webb's brigade) into the fight. The Massachusetts men were repulsed with heavy losses, and Wadsworth himself was mortally wounded. The break in Webb's brigade could not be rectified, for it was at that moment changing formation.† Field's division hustled the scattered Union regiments backwards, as they had hustled Hill's in the early morning. Even Hancock's personal influence was of no avail; the men, although not actually terror-stricken, had

---

* It will be remembered that this division, which had belonged to the old III. Corps, had given way on the 5th. It was largely composed of troops about to leave the service on the expiry of their term. Humphreys defends its conduct warmly; he had commanded it at Gettysburg and knew it well. He says that they only did what all other troops did, viz. fall back hurriedly when they were "flanked".

† Wheeling to the left under Webb's direction so as to face up the Plank Road, the 20th Massachusetts being the pivot of the wheel. The officers of that regiment protested against Wadsworth's order, but the general, whose blood was up, said they were afraid, and jumped his horse over the entrenchments, lately Hill's, that the regiment occupied. The men followed, and Wadsworth was almost instantly shot. He died in the enemy's hands on the 8th. General Webb's report provides one very interesting fact for the student of military psychology. His first misadventure having led to his changing front "right back", he found when he was trying to resume his original line, that is, to change front left, facing directly up the Plank Road, that his men had lost confidence in that line, and could not be relied upon to maintain it.

had enough, and disregarding their officers, retreated in a mob to their entrenchments on the Brock Road, and in bitterness of spirit Hancock gave the order, that he had never before given to the II. Corps, to retreat.

The method of retirement was usually that which may be called "break and rally" or "fall out and fall in". Webb says of one corps: "The regiment stood there until I gave it orders to break like partridges through the woods for the Brock Road".

The responsibility for the collapse of Hancock's offensive is attributed by Humphreys partly to the failure of Barlow to advance as ordered, and partly to the failure of Birney to guard the left of his line while engaged in the battle on the Plank Road. As to the former, it is pointed out that the railroad bed would have served the Federals as well as it did the Confederates for a covered approach to the enemy's flank. It was known to Hancock by 7.30 that his left was approximately level with Longstreet's right; Barlow's advance was ordered shortly afterwards. Barlow must have found and utilized the railroad bed, and his advance would have struck the forces on the Plank Road in flank, met Longstreet front to front, or struck the flank of Longstreet's flank attack— in any case with satisfactory results. As it was, Frank's single brigade, moving a little up the Brock Road before taking to the woods, blundered through them with its flanks unsupported. As to Birney's neglect of the local security of his own left, it can only be attributed to his being

BATTLE OF THE WILDERNESS 187

entirely, if unconsciously, absorbed in events on the front.

Hancock's corps retired into its breastworks, practically unpursued within effective rifle range. He has been criticized for constructing these works on the afternoon of the 5th—rightly or wrongly, this is not the place to consider—but they proved the salvation of half the Union army on the 6th.

The Confederates' attack came to a dismal end owing to a serious mishap within their own lines. Longstreet, Lee's "old war horse", was riding with his staff along the Plank Road at the head of Field's division and making arrangements to press home his victory, when suddenly, sixty or seventy yards away to the right, some friendly troops— the very troops that had made the successful flank attack from the railroad bed and were now reforming—fired one disastrous volley into the cavalcade. General Micah Jenkins, the gallant officer who commanded Field's leading brigade, and several others were killed outright, and Longstreet severely—it was thought at first fatally—wounded.[*] The fire was checked at once, but it had cost Lee the services of his second in command at the crisis of the first great battle. The joyous advance of Longstreet's men, who loved their commander, stopped abruptly. After a time a few troops tentatively approached the Federal breastworks, giving back at once when Leasure's brigade of the IX. Corps made a dashing counter-stroke under

[*] Two miles away in this same forest, just a year before, Stonewall Jackson had fallen a victim to a similar accident.

Hancock's orders.* Lee himself rode up, sent for R. H. Anderson to command Longstreet's corps, and postponed the attack on Hancock's works to a later hour. The Confederates were now formed in the original (Hill's) log-works lost in the early morning battle, and the right was extended to the railroad bed. The two corps, Longstreet's and Hancock's, were thus on equal fronts once more.

The agglomeration of units of different corps under Hancock's command calls for a word of comment. It was solely the result of the consolidation of five corps into three. Economy of force at indecisive points and accumulation of it at the decisive point was good generalship, and Grant overrode personal considerations † to enforce it. But he enforced it only at the cost of breaking up two out of the three corps, making ineffective two out of the three presumably most experienced generals in the army, and forcing upon some divisional commanders the responsibilities without the authority of a corps commander. The former five corps could have been distributed with the greatest ease, Hancock having three and Sedgwick and Warren one each.‡

---

* The brigade was drawn out of the works and formed at right angles to them, as if for a march-past with the line of the II. Corps as saluting base. Leasure then swept along the front from left to right at the double.

† Unlike Moltke on the 2nd July, 1866, in Bohemia. See Bonnal's *Sadowa*, Chapter IV., ii.

‡ Longstreet's and Hill's corps were much intermingled also, especially on the extreme right. But, in general, Lee and his corps commanders strove hard to re-establish the proper order of battle. Hill's corps (*i.e.* Heth and Wilcox) was reformed as well as possible and formed on a new line between Longstreet's left and Ewell's right,

BATTLE OF THE WILDERNESS

The original attack came to a standstill at the critical moment when the enemy was actually deploying his last intact corps. This in itself indicates the magnitude of the lost opportunity.

While Hancock's part in the programme was carried out with remarkable success, Burnside's never received even a beginning of execution.

The IX. Corps, which had been severely tried by forced marches on the 4th and 5th, had moved off even before the hour (2 A.M.) mentioned in Grant's orders, leaving the corps troops (infantry and cavalry) and Ferrero's division behind between Germanna Ford and Flat Run. From Wilderness Tavern, Burnside took the wood road past Lacy's house to Parker's Store that Crawford had used on the 5th. Wilderness Run was crossed at daylight, and the corps plunged into the forest that had already absorbed Wadsworth's men, Potter's division leading and Willcox's in line of battle in support of Potter.

But the fate of the Union attack on the Plank Road had been put to the touch, and lost, long before the head of the belated " mass of manœuvre " appeared in the neighbourhood. The battle in its original form was at an end, and all that the chief commander could do was to direct all the troops he could still control towards the most important target that had offered itself, ere they too slipped from his grasp.

Grant wasted no time in recriminations, then

---

and Anderson, who had come up behind Longstreet, was placed on Field's left so as to bring him into the sphere of influence of his own corps commander, Hill.

or afterwards,* but instantly sent a staff officer to stop Burnside's movement on Parker's Store, which point had no relation whatever to the new military situation, and to bring him in towards Hancock's battle. Moreover, Stevenson's, the rear division of Burnside's column, was broken off from it and halted near Wilderness Tavern as general reserve.

His advanced troops were actually feeling the enemy near Chewning's, the division commanders and brigadiers happy to have found open ground for their fight, when they were once more plunged into the forest. Lieutenant-Colonel Comstock of Grant's staff guided the troops to a new line on the right of Wadsworth's supposed position.

At 10 A.M. Comstock reported to headquarters that Burnside's lateral movement had progressed one and a half miles from Chewning's towards the presumed position of Wadsworth's right. Hancock's firing was heard about a mile away. At this hour, it will be remembered, the second attack of the Federals on the Plank Road was in progress.

On the side of the Confederates, Anderson was placed in the north-west corner of Tapp's Field, and as soon as Hill's other divisions (Heth and Wilcox) had reformed they were led off the Plank Road and formed on Anderson's left. Thence extending leftwards in the Wilderness—more familiar to them than to the young soldiers of the IX. Corps on the other side—they met Ewell's right, halted, and entrenched. Thus the Army of

* Note the kindly wording of Burnside's orders in the quotation from Grant's memoirs that stands at the head of this chapter.

BATTLE OF THE WILDERNESS

Northern Virginia was, for the first time, connected in one line of battle in order from left to right, Ewell, Hill, Longstreet.

The flank march of the IX. Corps was a delicate operation, for matters at Chewning's had gone so far by 9 A.M. that the skirmishers had fallen back into the ranks for the assault. Slowly Potter was moved direct to his left, Willcox's division, in line of battle abreast the Lacy–Parker's Store road, holding off the enemy during the flank march. After this was accomplished, Willcox continued to hold the wood road for some time, and was then directed to file off to the left to join Potter. It was 2 P.M. before all this was effected, and Willcox's men, all young soldiers, had to endure shell fire from the Confederates at Chewning's for perhaps four hours.

The main body of the IX. Corps, after two days' hard marching, was under arms and on the move almost exactly twelve hours before it took an effective part in the battle. Five of these twelve hours of course were consumed in extricating Burnside from the fight he had begun at Chewning's, and bringing him into the main Union line. But this does not explain his slowness in the earlier part of the morning, viz. before coming within sight of Chewning's. His hour for attack was the same as Warren's, Hancock's, and Sedgwick's, 5 A.M., and it was probably three hours after that time when his skirmishers came into action at Chewning's. How much of the responsibility for this must be assigned to Burnside for mismanaging, and how much to Grant for overworking the IX. Corps, it is impossible to say. The delay, to whomever it was due, was calamitous.

In view of Burnside's movement from Chewning's to Tapp's clearings, Warren was warned (3.15 P.M.) of a gap, corresponding roughly to the Parker's Store road, between the left of the V. and the right of the IX. Corps, and authorized to call upon Sedgwick for assistance if an advance were required to relieve Burnside or to fill the gap. The necessity did not arise, but it was provided for.

Burnside, with Willcox's and Potter's divisions, was now more or less in touch with the right of Hancock, and about two, Potter, with a portion of Willcox's division on his right—the rest were still moving westward from Chewning's clearing—attacked a part of R. H. Anderson's division with a certain amount of success, though Willcox's men and some of Potter's were raw,* and the enemy were entrenched on rising ground behind a swampy stream.

On the front of the V. Corps there was no event of importance from the time when Warren was ordered to suspend his attack (10.30). That general henceforward acted, punctually and with almost eager loyalty, as a depôt for the supply of troops to other commands, and occupied himself with the formation of a solid and properly traced

---

* "When it is remembered that the regiment had been but fourteen days in the field, so constantly marching that it had been drilled as a battalion but twice, and that it numbered only 313 muskets on the morning of the battle, I believe I may submit its record without comment."—Report of Officer Commanding, 17th Vermont.

BATTLE OF THE WILDERNESS

line of entrenchments.* The tool carts were brought up to the front, which seems to have been an unusual procedure. The normal method of entrenching was independent of engineer assistance,† the implements being axes, bayonets, and the hats or hands of the men to throw up the earth.

On Sedgwick's front also nothing of importance occurred till later in the day. It is suggested that Ewell was doubtful of the movements of the Federal IX. Corps, last heard of near Germanna Ford, and feared for his left flank. The somewhat erratic movements of Ferrero's division on Sedgwick's right rear had, therefore, no little effect on the course of events. Gordon, Early's energetic brigadier, who had been transferred overnight from the scene of his forest fight with Wadsworth and McCandless, found and reported a good position whence to attack the right of the VI. Corps, but his superiors preferred to await definite information as to the IX. Corps before committing themselves to a forward move against Sedgwick. Thus the IX. Corps was almost as uncertain and disquieting a factor for Lee as Longstreet's was for Grant.

We turn once again to the front of Hancock's

---

* Warren himself rode hither and thither attending to details, in accordance with his temperament. Headquarters seem to have realized this, and most of their notes bear such instructions as—"To be shown to General Robinson in General Warren's absence", "Commanding officer V. Corps", "General Warren or the chief-of-staff".

† The engineers of the Army of the Potomac, it may be remembered, had been assigned to duty with the V. Corps as infantry. It was found, then and thereafter, more profitable to employ these highly trained specialists in their proper work. Warren himself was an engineer officer.

motley command, no longer on the Plank Road, but behind its entrenchments along the Brock Road, and engaged in reforming and replenishing ammunition after its heavy morning's work.

At two, the hour of Burnside's first attack, Lyman sent word to Meade, "General Hancock has a continuous line, but not organized enough to attack". Reinforcements had already been sent over from Warren (Robinson with one brigade of his division and two regiments of heavy artillery), and though it was merely left to his discretion to co-operate with Burnside's present movement, Hancock was ordered (3 P.M.) to give his men a rest until six, when the attack was to be resumed by Burnside and Hancock together.

The Confederate attack, however, came first.

Longstreet's plan of pressing up to the front of the breastworks and turning their left * by way of the railroad bed that had done such good service already was not acceptable to Lee, who was much impressed by the visible wreck of battle on the Plank Road, and, of course, in ignorance of how things stood in the interior of the forest. Southern soldiers claim that, had they pressed Hancock as Longstreet intended, they would have made an end

* General M. L. Smith, Chief Engineer of the Army of Northern Virginia, who had designed the morning movement and conducted the four brigades to the position whence they routed Birney, had left Colonel Sorrel, of Lee's staff, to supervise the actual attack, and had himself gone on to the Brock Road. Returning after a careful examination, he reported in favour of a second flank attack upon the left rear of the Union entrenchments, by the routes he had reconnoitred. He had rejoined Longstreet and received that general's assent when the party was fired into, as already narrated, by the 12th Virginia.

BATTLE OF THE WILDERNESS

of the Federal left wing before night, but they admit that attacking as they did after some hours' rest they got only hard knocks.*

The criticism has also been made that it was then too late in the day to achieve important results before nightfall. If this be so, what is to be said of Grant's orders to Hancock and Burnside to attack at six? The explanation and justification of both commanders, Lee and Grant, are to be found in moral rather than in material factors. Each sought to impose his will upon the other, to answer his last effort with a better, and to leave upon the minds of his wearied soldiers the fatal impression of defeat.

For four hours there was no move of importance. Then, at 4.15, the firing swelled again to its loudest. The Confederate line of battle came up to within a hundred yards of the breastwork on the Brock Road. But the fire of men that have been fighting for many hours is wild and unsteady, and half an hour elapsed before the Union losses became serious. Then a rift appeared at that part of the line held by the wrecks of Birney's and Mott's divisions. Mott's was thus broken for the third time in two days, once through its own default, and twice, after it had retrieved its good name, by the fortune of war. The woods in front were on fire in parts,† and heavy clouds of smoke

---

* General Alexander goes so far as to say that the result of the afternoon's battle was that Hancock's men were forced to expend more ammunition than they otherwise would have done.

† Many wounded perished in the flames, chiefly, it would appear, by the more merciful process of suffocation. Frank Wilkeson, of the II. Corps, records that some of his comrades kept back a cartridge for

and flames were driven by a west wind on to the Union breastworks, the logs of which presently caught fire also. Unable to face the fire and smoke as well as the enemy's bullets, Mott's men gave way. The grey line of battle came on and planted its crimson battle-flags on the Brock Road, but only for an instant. The fire of the Union second line opened at full intensity, and Carroll's brigade, gallantly led as ever by its ardent brigadier, came down between the two Union lines at the double and drove out the intruders. Brooke's brigade of Barlow's division also assisted to re-establish the line,* and Mott's men, who were by no means defeated, rallied. The attack was over and repulsed at all points by 5.30.

Burnside played his part in the last act gallantly and with energy. He was ordered to "go in" with Hancock at six o'clock, and was regulating his final preparations accordingly. But when it became evident towards five that the Confederates had themselves attacked Hancock, he acted on his own initiative.

"The enemy opened upon General Hancock, thus rendering it important that our attack should be made earlier. General Willcox formed the lines quickly and at 5.30 commenced the assault, forcing the enemy, who had come out of his entrenchments, back to them and breaking his line

their own use in case of being wounded and abandoned in the burning forest.

* Hancock mentions the effective support of Dow's battery (6th Maine) at this crisis. This battery and Ricketts' were the only guns in the II. Corps seriously engaged during the whole battle.

BATTLE OF THE WILDERNESS

on the left". However, after a close struggle, Willcox's men were forced back to their original position.

This ended the fighting of the IX. Corps. It could claim that, arriving late as it did after much marching and counter-marching, it still managed to make its presence felt. The enemy's attack on Hancock in the evening was undeniably weakened by their having to detach troops to oppose Burnside. One division (Stevenson's) fought under Hancock all day, while the other two white divisions came into action only for two or three hours, yet the total losses were almost equally divided between the three.

"The best thing Old Burn did that day", was the judgment of the Army of the Potomac on this last episode of the battle on the left.

At 5.45 the order for a general attack by the Union forces on the Brock Road was cancelled, much to Hancock's relief, for ammunition had again run short, the old fear of an attack on his left rear had been revived by the reports of prisoners, and the woods were still on fire in his front. The battle, so far as directed by the superior leading, was over.

There was one more episode, of a quite unforeseen kind, on the far distant right of the Union army. It has been mentioned that Gordon had found and reported a good position whence to attack Sedgwick's right, and that Early and Ewell, uncertain as to the whereabouts of the IX. Corps, refused all day to allow him to advance. In the midst of a somewhat heated discussion between Ewell, Early, and Gordon. Lee himself appeared and asked, "Cannot something be done on this flank to relieve the pressure on our right?" This was about 5.30, the noise of Hancock's and Burnside's fighting contrasting strangely with the silence of Ewell's lines. Lee, after listening to Ewell's and to Early's objections, gave Gordon direct orders to take his own brigade and Johnston's (newly arrived from Hanover Junction) and to put his plan into execution. The two brigades attacked the extreme Union right just at sunset, and Gordon's arrangements had been so complete and exact that the first rush of his line of battle carried all before it. Two brigadiers, Seymour and Shaler, of the VI. Corps, with several hundred men were taken prisoners, and a strange panic fell upon the veterans of Sedgwick's corps. Staff officers who had lost their heads galloped up to Wilderness Tavern with alarmist rumours. Humphreys hastily sent for troops from Warren and Hancock, and with the provost guard and escort improvised a line of battle, facing north, across the Germanna Road. Order was at length restored, and the line re-established somewhat to the rear, thanks not a little to Humphreys' coolness and Meade's own powers of sarcasm. Tales of disaster continued to come in from the VI. Corps, even after Grant had gone to bed. Meanwhile, Gordon, who had caused all this commotion, drew off with his prisoners, expecting every moment to be attacked in force before he could reform his disordered ranks.

It would appear that the same ground that so

BATTLE OF THE WILDERNESS 199

favoured Gordon would have equally favoured an attack on Gordon by Wright at any time during the day. Wright actually suggested this to Sedgwick, but Sedgwick had received orders that the

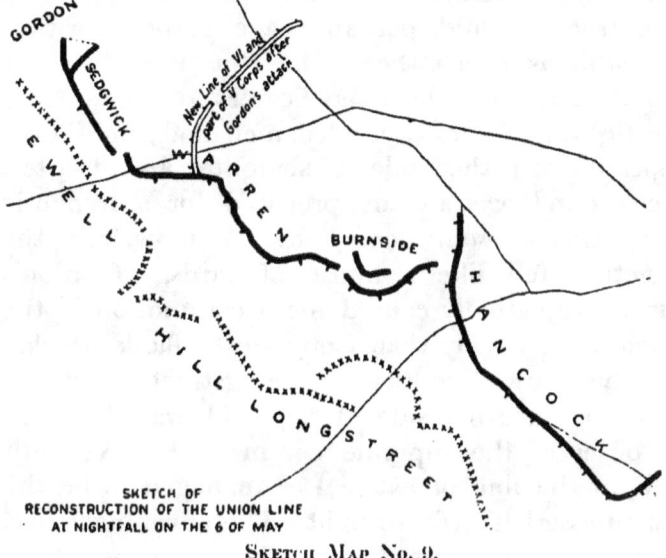

SKETCH OF RECONSTRUCTION OF THE UNION LINE AT NIGHTFALL ON THE 6 OF MAY

Sketch Map No. 9.

Union right wing was to suspend its advance* and to hold all but the bare minimum of troops at the disposal of superior authority for the reinforcement of Hancock and Burnside.

The student of military psychology will find much food for thought in this last episode of the battle. Panics are not rare on the evening of a great battle, even when the troops affected have not been seriously engaged. Imaginary terrors are far harder to endure than real ones, and the mere

* 10.30 A.M., Humphreys to Sedgwick and Warren.

act of waiting produces an intense and prolonged nervous strain. The dim forest, the unseen sniping enemy a few score yards in their front, and the roar of the main battle* away to their left had effectually shaken the self-control of the right wing. The troops would perhaps have rushed forward as readily as in fact they fled. But they could not stand still, and when the bearers of news from the fighting front—wounded men and fugitives—appeared with their tales of slaughter and disaster, the ground was already prepared for a hypnotic suggestion of *sauve qui peut*. A blow, and the structure fell like a house of cards. Gordon's adventure actually caused more commotion in the whole Union army than Longstreet's flank attack.

This blow, like that of Longstreet's corps at 4.30 on the other side of the field, was delivered by order of the supreme commander. At both ends of the line of battle Lee managed to be the last to assert his will to fight. The advantages that he gained thereby may be told in Grant's words.†

"Lee was in distress.‡ His men were in confusion, and his personal efforts failed to restore order. *These facts, however, were learned subsequently, or we would have taken advantage of his condition and no doubt gained a decisive success.*"

---

* The musketry reverberating over the woods made up for the absence of artillery fire, and Humphreys tells us the noise of Hancock's battle "sometimes approached the sublime".

† Grant had hoped to secure for himself the same opportunity of showing his will to fight and to deliver the last blow, by his orders to attack at 6 P.M. This attack was not delivered, owing to the Confederate attack on Hancock at 4.15, the consequent expenditure of ammunition, and the now widespread conflagration in the woods.

‡ *Personal Memoirs of U. S. Grant*, ii., 201.

BATTLE OF THE WILDERNESS 201

In the Cavalry Corps, too, the 6th was a day of vicissitudes and of final disappointment. Meade's order to Sheridan (6 P.M. May 5) ran as follows: "If Gregg and Wilson [this referring, of course, to the fighting about Todd's Tavern on the 5th] are compelled to fall back, the commanding general directs that you cover our left flank and protect the trains as much as possible. The left flank at present rests at the intersection of the Brock and Orange Plank roads [this, it will be observed, is a very loose description of Hancock's position on the 5th]. The infantry has been heavily pressed to-day along the whole line. If you gain any information that leads you to conclude that you can take the offensive and harass the enemy without endangering the trains you are at liberty to do so".

The restless activity of the cavalry leader was thus definitively repressed, and there was the less need for it on the 6th, as the opportunity for striking at the enemy's cavalry had gone by. In the absence of the train guards, then, Sheridan took his responsibilities more seriously perhaps than Meade imagined he would. Custer, with his own brigade and Devin's, of the first division,[*] was at the exit of the cross-road from the Furnaces to Todd's Tavern, Gregg's division at Todd's Tavern. Wilson's had gone back to Chancellorsville to replenish ammunition and forage. It was not long

[*] Torbert, who was suffering from an internal abscess, gave up the command of his division on the afternoon of the 5th, and did not return to the front until May 16, after undergoing an operation. Merritt was not assigned to the temporary command of the division until the 7th. On the 6th Merritt's own brigade was kept back in reserve.

before the enemy's cavalry under Fitz Lee appeared in front of Custer. Custer, who had at first his own brigade only, lured the enemy into charging a small force that acted as bait, and himself charged from cover and overthrew the Confederates, establishing himself in a long ravine on the enemy's side of the Brock Road, where he defended himself by fire action —the horses having excellent cover in the ravine and the men lining the edge of it towards the enemy —until his right was threatened, whereupon he resorted once again to a counter-stroke, sending Colonel Russell Alger* with two regiments to eject the enemy's turning force from the woods. At this point horse artillery arrived from Gregg, and also Devin's brigade. Custer reinforced Alger and told off a force from Devin's command to look after the left flank; then, ordering rapid fire from his eight horse artillery guns in front, he sent forward three regiments on the right dismounted, and completed a smart little engagement by a mounted charge of the squadron that had in the first instance acted, dismounted, as bait. The Confederates gave way and retired rapidly at all points towards the Catharpin Road. Custer's pursuit was stopped by orders not to proceed any further.

On Gregg's front there was heavy skirmishing during the whole day.

The effect of Custer's fight on the main battle has been already noticed. That of the main battle on the operations of the cavalry was hardly

* Commanding 5th Michigan cavalry; Secretary of War in President McKinley's cabinet during the Spanish-American War of 1898.

BATTLE OF THE WILDERNESS 203

satisfactory to the more restless spirits in Sheridan's command. After twice reporting the enemy "driven" and "handsomely repulsed", Sheridan received at 1 P.M. the following: "General Hancock has been heavily pressed and his left turned*... draw in your cavalry so as to secure the trains". Sheridan had already forbidden Custer and Gregg to go too far out; he had less means even than headquarters of knowing that it was Hancock's advance, a mile and a half out on the Plank Road, and not his defensive line on the Brock Road that had been turned by the enemy, and he drew back hastily.

"I obeyed this order and the enemy took possession of the Furnaces, Todd's Tavern, and Piney Branch Church, the regaining of which cost much fighting on the 6th and 7th, and very many gallant officers and men", are the bitter words of Sheridan's report, and he characterizes the report of Hancock's left being turned as "false", confusing in his disappointment the mere rumours which pinned Gibbon to the Brock Road with the tangible fact of Longstreet's attack from the railroad bed. Custer's right (Devin) communicated from time to time with Hancock's left along the Brock Road, but reports, orders, and information circulated very slowly between the division

---

* Sheridan had informed Meade that there was supposed to be infantry in front of Gregg and Custer, but none on the Brock Road (11 A.M.), but whether this report ever filtered through to Hancock and Gibbon and Barlow I cannot ascertain. Humphreys' dispatch here quoted refers, of course, to the flank attack from the railroad bed, though the idea at headquarters was evidently that there was danger on the Brock Road itself.

and brigade commanders at the front, Sheridan at Chancellorsville, and Meade at Wilderness Tavern. During the reconstruction of the cavalry line to the rear the enemy's cavalry again attacked and were repulsed. In the afternoon Sheridan was chiefly concerned with regulating traffic along the Chancellorsville–Ely's Ford Road, still congested by the wagon train.

It was evident that in Sheridan Meade had acquired anything but a docile corps commander. Sheridan himself tells us that he "took up the idea" of fighting the enemy's cavalry, leaving the infantry to fight infantry. He had the opportunity of doing so in due course, but for the present he was required to assist the infantry, and the commander of the Army of the Potomac, who did not desire to abdicate all control over his thirteen thousand sabres, was as capable of enforcing obedience and of "saying unpleasant things" in the case of Sheridan as in that of his infantry generals.

Nearly every great cavalry commander in history has been "hard to hold"—amongst them Sheridan's present opponent, the brilliant "Jeb" Stuart. Only in such armies as Frederick the Great's, Hannibal's, Gustavus's, where the commander-in-chief himself is as bold and as skilful a cavalry leader as his subordinate, has the contrary been the case.

The second day in the Wilderness was thus, in the Cavalry Corps, a day of sullen obedience, relieved, it is true, by the brilliant episode of Custer's fight on the Furnace Road, but none the less unsatisfactory. It is difficult fully to sympathize with Sheridan. He tells us that owing to the ideas as to cavalry work prevailing in the Army of the Potomac, "we had to bide our time", but this is scarcely adequate to express his mental attitude on the 6th, and after all, why should Sheridan, any more than Warren or Sedgwick or Burnside, take offence because he received new orders in consequence of the reverse to Hancock?

In his memoirs Grant thus summarizes the results of the battle: "As we stood at the close, the two armies were relatively in about the same condition to meet each other as when the river [Rapidan] divided them. But the fact of having safely crossed was a victory".

If by "victory" Grant means the mere achievement of something which it was to the enemy's interest to prevent, the Wilderness was an undeniable Union victory. But Grant was always more concerned with achieving his own objects than with denying Lee's hopes, and if this is all that, looking back upon the war, he cares to claim for his operations in the Wilderness, it is fair to say that he virtually admits failure in respect of his real and more important objects.

Let us see, however, whether in fairness he could not with justice have claimed something more than a logistic success.

As for the losses, of 100,000 men put into action, the Union army lost about 18,000. The enemy's loss cannot have been much less, for they fought in the open—that is, outside entrenchments

—and attacked quite as often as the Federals, and in the past, under these conditions, they had suffered in due proportion. The *Medical and Surgical History of the War* gives the Southern losses as 11,400, but Colonel Livermore, a high authority, says that this is probably the lowest reasonable estimate, and we must bear in mind that Confederate commanders had every incentive to return low figures, so as to prevent discouragement at home and in the army alike. Even this represents 17 or 18 per cent. of the force engaged (say 65,000), and considered in connection with the policy of " mere attrition " foreshadowed by Grant, such a result would have been eminently satisfactory to the Union commander.

The explanation of Grant's statement is to be found in the character of the memoirs themselves. He wrote, almost on the last page, " I feel we are on the eve of a new era when there is to be great harmony between the Federal and Confederate. I cannot stay to be a living witness, . . . but I feel it within me that it is to be so". These memoirs are Grant's last public service, written by a dying man and dedicated to the purpose of healing the wound in the body politic, and before they were written the events in the Wilderness had been the subject of much historical and controversial discussion.

His general report as Lieutenant-General commanding the armies reads very differently: " It was evident to my mind that the two days' fighting had satisfied [Lee] of his inability to further maintain the contest in the open field". This idea.

upon which Grant's subsequent operations were based, is not far from the truth. Lee did, as a matter of history, henceforward await Grant's assaults behind entrenchments.*

Here, then, is an important result, a result which no former Union commander had been able to compel Lee to accept. Lee did not dare to act on, say the 9th of May, as he had dared to act on the 5th, and no reason can be assigned for the change in Lee's outlook other than the sum total of events in the battles of the 5th and 6th of May. The Wilderness was a qualified and indecisive victory indeed, and the results achieved fell, from one cause and another, far short of those justifiably anticipated from the numerical superiority of the Union army, but it was still a victory. If we regard it, as most historians and participants regard it, as a trial of strength, there can be no question as to which proved the stronger. Critics can only differ as to the extent of the margin of superiority possessed by Grant.

There were other results. Grant remarked on the morning of the 7th, when he found Lee still in front of him, "Joe Johnston would have retreated after two days of such punishment!" to the great satisfaction of the officers of the Army of the Potomac who heard the remark. His eyes were opened to the truth that was hidden from the Western officers. He saw that he had in front of him a general of the highest rank and an army of the finest temper. But his recognition of this

* We are not concerned for the moment with discussing the use Grant made of this moral superiority, but with establishing its existence.

fact implied recognition of the work of the army that had so often fought with honour against Lee and Lee's army. Whatever may have been his preconceived ideas he saw, and frankly admitted, that the Army of the Potomac was not below the level of its task. There is no further record of Meade's "hearing the bravery of his army questioned", and thus Lee's first attempt to break the "war spirit" of the Union ended with little more than the loss of 18 per cent. of his small army and the confirmation of his opponent's resolution to renew the battle.

CHAPTER X

THE 7TH OF MAY

THE work of the Federal infantry on the 7th, after two such days of fighting, is easily summarized—

"On the morning of the 7th, reconnaissances were made of the enemy's position, which was found to be well intrenched. . . . To attack a position of such character situated as this was and covered by a tangled forest that inevitably disordered the attacking forces as they advanced, was not judicious: it promised no success."—(Humphreys.)

The original order of battle was gradually reconstituted. Units marched to and fro on the narrow roads to find their proper commands, and from time to time a volley or a gun report sounded through the woods when a reconnaissance on one part or another of the line felt the enemy.

At headquarters, while the Adjutant-General's and Quartermaster-General's officers were busily engaged in the multifarious duties consequent upon a great battle, Grant, Meade, and Humphreys were considering the military situation, interrupted only by alarms on the left, on the extreme right,* and again on the left.

* General Meade placed a colonel of cavalry under arrest for "giving false information in respect of the enemy" in this quarter.

Newspaper correspondents stated at the time that Meade advised a retreat over the Rapidan.* There seems to be no truth whatever in the suggestion. Had Meade been the bearer of the whole responsibility it is quite possible that he would have, according to precedent, rested and refitted his army in safety, even at the cost of acknowledging another failure. But with Grant to take on his shoulders the burden of the decision he had only to advise, and it may safely be assumed that Meade's advice was soldierly and resolute. Of the feeling of the army on the subject an incident of the evening of the 7th, presently to be narrated, may be taken as a good indication.

Short of an attack by Lee—and Grant rightly considered this most unlikely, though he did not omit to order Meade to be ready for a counter-stroke—there were three courses open to the Union commander—to stand still, to retire, or to advance still further to the south and south-west. The choice between them depended upon his general military policy.

As director of operations in Virginia, Grant's aim was to place the Army of the Potomac between Lee and his centre of operations; as generalissimo he had to screen Butler against a sudden and overwhelming blow. In respect of the tactical object of inflicting a decisive defeat on Lee's army, his task was to bring about a battle

* Wilkeson relates that at Cold Harbor a newspaper correspondent was led up and down the lines under fire, carrying a board with the inscription "Libeller of the Press". His offence was that he had written to his paper saying that Meade counselled a retreat after the battle of the Wilderness.

upon ground suitable for the attainment of that object.

It was clear, to a mind which was capable of looking unvaryingly to the main object, that another movement by the left flank, a repetition, in fact, of the original manœuvre, was called for by the situation.*

Of the alternatives, that of standing still was out of the question. The faint chance of Lee's attacking the Union entrenchments, and the almost equally faint chance of bringing off a decisive counter-stroke in the Wilderness, were all that could be urged in favour of the policy of marking time, against which there was the fatal objection that Lee would not fail to turn to his own purposes the initiative thereby surrendered to him. He would probably decamp in all secrecy and, provided that his rearguard or containing detachment did its duty, he would gain at least three days' start in whatever manœuvre he chose to undertake. The probable result of such a shift in the centre of gravity would be either a disaster to Butler, or a "scare" invasion of the North, coupled with the annihilation of the Union forces in the Valley, as in 1862 and 1863.

The alternative of a retirement towards Fredericksburg was tempting, but specious. Open

---

* Some writers have said that Grant practically abandoned fighting and reverted to "manœuvre", so-called, after this one experience of Lee's powers, and that "we hear no more of making Lee's army the objective point". This rests on nothing more than the fact that he manœuvred to place his army between Lee's army and Richmond. His invariable object in so doing was to isolate the army, not the city—to deprive Lee of Richmond, not Richmond of Lee.

battle-grounds lay in that quarter, the lower Rappahannock was patrolled by the Federal gunboats, and a new centre of operations could be arranged at Fredericksburg for the second forward move. But this, again, surrendered the freedom of manœuvre to a daring and skilful enemy. Moreover, it would be impossible to disguise the fact that the movement was retrograde.

It is hardly necessary to say that a retreat over the Rapidan had nothing to recommend it as a solution of the strategical problem. It would have been an admission that the problem was insoluble. Yet such an admission is the most common result of the nervous depression that is the inevitable sequel of a day of battle, when the combatants have expended the last physical and moral efforts of which they are capable. "We were glad to see them go", wrote an officer of a victorious army long ago, "for if they had not, I know who had within the hour". The Army of the Potomac had retreated more than once, after such costly and unsatisfactory battles as this of the Wilderness.

Grant, however, possessed strength of character, which is virtually the power to resist the pressure of disturbing influences, and thus to solve the immediate problem on its merits and to impose his theoretical solution on the weary men who would be charged with its execution. As these disturbing influences are most potent and insistent during a battle, and meet with the least resistance after one, the measure of Grant's strength may be taken from the rapidity with which he formed the resolution to go forward—a resolution which, as the enlisted men realized with gladness, sealed the fate of the Confederacy.

Badeau states that even on the 6th, while Hancock and Burnside were fighting hard on the Plank Road, Grant lay under the trees near Wilderness Tavern revolving in his mind plans for a further southward advance. Be this as it may, his directive, upon which Meade framed the orders for the march on Spottsylvania, was written as early as half-past six on the morning after the battle. It ran as follows :—

"Headquarters, Armies U.S.,
May 7, 1864, 6.30 A.M.

"Major-General Meade, commanding Army of the Potomac.

"Make all preparations during the day for a night march to take positions at Spottsylvania Court House with one army corps, at Todd's Tavern with one, and another near the intersection of Piney Branch and Spottsylvania road with the road from Alsop's to Old Court House. If this move is made the trains should be thrown forward early in the morning to the Ny River.

"I think it would be advisable, in making the change, to leave Hancock where he is until Warren passes him. He could then follow and become the right of the new line. Burnside will move to Piney Branch Church. Sedgwick can move along the pike to Chancellorville, and on to his destination. Burnside will move on the (Germanna) plank-road to the intersection of it with the Orange and Fredericksburg plank-road, then follow Sedgwick to his place of destination. All vehicles should be got out of hearing of the enemy before the troops move, and then move off quietly.

"It is more than probable that the enemy concentrate for a heavy attack on Hancock this afternoon. In case they do we must be prepared to resist them, and follow up any success we may gain with our whole force. Such a result would necessarily modify these instructions.

"All the hospitals should be moved to-day to Chancellorville.

"Respectfully, etc.,
"U. S. GRANT,
"Lieut.-General.
["Copy to General Burnside."]

The movements ordered were, of course, understood to be merely preliminary to a further advance to the southward.

Grant's own statement of the objects pursued in this second manœuvre is as follows: "First, I did not want Lee to get back to Richmond in time to attempt to crush Butler before I could arrive there; second, I wanted to get between his army and Richmond if possible, and if not to draw him into the open field".

The first object he proposed to attain not by watching, but by forestalling, Lee's movements. The third, specifically the task of the Army of the Potomac, implies a battle in the open field, that is, not only in clear ground but also outside entrenchments. The way to attain this with certainty, and to make the best use of the victory when won, was to "get between Lee's army and Richmond". If this last fell short of execution, the very act of preventing the manœuvre would, of itself, draw Lee out of his forest stronghold.

The idea, and the method of execution, were largely influenced by the events of the 5th and 6th.

First, Grant had decided in his own mind—

more or less accurately as the event proved—that Lee would not fight again in the open except under pressure of necessity. He hoped to bring about that necessity by placing himself between Lee and Richmond by a southerly march viâ Spottsylvania towards Chilesburg.

Secondly, though a sweep as wide as or wider than that of the 4th and 5th of May is projected, it is intended to carry it out, not by relatively disconnected columns, but by the army as a unit. And preparatory positions with this object are to be taken up by all four corps before they move southward to the hoped-for battle-ground on the North Anna. Owing to the lie of the roads, it was possible for Lee to carry out on the first day a counter-move towards Spottsylvania that would prevent the development of the manœuvre on the second. Such a move on Lee's part might bring on an encounter on the first day (8th May), and as all Grant's manœuvres were directed to this end, he would be well content if Lee should voluntarily offer him the target that otherwise he would have to gain by his own manœuvres. But the experience of May 5 showed clearly that the army must be so distributed as to take advantage of such an opportunity, and also to be guaranteed against a serious check. Moreover, in view of what was thought the more probable event of Lee's retirement to the North Anna, it was advisable that the various Union corps should retain their marching formations, that is, their power of manœuvre, as long as possible—in other words, that they should be ready to move out, at a moment's notice, along the three roads leading directly to the North Anna.*

The movement to Spottsylvania–Todd's Tavern was therefore a tentative expansion of the manœuvre area not too great for tactical purposes, not too small for strategical. The closed line of battle or the full manœuvre interval could be taken up on the 9th according to circumstances.

In the meanwhile, Grant had in mind the contingency of Lee's attacking him during the manœuvre towards Spottsylvania. He did not desire this, another battle in the tangled woods of the Orange Plank Road, but he foresaw that the preliminaries of the proposed night march might tempt Lee into an attack on Hancock. Meade was warned to be ready to exploit whatever advantage was to be gained from such a move on the enemy's part on the evening of the 7th. But the first sentence of the note defines exactly what Grant desired, namely, to bring the army, unopposed, to a half-extended position in readiness for another battle on the 8th/9th, or for a manœuvre on the 9th followed by a battle on the 10th/11th, Lee in either case being compelled to attack, or to defend, as the case might be, on open and unprepared ground.

At three o'clock in the afternoon, just before the issue of detailed orders to the Army of the Potomac, encouraging news was received of the doings of the Army of the James, which had started according to programme. This doubtless served to

* Old Court House—Mount Pleasant, Spottsylvania—Snell's Bridge, and Stannard's Mill—Thornburg (see Sketch Map 16).

THE 7TH OF MAY

accentuate the importance of the manœuvre towards the North Anna, and by implication the necessity of forestalling Lee at Spottsylvania Court House.

The centre of gravity of the army was now to be shifted to Todd's Tavern, Spottsylvania, and Piney Branch Church, and this being the sphere of action of the Cavalry Corps, Sheridan was the first to come under the influence of the new scheme.

At nightfall on the 6th that general, restless and angry at being drawn in to protect the trains "on false report that Hancock's left had been turned", was at The Furnace—Aldrich's–Chancellorsville. The 3rd Division (General Wilson), which had fought the long running fight from Craig's Church to Todd's Tavern on the 5th, was held back on the 6th and 7th and took no part in the fighting of those days at The Furnace and Todd's Tavern. On the morning of the 7th, being then in bivouac at Chancellorsville, Wilson went out with McIntosh's brigade to investigate alarmist reports from Burnside's cavalry * as to the situation at Germanna Ford. It was on this occasion that Meade, as before related, put a colonel under arrest for giving false information of the enemy. At the same time Lieut.-Col. Hammond, of the 5th New York, who had distinguished himself on the 5th, was ordered by Meade, with his own and two of the IX. Corps regiments, to watch the ground between Sedgwick's right and the Ford. After a time the alarm died away without serious fighting.

* This had not moved with the rest of the IX. Corps into the Wilderness.

Wilson and McIntosh had already returned to Chancellorsville and the trains, Chapman's brigade meanwhile executing a short and unopposed reconnaissance towards Spottsylvania. The 3rd Cavalry Division, after an easy day, went into bivouac at Aldrich's. Hammond's command continued to watch the right flank during the assembly of the army towards Spottsylvania, and on Sheridan's departure on the 9th it remained behind, with other details,* at headquarters.

Gregg and Torbert (Merritt) had meantime been engaged in what Sheridan calls the battle of Todd's Tavern.

"On the 7th", says Sheridan, "the trains of the army, under directions from headquarters Army of the Potomac, were put in motion to go into park at Piney Branch Church. As this point was in the hands of the enemy, I was confident that the order had been given without fully understanding the condition of affairs, and therefore thought the best way to remedy the trouble was to halt the trains in the vicinity of Aldrich's, attack the enemy, and regain the ground". There seems to be some difficulty in tracing this order. The general trains did not begin to move until long after Sheridan's battle had opened, and a study of the available documents leads to supposition that the loosely

---

* The Germanna line was not yet abandoned, although the bridge had been taken up and relaid at Ely's Ford for the transportation of the wounded to Rappahannock Station for Washington. Belated corps of the IX. Corps cavalry came in during the morning of the 7th, and by degrees a force of about a strong brigade was assembled at or near Germanna. The destination of the wounded was, however, as a consequence of the alarm on the right, altered during the 7th, and on the 8th they were sent home by way of Fredericksburg.

THE 7TH OF MAY

worded phrase in Grant's 6.30 A.M. directive, " the trains to be thrown forward to the Ny river early in the morning", *i.e.* of the 8th, reached Chancellorsville very early in the form of an order (afterwards cancelled) for the trains to go forward at once. Be this as it may, Sheridan, now relieved of much of his anxiety for the trains, owing to the arrival of the coloured division under Ferrero, stopped them practically before they moved off, and advanced at once, shortly after 7 A.M., to clear the front. By noon Custer had fought his way, dismounted, along the Furnace Road to beyond the Brock Road. The rest of the 1st Cavalry Division followed up, and Custer having cleared the way, Merritt sent his own brigade, now under Colonel Gibbs, down the Brock Road towards Todd's Tavern, where the enemy's cavalry was in force. Sheridan, meanwhile, had sent forward Gregg with one of his two brigades, by the Catharpin Road, to the same point; and when Merritt, continuing to drive the enemy along the Brock Road towards Spottsylvania, had cleared Todd's Tavern, Gregg crossed his track, moved along the Catharpin Road towards Corbin's bridge, and gradually pressed back the Confederate cavalry under Hampton. The other brigade of Gregg's division operated on the Piney Branch Road, in connection with Merritt, towards Spottsylvania, Fitz Lee's cavalry opposing both. Sheridan was well satisfied with the result, and without difficulty convinced himself that he could " whip Stuart ".

When the fighting degenerated into picket firing—it never ceased altogether on this fateful night of the 7th/8th May—Merritt had with him Gibbs's and Devin's brigades,* on the Brock Road, facing towards Spottsylvania, and Gregg was with one brigade on the Catharpin facing towards Corbin's bridge. The main bodies of both were massed in the fields round Todd's Tavern. Davies's brigade of the 2nd Division was on the Piney Branch Church–Spottsylvania Road in touch with Merritt's left and looking towards Spottsylvania. Wilson's was at Aldrich's, well closed up, refreshed and ready for the service it was soon to be called upon to perform.

The following orders were issued for the movements of the Army of the Potomac, at 3 P.M. on the 7th.

Movements ordered for to-day and to-night:—

1. The trains of the VI. Corps authorized to accompany the troops will be moved at four o'clock P.M. to Chancellorsville and parked on the left of the road, and held ready to follow the VI. Corps during the night march.

2. The trains of the V. Corps authorized to accompany the troops will be moved at five o'clock P.M. to Chancellorsville, following the trains of the VI. Corps and parking with them, and held ready to follow those trains in the movement to-night.

3. The trains of the II. Corps authorized to accompany the troops will be moved at six o'clock P.M. to Chancellorsville and park on the right of the road, and held ready to move at same hour with the other trains by way of the Furnaces to Todd's Tavern, keeping clear of the Brock Road, which will be used by the troops.

4. Corps commanders will send escorts with these trains.

5. The reserve artillery will move at seven o'clock, by

* Custer's was still on the Brock Road, where it had fought in the forenoon.

THE 7TH OF MAY

way of Chancellorsville, Aldrich's, and Piney Branch Church, to the intersection of the road from Piney Branch Church to Spotsylvania C.H., and the road from Alsop's to Block House, and park to the rear on the last-named road so as to give room for the VI. Corps.

6. At half-past eight P.M., Major-General Warren, commanding V. Corps, will move to Spotsylvania C.H. by way of the Brock Road and Todd's Tavern.

7. At half-past eight P.M., Major-General Sedgwick, commanding VI. Corps, will move by the pike and plank roads to Chancellorsville, where he will be joined by the authorized trains of his own corps and those of the V.; thence by way of Aldrich's and Piney Branch Church to the intersection of the road from Piney Branch Church to Spotsylvania C.H., and the road from Alsop's to Block House. The trains of the V. Corps will then join its (*sic*) corps at Spotsylvania C.H.

8. Major-General Hancock, II. Corps, will move to Todd's Tavern, following the V. Corps closely.

9. Headquarters during the movement will be along the route of the V. and II. Corps, and at the close of the movement near the VI. Corps.

10. The pickets of the V. and VI. Corps will be withdrawn at one o'clock A.M., and those of the II. Corps at two o'clock A.M., and will follow the routes of their respective corps.

11. The cavalry, now under the command of Colonel Hammond, will be left by General Sedgwick at Old Wilderness Tavern, and upon being informed by General Hancock of the withdrawal of his corps, will follow that corps.

12. Corps commanders will see that the movements are made with punctuality and promptitude.

13. Major-General Sheridan, commanding Cavalry Corps, will have a sufficient force on the approaches from the right to keep the corps commanders advised in time of the approach of the enemy.

14. It is understood that General Burnside's command will follow the V. Corps.

By command of Major-General Meade,
S. WILLIAMS, A.A.G.

The first point to observe in these orders is the fact that they were issued at 3 p.m., eight hours after the directive which inspired them. Grant, it may be said, was in no greater hurry than Meade, for Burnside's order to follow the VI. Corps to Piney Branch Church was issued at two. Three-quarters of this delay was due probably to a natural desire to have the army sorted out into its proper commands before working out its ulterior movements, and also to obtain the latest information from Sheridan.

Generally, military history warns us against a premature issue of operation orders,* but in the present case it was not an operation against the enemy that was immediately intended, but a regrouping of the army with an ulterior motive, and the protection of the army during this regrouping. So far from 3 p.m. being too early an hour for the issue of orders of this character, the question is, was it not too late?

It was certainly as late as possible, considering that it involved the moving off of the first line trains practically at once (paragraphs 1–4). But more important than this was the fact that no special instructions were given to Sheridan, then fighting around Todd's Tavern. Paragraph 13, which concerns the action of the cavalry, is at once vague—because the engagement in progress rendered impossible detailed instructions for its sequel—and misplaced—because it is a directive for military operations interpolated in positive orders

* *Cf.* the 17th of August, 1870, for which see Hoenig's *Twenty-four hours of Moltke's Strategy.*

for a march. It seems clear that 3 P.M. was too late for a directive and too early for an order, and that special instructions for the action of the cavalry should have been framed as early as possible, so as to enable the cavalry commander to glean and to forward information relevant to the projected move, and to give his own action the most suitable direction with the least possible delay.

There is no reference to the army trains. They were not to move that day, but to be thrown forward in the morning to the Ny, in accordance with Grant's directive.

The first movement ordered is that of the first line transport for Chancellorsville. This would, of course, soon come to Lee's notice, as was expected by the Union staff. Lee could not surmise with certainty therefrom that Grant was manœuvring. It was within the bounds of possibility, as defined by experience, that he was merely retreating on Fredericksburg.

In this case Lee's alternatives were, to shift his army eastward to cover Richmond directly, to "go North on a raid", or to turn on Butler. As the result of the battle of the Wilderness had not been so encouraging as to warrant him in adopting the second course, and the third could be carried out at leisure if Grant were really retreating, the only immediate movement on Lee's part that the dust-clouds of the Union trains could provoke was one towards Spottsylvania, the object of which would be to place the Confederate army astride of the

Richmond-Fredericksburg road. In short, Grant's scheme accepted the possibility of Lee's attempting, for whatever reason, to forestall the Army of the Potomac in its preliminary positions, and no inference from the early movement of the trains could justify Lee in adopting a line of conduct that his opponent had not foreseen from the beginning.

The question then was one of time and space. Could Lee forestall the Army of the Potomac in its projected positions?

The head of the V. Corps had thirteen miles to march after 8.30 P.M., and could not be expected to reach the Court House before 2 A.M. even if unopposed. It would be five or six before the corps was massed, and perhaps eight or nine before it was wholly in position and entrenched.

The VI. Corps from Wilderness Tavern *via* Chancellorsville to the position near Alsop's, would have to march about thirteen and a half miles, and could not arrive there before two. It would probably, allowing for the necessity of taking in and marshalling the fighting trains of the two corps, arrive at Alsop's about the same time as the rear of the V. Corps passed that place—say 5 A.M.

The II. Corps was to stand fast to cover Warren's movement and then to follow closely. The head of the corps would be due to start about one o'clock and to arrive at Todd's Tavern before three.

This was the best that could be anticipated. Difficulties of night marching, being common to both sides, may be omitted from consideration.

THE 7TH OF MAY

But the enemy's cavalry, with which Sheridan was engaged until after nightfall, might have to be driven in while his infantry marched in peace. And considering that Hancock's left and Lee's right were nearly equidistant from the point aimed at, the only chance of Warren's corps—which had 3 or 4 miles more to march than the II. would have had—reaching Spottsylvania before Lee's infantry, lay in the activity of Sheridan's cavalry in carrying out paragraph 13, and "having a sufficient force on the approaches from the right.", that is, gaining time, more than ever essential in so complicated a manœuvre as that ordered. Sheridan's dispositions, as a matter of fact, would have met the case. Gregg and Merritt were to move across the Po, and to head for Block House as a flank guard—the Brock Road being left free for Warren's infantry—and Wilson, refreshed by a day's rest, was to eject the grey cavalry from Spottsylvania Court House and to occupy all the southern approaches. But these orders were never executed, for they were issued at 1 A.M. on the 8th, and the movements ordered were to begin four hours later still.

Now, the army order must have reached Sheridan not later than 5 or 5.30 P.M., and seven or eight hours elapsed before his own orders were issued to give effect to them. This delay was of grave importance, but it may be accounted for in part by the fact that Sheridan was preoccupied with the fighting on his own front, and awaited the reports of his subordinates before issuing corps orders for the 8th. Still, when finally drafted, the orders were well considered and framed in cold blood for the execution of Meade's instructions. Now, in these circumstances calculation was possible, and it was a matter of calculation that the infantry, whose movements Sheridan was to protect, would be on the march from 8.30 p.m. to the time of Warren's arrival at Spottsylvania, and that at 1 a.m. or thereabouts Warren would enter the danger zone. That Sheridan realized the best possible military measures to ensure Warren's safety is obvious from the orders he actually issued. That he ignored calculations of time and space is equally obvious from the fact that he fixed the hour of starting for all his divisions at 5 a.m., which was demonstrably four hours too late.*

This was the extent, and the wide extent, of Sheridan's responsibility for the blunders that followed.

* There was no necessity for sparing the horses, as the fighting on the 7th had been wholly dismounted.

CHAPTER XI

THE NIGHT MARCH ON SPOTTSYLVANIA AND THE FIGHTING OF THE 8TH OF MAY

THE columns of the Union army began to move at 8.30 as ordered. Warren personally drew off his corps unit by unit out of their lines—in order of divisions, Robinson's, Griffin's, Crawford's, Cutler's—remaining behind to superintend the delicate operation of withdrawing from contact with the enemy. As ill-luck would have it, however, his presence was soon urgently required at the head of his column, for at the Brock and Plank cross-roads it found the road blocked by the Provost-Marshal's mounted troops and the staffs and personal escorts of Grant and Meade, which had halted while those officers were conferring with Hancock. After a delay of, as stated by Warren, an hour and a half, headquarters, seeing no other way out of the difficulty, set out for Todd's Tavern at the gallop. The passage of the Lieut.-General, with his horse's head turned *southward*, aroused a feu-de-joie of cheers from Hancock's men, who lay in line of battle along the Brock Road, the noise and the light of torches drawing a wild and ineffective fire from the Confederate outposts.

At Todd's Tavern, where they arrived about midnight after taking a wrong turning in the road, the commanding generals found more difficulties.

Gregg's and Merritt's cavalry divisions were bivouacked there, Gregg on the Catharpin, Merritt on the Spottsylvania Road. On inquiry, Meade found that neither of these officers had received any orders from Sheridan, and at 1 A.M. he gave them instructions which were afterwards the subject of much controversy, for precisely at that moment (1 A.M.) Sheridan was issuing orders for Gregg to proceed *viâ* Corbin's Bridge towards Shady Grove Church, for Merritt to follow Gregg, and then, turning off to the left, to ride to the Block House, Gregg following, and for Wilson to move from Aldrich's, *viâ* "The Gate" to Spottsylvania Court House, these movements to be begun at 5 A.M.

Meade's orders were different. Merritt was to continue towards Spottsylvania (Meade, of course, knew nothing of Wilson's movements), gaining ground as rapidly as possible, so as to clear the way for the infantry. After reaching the Court House he was to picket all the roads beyond, and in particular to have a brigade at the Block House. General Humphreys suggested that Merritt should be ordered to guard the bridge over the Po, west of Block House, but Meade replied, somewhat curtly, that the object of the order was plain, and that Merritt would certainly push out a force to the bridge. Gregg was ordered to move out along the Catharpin Road to the vicinity of Corbin's Bridge, to

THE 8TH OF MAY

watch the roads from Parker's Store, and when Hancock's corps should arrive at Todd's Tavern, to send a force to the Brock Road to watch his right.* In spite of the claims made by General Sheridan in his report, it is hardly questionable not only that no orders whatever to be acted upon so late as 5 A.M. would have been possible of execution, but also that Meade's orders and Sheridan's were already at 1 A.M. too late. At that hour, the head of Longstreet's (Anderson's) Confederate corps, and all Hampton's cavalry division, were in front of Gregg, and Fitz Lee's cavalry division on the Brock Road in front of Merritt.

However, Meade's orders were obeyed. Gregg moved out towards the bridge, Merritt roused his men and resumed his march down the Brock Road.

Warren, meanwhile, had ridden up to the head of his column, though his last division only drew out of the Wilderness lines at half-past twelve. The march went on—with several checks and with much straggling, for the night was hot and close and the men were tired—until at 3.30 General Warren came up with General Merritt, two miles beyond Todd's Tavern, and found a heavy skirmish in progress.† Fitz Lee's stubborn troopers had to be dislodged from every tree and every thicket. They had felled trees to obstruct the road, and after a severe and painful struggle the Union

---

* Sheridan was notified of these orders at the same time.

† Merritt was still without Custer's brigade, which was on the Furnace Road.

cavalry were still, at 6 A.M., three miles short of their objective. Now that daylight had come, it was imperative to show by a display of resolute infantry that the Army of the Potomac meant to go forward at all costs. Merritt, therefore, called upon Warren, who had closed up and halted for a rest, to take the work of driving Fitz Lee's cavalry and capturing Spottsylvania upon himself.

Warren agreed to do so, though doubtful whether he would be able "to do anything expeditiously in the woods", and desirous of sparing his men after their long march. He himself went up to the front, notifying headquarters that Crawford was to succeed him if he were himself disabled.

There was some difficulty in replacing Merritt's troops by Robinson's, in the course of which Merritt lost some men by the fire of the leading regiment or regiments of the infantry, which, tired and hungry as they were, had become nervous and fretful at the long delay and the mysterious fighting in the dark woods.

It was a little beyond the Hart house that Robinson's infantry deployed and took up their task. Contrary, perhaps, to Warren's expectations, there was at once a difference in the rate of progress of the Union troops, for it was an infantry attack by daylight instead of a cavalry skirmish in the dark. The Confederates were driven through the wood, and two horse artillery guns had a narrow escape from being captured. At eight Warren reported that the opposition to him was "almost nothing", but he was by no means

THE 8TH OF MAY

confident about his own men. "They are exceedingly hesitating, I think", he says, which must be attributed almost as much to the fact that they were fighting without breakfast as to the long night march from the Lacy house.

At 8.30, or thereabouts, reaching a fork in the Brock Road near Alsop's, the V. Corps divided, Robinson taking the left-hand road, and Griffin, when he came up in turn, the right-hand. The column was not destined to be reformed.

Meanwhile, pursuant to his abortive scheme for covering the right of the army, Sheridan had moved Wilson to Spottsylvania Court House, *viâ* "The Gate". Wilson marched off at 5 A.M., and by nine o'clock was able to send to Sheridan the following exultant dispatch :—

"Have run the enemy a mile from Spotsylvania C.H. Have charged them through the village. Am fighting now with a considerable force supposed to be Lee's division. Everything all right."

Later, he gave details :—

"We cleaned out Wickham's brigade in about two minutes. Scattered him in all directions. . . . Our artillery had an admirable chance."

The Union troops, however, did not long remain there. An officer of Sheridan's staff appeared with a fresh order, directing the evacuation of the Court House, and information to the effect that the 1st and 2nd Cavalry Divisions and the V. Corps were heavily engaged on the side of Todd's Tavern, and that the IX. Corps was not following him to Spottsylvania as he understood was to be the case. The enemy was in force, and Wilson then withdrew with his prisoners, some of whom belonged to Longstreet's infantry.

Anderson's corps had in fact won the race to Spottsylvania, though by a narrow margin, and, indeed, unintentionally. Lee telegraphed to Richmond on the 8th that the enemy had abandoned his position and was moving to Fredericksburg, and that the Army of Northern Virginia was following on the right flank. He had, indeed, ordered the following movements for the 8th: Anderson to march by the Catharpin and Shady Grove Roads to Block House and Spottsylvania; Hill to follow Anderson as far as the Catharpin Road, then to turn towards Todd's Tavern and to reach his objective by way of the Brock Road; Ewell to follow the others by a more westerly route when it became known that the Army of the Potomac had left his front. The assignment of the Brock Road as an available Confederate route to the new positions, and the fact that 3 A.M. on the 8th was fixed by Lee as the hour of starting, are conclusive as to Lee's initial misapprehension of his opponent's move. But fortune intervened to redress the balance. As a preliminary to the movement, Anderson was to draw out of his works overnight and to bivouac in mass, ready for an early start. But finding the woods on fire, he decided to march on at once, hoping to find camping ground on the way. Starting therefore about 11 P.M. he moved to the Catharpin Road, then (covered by Hampton's

THE 8TH OF MAY

cavalry) across Corbin's Bridge, and so to Block House Bridge (7 A.M.). Here he found the desired bivouac, and was beginning to mass on the head of the column when urgent appeals were received from Fitz Lee and from Rosser, who were opposing Warren and Wilson respectively. The corps was at once broken up, one division being sent up to the Brock Road and the other to the Court House as fast as the tired men could be urged forward,* and so it came about that before nine Warren found himself opposed by well-covered infantry.

Robinson, deployed in line of battle across the left-hand fork of the Brock Road, had passed Alsop's field, and cleared the wood beyond without difficulty, and Griffin, on the right of him and further back, had emerged into the open ground, facing Spindler's house, one brigade leading in line, the remainder following in mass on the road itself (see Sketch Map 10). Anderson's infantry opened fire, greatly to the surprise of the Union troops, whose moral and physical fitness for battle was already much impaired by the long night march and three hours' cross-country skirmishing. Robinson pleaded for a little delay, but Warren, saying that his orders were to go to Spottsylvania Court House, ordered him forward at once.

The direction of the attack was towards Spindler's. Robinson, knowing that his infantry was no longer capable of facing artillery, ordered an immediate charge. "We must drive them

* The corps artillery came from Parker's Store, where it had been during the battle of the Wilderness, past Shady Grove Church, to Block House.

from there or they will get some artillery in position ", he said, and rode up to lead the attack personally, hoping that so at least his men would follow. The heat was intense, and there had been not a few cases of sunstroke.

The left of the line (Lyle's brigade) broke cover first. It had five hundred yards of rough open ground to cross at the double under the fire of a closed line of infantry and two horse artillery guns. Actually these brave men, with heavy losses (especially in officers), reached cover thirty yards from the hostile log-works, where they rested awhile, keeping down the fire of the enemy, who were as tired as themselves. On their right the Maryland brigade had been less successful. This brigade had been severely handled on the 5th of May, and its term of service had almost expired. Even so, encouraged by Robinson, and closely supported by Coulter's (late Baxter's) brigade, they passed half the deadly zone in front of the log-works before the advance was stopped. But General Robinson fell wounded. The spirit died out of the attack at once, and the men drifted backwards. Lyle's men, seeing the repulse of their comrades, soon ran back over the quarter-mile of open ground to the shelter of the woods.*

Griffin, further back on the right-hand road, had come under fire about the same time as Robinson's charge had begun. There was some

* The Maryland brigade lost two successive commanders in a few minutes. Lyle's brigade came out of action under Lieut.-Colonel Peirson.

THE 8TH OF MAY

unsteadiness consequent upon Robinson's retreat and the unexpected sight of Confederate infantry, but the men quickly reformed in a hollow, and about 10 A.M. advanced smartly and in good order towards the enemy, taking up and entrenching a line opposite Spindler's. An isolated attack after Robinson's repulse would have been futile and costly.

The arrival of Crawford on the left of Griffin's line re-established the front lost by Robinson, and he drove out of the woods a Confederate brigade that had attacked Lyle's left. Cutler's division, coming up after a good rest and a meal, effectually checked a Confederate counter-attack from the pine woods on Griffin's right, taking position there on the ground gained and connecting with Griffin. But for a time, at any rate, the V. Corps had come to a complete standstill. Wilson had already begun to retire from the Court House over the Ny, and a whole corps of Lee's army was on the ground of which Grant had desired to possess himself at daylight.

The failure of the Union attempt to take up the Spottsylvania–Todd's Tavern line was due, as we have seen, to an accident. But Grant and Meade must have calculated in advance that Lee might act of design as, in fact, fortune acted for him, viz. move off overnight towards Spottsylvania. The event proved that but for the two successive checks to the head of the V. Corps, even accident would not have enabled Longstreet's corps to come up in time to help Fitz Lee. If, therefore, the Union manœuvre was so well planned that, short of failures in execution, Lee's promptest movement—whether designed or accidental does not signify—would be too late, the reason must be sought in errors of execution. First of all, Fitz Lee's holding power was probably under-estimated. The consistent note of triumph in Sheridan's dispatches of the 7th seems to have hypnotized the army staff, and to have given rise to the idea that Fitz Lee and Hampton would merely have to be held off, not *driven* off, the infantry routes. Secondly, the actual delays encountered by Warren were caused first by the headquarters retinue, and afterwards by the cavalry. The former, it will be remembered, blocked the Brock Road close to the Plank Road crossing, and there was nothing apparently to prevent the officer commanding the headquarters from shunting his column eastward into the Plank Road, when he found that he was in the way. The cause of the second block—the presence of the cavalry at Todd's Tavern—has already been discussed; it was due probably to a failure to give special instructions to Sheridan in advance of the general army order. Both these fatal mischances would seem, therefore, to have been avoidable. Luck was entirely on Lee's side, but it only gave him back, after all, time that was his own and that he had thrown away.* That he was actually able to *gain* time was due not to luck, but to the errors of his opponents.

* This is not intended as a criticism on Lee's action, nor is "thrown away" to be read as meaning "wasted". He "threw away" the hours between 11 P.M. and 3 A.M. because, rightly or wrongly, he saw no advantage in employing them.

THE 8TH OF MAY

At 10.15 Warren reported these events to headquarters, not glossing over the demoralization of Robinson's command but dwelling hopefully on the fine conduct of his other divisions. He reported prisoners from Longstreet's corps, and in reply, Meade informed him that one division of the VI. Corps had been sent to him and that he could have another if necessary. Meade was not, however, very hopeful of good results from a new attack, owing to the condition of the V. Corps.

General Grant took a different view. At this moment both armies were on the move and at large in the open field. His intention was to maintain this state of things, to press forward towards the North Anna and to attack promptly any part of Lee's scattered forces that he met. This amounted to nothing less than a "strategic pursuit". Warren and Sedgwick were to fasten themselves upon Anderson, and the other corps were to make their best speed southward in search of a target. In the course of the morning a project for the march to the North Anna was prepared, and at 1 P.M. it was issued. Warren, reinforced to the needful extent by Sedgwick and even Hancock, was to attack whatever force Lee might have at Spottsylvania.* Next day or earlier, Hancock and Burnside were to pass round the flanks of the Spottsylvania position, Hancock by

---

* The army staff, as appears from Meade's endorsement to Warren's 10.15 dispatch, still hoped that the enemy there were only parts of Longstreet's corps, perhaps mounted for the nonce and hurried up to assist Stuart.

Old Court House towards Three Cornered Handkerchief (see Sketch Map 16), Burnside by "Gate" and Anderson's to Stannard's Mill, Thornburg, and beyond. When affairs were cleared up at Spottsylvania, Warren was to follow Hancock, Sedgwick to pass through the Court House and over Snell's Bridge to Mattapony Church. Army troops were to follow Sedgwick, the general trains Burnside. The time of starting was to be notified later. It would depend very largely on the results of Sedgwick's and Warren's attack and on information from Hancock at Todd's Tavern. Meanwhile the IX. Corps was ordered (9 A.M.) to stop at Aldrich's, to cover the main army trains from possible attack by way of the Orange Plank Road.

The immediate task, of course, was the attack on Anderson's corps. This had for its ulterior objects, to prevent the enemy concentrating upon Longstreet (Anderson) and to prevent Anderson from interfering with the development of the Federal manœuvre. The present object was to fight one of Lee's corps, outside its works, with two of the Union army.

At 1 P.M. Sedgwick, who had just reported that Warren had called upon Wright's division for assistance, was ordered to proceed with his whole corps to Spottsylvania Court House and to join Warren "in a prompt and vigorous attack on the enemy now concentrating there". Both Sedgwick and Warren (1.30) were notified of the necessity of speed.* Meade had already ordered Warren to

---

* Warren's ammunition having run short, no less a person than General Ingalls was detailed to procure him a fresh supply.

let his men know that " it is our interest to prevent a concentration to stop our march, and that they should drive them ". The available force consisted of Warren's corps, the harassing adventures of which we have traced above, and Sedgwick's. The latter had left its lines beyond Wilderness Tavern about 9.30 on the evening of the 7th, and had apparently encountered some delays owing to the movements of the 1st line trains. It was in its assigned position north-west of Alsop's house — one division, however, being kept back at Piney Branch Church — considerably before midday, though the men were very tired.

Hancock, like Burnside, could not move freely until it was certain that the two-thirds of the Army of Northern Virginia still unaccounted for had left the Wilderness lines. The operations of the II. Corps will be dealt with later.

Headquarters had been established at Piney Branch Church, where Meade, whose temper had broken down under the strain of disappointment and waiting, sent for Sheridan and reproached him freely and bitterly for leaving Gregg and Merritt in the way of the infantry. Sheridan's quick temper was roused and he replied, with many expletives and almost uncontrollable rage, accusing Meade of interfering with his arrangements and asserting that Warren had allowed himself to be imposed upon by an almost imaginary force of the enemy. Meade then tried to calm his subordinate, even admitting frankly that he himself had spoken too strongly, but Sheridan, abruptly throwing off Meade's hand, answered, still defiant, with the words, "If I am allowed to cut loose from this army I can draw Stuart after me and whip him too!" Meade thereupon went over to General Grant's tent and reported the incident. Grant listened quietly, as was his wont, and then, having a strong belief in Sheridan as well as in maintaining discipline, told Sheridan to concentrate his command and "cut loose" as he desired. This was obviously in accordance with the general plan of the "strategic pursuit", and moreover was the only way by which it was now possible to retain the services of both Meade and Sheridan with the army in Virginia. On the morning of the 9th (see Chapter XIV.), in pursuance of the idea he had formed of fighting cavalry duels on a large scale, Sheridan began the so-called "Richmond Raid".

The strategic pursuit, as we have called it, was never executed. While these schemes were being worked out, Warren in front of the enemy became more and more anxious. At 12.30 he reported that he could not advance with the force he had unless he found a weak spot on the enemy's left — in other words, he hoped for nothing except from Cutler's division, which was less shaken than the others. He had lost no prisoners, he continued, but the straggling was very heavy owing to fatigue and the heat of the day. He suggested that Sedgwick and even part of Hancock's corps should be closed up in his rear, mentioned his want of ammunition, and considered the situation from a defensive standpoint, concluding with the curious phrase, "You [Meade] can best judge whether I can be spared more assistance from General Sedgwick by being informed of our necessities elsewhere". Towards two o'clock, however, Warren became more hopeful. "I feel the less apprehensive of an attack than I did after considering the matter from my own point of view. The rebels are as tired out as we are", he wrote at that hour, promising to "do his best to smash Longstreet up when General Sedgwick comes".

But Sedgwick's men were almost as tired as Warren's, and new to the ground. Wright arrived first and made his way through the woods to form up on Crawford's left; Ricketts followed Wright, and it would appear that in the end an attacking mass several lines deep, chiefly of Crawford's and Ricketts' troops, was got together in the wood. Getty came up last of all and was placed in second line.

It was 6.30 when the attack, so-called, was delivered. Warren's responsibility was practically at an end, for Sedgwick was his senior, and Meade himself appeared on the scene. Neither of these officers failed to realize that the enlisted men had had enough for the day, and the assault was allowed to become a mere reconnaissance in force, productive only of information as to the strength of the enemy's works. On the left, however, there was a gleam of success; Crawford's command, composed of troops of both corps, passed across the open ground into the woods beyond Anderson's flank, and by good fortune struck a marching column of Rodes's division, Ewell's corps, with great effect. But being unwilling to venture far into the dark woods held by the enemy, Crawford soon fell back to the main line of the V. Corps, bringing with him a colour and a number of prisoners.

The following dispatch from Grant's headquarters to Burnside, sent at 7.30, even before Warren's battle had died away, marked the end of the attack and the collapse of the intended manoeuvre :—

"Dispose of your command so as to most easily and effectively guard the trains in your convoy, and at the same time be in readiness, on receipt of orders, to send two divisions *to try and help drive the enemy from Spotsylvania Court House*, where he appears to have made a stand in very considerable force."

Ewell's corps was arriving rapidly from Block House and deploying to the left to prolong Anderson's line northwards. Long before this the division of Anderson's corps which had gone to Spottsylvania Court House early in the day, had rejoined, and it aided in repulsing Warren's second and third attacks.* Both sides entrenched heavily after dark.

It remains to consider the day's events around Todd's Tavern, which concerned Hancock's corps and Hill's (commanded temporarily by Early).

The II. Corps remained in the Wilderness all

* Various minor counter-strokes by small units have not been mentioned, not only for want of space but also from the absence of data upon which to reconstruct the incidents of those confused and resultless fights.

night, for although Hancock had expected to be able to start for Todd's Tavern about eleven, Warren's column occupied the Brock Road until daylight. About nine o'clock Hancock arrived at Todd's Tavern, and found Gregg's cavalry engaged with the enemy's (Hampton) a little distance out on the Catharpin Road, but before 12 the skirmishing died away. Hancock entrenched his corps round Todd's Tavern, sent Miles's brigade towards Corbin's Bridge to reconnoitre, watched the Furnace Road with infantry, and used his cavalry (Gregg's division and Hammond's provisional brigade) to scout his front and right.* A column of dust parallel with the march of the II. Corps and in the same direction was observed and reported.

A little after noon, in answer to an urgent appeal from Warren, Hancock ordered Gibbon's division to prepare to march. This division was later moved to replace, at the Alsop cross-roads named in orders, the troops of the VI. Corps that had gone forward to join Warren, and Warren was authorized by Meade to call upon Gibbon also if necessary, though not otherwise.†

Miles's reconnoitring force, of all arms, reached the heights overlooking Corbin's Bridge, and actually passed a party of a hundred men over to the other bank of the Po. More dust clouds, moving south, were visible towards Craig's Church.

* Rations were issued on the evening of the 8th and the morning of the 9th for the first time since crossing the Rapidan.

† Warren did not, as a matter of fact, send for this division to take part in his sunset attack.

He had no report of Anderson's night march, although he actually occupied the route of that corps.

The dust cloud moving parallel with Hancock's column was Hill's (Early's) corps, that towards Craig's Church, Ewell's.

The latter officer had taken over the whole front in the Wilderness from north of the Pike to the Plank Road, and finding no enemy in front at daylight, as ordered, he set his corps in motion *viâ* Parker's Store for Spottsylvania Court House. On the march there was a certain amount of redistribution of brigades consequent upon Early's departure to take command of Hill's corps. Gordon succeeded to Early's division.

Early had been ordered to move to the Court House *viâ* Todd's Tavern and the Brock Road as soon as his front was clear of the enemy.

In order to carry out this order, he reopened a wood-road to the Catharpin Road, and his leading division, Mahone's (late Anderson's), approaching the Catharpin Road, met the cavalry vedettes of Miles's force. This was a little after five in the afternoon, when Miles was retiring leisurely from his reconnaissance of the bridge. Hampton's cavalry at once showed renewed activity, and when Miles swung round to meet Mahone, pressed up the Catharpin Road to cut him off from Todd's Tavern. Hancock was informed, and at once caused his men to stand to arms, detailing Barlow to extricate his adventurous brigadier if necessary. Miles, however, handled his troops neatly and skilfully, repulsing Mahone and Hampton in turn, and then withdrew by order of his corps commander to the Tavern. Early, realizing that the route he had been ordered to take was strongly held by the enemy's army, halted and entrenched in line of battle across the Catharpin Road, facing Todd's Tavern.

The criticism has been made that Grant and Meade, by retaining Hancock at Todd's Tavern, deprived themselves of the presence of the best and freshest corps of the Army of the Potomac on the battlefield. But Grant's 1 P.M. plan looked to a far-ranging encounter-battle well to the south, not to a decisive concentration of force at Spottsylvania. Nevertheless, in view of the possibility of events taking an unexpected turn there, Hancock was called upon for a division to aid Warren, and ordered to be in readiness to follow it up with his whole corps if required to do so. When later, the manœuvre was abandoned and a battle accepted on the Spottsylvania ground, the day was too far spent for the effective employment of the II. Corps as a unit. Warren, as we have seen, did not even employ the division Hancock actually sent. In any case the II. Corps was carrying out Grant's oft-expressed principle, and " doing good service by holding a force equal to its own in front of it ".

CHAPTER XII

SPOTTSYLVANIA—THE BATTLE OF THE 10TH OF MAY

ON the night of the 8th the fatigue of the V. and VI. Corps was extreme, and its influence mastered even Grant's doggedness. Warren's last message to Meade, after the battle was over, seems to indicate a faint impersonal amusement at the course events had taken, and concludes with the phrase, " I am too sleepy to write intelligently ".

The same drowsiness overcame the Confederates. Ewell's corps, indeed, continued to arrive after dark, and as a matter of habit, the men threw up log-works wherever they happened to make their final halt in the blind woods.* Its right division was moved hither and thither for some time seeking to form a well-connected line of battle, the generals and colonels displaying commendable energy, but ere long they too submitted to the prevailing spell.

---

* The amazing complication of earthworks on this ground arose out of, first, the arrival of both armies in the dark, and secondly, from an ingrained habit of making a new entrenchment at every change of position, even within the brigade and away from the front. On the 9th no less than five successive works were constructed by one of Robinson's brigades. In most of the published Spottsylvania maps, the student is still further confused by the fact that works belonging to four distinct periods in the operations, which often cross one another, are shown indiscriminately.

THE 10TH OF MAY

On the Union side, army orders for the 9th were to the following effect:—

Headquarters A.P.   May 8, 1864, 11.5 P.M.

1. The army will remain quiet to-morrow, 9th inst., to give the men rest and to distribute ammunition and rations.

2. Corps commanders will strengthen their positions by intrenchments. The chief engineer and his assistants will aid in making the necessary examinations and in throwing up the works.

3. Corps commanders will return to their proper commands troops of other corps temporarily assigned to them.

4. They will make field returns of the number present for duty.

5. Will send an estimate of casualties during the recent operations.

6. Every effort will be made to bring up the stragglers.

By command of Major-General Meade,

S. WILLIAMS, A.A.G.

The positions of the corps were as follows:—

II. (Hancock), headquarters and Barlow's, Birney's, and Mott's divisions, Todd's Tavern, Gibbon's division at the junction of the Piney Branch and Brock Roads.

V. (Warren) and VI. (Sedgwick), much mixed up, entrenched on the battlefield.

IX. (Burnside) and the army trains, between Aldrich's and Chancellorsville, Willcox's division posted as rearguard to cover the evacuation of the Union wounded towards Fredericksburg.*

---

* The movement of the army from the Wilderness left many of the wounded to their fate, and also most of the dead unburied. Hammond's cavalry brought in all the wounded who could be found. Willcox exchanged some shots in the morning of the 8th with troops of Lee's army, presumably the rearguards of Ewell's or Hill's corps.

Cavalry Corps (Sheridan), concentrating at Aldrich's for independent operations.

On the 9th, as ordered, the V. and VI. Corps were sorted out, the V. on the right, the VI. on the left, and the men rationed and resupplied with ammunition. Crawford's division was brought over to the right in exchange for troops of the VI. Corps. Robinson's division, now without a leader and severely shaken, was broken up, the Maryland brigade* being retained as corps troops. The order of divisions was now—from right to left—Crawford, Cutler, Griffin.

Crawford's right connected with Gibbon, of the II. Corps. During the morning Hancock's command, *pari passu* with the disappearance of Early's corps from its front, was extended along the Brock Road until only Mott's division and the heavy artillery brigade, temporarily assigned to him, remained at Todd's Tavern.

The skirmishers on both sides were very active, and the Union army lost a life that, according to Grant, was worth a whole division of troops. General Sedgwick was killed by a Confederate rifleman, at six hundred yards range, while standing near the left of the VI. Corps works near the Brock Road. No officer in the army was more loved and respected than this gallant old dragoon. Having just been assigned to command the V. and VI. Corps as a wing of the army, he had told Warren to "go on and command his own corps as

---

* Most of its regiments were nearly time-expired.

THE 10TH OF MAY

usual". "I have perfect confidence that he . . . knows what to do with his corps as well as I do", he said to Warren's aide-de-camp. He was hit while walking with McMahon, his chief-of-staff, and conversing gaily and kindly with some of the enlisted men of Penrose's brigade.

General H. G. Wright, an engineer officer of good reputation, succeeded him. Ricketts waiving his seniority out of respect to General Sedgwick's known wishes. Brigadier-General Morris, of the VI. Corps, was wounded later in the day. Russell succeeded to Wright's division. Warren took charge of the right wing up to Hancock's arrival.

During the morning the skirmishers of the V. and VI. Corps were pushed forward to gain information as to the enemy's works in their front.

Anderson's corps, having improved its lines and also having a good field of fire, had now fully extended, and occupied the line from Perry's house near the Po* to a point some distance beyond the Brock Road.

Opposite the VI. Corps, and extending considerably further to the north-east, was the line of Ewell's corps. Ewell's left (Rodes) joined on to Anderson's right. His right division (Johnson's) had already abandoned the useless log-works constructed in the woods during the night, and fallen back into the line (designated by engineers of the

---

* The woods in front of this house, the first position of Anderson's left that had been cleared by Cutler's attack, were not reoccupied by the Confederates. They served, however, to break the force of every subsequent attack on this front.

corps and army staffs), thereafter called the apex of the Salient.* Warren's artillery was able to enfilade in part both the original log-works and the Salient, and in the course of the day Johnson's division lost a brigadier-general (Hays) wounded.

An accurate general idea of Lee's position was formed from the reports of these reconnaissances. His line was understood to be facing north-west, with its flanks on the Po and the Ny, the right being refused along the last-named river.

So much had already been surmised on the 8th, from the mere fact that Anderson was facing the V. and VI. Corps directly. Ewell's arrival, and the presence of Hill (Early) near Todd's Tavern, left no Confederate forces to be accounted for, and the Union plan of battle for the 10th naturally aimed at attacking Lee's front with the Army of the Potomac, while the IX. Corps, the one free mass of manœuvre at Grant's disposal, swung in upon Lee's right rear.

As a preliminary, this corps was, early on the 9th, to work over to the Fredericksburg–Spottsylvania Road, its natural line of advance towards the enemy's rear or refused wing. Burnside's orders, emanating directly from Grant, were to the effect that two divisions of the IX. Corps were to be got up to " Gate " by 6 A.M., preparatory to an advance on the Court House. His column was, however, to go no further than the point mentioned unless ordered. Communication was to be opened with the left of the Army of the Potomac. The third of

* The continuation of the works to the south-east, which completed the Salient, were not constructed until the early morning of the 10th.

THE 10TH OF MAY

Burnside's available * divisions was held as general reserve at Piney Branch Church, and corps details under Colonel Marshall at Aldrich's.

Accordingly, Burnside set his corps in motion very early on the 9th, towards "Gate". But the point so called on the map was a mere gate in the fence by the roadside, and naturally failing to distinguish it, the head of the IX. Corps passed on by the Fredericksburg–Spottsylvania Road to the Ny and beyond. About seven, Willcox, whose division was leading, reached a farm-house, which he learned was called Gayle's.† It was not difficult to assume a misprinted *l* on the map, and Willcox and Burnside believed that they had exactly carried out their orders.

Ere long, however, the advance of this heavy mass of Union troops was observed and reported by the Southern cavalry, and Willcox found himself involved in a skirmish with cavalry and, it was thought, infantry as well. This information being passed on by Burnside to Grant, who understood "Gayle's" to be "Gate", was read as implying not that Burnside had gone too far southward, but that Lee was moving north towards Fredericksburg.

The first result was that Grant authorized

---

* Ferrero's had now definitively become the escort for the trains.

† In reality this house was one of those called "Beverly" on most of the maps, and it is shown under that name on Sketch Map 11 and Map II. "Beverly" appears as "Gayle" on some of the Confederate field sketches reproduced in the atlas to the *Official Records*. The "Gayle" house further down the Ny, which will figure in the later operations, is shown as such in Michler's map and on the maps redrawn from it in the present work. It does not figure in history up to May 14.

Burnside to close up his three available divisions for action "without hesitancy or reference to previous orders". At such moments Grant's mind worked rapidly. Without, for the present, making any alterations in the actual positions and movements of Meade's army, he decided, in a few minutes, on the course to be taken if the news were confirmed. At 10.15 he wrote to Meade:

"You will see by this dispatch that Willcox has met a force not far from Gate. Under the circumstances I think it advisable to send out scouts over to the road from the Gate to Spottsylvania Court House to discover if there is any considerable force moving in this direction. Should there prove to be, it would become necessary to recall the trains and to push the enemy's left flank vigorously."

Three hours later (12.45) Burnside reported that Willcox had been engaged for some time with equal or superior forces, and informed the Lieut.-General that Stevenson's division had gone up to the front to aid Willcox's. The division from Piney Branch Church (Potter's), by leave of General Grant, was moved over about a mile towards Burnside. By now, too, the reports from Hancock indicated the disappearance of the Confederates from the Catharpin Road, and this, taken along with information of heavy fighting at the Gate, which was emphasized by the sound of Willcox's field artillery, seemed fully to confirm the surmise that Lee was bringing in his left and extending his right towards Fredericksburg.

Grant had decided upon his new plan of battle three hours in advance. The orders were issued within a few minutes after the receipt of Burnside's

THE 10TH OF MAY

last message. The plan was Napoleonic in its simplicity.

"The enemy has disappeared from our right, moving in the direction of Gate evidently, which will enable us to follow from here.

"*Direct Willcox to entrench and hold his position strongly, only falling back at the last extremity, expecting the enemy, if they have gone in force towards him, to be attacked from here.*"

At the same time (12.45) Meade was told to have the Army trains turned back (they were heading south from Chancellorsville and Aldrich's) so that "we [? they] may if it should be decided upon make a rapid march on Gordonsville". "If", says the note, "the enemy is moving towards Gate, *we must follow and attack vigorously*". Burnside was shortly afterwards ordered to take immediate charge of his corps at "the Gate"; he had already ordered Willcox to hold his position to the last. The purport of these orders is unmistakable. The IX. Corps was to be the anvil, the Army of the Potomac the hammer.

Meade, however, misread the sense of his own orders, and the orders to Burnside did not pass through his hands. Instead of sending over scouts to the Fredericksburg Road as ordered, to gain information as to Lee's movements, he directed Humphreys to reconnoitre the *roads towards Gate*, "as it may be necessary to *reinforce Burnside*".*

---

* Humphreys, in his book, makes no direct comment on this incident, but precisely at this point in his narrative he introduces a footnote remarking upon the want of cohesion that resulted from two officers commanding the same army. Meade undoubtedly misunderstood

Shortly after noon, too, he ordered Hancock at Todd's Tavern to prepare to move "towards the V. Corps". "This presupposes", he continued, "that the enemy are not in great force in your front. . . . All information leads to the belief that they are passing to our left and *you will be needed here*".

Let us see how Grant's plan fared in execution.

Hancock's corps, so far from "moving towards the V. Corps",* was to be used with the utmost energy on the offensive, irrespective of everything but driving the enemy's left wing. Lieut.-Colonel Comstock, of Grant's own staff, was sent to General Hancock to act as guide, to interpret the views of the general-in-chief and to keep the latter well informed as to the progress made.

The way to the enemy's left was by the Shady Grove Road and Block House, and Hancock was ordered to cross the Po and then to make for Spottsylvania Court House.

Shortly after noon Birney and Barlow moved from the lines at Todd's Tavern down the Brock Road to join Gibbon, who had been sent towards Warren's line during the battle of the 8th. Mott was left at Todd's Tavern and reinforced by the reserve artillery (acting as infantry) from Piney Branch Church. Birney, Barlow, and Gibbon then

---

the spirit both of the 10.15 directive and of the 12.45 order. But the real cause of failure seems, to me, to be that stated above, viz. that there were two *armies* as well as two generals. Had Meade seen the orders to Burnside, no misconception would have been possible.

* In the orders for the development of the manœuvre, issued that night, no *rôle* is assigned to the V. Corps but that of being held in readiness.

THE 10TH OF MAY

struck off to the right towards the fords of the Po, forming in line of battle overlooking that river during the afternoon.

About 5.30 the three divisions began to cross at three points, Tinder's Mill, Talley's, and Pritchett's, Birney meeting a certain amount of resistance from Hampton's dismounted cavalry at Tinder's Mill. Once more the Confederate troopers gained priceless hours by rearguard tactics, and Hancock was obliged to proceed carefully, with a skirmish line searching the ground (mostly woods) in front of each division. Thus nightfall came before the II. Corps had reached the Block House bridge, its objective point, and the corps commander, knowing though he did that General Grant desired that the advance should be pressed up to and over the bridge, felt obliged to halt and bivouac in the woods. Gibbon, his left wing, and subsequently (when each division wheeled to its left independently) his advanced guard, was actually in sight of the bridge, and some of its outpost sentries sounded the stream for fords, though in vain.

Bridges were constructed at the three points of crossing used by Birney, Barlow, and Gibbon; these were finished early on the morning of the 10th.*

The other corps of the Army of the Potomac were not affected, on the 9th, by the change of plan.

---

* Mott's division was directed, when finally called in from Todd's Tavern, to take position on the left of the VI. Corps, but this movement was not to take place until 3 A.M. on the 10th. The heavy artillery with his command was to rejoin the general reserve of artillery at Piney Branch Church.

Although the manœuvre had not been carried, before nightfall, to the point that Grant desired, it was to be continued on the 10th. No change was reported in the situation in front of Burnside, and the real position of the IX. Corps seems still to have been unsuspected, the more easily as Grant was now convinced by the frequent repetition of "Gayle" or "Gale" that the name "Gate" was a misprint on the map. The plan of battle was, as before, that Burnside was to hold his ground, Wright and Warren to stand fast, but to be ready to move forward, and Hancock to *attack*.

The actual instructions to Burnside were to the effect that he might use Mott's division if necessary, and that he was to hold his Gayle position if he could, *otherwise to withdraw to Alsop's*, i.e. to clear the front and to bar the western outlets to Lee's army.

But of the leading idea in all this there is still no trace of this in Meade's orders to the Army of the Potomac, which directed " the several corps to be held in readiness", and Hancock " to endeavour to ascertain the position and force of the enemy in his front and the location of his left flank ".

Even Mott was misdirected. Instead of being ordered to be ready to assist Burnside if called upon, he was told to move to Burnside's assistance *in any case*, " on hearing heavy firing in that direction ".

At early dawn on the 10th, Hancock resumed the march that had been interrupted by nightfall. But Meade's instructions were not such as to lead to great results. Hancock was evidently puzzled by the discrepancy between Grant's wishes, as represented by Comstock, and the order he received from the army commander, and at 6.45 he wrote a note to Meade, every line of which reflects sheer mystification. " I am anxious to meet your views, but I desire to explain the causes of delay. Now, if it is a positive order to make the crossing, my troops will do it as well as any. But. . . .", and with little idea of what was required of him, Hancock went forward very cautiously. A careful examination of the Block House bridge revealed trenches well manned by infantry on the other side of the river. Brooke's brigade of Barlow's division, with some artillery, was thereupon sent down stream to find a ford. He did so, about half a mile below the bridge, and crossing, made for the bridge by the enemy's bank of the river. But he came upon more trenches, and Hancock having sent in to headquarters as requested information as to the strength and position of the enemy's left wing—which proved to be two divisions of Hill's (Early's) corps brought over from Burnside's front—the advance of the offensive wing was given up without an effort to press it (10 A.M.). Hancock's crossing on the evening of the 9th certainly gave the enemy warning of the coming attack, and thereby caused the failure of the whole plan, which presupposed that Burnside could draw upon himself the weight of the opposition. But as this plan was based on the mistaken idea that Lee's advance was at the "Gate", viz. further towards Fredericksburg than was actually the case, it was of vital importance, on that understanding, to hurry on the outer flank of the wheeling army. And it may be that a little less delay in crossing and deployment would have given full effect to the blow of this moving flank.

Grant wasted no time in regrets. The hypothesis upon which his plan was based having collapsed, and all indications being that Lee was concentrating on his left, the lieutenant-general at once framed a new plan for the new situation. Hancock was to withdraw and join Warren and Wright for a decisive attack on the enemy's centre.

At 10.30 the following order went to Burnside.

Colonel Porter carried it, running the gauntlet of a good deal of Confederate marksmanship, and remained with Burnside to explain the views of the general-in-chief.

"A general attack will be made on the enemy at 5 P.M. to-day. Reconnoitre the enemy's position in the meantime, and if you have any possible chance of attacking their right do it with vigour and with all the force you can. Do not neglect to make all the show you can as the best co-operative effort."

This and instructions to get touch with Meade's army, mark the definitive close of the first abortive manœuvre.

The choice of the centre as the point to be attacked seems to call for some discussion.

The modern German, working on the idea that "the resolute execution of a scheme, even though this be not the best possible, will always secure good results",* would probably have reinforced Hancock for a battle at the Block House bridge.

* *Der italienische Feldzug, 1859*, by the German staff.

Humphreys considers that this would have been the correct procedure in the present case.

But Hancock's corps was a mass of manœuvre, and its position towards the lower Po was only favourable for manœuvre, not for fighting. Now, owing to the unexpected extension of the Confederate line on that side, a further advance would not be a manœuvre but an attack, and Grant may be assumed to have weighed the advantages and disadvantages of an attack on Block House bridge before giving up the scheme. The problem before him was now to select the best point of attack on the enemy's line from Block House bridge to Landron's. The front held by Early's corps was only hastily fortified, but it was by far the most difficult of approach. It might be turned. But in that case the II. Corps would find itself separated from all possible support by two reaches of the river, and liable to complete isolation should the enemy advance over Block House bridge. If provision were made against this last contingency, not more than half the corps would be free to make the turning movement, and to despatch such a force into the heart of the enemy's position would be to expose it to annihilation.

On the left of the line, Wright and Mott were too widely extended to be able to deliver a really heavy attack. Burnside was so far separated from the Army of the Potomac, and the state of things in his front so obscure that nothing could be calculated as to the chances of success there.

There remained the V. Corps, closely concentrated in its lines on the Brock Road. The enemy's centre, so vainly assaulted on the 8th, was undoubtedly the strongest point on Lee's whole line, by reason of its wide field of fire and the labour spent on its works. It was, however, the only point on the line opposite which a sufficiently heavy assaulting mass could be collected in time. There was reason to hope that as Lee had drawn so many troops to the Block House, the strongest position of his line and not the weakest had been called upon to find these troops. Better results, in case of success, were to be expected from the employment of two corps here than from that of one, or even a less force, at weaker points on Lee's line, and Grant was ever ready " to put it to the touch, to win or lose it all ".

As to the attack on earthworks in general, there had been nothing hitherto to show that it was impossible to succeed with well-massed troops. The enemy's lines at Spindler's were strong, but by no means impregnable, and given the two conditions that the stormers were well supported, and that the enemy was prevented from concentrating at the breach, there was no reason to suppose that the assault would fail. Grant and Meade met the conditions by choosing a point of attack opposite their heaviest mass of troops, and by ordering a simultaneous attack of all troops along the whole line.

On the rest of the front, the morning of the 10th, like that of the 9th, was chiefly devoted to costly and resultless skirmishing. In the IX. Corps another excellent general officer, Stevenson, like Sedgwick the previous day, met his death from a sharpshooter's bullet. Hitherto six Union general officers had been killed and wounded in front of Spottsylvania.

Along Warren's, Wright's, and Mott's front all the morning there was skirmishing, rising occasionally to sharp fighting of artillery and of infantry in single rank as well as of thin lines of skirmishers.

The hour fixed for the general attack, which was to be made as heavily as possible by Hancock and Warren, and more or less vigorously in proportion to their means and positions, by Wright, Mott, and Burnside, was 5 P.M. The seven hours (10–5) allowed for preparations were designed chiefly to permit of the gradual withdrawal of Hancock's corps over the Po to join Warren.

A hasty withdrawal would have defeated its own object, for the Confederates would not have indulged in a useless foray towards Tinder's Mill, but would have returned as quickly as possible to the decisive point on the main line of battle, whereas a slow retirement, and best of all a well-timed rearguard fight, would keep them occupied all day on the Shady Grove Road, where they could have no influence on the fate of the battle on the Brock Road.

Accordingly, General Meade ordered Hancock to recross two of his available divisions, leaving the other to maintain a threatening attitude on the side of the Block House or Shady Grove Road. The adventures of this division will be described later; here it is sufficient to say that it occupied rather more than its own weight of the Confederate army for the rest of the day, and in so far, brilliantly fulfilled its mission.

Hancock was to command his own and Warren's corps, or five divisions out of ten on the ground, and it was hoped that he would break Anderson's weakened * line at one blow. The hour of attack was fixed at 5 P.M.

Wright and Mott were instructed to attack at the same hour. The orders to Burnside have been given above.

One critic † says that the assaults which followed were of such a character that no troops in the world could be expected to succeed in them unless they were brought up to a high pitch of enthusiasm, exceptionally well officered, picked men, and sure of being supported, and that " such work as this is no part of the ordinary duty of a soldier. It is exceptional in its character, and any attempt to make it part of the daily task is sure to result in failure". But, hitherto at any rate, there seems little reason to condemn the policy of assaulting works. The assault was originally ordered at five, to be carried out by Hancock with six divisions, and Wright and Mott with four, simultaneously. Such a force would very likely have driven Anderson as it had driven Hill on the early morning of the 6th in the Wilderness. But headquarters eagerly caught at the first chance of gaining a foothold in the works, and Warren

---

* As a matter of fact it was Hill's (Early's) corps, from Spottsylvania, that was shifted to the Block House Bridge lines. Anderson's line was maintained in full strength.

† J. C. Ropes in *Mil. Hist. Soc. Mass*.

having reported a good opportunity of doing so, the order was given to assault at once before the whole of Hancock's force had arrived. The result seems to show that Warren was right in reporting that he could take the works, and that headquarters were wrong in allowing him to make the attempt.

The attack was made, then, at four, on the so-called "Laurel Hill" front—that is, between Spindler's and the Po—by Crawford's and Cutler's divisions of the V. Corps, and Carroll's and Webb's brigades of Gibbon (II. Corps). Wright and Mott were ordered to attack at the same time, instead of at five. Mott's orders to move to the sound of Burnside's guns had of course been cancelled.

Warren, as usual on battle days, wore his full uniform, and with deliberate personal bravery led his assault in person. The men certainly needed encouragement for the task in front of them, the nature of which they knew well enough after the morning's work of close reconnaissance.*

The assault itself was bravely made, though without the contagious enthusiasm of the two later attacks at the Bloody Angle. The right brigades had to pass through a wood of stiff dead pines to reach the Confederate works at Perry's farm, and many men were killed and wounded by the trees that the rapid fire of the hostile artillery cut down. There was much confusion and wild firing, and not all the line went forward from the wood. But parts of Carroll's brigade and of Crawford's division certainly reached the works,

* Two reconnaissances in force had been made by the V. Corps, the second to relieve the pressure on Barlow's rearguard (see below).

and the bravest, Brigadier-General Rice of the V. Corps amongst them, were killed inside the enemy's lines.

The attack was unsupported, however, and the two and a half divisions that had made it gave back in considerable confusion.

Hancock was not present, nor did Birney's division take part in the attack. The fighting of Barlow's division south of the Po absorbed the corps commander's attention and required him to hold Birney in readiness to assist. But even if he had marched his whole corps to Warren's position, beginning at 10.30, he would scarcely have been able to take a preponderant part in an assault made along the Brock Road as early as four. The 4 P.M. attack was necessarily an isolated venture of the troops immediately available. As such it presented fair chances of success on the understanding that the enemy's line was weakened, but in fact it encountered such resistance as only a general assault—for which four was too early an hour—could hope to overcome, and it failed, to the serious detriment of the moral of the much-tried V. Corps.

It was the first of those frontal assaults on entrenchments, which are the stock-in-trade of criticisms on Grant's leadership, but it was distinctly a misadventure, not a defeat, and it is difficult not to assign to Warren the responsibility for a serious error in judgment which led him to miscalculate the chances of the enterprise.

It is a significant fact that Grant did not blame Warren for this assault as he blamed him for his

THE 10TH OF MAY

failure of the 8th. It may even be that the resolution displayed by the commander of the V. Corps, in spite of its consequences, reinstated him in Grant's estimation as a capable leader of troops.

Wright and Mott took no part in this attack. Wright was busily engaged in preparing for the five o'clock assault by a careful reconnaissance, and Mott was too much extended in his search for Burnside's right to be readily brought back in sufficient force for an attack as early as four, besides which the order was not sent from Meade's headquarters until twenty minutes or so before that hour. Wright, it should be said, had all day been gaining ground in the woods on his left.

It was 5.30 or thereabouts when the attack of the V. Corps broke up. Not long after that hour Wright's front became the scene of a memorable achievement, one of the classic infantry attacks of military history.

At this time Lee's entrenchments extended from the heights commanding Block House Bridge, through Perry's and Spindler's, to Harrison's, then curving round McCool's house (The Salient), it turned southward and ended near the church with a short defensive return. The works were continuous except for the break between Ewell and Hill, east of Harrison's. This was held by a skirmish line. Hill's section (astride the Fredericksburg Road) was at the moment held only by a long thin line of Wilcox's division; the other two divisions of that corps constituted Lee's army reserve or mass of manœuvre, and were shifted from left to right and back as required.

The celebrated Salient itself was not the result of deliberate siting, but was accidentally formed by the rectification of the haphazard entrenchments made on the night of the 8th/9th May. It is generally considered as a blunted redan of wide salient angle, the defenders of the blunted apex facing somewhat west of north, those of the west face north-west, and those of the east face north-east. The base of this irregular redan was about half a mile across, the western half of the interior chiefly comprising the open ground of Harrison's and McCool's farms, and the eastern being thickly wooded. The troops of Ewell's corps occupying the Salient were Rodes's division, from Anderson's right to the west angle and Johnson's division along the apex and the east face. In front of Rodes there were woods, but a field of fire had been obtained by a "slashing". In Johnson's front along the apex there was a very favourable field of view and fire towards Brown's and Landron's farms. From the east face the woods were held chiefly by skirmishers until the left of Wilcox's division was reached, whence the field of fire was generally open to the end of the line. A retrenchment cut off the whole of the McCool salient. The value of this retrenchment was to appear presently, but the occupants (Gordon's, late Early's, division of Ewell's corps), incommoded by the enfilade fire of Warren's guns, had drawn out into the salient and stood in close order as a reserve. The three divisions, Rodes, Johnson, Gordon, were what remained of Jackson's unsurpassed "foot-cavalry". Besides the principal retrenchment there

THE 10TH OF MAY

were a few short lengths of log-works constructed by Gordon in the interior of the Salient.

Opposite Rodes and Johnson respectively were Wright and Mott. Wright had ordered, and personally supervised, a thorough reconnaissance of the ground on the west side of the salient. It was decided that the west angle—soon to be immortalized as the Bloody Angle—should be the point of attack for the VI. Corps and the apex itself for Mott.

The VI. Corps column of attack was not as strong as it might have been, for Wright had to provide for the defence of his own lines, now somewhat prolonged to the north towards Shelton's, and it would appear that demands for supports to the V. Corps were made upon him. Mott, too, had to go forward before he was able to close in the regiments which had extended towards Burnside.

Colonel Upton was assigned to command the twelve selected regiments that were to storm the angle. He massed them in four lines (Sketch Map 12).

All preliminaries were carried out quietly under cover of the wood. The exact alignment was taken up with the assistance of engineer officers from headquarters. Units were moved into position singly and halted and fronted by signal.* The enemy seemed to be absorbed in watching the formation of Mott's line far away at the Brown house. All the mounted officers sent their horses

* There was no deployment, each regiment moving in in column of fours and turning to its front.

to the rear. By Wright's orders every regimental commander had examined the ground. The rifles of the first line were loaded and capped, those of the rest loaded but not capped, and the whole fixed bayonets. On passing over the enemy's works, two regiments of the first line were to change front to the right and to charge down the line towards a battery or small re-entrant known to be on the west face, the third to change front left and to enfilade the apex: the second line was to halt at the works and to beat down any counter-stroke of the enemy from the interior. The other two lines were held in reserve. The third was to be close behind the second, the fourth at the edge of the wood ready to change front to the left in order to fire obliquely upon the apex. "All the officers were instructed to repeat the command 'Forward' constantly from the commencement of the charge till the works were carried." The guns, which had meanwhile taken the angle and the apex under their fire, ceased by arrangement at six, and Upton's men moved through the wood up to the further edge in the breathless silence of excitement, every officer and man in the twelve regiments tuned to respond to the single word of command.

At ten minutes past six it was given.

"With a wild cheer and faces averted", says their commander, "the men rushed for the enemy's works, swept from both flanks and from the front by bullets and case shot. But the parapet was reached.

"The enemy, sitting in their pits with pieces

upright, loaded, and with bayonets fixed ready to impale the first who should leap over, absolutely refused to quit the ground."

The brave Union volunteers who first mounted the parapet were shot or bayoneted, and for a few seconds there was a murderous hand to hand fight, Federals and Confederates stabbing and shooting vertically downwards over the parapet that divided them. But the wrecks of the first assailing line were soon pushed forward by the second and third, and the Union battle flags were up and over the entrenchments.

Even at this moment of intoxication the colonels managed to fulfil their instructions. The first line and parts of the second swung away to the right and left, storming the re-entrant on the right, firing wildly into the rear of Johnson's line and crowning the second short line of defence in front.

But the rest of the VI. Corps was not there to follow up the success of the stormers. Ewell's reserves, with Gordon at their head, hastened up, and Upton soon found himself attacked on all sides. He fought hard to retain the captured works, but Mott's assault, made from Brown's house in full view of Johnson's line (the apex), had been brought to a standstill some distance from the works, and finding himself unsupported, Upton held out until night and then, on a written order from General Russell, withdrew, with his prisoners and trophies, into the wood and thence to the lines of the VI. Corps. He had lost about a thousand men, but he had inflicted a loss of perhaps 500 in killed and wounded on the enemy, and in addition brought off fully a thousand prisoners, as well as several colours.

General Grant had been authorized to promote officers on the spot for special acts of gallantry, and he made Upton a brigadier-general the same evening.

On the other flank, earlier in the day, there had been another example of faultless troop leading.

The withdrawal of the II. Corps over the Po was covered by Barlow's division. This was perhaps the best in the army, and was moreover in full strength, having scarcely been engaged since the 5th. On receiving the order to retire Barlow fell back from the Shady Grove Road into the woods, where Heth's division (Early's corps), approaching from Glady Run, pressed him closely. The woods as usual caught fire,* but the division retired steadily by pairs of brigades, inflicting heavy loss whenever the enemy attempted to close. The firing was so heavy that at one moment Birney's division was brought back from Warren's lines to the Po to cover Barlow's crossing. An artillery mass of the II. Corps also came into action, facing south on the heights near Pritchett's, and kept up a heavy fire on the advancing Confederates and on the guns near Block House Bridge. On leaving the woods and emerging into the open field near the river, the division came

* One gun was abandoned in the woods, having been immovably jammed between two trees. General Hancock says that this was the first gun lost by his corps.

under enfilade shell fire from Mahone's guns on the Block House position, but the men maintained their order as if on parade. Miles's brigade was the last to cross, and repulsed a final advance of the enemy before doing so. On recrossing after this exploit, Barlow was moved into the woods on the right rear of the V. Corps.

Hancock says of this action, "The enemy regarded this as a considerable victory, and General Heth published a congratulatory order to his troops. . . . Had not Barlow's fine division, then at full strength, received imperative orders to withdraw, Heth's division would have had no cause for congratulation".

At the time of Warren's attack (4 P.M.), Hancock was superintending the withdrawal of the last of Birney's covering force on the Po. He reappeared on the front of the V. Corps about 5.30, when the attack there had spent its force and was showing signs of flagging.

It was not long before he received an order to assault a second time. Upton's success being reported at headquarters, Grant was intensely anxious to help him by pressing up to the entrenchments elsewhere, so as to prevent the enemy from denuding their lines to concentrate on the gallant handful at the Angle. Meade therefore ordered the second assault for 6.30. This was quickly countermanded owing to the false report of a hostile advance against the extreme left (Barlow), but it was as quickly re-issued, and the assault took place only half an hour later than the time originally fixed. It was bravely made by Birney and Gibbon and a part of the V. Corps, over the same ground and with the same result as the first charge. This time the Union troops did not advance beyond the wood.

They were " fought out ", and knew the ground in their front only too well. But the assault certainly achieved its purpose. Not a man of Anderson's corps was detached to aid Ewell at the Salient, and this result may well have been worth the cost. It was the duty of Wright and Mott to support Upton, and Hancock's and Warren's men, after the failure of the afternoon's assault on their own front, had only to give their lives to ensure success elsewhere.

As to the attack of the IX. Corps, the hour was the same as that fixed for the others, viz. 5 P.M. It was left to Burnside's discretion to advance in one long line from Mott's left to the Beverly house or in one mass of three divisions along the main road. Colonel Porter, who was with Burnside, strongly urged the latter course, but Burnside preferred to obtain a decision from General Grant himself. It is hardly necessary to mention that the answer was in favour of the massed attack. However, by the time it arrived, it was too late to bring up the rear division. It was also too late to co-operate effectively with the V. and VI. Corps, and only the two divisions actually on the ground went forward. In these circumstances the attack was no more than a reconnaissance in force. But, as far as it went, it was methodically and carefully conducted, and the outpost line was ultimately established within twelve hundred yards of the Court House itself.

The losses of the Union army in this battle were somewhat over four thousand, of which Upton's share was about one thousand, and Warren's and Hancock's about nine hundred each. The casualties in the II. and V. Corps do not seem heavy enough to justify the commonly accepted belief that Grant's frontal attacks on earthworks were mere massacres.*

The most significant feature of the battle, however, is not these frontal attacks on entrenchments, but the manœuvring of Early's corps on the defender's side. This " mass of manœuvre ", handled by Lee in the most masterly fashion, was brought in from Córbin's bridge to form the refused right wing of the Army of Northern Virginia at Spottsylvania Court House. Thence it made its presence felt on the front of the IX. Corps, and after that at different points of the line, always with striking effect. First of all, it inspired and then it checkmated Grant's bold scheme of a hammer and anvil battle, and as we shall see its third manœuvre gave a special and unfavourable character to the great Union attack on the 12th, and its fourth (on the 19th) delayed by two days the execution of a manœuvre that Grant had hoped would be decisive. And in achieving all this —in tempting the Union general into false deployments, and in nullifying every calculation of time, space, and position—Early was not once compelled to fight his corps *à fond!* He was aided, of course,

* Colonel Livermore.

by good luck—the mistake as to the position of "Gate", for instance, led to the belief that Burnside had only to stand still to ensure Lee's attacking him—and by the co-operation of the cavalry near Tinder's Mill on the evening of the 9th. But enough has been said above in the chapters on the 4th and 5th of May to indicate that modern strategy knows of means whereby it is possible to guarantee one's self both against ill-fortune of this character, and against kaleidoscopic changes in the military situation.

CHAPTER XIII

SPOTTSYLVANIA—THE BATTLE OF MAY 12

On the morning of May 11, General Grant bade farewell to a member of Congress, Mr. E. B. Washburne, who had been staying at headquarters, and in response to Washburne's request for a message to the President he went to his tent and wrote an official letter, which the visitor carried with him to Washington.

"We have now ended the sixth day of very heavy fighting. The result to this time is much in our favour. But our losses have been heavy as well as those of the enemy. . . . I think the loss of the enemy must be greater. . . . I am now sending back to Belle Plain all my wagons for a fresh supply of provisions and ammunition, and propose to fight it out on this line if it takes all summer."

The letter was intended as a brief statement of events and of his intentions in the future, but when it reached Washington the significance of the last phrase was not lost upon the cabinet, and the letter, with the confidential portions omitted, was published at once. The effect was instantaneous. It is hardly too much to say that from that moment dated Grant's real ascendancy over the people he represented.

On this morning favourable news came in from Butler and from Sheridan. Grant expressed particular satisfaction on learning that the cavalry general had broken the Virginia Central Railroad between Lee and Richmond, and this not because a line of communication was interrupted—that signified little as compared with cutting off Lee from his centre of operations by the living barrier of the Army of the Potomac—but because Lee could no longer use the railroad to concentrate against Butler. Butler's success was apparently greater, but Grant attached relatively little importance to operations south of Richmond, provided only that the Army of the James did not expose itself to disaster. Good news had also been received from West Virginia and from the Western armies on the Georgia border.

The results of the engagement of the 10th, though unsatisfactory, seemed to Grant to afford data upon which a carefully prearranged battle could be fought to a better, he hoped even a decisive, result.

Burnside was ordered to fill the interval between himself and Mott with his third division. This meant that the corps were to be disposed, no longer at intervals of manœuvre, but in line of battle. Corps commanders were ordered to report the number of men available for free offensive operations after the garrison of the lines had been provided for, and to reconstruct their lines if necessary with a view to their being held by a minimum force. Meade and Burnside were ordered to

THE BATTLE OF MAY 12

replenish every cartridge box, to issue as much of the food in the supply train as the men could carry in their haversacks, and to send every wagon that could be spared back to Belle Plain. Meade was given permission, if he chose to do so, to send away the reserve artillery as well. There was no provision made for guarding the wagons when they should return from Belle Plain.* "All the infantry you can rake and scrape" had been ordered to Belle Plain to reinforce the Army of the Potomac, and would furnish sufficient escort for a long cross-country march. The wounded with the army were evacuated to the rear for transportation to Washington. Slight cases were, however, required to accompany the army, travelling in the field ambulances.† All these measures pointed to a pursuit consequent upon a victory. The Federals were, contrary to precedent, to make this pursuit in the lightest possible marching order.

There were few events on the 11th. Birney was ordered to join Mott, and the two, under Birney's command, were to march across country sweeping everything before them until they found and connected with Burnside; but on Mott having established the connection alone, the order was rescinded. Burnside, whose corps appeared to

---

* General Halleck, more prompt than he had been on a former celebrated occasion, had anticipated Grant's orders, and had had a bridge constructed at Fredericksburg.

† On this day orders were issued for the mustering out of those units whose term of service was at an end. Not long before this, the commanding general had dealt very severely with soldiers who refused to do duty on the ground that they were time-expired, but incidents of the battles of May 5, 6, 8, and 10 had shown that troops with a grievance could not be relied upon for whole-hearted devotion.

Grant to be too much isolated, was ordered to retire beyond the Ny. Miles's brigade reconnoitred the Brock Road as far as Todd's Tavern, and Barlow sent a force over the Po towards the Shady Grove Road to see whether the situation on the side of Block House Bridge had undergone any serious modification. These troops found entrenchments in front of, as well as those overlooking, the bridge, but retired unharmed.

Wright, Mott, and officers of the headquarters staff, spent the morning in collecting additional information as to the Salient, the weakness of which Upton's secondary attack on the 10th had so startlingly developed, and on this information General Grant based his plan of battle for the 12th. At three in the afternoon, Meade received the following directive:—

"Move three divisions of the II. Corps by the rear of the V. and VI. under cover of night so as to join the IX. Corps in a vigorous assault on the enemy at 4 A.M. to-morrow. I will send staff officers over to-night to stay with Burnside and impress him with the importance of a prompt and vigorous attack. Warren and Wright should hold their corps as close to the enemy as possible to take advantage of any diversion caused by the attack, and to push in if any opportunity presents itself. There is but little doubt in my mind but that the assault last evening would have proven entirely successful if it had commenced one hour earlier,[*] and had been heartily entered into by Mott's division and the IX. Corps.

"U. S. GRANT,
"Lieut.-General."

At four, accordingly, Meade ordered the II.

[*] It will be remembered that the hour for the general attack was five, and that Upton advanced at 6.10.

Corps to move as soon after dark as it could be done without giving the alarm to the enemy, to Mott's front, and thence "at 4 A.M. as promptly as possible" to assault the enemy's lines. Gibbon's division, being close to the enemy at Spindler's, was at first ordered to stand fast, but was eventually released to follow the others. Hancock's circular to his division commanders, amongst other details of the march, insisted upon the necessity of keeping the marching column well locked up, and forbade the lighting of fires on the position of assembly at the end of the march. The artillery was to go by a separate road. All other wheeled vehicles (except three tool wagons) were to move to the rear as soon as the troops had marched off.

At 6.30, Warren was ordered to be ready to take over the lines of the II. Corps in addition to his own. Yet, even so, says Humphreys, "it was not designed to change the concentrated formation of the V. Corps", and he was to shorten his lines wherever it could be done, and to have his troops "in readiness" at 4.30, the hour at which it was expected that Hancock's and Burnside's attack would be in progress.*

VI. Corps orders (5 P.M.) assigned to Ricketts (and Mott) the guard of the trenches, and to Neill and Russell a more mobile rôle, for which they were to prepare by drawing out of the trenches and taking up assembly formations in the woods behind.

* The reference in Meade's order to the troops of the V. Corps being held *ready to meet an attack by the enemy* on the Union right, must be considered injudicious, psychologically, as tending to turn Warren's mind in the direction of a cautious defensive.

Burnside's retirement over the Ny, then in progress, was stopped, and the troops brought back to their old positions at Beverly's. He was informed of Hancock's movements, and ordered to move against the enemy with his entire force,* " promptly and with all possible vigour ", at precisely four o'clock on the morning of the 12th. All preparations were to be made with the utmost secrecy, and two of Grant's confidential staff officers, who were conversant with the situation along the whole front and with the Lieutenant-General's intentions, were to remain with Burnside and Hancock during the attack. He was further told that Warren and Wright were to " hold their corps as close to the enemy as possible to take advantage of opportunities ".

The plan of battle, then, was as follows. The left wing of the Union army, seven divisions, was to attack with all its might, four of them massed on a narrow front opposite a part of the enemy's lines that was known to be assailable. On other parts of the field, two divisions were to be held in readiness to go wherever their services might be required, and the other four were to garrison the lines, to fix the enemy by the ever-present threat of an assault, and to seize any opportunity of " pushing in " that might present itself.

We now turn to the execution of the scheme.

There was the usual severe picket firing along the front of the II., V., and VI. Corps until

---

* It is not at all clear that Grant did not actually intend the II. and IX. Corps to act as a unit under Burnside's command.

THE BATTLE OF MAY 12

evening. Rain began to fall heavily in the afternoon, and hardly ceased all night. The warm, almost stifling heat of the past days gave place at nightfall to bleak cold. A brief sleep on the ground around half-drowned bivouac fires was not the best preparation for a day of battle, and some of the Union soldiers were not even thus fortunate. Hancock's corps in particular was on the march or under arms from nightfall to 2 A.M. Miles's brigade, returning from Todd's Tavern, found the corps already on the move, and went on with it to its new position near the Brown house.

The march of the II. Corps in the muddy roads through a dark and rainy night began about 10 P.M. and took about two hours, forming up in Brown's field another two, and the men lay down in the ranks to snatch two hours of comfortless rest before daybreak. General Barlow says that he himself knew nothing of the scheme, save that it was an important movement, and that the country might be expected to be grateful to those who should contribute to the success of the enterprise, and he also says that the staff officers guiding the column knew little more than he. The situation seems to have appealed to the sense of humour of some of the higher officers, and to the grumbling instinct of others, but the men were very quiet as they trudged through the rain.

The direction of the attack had been ascertained on the morning of the 11th by taking a compass bearing on McCool's house in the interior of the Salient.

The formation taken up by the corps is shown

in Sketch Map 13. Barlow threw out a regiment some distance to his left, which marched in column of fours (right in front) as flank guard. Field and general officers were on foot.

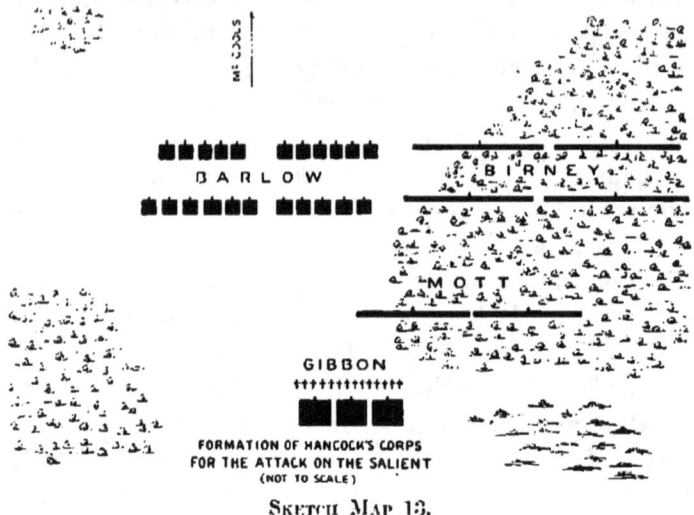

Sketch Map 13.

On the other side, Ewell's outposts heard and reported heavy forces of infantry forming up in Brown's field, and Johnson's division manned the trenches at 3 A.M., Gordon's division being also put under arms in support.

Hancock waited, owing to the mist, until 4.35, when he gave the word to advance. Without a sound, the II. Corps moved forward from Brown's field, through Landron's, towards the McCool house. Nothing could be seen in front through the drizzling mist, but the assaulting mass moved on the ascertained compass bearing and presently met a skirmish line of the enemy, which fired a

THE BATTLE OF MAY 12

few wild shots and scurried back to the main defences. One excited voice in the ranks raised a cheer, which was instantly taken up by the nearly twenty thousand others. The pace was increased to a run, Barlow's line of columns in the open dissolving at once into a formless mass, Birney's deployed regiments in the wood maintaining a ragged alignment and struggling to keep pace with their comrades. The Confederates were now firing, and when the corps was still one hundred and fifty yards from the works an abatis was met. But the excited men pulled it aside, or blundered through it, and then encountered a storm of bullets from the apex of the Salient. Seeing an angle, and making instinctively for the obvious weak spot, the mass swayed to the left, and so Barlow's columns crowded upon the east angle, while Birney's line struck the westerly part of the apex and Mott's pressed in between them. There was a moment's hesitation, for the Confederates stood up and fired two or three rounds from every rifle with deadly effect, and then the entrenchments were stormed. Bayonets were crossed for an instant, but the thin line of Ewell's corps gave way before the flood.

It was the greatest success that ever fell to the lot of a corps in the Army of the Potomac. In the interior of the Salient the Union troops gathered up thousands of prisoners, twenty guns,*

---

* Misled by Burnside's momentary withdrawal beyond the Ny and by the activity of Miles and Birney on the other flank, Lee had withdrawn most of Ewell's artillery from the Salient to be ready to act on the side of Block House Bridge, whence Early's outposts had sent in alarming reports. On receiving Johnson's reports from General Ewell,

and over thirty colours. One division (Edward Johnson's) was taken *en masse*, and in it was the famous Stonewall Brigade once led by Jackson. Beyond Barlow's left Owen's and Carroll's brigades of the reserve raced forward and entered the east face of the Salient, capturing Brigadier-General Steuart and most of his men.

In the interior of the Salient the whole II. Corps was soon a mob of excited soldiers, cheering wildly and almost completely out of hand. Practically all the reserves had been swallowed up in the rush, as Upton's had been on the 10th, and the advance of Gordon's division, fresh and in excellent order, to check their further advance, brought on a second conflict of extraordinary and pertinacious bitterness, which gave its historic name to the "Bloody Angle".

Gordon's leading brigade, coming into action before the force of the attack was spent, was severely handled, and the division had to be re-formed in the retrenchment at the base of the Salient. Thence the gallant young general led it through the McCool woods, and began to press back the foremost groups of Barlow's and Gibbon's men. Birney's and Mott's men along the apex and at the west angle began to roll up Rodes's right, but were stopped by a gallant counter-stroke by Daniel's and Ramseur's brigades of Rodes's division. General Daniel was killed. But this

Lee ordered the guns "to be back at daylight". They returned at the gallop, but were swamped, with their teams and wagons, by the first rush of the Union infantry.

THE BATTLE OF MAY 12 285

first counter-attack was not made, it would appear, until an hour or so after the works were stormed, and during that hour something had been done by the Union division and brigade commanders to restore order. Most of the prisoners and trophies had been cleared away to the rear, and a skirmish line thrown forward, at any rate on Barlow's front.

By 6 A.M., however, Hancock felt obliged to send to Meade for support, and the two divisions of the VI. Corps that were held in readiness were brought up at once. At the moment of their arrival, the fighting had become desperate.* The Union troops stood on the outside, the Confederates on the inside of the captured works, fighting hand to hand, stabbing over the breastworks, even leaping on to them from time to time and making prisoners by sheer wrestling and strength of arm.

The battle is indescribable, except by a catalogue of those deeds of individual heroism that happened to be noted and to be remembered in quieter hours. It must suffice to say that the men of the II. and VI. and later some of the V. Corps, struggled all day in the rain against every brigade that Lee could spare to attempt the recapture of the lost entrenchments,† and that after *twenty*

---

* Artillery was freely used on both sides, and on the Union side a regular battery galloped up to the Salient and fired until the last horse and almost the last man were killed and wounded. The main body of Hancock's artillery was posted in rear, firing over the heads of the troops and sweeping the interior of the Salient to break up the enemy's supports as they advanced.

† Lee himself, as at the crisis of the Wilderness battle, rode forward to lead a brigade in person, but was restrained by the protests of the men from doing so.

hours under fire the II. and VI. Corps were allowed to hold the captured lines without further contest.

On both sides troops were relieved from time to time in order to reform and to replenish ammunition, but the fighting lines were never less than crowded. The front of battle of the six or seven Union divisions was hardly a mile. Parts of the VI. Corps filled their pouches four times over, that is, fired two hundred rounds of ammunition per man. The name " Bloody Angle " is distinctively applied to the west angle. Of the fighting here, Brigadier-General L. A. Grant, of the VI. Corps, says : " It was not only a desperate struggle, but it was literally a hand-to-hand fight. Nothing but the piled-up logs or breastworks separated the combatants. Our men would reach over the logs and fire into the faces of the enemy, would stab over with their bayonets ; many were shot and stabbed through the crevices and holes between the logs. Men mounted the works, and with muskets rapidly handed them, kept up a continuous fire until they were shot down, when others would take their places and continue the deadly work. . . . Several times the rebels would show a white flag . . . and when our fire slackened jump over and surrender, and others were crowded down to fill their places. . . . I was at the angle next day. The sight was terrible ". All eye-witnesses record it as a fact that the dead were piled up several deep.

We now turn to events elsewhere, always keeping in mind the existence and predominating

THE BATTLE OF MAY 12

influence of this unvaried and unrelenting soldiers' battle.

At early dawn Grant sat in front of a dying camp fire awaiting news. The headquarters baggage was packed and ready to start.* Burnside's guns were heard, then musketry on Hancock's front, but nothing was visible, and it was only after an hour's suspense that the first galloper came up from Hancock. Grant's first thought was to urge Burnside forward. In reply to an order to push on with all possible vigour, Burnside sent word (6.15) that he had advanced two miles from his original lines. Later, at eight, Grant hearing that connection had been lost between the II. and IX. Corps, hastily pencilled another note to Burnside: "Push the enemy with all your might. That is the way to connect. We must not fail". The gist of these orders was iterated and reiterated in one dispatch after another, until afternoon.

Burnside's attack, as a matter of fact, opened before Hancock's. It was delivered due westward across country from Beverly's house. On the right Potter's division carried the left of the eastern lines, held by part of Wilcox's division, Hill's (Early's) Corps, but was driven out again by a counter-stroke. At a quarter past nine, in response

---

* General Edward Johnson was sent in to headquarters, and courteously received by Grant and Meade, both of whom knew him in the old army. When Johnson was present, Grant, out of consideration for his feelings, passed round the dispatches from Hancock instead of reading them aloud. Steuart, on the other hand, when brought to Hancock, lost his temper and refused to shake hands with his former comrade, after which Hancock left him to find his way to the rear on foot.

to Grant's urgent orders and Hancock's equally urgent messages from the Salient, Burnside attacked with Potter on the right, and Major-General Crittenden (Stevenson's successor) in the centre without success. Willcox on the left, feeling himself to be the extreme left of the whole army, consumed much time in refusing his exposed flank and arranging with the corps troops infantry (Marshall's provisional brigade) and reserve artillery to give it additional protection. He then moved forward, about 9.15, Potter having meantime reported that he had gained touch with the II. Corps. His objective point was a small salient, and he advanced to close rifle range through the pine woods. But Early's two divisions (Heth and Mahone) that had spent the night in the entrenchments around Block House Bridge, were now back in position to help the third (Wilcox's), and after a severe fight with most of Heth's and a part of Mahone's division, Willcox had to retire. For the rest of the day Burnside's line was engaged in heavy skirmishing, the right close up to the enemy, the left somewhat retired and the extreme left refused to protect Beverly's house and the bridge over the Ny.

The end of its *rôle* as part of the decisive attack is marked by Grant's orders of 3.15, to "keep your division commanders on the look out to take advantage of any weakening on your front".

Grant was disappointed with the result of Burnside's attack, but the opposition the IX. Corps had met was more considerable than headquarters knew at the time, and it occupied all

THE BATTLE OF MAY 12

except three or four brigades of Early's command all day.

On the other flank Warren had been ordered to be "in readiness", and soon after daylight opened a heavy artillery fire on Anderson's line on his front, following this up with the advance of his skirmishers. At 6 A.M. he was ordered to keep up as threatening an attitude as possible. "Wright must attack and you may have to. Be ready and do the best you can".

It was not long before the concentration of the VI. Corps on the Salient depleted the lines of that corps nearest to Warren; General Meade therefore ordered Warren at 7.30 to extend somewhat to his left towards Wright. The V. Corps had already taken over the old lines of the II. Corps as well as its own, but owing to its concentrated formation not having been abandoned Warren was still, after sending away a brigade to his left, able to use Cutler's, most of Griffin's, and a portion of Crawford's divisions in the open. At eight the order to attack came in definite terms: "Attack at once with all the force you can and be prepared to follow up any success with the rest of your force", but it did not find Warren in the best frame of mind for its simple and whole-hearted execution, for his engineer's eye had noted the "key points" on the left and the right of the enemy's line that were ready to enfilade him on both flanks.

At 9.15 and 9.30 Humphreys sent Warren two notes. The first was curt and precise—

"The order is peremptory that you attack at once with your whole force if necessary".

the second full of the kindly encouragement of the older and more experienced soldier—

"Dear Warren,
"Don't hesitate to attack with the bayonet. Meade has assumed the responsibility and will take the consequences.
"Your friend,
"A. A. H."

Already an hour and a quarter had elapsed since the original order, and the attack had not been made, though the skirmishing had become heavy and continuous. It is not perhaps unjust to Warren to attribute the delay to his habit of superintending everything himself. But he passed on the last peremptory orders to the subordinate generals, and the disposable forces of Griffin, Cutler, and Crawford* moved out of their works in lines of battle. Nothing came of Crawford's attack but a heavy skirmish. On his front was the deepest and most densely wooded part of the ravine which separated the opposing entrenchments. Matters were made worse by the overlapping of the left wing with Cutler's right.

Cutler assaulted on the wooded hill-side so often passed over by the Union troops on the 8th and 10th. About an hour after his attack, which was not simultaneous with Crawford's, opened, Warren called for a report as to the practicability of

* Of the troops immediately at the disposal of the corps commander the Maryland brigade was assigned to Crawford and the Heavy Artillery sent away to the VI. Corps.

THE BATTLE OF MAY 12

pressing the assault forward, and received the reply (10.45): "My brigade commanders report that they cannot carry the works; they are losing badly and I cannot get them up the hill".

Griffin's attack was delivered in good style, though without enthusiasm. Passing over the open ground of Spindler's, his two lines of battle arrived almost unharmed within one hundred and fifty yards of Anderson's line,* from which rapid fire was then opened, instantaneously and in full volume. The assailants were checked, and then gave back in some disorder, some finding cover in the lines whence they had come, others sidling away to the right into the ravine and there disappearing from view.

There were now, about eleven, the greater part of three divisions in this ravine. All were in considerable disorder. The attacks had not been simultaneous, and in several cases the lines had passed through each other, causing the greatest confusion. Above them, after a few random shells, the Confederate fire was silent for want of a target. A few skirmishers daringly crept forward to look into the ravine, and it is said found that there was something approaching a panic in the interior, and that the Union soldiers were firing up the hill-side at an imaginary enemy. Bratton, one of Anderson's brigadiers, states that so great was the noise of their firing that he thought the Federals were fighting each other.†

---

* At this moment only one brigade had been taken from Anderson's front to help Ewell.

General E. P. Alexander (*Military Memoirs of a Confederate*,

Meanwhile, Grant had with unfeigned regret come to the conclusion that Warren was "not as efficient as he had believed". At 10.40 he wrote to Meade: "If Warren fails to attack promptly, send Humphreys to command his corps, and relieve him". Meade concurred in this course, and Humphreys directed the operations of the V. Corps for the rest of the day.

Before this, about ten, Warren's dispatches had sufficiently indicated the likelihood of the V. Corps attack failing.

"May 12, 1864, 10.5 A.M.

"Commanding Officer V. Corps.

"The Major-General commanding infers from the tenor of your dispatches that in your judgment your attack will not be successful. Should it fail, make your dispositions to draw in your troops and send them as fast as possible to support General Wright and General Hancock.

"A. A. Humphreys,

"Major-General and Chief-of-Staff."

Meade then rode over to Hancock's front, leaving Humphreys at headquarters with instructions to "attend in my name to the shortening of the line and the sending of reinforcements to Wright and Hancock" (10.30). This was apparently sufficient answer to Grant's note a little later, for Humphreys says " the after

p. 524) accepts Bratton's theory as the explanation of Warren's misadventures, but it rests on no more than a single Confederate report and the absence of all details in the Union reports, which is certainly curious, but may or may not signify that the details have been suppressed. The V. Corps reports are far from satisfactory throughout the campaign, and at best this was not an incident to be dwelt upon with satisfaction.

movements of the V. Corps were made under verbal orders issued by me ".*

By that time it was certainly necessary to take strong measures. But Humphreys' tact and Warren's loyalty were equal to the strain imposed by the new relation, and gradually Cutler's and Griffin's divisions were got out of the ravine, reassembled, and sent off to take part in the fighting at the Salient, Cutler soon after noon, Griffin two hours afterwards. Crawford followed, and as evening came on there was nothing but an attenuated skirmish line in the whole of the II., V., and VI. Corps works.

Long before this the VI. Corps had been entirely involved in the fight at the Angle. Two of its divisions had moved up before 8 A.M., and the last (Ricketts') had drawn out of the trenches and joined the others about ten, Warren's (Griffin's) left brigade extending a thin skirmish line to occupy the right of the VI. Corps works. General Wright was wounded early in the day, but refused to leave the field. The corps was partly in rear of Hancock's right at the Apex, partly at the Bloody Angle, and after Ricketts' arrival somewhat to the south-west of it along the western face of the Salient.†

---

* Quoted by Badeau. Does not appear as an endorsement to the dispatch in the Official Records.

† The prolongation of the Union right at a tangent to the curve of Lee's line, shown in Sketch Map 14, was Wright's or Hancock's reply to a very serious counter-attack made by Rodes' division. There was severe fighting at this point, as both parties were "outside works" as well as at close rifle range.

The V. Corps reinforcement was intended, not as a reservoir for maintaining the defence of the captured works, but as a column of attack. So, however, General Wright did not regard it, and a little after 6 P.M., fighting being still severe, he abandoned the idea of an attack and informed Meade, who approved and ordered him to "rectify his lines and connect with Warren". At the same time word was sent to Burnside that he was to "strengthen his position so as to hold it against any attack of the enemy", and a few minutes later Grant suggested that he should swing back his left to the Ny and put his artillery beyond that river. And in fact, except for the fighting at the Angle and the Apex, which were the arena for the duels of successive brigades or regiments on each side, the evening of this day of slaughter was spent by both sides in rectifying alignments and redistributing forces on the accepted result of the battle, viz. the capture of the Salient and of a whole division of Lee's army. The losses of the Army of the Potomac and the IX. Corps are stated as 6020 killed and wounded and 800 missing. Two-fifths of this loss, about 2700, fell upon the II. Corps; then came in order the IX. Corps with some 1500 casualties, the VI. with 1350, and the V. with 1200. These figures (based on Humphreys') seem excessive in respect of the IX. Corps, and somewhat surprising for the V., and are offered only as an approximation. Lee's losses are stated by Humphreys at 4000 to 4500 killed and wounded, and 4000 prisoners. A margin of 2000 against the Confederates was

THE BATTLE OF MAY 12

undeniably satisfactory as the result of "attrition". According to Livermore's calculations, the total Confederate losses, 8th to 12th May, represent nearly 20 per cent. of their original effective force, as against the Union 12·5 per cent. Hitherto, at any rate, it may be admitted that criticisms on Grant's wastefulness of human life are to be regarded as based on mere aggregates instead of proportions and results, and as having its roots in the reaction and disappointment felt in the Union army at having no decisive tactical success to show in return for nearly 35,000 casualties.

The battle of May 12 is interesting from the tactical, and still more from the psychological, standpoint.

It was fought in accordance with the idea to which Upton's success on the 10th had given rise, viz. that the lines could be broken by a resolute and well-supported attack at the Salient. Considered as a conception of tactics the scheme of battle was not a manœuvre, but a modification of the existing tactical equilibrium. The object of this was to bring the greatest weight of the attack opposite the weakest point of the defence. The result of making such a breach would be far greater than that offered by any other form of attack, *e.g.* a manœuvre round either flank. The quick orderly retreat of Lee's army to the North Anna was the last thing desired by the Union generals. The result expected and desired from the forcing of a breach in Lee's centre was nothing less than the *flight* of Lee's broken army to the North Anna, with a sharp pursuit at its heels.

It should be observed, further, that the centre of gravity was once more shifted to the Union left and the Confederate right.* Grant, not having succeeded as he hoped in exploiting the dissemination of Lee's army on the 8th, or in using Burnside as an anvil on the 10th, now moved his four corps to their natural positions, Warren and Wright being ordered to hold their corps close to the enemy, and Hancock and Burnside to *attack* straight to their front.

Tactically the idea was to break the line of defence at a selected point, and by pressing forward through the gap to force the Confederates into a confused retreat. How far was this carried out?

Hancock's initial success was as complete as could be desired. But sufficient care had not been taken to ensure its being utilized. The conditions of Upton's attack were not reproduced. Upton had sufficient force to gain a foothold, and an entirely separate body (Mott) was told off to co-operate to make it good. If the idea of the superior leading was to repeat Upton's success, Barlow, or at most Barlow and Birney, should have been sent against the Apex at dawn on the 12th and the other divisions should have been held in hand and ready to follow. As it was the whole corps was let loose together, and, as Upton had found on the 10th, the so-called "reserve" vied

---

* Anderson's front had to be maintained intact because it was the pivot, not of a forward move of Lee's other corps, but of a swinging back of the whole line so as to face east.

THE BATTLE OF MAY 12

with the other lines in racing forward to the enemy's works. By 5 A.M., or thereabouts, Hancock had only one brigade (Webb's) intact and in hand. Barlow complained bitterly that the massing of troops, and, in particular, troops of the VI. Corps, behind him prevented him from re-forming, and if we can believe the evidence of the participants there were ere long twenty thousand Union soldiers and four thousand Confederate prisoners, as well as the guns, wagons, and teams of four or five batteries crowded into a few acres of rough ground.

There is no question that four thousand prisoners and twenty guns were a notable tactical gain, and that the II. Corps did not suffer a disproportionate loss in obtaining it. But that corps was as broken by its own success as it would have been by a heavier loss in killed and wounded, and we may well accept General Alexander's judgment as to the lesson of the attack on the Salient, viz. that there is a maximum limit to the force that can be advantageously used in any one locality and that a superfluity may paralyse all efforts. Of course the II. Corps was formed in great depth from perfectly justifiable reasons. The Salient might have been so strongly held as to necessitate an attack in form over the open. The mistake was in not maintaining the rear lines in a fit condition to manœuvre. The temptation to make sure of adequate support, so as to avoid a repetition of the fiasco of the 10th, was too strong to be resisted, and the ardour of the American volunteer was not sufficiently taken into account. It is noteworthy that Carroll, who had so distinguished himself in the Wilderness, was almost the first to reach the East Angle, though he was in the reserve line of the corps at the beginning of the advance.

Burnside's part in the original attack appears to have been to take advantage of the presumed absence of part of Early's corps on the Block House side, and for this and other reasons the IX. Corps was not as closely massed as it might have been. It was practically in one long line of battle without reserves, and the first local success of Potter's division could not be made good. Still, on the not unlikely supposition that the resistance would not be serious, it is easy to understand that this disposition would appear satisfactory.

The ease with which the mass that had carried out this brilliant and successful charge was borne back by the enemy's first slight counter-stroke affords a remarkable illustration of Ardant du Picq's aphorism that "a general or captain who employs every man he has to take a position may count upon seeing it recaptured by the resolute offensive return of a corporal's guard".

Through this short intermediate stage the original attack developed into a succession of murderous brigade duels at the Angle, and when this was realized the general plan of battle was modified accordingly.

First, the fighting was so severe at the point of contact that Grant was convinced that Lee's lines elsewhere had been denuded of their defenders. He therefore ordered Warren to attack, and

THE BATTLE OF MAY 12

reiterated that order more and more urgently until at last he sent Humphreys to take the effective command out of Warren's hands. Later, this impression was strongly confirmed by the passivity of the enemy during Warren's withdrawal.

Thus Grant, in spite of his reasoned idea that Lee would not fight again in the open, reverts to his own instinctive and unbridled offensive, and presumes that his opponent is as willing to attack, and as free to do so, as he is himself.

Lee, however, acted otherwise. No appreciable force was sent from Anderson's front, which was maintained at full strength as a pivot upon which if necessary to swing back the Confederate army, and in any case in order to keep the Federals from entering the Salient by the gorge. Lee also considered it necessary to leave an adequate force in front of Burnside. How then did he manage to keep up so desperate a fight in the centre?

The attempt to do so, at any rate, was imposed upon him by hard necessity. His alternatives were, success at this point and disaster at all points. It was of vital importance to keep the Federals at the Angle so fully occupied that they could advance no further that day, and the one way of doing this was by attacking again and again. If once the II. and VI. Corps organized a fresh and well-massed attack, the new works at the base of the Salient (see Sketch Map 15), at which Lee's artillerymen were labouring with feverish energy, must be overrun as the outer line had been, and nothing would then be left for the Confederates but a *sauve qui peut*. "To bring about the withdrawal, and the disaster that must ensue", was, Humphreys tells us, Meade's object in hammering at the Salient, and in the hope of compelling this the VI. and later the V. Corps were added to the corps that made the first assault. Yet, in spite of all, Lee's desperate holding attack of twenty hours' duration was successful. Under cover of these ceaseless counter-strokes the new strong line of defence was made ready in time. The problem is, then, not how to explain or to defend Lee's and Meade's pertinacity against the attacks of some later critics, but how to account for Lee's success and Meade's failure.

On neither side were the soldiers found wanting in heroism. It is a very remarkable and significant fact that neither Lee nor Hancock found it necessary during the day to engage personally in the front line.

On the Union side the crowd at the fighting point numbered in the end some 45,000 men. General Barlow says that, viewed from the rear, the troops at the Apex seemed in places to be forty deep.

The losses, distributed over the whole day, show the startlingly low average of 1 per cent. per hour, or between 18 and 20 per cent. in all—which would certainly not have sufficed to stop a charge of either the II. or the VI. Corps across open ground.

The positive results of the day's work, after the trophies and prisoners secured in the first rush had been removed into safe keeping, were practically *nil*.

THE BATTLE OF MAY 12

These five components of the "soldiers' battle"—bravery, numbers, physical and moral endurance, small losses and absence of results—if taken together as material facts governed by a material rule of cause and effect, are inexplicable. Taken as manifestations of moral, they can be examined and in a measure at least accounted for by comparison with the battles of the ancient world, which represent the moral of close-quarter fighting in its purest form.*

In ancient battles, as in this,† the fighting was entirely between the foremost ranks of the two opposing corps. The ranks in rear, whether five, ten, or twenty in number, had to wait until their comrades in front had been killed or wounded before they themselves engaged. Inactive spectators, and so the prey of every passing wave of exultation or fear, they had to watch the slow approach of danger and defeat (for the battle never

---

* The following analysis of the ancient battle is derived from *Études sur le Combat*, by Colonel Ardant du Picq, who was killed on the 15th of August, 1870, and after death became revealed as one of the great soldier-philosophers. From him, and, on the other side, from the so-called psycho-physiologists of a later generation, Le Bon and Ribot, descends the new military psychology of the present day. Details, and an application of its principles to the Anglo-Saxon temperament will be found in *War and the World's Life*, by Colonel F. N. Maude, C.B., to whom, personally, the author owes his first ideas as to the existence and potentialities of a science of "moral". The far-reaching influence of this intensely modern and scientific school of thought over French soldiers of all ranks is obvious from a glance at their military literature, whether it be the strategical works of General Bonnal, a character study such as Colonel Biottot's *Jeanne d'Arc*, or a regimental officer's contribution to a service periodical on such a subject as the indication of targets to an infantry firing line.

† Hancock's artillery, of course, only shelled the interior of the Salient, not the actual points of contact.

approached them if their front rank was victorious), and consequently, they gave way and fled before their turn came. It was thus that the decision was obtained in the open field between Greek and Greek—by the fighting of the front ranks and the moral impression produced thereby on those in rear. Such battles, however desperately fought, were rarely costly; often the losses of the victors could be numbered by dozens instead of thousands. It was when the decision had been obtained by the killing of the front ranks and the panic of the rest, and the beaten side suffered itself to be massacred almost unresistingly, that the numbers of the slain reached the appalling aggregates that we know. At Cannae (216 B.C.), which was more closely contested than most battles, the loss of the victors was about 6000, that of the vanquished 65,000 at least.

Here, at the Salient, however, there was no beaten side, for owing to the barrier between them the front ranks were unable to progress and the rear ranks thus escaped the steady moral pressure that at the "psychological moment"—on the approach of the victorious enemy with uplifted weapon—would have turned them into a flock of frightened sheep. There was consequently no massacre, in the ancient sense, and each side had only to endure the losses due to actual shooting and stabbing at close quarters. Equally, too, there was no decision, for the moral of neither side gave way. Desperate as it was, the fighting of the front ranks went for little, for the troops in waiting on either side were worked up to a high

THE BATTLE OF MAY 12

nervous tension, and, in the absence of the fatal suggestion of *sauve qui peut*, success delayed only made them the more eager.

A Greek battle, too, was of short duration, for two front-rank champions face to face could not fight for very long before one was disabled. Here, however, the breastwork made it difficult to kill at all.

We have, in short, an example of a hand-to-hand battle in the old manner, but without a decision and without a massacre of the beaten side. Had it not been for the four-foot entrenchment that as a rule separated the combatants, the Salient would have been the scene of a *caedes*, a slaughter, not of a prolonged battle, and this is the justification of Meade's persistent efforts to force the contest on to open ground and of Lee's to confine it to the breastwork.

The last point in the comparison is in the actual conduct of the fight by the superior leaders. The superiority of Roman tactics over Greek lay in this, that all the troops not actually fighting were kept as far as possible from the turmoil, in small closed bodies, instead of being sent forward at first in one large mass. As Ardant du Picq puts it, "R (resolution) is $>$ all the MV^2 in the world". Lee's exact knowledge of the tensile strength of his materials enabled him to use them to the best possible advantage in succession. Meade and Hancock, however, having in the first instance allowed their whole force to slip from their grasp, were unable to do more than extricate their brigades, reform them, and give them a respite, one or two at a time. Both commanders, we may assume, did their best in the circumstances as they found them, but the waste of force in the original assault had as one of its evil results that of compelling Hancock to undertake a hand-to-hand battle not with fresh, but with rallied, troops.

All this, however, does not account for the actual devotion of the actual combatants. The conditions at the points of contact were certainly such as no man could have endured for long. Those men who were naturally the bravest, or who naturally responded most easily to the impulse of the collective will, " paid in person ", as the French say, for acts of almost incredible heroism such as those mentioned by the general officer we have quoted. But the average soldiers fought and endured with a bravery unsurpassed even in this brave war. Sometimes they stood back to fire, and their bullets whipped the head logs* of the entrenchment "into basket stuff". Then, again, they would crawl up to the entrenchment and shoot and stab through the crevices. Whatever the method at any moment or any place, all fought their hardest. As they were spared the last intolerable trial of seeing the victor advancing upon them to begin the massacre, the instinct of "fighting it out", called into activity by the need of the race and made paramount over other instincts by the collective will of the mass, sufficed. It must

---

* The top of the solid breastwork of earth and logs was furnished with rough head cover, in the shape of stout logs, supported at intervals by billets of wood, sand-bags, etc. As an example of the intensity of the fire, it is usual to quote the celebrated tree, twenty inches in diameter, which was literally cut through by the bullets.

be remembered that in the old days the bravest fought in the front rank as a matter of course, and that to-day there is a process of elimination whereby a firing line eventually consists only of the men who intend to "fight it out". At the Salient, however, the heroes, the average volunteers, and the "coffee-boilers" of each brigade in turn bore the brunt of the action.

CHAPTER XIV

LATER OPERATIONS AROUND SPOTTSYLVANIA COURT HOUSE—THE RICHMOND RAID

AFTER the critical day of the 12th, with its partial successes, and more than partial expenditure of effort, headquarters were busied with sorting out the troops that had fought at the Salient, with connecting up the line from Warren's right to Burnside's left, not only with works but with roads also,* and, above all, with collecting information as to Lee's new position *in view of another battle*. With this object each corps was ordered to press up its skirmish line as near as possible without bringing on a battle. The rain continued to fall heavily at intervals, and the roads became more and more difficult.

The information obtained on Burnside's front was meagre, but pointed to no important change.

On the front of the II. Corps the battle-ground of the 12th was found to have been abandoned, and Lee's new line across the base of the old

---

* In all these operations before Spottsylvania, after the 8th/9th, the field telegraph was extensively employed to connect army, corps, division, and even brigade headquarters. It was used thenceforward in practically every position that the army occupied to the end of the war.

Salient, to maintain which he had expended so much effort and so many precious lives, was more or less accurately defined by the reconnaissances of Carroll's brigade, that energetic officer receiving a severe wound.* Amongst administrative measures of this day was the consolidation of Mott's unlucky division with Birney's.† It had lost heavily in various actions, and contained many men whose period of service was almost expired. But the true reason for its amalgamation was Hancock's own feeling that the division will soon "be of no service under its present commanders, who seem not to control their men". The resentful III. Corps was now represented only by Birney's division.

On Wright's front the enemy was reported to have disappeared. On Warren's the skirmishers were pressed close up to Anderson's lines, and there was some desultory fighting. Crawford reported ‡ that the lines opposite the V. Corps were still occupied, and this dispatch, after receiving endorsements from Warren and Meade, reached Grant, who penned thereon—

"I do not desire a battle brought on with the enemy in

* He was recommended, along with Upton (already provisionally promoted), Miles, Brooke, and other colonels commanding brigades, for the rank of brigadier-general.

† Mott resumed command of the brigade he had formerly had, and before many months had passed he rose once more to the divisional grade.

‡ This was known by the fact that all along the Confederate line the men fired their muskets into the air to clean them, a practice not unknown in Napoleon's day. The "thinking bayonets" doubtless thought, each man on his own account, that neither side could possibly be ignorant of the other's force and positions.

their position of yesterday, but want to press as close to them as possible to determine their position and strength. We must get by the right flank of the enemy for their next fight."

A little later Warren received a welcome note from Meade, expressing satisfaction with the close reconnaissances of the V. Corps. This must have comforted the recipient after his bitter experience of the day before, for he shortly afterwards writes to headquarters in his old vein, recommending a resumption of the former plan of attacking *viâ* Block House bridge.

"This was not desired", says Humphreys. It would probably have caused Lee's retirement to the North Anna; and Grant's intention was to fight his next battle—strictly in accordance with precedent—in such a way as to press Lee's inner flank, and to place his own back to the coast.

Towards five o'clock in the afternoon sufficient information had come in for the issue of a directive looking to a battle on the 14th—the sixth since May 4th.

Lee's position was known to be strongest at its left (Anderson) and centre (Ewell's new works), and probably weak and much extended on Early's (the east) front.*

---

* The new line across the base of the lost Salient " was a curiosity of fortification ", says Colonel Lyman, who visited it after the war. "The high parapet was not only traversed as often as every ten or twelve feet, but was enclosed in the rear, so that the line was divided into a series of square pens, with banks of earth heavily riveted with oak logs. From space to space was what looked like a camp chimney, an elevated post for sharpshooters, with a loophole in front. I never

General Warren was, for the third time, to have the advance. The V. Corps was to move after dark past Shelton's and Landron's, to a ford on the Ny, which it was to cross, and then, turning eastwards, to strike the Fredericksburg road, whence he was to move on Spottsylvania C.H., and to form up his corps for attack on Burnside's left, near the Beverly house. His artillery was to take what roads it could find further to the rear, and, to provide against mischance, Burnside was at the same time ordered to hold his reserve artillery at Warren's disposal.

In case the ford of the Ny, like so many other points on the maps in use, proved to be non-existent, the V. Corps was to pass close along the rear of the IX. after leaving Landron's. The order was for the V. Corps to attack at 4 A.M. directly down the road to the Court House. It was apparently given verbally in the course of an interview between Grant, Meade, Humphreys, and Warren, at headquarters.

General Wright's infantry and artillery were directed to follow those of the V. Corps on the same routes. " From Beverly's a guide will lead you to the Massaponax Church Road over an open country. Upon this road your attack is to be made ".*

Hancock and Burnside were to be in readiness

saw any like them". The strength of these works against enfilade was doubtless due to the menace of the V. Corps artillery, which had, as early as the 9th, caused Gordon's division some inconvenience in the old retrenchment.

* "I will send you my map to look at. Please return it", Humphreys' message concluded.

to attack at four, but they were not to do so until ordered.

Once more, therefore, we have a night march as a preliminary to serious fighting. Thwarted before by the heat of an unendurable summer night on a good but dusty road, Warren was now to be confronted with the difficulties of bad wood roads and rough open ground, upon which rain had fallen for forty-eight hours and was still falling. Moreover, the order to move seems to have, in a measure, taken the corps by surprise, for wagons were coming and going upon the road that the artillery was to take.

The result of all these unfavourable conditions may be guessed.

"The night set in dark and rainy. Every precaution was taken by General Warren to mark out the line of his march; men were posted at short intervals and fires built along the line, but the rain and heavy mist extinguished them. The mud was deep over a large part of the route; the darkness intense, so that literally you could not see your hand held before your face. . . . In spite of all the care taken to prevent it, men lost their way and lay down exhausted. . . . At six the head of General Warren's column arrived at the point where they were to form for attack, but the column was broken and scattered and it was not practicable to get the command in condition for offensive operations that day."—(Humphreys.)

The VI. Corps started at 3 A.M. and followed the V. through the miry roads. After crossing the Ny near Landron's it was led to a covered rendezvous position on the Massaponax Church Road. Thence Upton's brigade (now but 800 strong) was sent forward to occupy the high open ground at Gayle's.* Warren, or rather Griffin, at the head of Warren's column, had already sent a regiment to seize this point. Hostile cavalry had been reported on the Massaponax Road on the evening of the 13th, and these now opened a brisk skirmish with Upton, who, however, made good his footing on the hill. A more serious attack began about 4.30 in the afternoon. Parts of Early's (Hill's) corps which, when Anderson reported the evacuation of the V. Corps lines on the Brock Road, had been brought over from the Block House side in the early afternoon, attacked the Gayle hill in some force. Upton was soon driven off, but Wright prepared at once to retake the lost hill, and cannonaded it from the farther (left) bank of the Ny. Meade ordered Warren to aid him, and the response was prompt and efficient. By the time Wright's men reached the hill they found Ayres's brigade of the V. Corps in possession (about 7 P.M.). Both Grant and Meade desired particularly to efface the impression of past censures from Warren's mind, and Meade wrote, "Orders sent to Wright to relieve Ayres. I thank you and Ayres for taking the hill; it was handsomely done".

Wright was still somewhat uneasy at his position beyond the Ny. He brought across Russell's and Ricketts's divisions to the hill and had Neill's (Getty's) on his left flank east of Anderson's, but recommended that the whole corps should be withdrawn. Instead, he was ordered to make roads, not only to his rear, but towards Warren at Beverly's.

* This is the "Gayle's" usually marked on the maps. It is also called Jett's, Myers', and Bleak Hill.

The Union army was now posted (in order, from right to left, Hancock, Burnside, Warren, Wright) in one connected line of entrenchments from the Salient to Gayle's. On the other side Anderson's skirmishers entered the Brock Road works, abandoned by Warren, shortly after noon, but Field's division was not brought over to the Court House until late in the day, and Kershaw's only on the morning of the 15th. It is evident, therefore, that luck was against the Union army, for had Warren and Wright had good weather they would almost certainly have carried the lines in their front without difficulty. Still, the operation was one which was planned and begun in the worst conditions of weather, and even if Warren was in position, the chances were greatly against Wright's having reached the Massaponax Church Road in time to co-operate. Grant would doubtless have liked to repeat on the 14th the success of the 12th, but it is probable that he was not greatly disappointed. His whole army, after all, managed to change its position unmolested, and to carry to its logical conclusion the shift of the centre of gravity already foreshadowed on the 11th. A further development of the same idea was seen on the morning of the 15th, when Hancock took Barlow's and Gibbon's divisions to a position in rear of the left centre of the army at Anderson's house.

On the ground so hotly contested three days before only Birney's division remained, and reconnoitring parties of the enemy actually recovered some artillery vehicles left in the old Salient, just as they had removed Griffin's two guns from the

Orange Turnpike after the departure of the Army of the Potomac from the Wilderness. Equally in accordance with the precedent of May 7, an ambulance train went out with a strong escort to look for wounded men on the positions occupied from the 8th to the 13th. These minor incidents signify little, but may be allowed as illustrations of the new "forward" spirit in the Army of the Potomac under Grant's direction. Only in the intervals of preparation for a battle or a fresh advance was there time to attend to the *débris* on the track passed over.

During all this time the trains, and Ferrero's division with them, had remained in the area Chancellorsville – Tabernacle Church – Aldrich's unmolested. The bridge at Fredericksburg being completed, the Belle Plain line of supply was definitely taken up on the 14th. On the 15th, the trains, hospitals, and artillery reserve were brought eastward to the neighbourhood of Fredericksburg. Thence the Fredericksburg – Spottsylvania road was, of course, the principal route to the front.

On the 15th, on the alarm of an attack on Birney and Burnside,* Warren and Wright were ordered to be ready to attack straight to their front, and Hancock's two divisions in support to be ready to move at a moment's warning. The troops spent three hours under arms, and were then allowed to break off, as nothing happened in the threatened

---

* Mott's men, now under Birney's command, came in for some artillery fire, and evidently endured it ill, for we find Hancock telling Birney that the colonels of regiments that break under a little shelling ought to be mustered out of the service.

quarter. In this time Warren had replied to the order to attack to his own front with a suggestion that it would be better for the V. Corps to reinforce Burnside if attacked, and so fight the enemy outside entrenchments. He received in return the following curt order:—

"Dispatch containing suggestions received. Your orders will be sent you when Burnside is attacked. Meanwhile they are unchanged."

The suggestion was conscientious and unselfish, like Warren's every act, but it infringed on the province of the supreme command, which had (unknown of course to the commander of the V. Corps) provided itself with Hancock's two divisions as a reserve to act, if necessary, in the sense indicated by Warren's far-ranging mind.

Later in the day, Burnside was directed to shorten his line and to throw back the right towards the Ny, in preparation for the removal of Birney to join the rest of the II. Corps at Anderson's.

The Confederate cavalry (Chambliss's brigade) was very active, in small bodies, on the left rear of the Union army towards Fredericksburg, but effected little. While Sheridan, for reasons to be told shortly, was many scores of miles away, Lee's cavalry was close at hand and giving ceaseless trouble to the small force of cavalry left with the Army of the Potomac after Sheridan's departure.

There was nothing of importance on the 15th at Gayle's. General Wright, like Warren, had his corps under arms for some hours under orders to advance if Burnside were attacked.

On the 16th, the available cavalry was freely used in scouting and obtaining information as to the country to the south-east. A reconnaissance ordered on the front of the V. and VI. Corps was given up when the Lieut.-General found that the skirmishers were already close up to the enemy. Burnside's lines were rectified and somewhat shortened, though Birney was not yet withdrawn. On this day the artillery was reduced by one-third, each six-gun battery sending two guns to Belle Plain. At the same time, the divisional artillery was discontinued, and division commanders were told to apply to the corps chief of artillery when guns were required for their divisions. "The 16th", writes an officer, "was a day that in comparison might be called quiet".

On the 17th there was more activity, though not more fighting, than on the two preceding days.

At this time appeared the first reinforcements that the army had received since crossing the Rapidan. They were not, however, more than 12,000 men in all, and the casualties had been, irrespective of sick and of time-expired men, over 32,000 in a fortnight. If we add 10,000 for the latter, and deduct 13,000 sabres absent with Sheridan, we obtain as a very rough estimate of Grant's disposable force on the 17th—$120,000 - 55,000 + 12,000 = 77,000$. Lee, on the other hand, had as yet received no reinforcements, and had lost perhaps 25,000 men. Allowing for sick, and for the absence of some at least of Stuart's cavalry, his effectives cannot have greatly exceeded 45,000, if indeed they reached that figure. These are very round numbers, but may serve as such, and as a test of the efficacy of "attrition".

The Union army had therefore a five-to-three numerical superiority still, and Grant was already considering a further manœuvre to the southward, with the now usual object of interposing between Lee and the places and armies on the James, so as to compel him to fight without entrenching.

But fighting was not yet over in front of Spottsylvania.

On the 16th, Grant wrote to Halleck as follows :—

"The roads have now become so impassable that ambulances with wounded men can no longer run between here and Fredericksburg. All offensive operations must necessarily cease till we can have twenty-four hours of dry weather. The army is in the best of spirits. . . . The promptness with which you have forwarded reinforcements will contribute greatly to diminishing our mortality list and ensuring a complete victory. . . . *The elements alone have suspended hostilities, and it is in no manner due to weakness or exhaustion on our part.*"

This is clearly a restatement of Grant's purpose to "fight it out on this line if it takes all summer".

The new plan was an attack by the left (Wright and Hancock) against the enemy's right, which was now extended to the Po, immediately below Snell's Bridge. Warren's line was modified accordingly, the right being swung back to cover the Fredericksburg Road. Burnside and Birney were to be ready to move from right to left, leaving only pickets in their lines. But a reconnaissance showed that the ground south-west of the Gayle house, where it was intended to make the attack, was dense "chapparal", and the scheme was abandoned in favour of the one proposed by Humphreys and Wright.

This was for a surprise attack on the new works at the base of the Salient. It was hoped that in extending his right Lee might have weakened his left, this idea being reinforced perhaps by the demonstrativeness of detachments of Ewell's corps on the 16th and 17th, and the presence of Confederate cavalry posts on the lower Po and the Mattapony, which latter the enterprising Hammond and other cavalry officers developed by extended reconnaissances.*

The fate of this venture can be described in a few words. Parts of three corps, the VI., II., and IX., attacked the enemy's new line punctually at 4 A.M. on the 18th. Warren kept up a brisk artillery fire to aid them.

"But the enemy was on the alert. . . . As the troops approached they were met with a heavy musketry and artillery fire . . . [they] pressed forward to the slashing and the abatis and made several gallant attempts to carry the enemy's lines, but without success.

"Upon its being reported to General Meade that there was but little probability of the enemy's lines being carried, he directed the attack to be discontinued, and the troops were accordingly withdrawn."—(Humphreys.)

The VI. Corps returned to the old lines near Gayle's, the II.—which had now been reinforced

* General Torbert returned to the army about this time, and was assigned to command all the cavalry that Sheridan had not taken with him on the 9th.

from Belle Plain by Tyler's command (temporarily called 4th Division, II. Corps) of heavy artillery serving as infantry—to its rendezvous formation east of the Ny. Moreover the IX. Corps was brought over to the extreme left flank, near Quesenberry's house. All these movements were carried out on the night of the 18th/19th May, and were preparatory to a new far-ranging manœuvre which was to bring the contending armies to the North Anna.

But the manœuvre referred to was delayed for two days by a sudden advance of the enemy's left wing. It seems doubtful if this advance was intended as a raid on the Union trains, or as a reconnaissance to ascertain whether the Union army was on the move to the south-east, but whichever it was Lee had the last word in the battles round Spottsylvania as he had had the last word in the Wilderness at nightfall on the 6th.

This last word was spoken with emphasis.

The Union troops were now arranged in a long connected line from the Ny to the Po, in order from right to left, Warren. Wright, Burnside. In rear of Wright was Hancock's corps in mass. Grant's, Meade's, and Hancock's headquarters were near the Anderson house. Beyond Warren's right, north of the Ny, the line was continued, so as to cover the Fredericksburg Road, by Kitching's brigade (artillery reserve, now attached to the V. Corps) and Tyler's division (II. Corps).

Nearly all these troops were heavy artillery

regiments serving as infantry, and the army therefore called this day's action the "battle of the Heavies". Some of Tyler's had been under fire for the first time in the abortive attack of May 18. The rest had never fired a shot in anger. Kitching's men, however, who had taken their full share in the battle on the Plank Road on May 6, may be accounted veterans.

All along the front there was quiet until late in the afternoon, the Union soldiers eagerly taking this their first opportunity of bathing, mending clothes, and writing letters, since crossing the Rapidan, for the "quiet day", so-called, of the 16th had been employed in energetic trench work. Suddenly about five o'clock heavy firing broke out to the north-west, and the II. Corps at Anderson's hurriedly stood to arms. Presently they were marched off towards the Fredericksburg Road without even packing up their scanty personal belongings.* Soon they met a mob of demoralized train-drivers and stampeded mules.

General Ewell had moved out of his lines with two divisions (Ramseur's and Gordon's), Kershaw's division of Anderson's corps taking over the guard of his trenches in his absence. Hill's corps, still under Early, was held ready to follow if required. The route taken by Ewell was circuitous and, it is said, impracticable for artillery.

Near the Harris house, about 5.30, he fell upon

* They appear to have recompensed themselves in their usual light-hearted manner by sweeping through the abandoned lines of a heavy artillery regiment and gathering up the new knapsacks and haversacks there deposited.

Tyler and Kitching, but they had already prepared to meet him and offered a steady resistance. Meade promptly ordered up divisions from Warren's and Hancock's corps. The whole line was infected with the alarm, and Wright sent Russell's division over to Warren. A time-expired regiment (the 1st Maryland) came back from Fredericksburg of its own accord to join in the fight, and after a sharp engagement, which lasted until 9 P.M., Ewell withdrew with a loss of at least nine hundred men. Considered as a reconnaissance, his adventure produced satisfactory evidence that the bulk of the Union army was still on the ground. Considered as an attempt to impair the moral of the Federals, it was an entire failure. Even the twenty-five wagons captured in the first rush near the Harris house were retaken by the Union troops, and the conduct of the raw regiments of Tyler's command was generally admitted to have been exemplary.

Russell's division of the VI. Corps was sent over the Ny during the night, and relieved the troops of the V. and II. Corps that had been engaged. Further to the Union right, on the Orange Plank Road near Salem Church, a Confederate cavalry force attacked about the same time as Ewell, but it was repulsed with little difficulty by two Union cavalry regiments.*

The losses of the Union army in these last

---

* Ferrero's division was formed up in support, and Badeau has a spirited account of the gallantry of the negro troops. But, as Humphreys tersely remarks, "the coloured division had no casualty of any kind, handled nobody, severely or otherwise ; in fact were not engaged". The two veteran white cavalry regiments were temporarily under Ferrero's orders.

THE RICHMOND RAID

affairs of the 18th and 19th were, according to Humphreys, 2023 killed and wounded. The battles around Spottsylvania were now at an end. The total losses of the Union forces on this ground are given as 17,723, exclusive of the slightly wounded who were retained in the ambulances instead of being sent to the rear. Hitherto, in round numbers, the Federals had lost 35,000 men, and the Confederates about 26,000.

During these two weeks in which the army lay before Spottsylvania, Sheridan's cavalry had been engaged in what is known as the "Richmond Raid". His orders, issued at 10 P.M. on May 8, must be considered in connection with the general concentration of both armies, at that date, in the cramped manœuvre area between the Po and the Ny. Quite apart from the personal differences between Meade and Sheridan, which rendered their separation for a time advisable, the cavalry could neither find charging room on the front nor manœuvring room on the flanks, and nothing could please Grant better than that Sheridan should fulfil his boast of drawing Stuart after him, and "whipping him too". It is to be observed that Sheridan's task, according to his orders, was to "proceed against the enemy's cavalry". The cavalry leader's idea was, however, to move towards Richmond in order that the enemy's cavalry should proceed against him—a manœuvre fundamentally the same as that which the Army of the Potomac itself carried out on May 21. Sheridan, as we know, proposed to fight cavalry with cavalry, and infantry with infantry, in this close Virginia country, and, vicious as such a proceeding was at times when the main army was manœuvring, it was undeniably the correct proceeding now that the necessity for co-operation no longer existed. Grant's view of the matter seems to have been that, as Sheridan could not fight in the Spottsylvania area, he should be given every opportunity of fighting elsewhere. Neither his own views nor the tenor of his orders, it should be observed, assigned the destruction of enemy's property, even of the railways connecting Lee with Richmond and Gordonsville, as an object of the expedition. The Union cavalry made for the North Anna region, to draw Stuart thither by threatening his one remaining forage area, to supplement the "half rations for one day"* with which it started, and the troopers employed, so to speak, their spare time in breaking up railways and depôts.

The raid need not be described in detail. Brilliant as it was, it was its results, and not its incidents, that affected the general course of the campaign. On the 9th, having formed his corps

* Before crossing the Rapidan, Army orders had provided for five days' forage to be taken with the troops. These rations were expended between the 4th and 8th of May, but the general trains of the army near Piney Branch Church were at hand and should have been called upon to make good the deficiency. The neglect of this precaution must be imputed to the Army staff, which ordered Sheridan to move "with his ambulances and such supply trains as were filled". It must be remembered that relations were strained after the quarrel in the morning of the 8th, and that the tendency of generals in all countries and at all times, under such circumstances, has been to obey the strict letter of their orders. (Compare the German I. Army on the 4th, 5th, and 6th of August, 1870.)

THE RICHMOND RAID

in one column thirteen miles long—stung by his experience on the night of the 7th, he refused to put his trust in the co-operation of many columns —Sheridan started. From Aldrich's he passed to the Telegraph Road, and thence, at the walk, to the North Anna at Anderson's Bridge (see Sketch Map 16 and Map III.). The rear of the column (Davies's brigade) was smartly engaged with the enemy's cavalry, as Sheridan expected, and at night the head (Merritt's division) was across the North Anna. On the 10th the fighting on the rear of the column involved both Gregg and Wilson, while Merritt at Beaver Dam put the torch to an enormous quantity of stores and rations destined for Lee's army. Before night the whole corps was safely between the Annas, heading south-east and collecting forage *en route*, and Stuart, on the other side, was "urging every horse to the death" to pass from the rear to the front of the Federals. On the night of the 10th/11th, Davies was sent to break the railroad at Ashland Station. On the 11th Stuart, though in these rapid movements he had never succeeded in gathering his corps as a unit for battle, stood to fight with the fraction at hand at Yellow Tavern, and was beaten. More serious than the momentary rout of a brigade or two of Confederate cavalry was the death of Stuart himself, the greatest cavalry leader of the South, in the action. The victor rode on to Richmond, passed the outer defences of that city in the dark (May 11/12), and coolly remained amidst the fortifications a whole day, to show the militiamen of Richmond that he was not afraid. Then, after some irregular fighting with the various bodies of the enemy all around him, he recrossed the Chickahominy. "For the balance of the day", he says in his report, "we collected our wounded, buried our dead, grazed our horses, and read the Richmond papers, two small newsboys having with commendable enterprise entered our lines and sold to the officers and men". There was no further fighting, and in accordance with his orders, Sheridan took the corps to Haxall's Landing on the James, when General Butler resupplied him with forage and rations. After three days' rest, the return journey was begun. Sheridan was unaware of the exact position of the Army of the Potomac and knew that reinforcements for Lee were passing up the Fredericksburg Railroad. He therefore crossed to the left bank of the Pamunkey—sending to Fortress Monroe for a bridging train for the purpose—and proceeded leisurely to Aylett's on the Mattapony. His losses aggregated only three hundred men and about the same number of horses.

It is often said that the results of this raid were insignificant, on no better ground than that the broken railroads were easily restored. It may be well, therefore, to repeat what has been said above, viz. that the "raid" was a successful manœuvre to bring about a cavalry duel, that the cavalry duel resulted in the defeat of the enemy's cavalry and, by the fortune of war, in the death of his greatest cavalry leader, and that Richmond was terrorized by the presence of the enemy at its gates and humiliated by his open defiance of the defenders. All this was achieved at the cost of less than three per cent. of casualties in men and horses.

On one point, already alluded to, this brilliant operation is open to adverse criticism. The necessity of the detour caused by the march to Haxall's Landing, which was the consequence of starting with inadequate forage,* kept Sheridan away from the Army of the Potomac for a full fortnight after his task was thus effectively completed, and left the enemy's cavalry free to return to the scene of the main struggle, where they would be opposed only by the weak and miscellaneous force of mounted troops under Torbert.

More important still was the fact that for want of forage the success of Yellow Tavern was not effectively followed up by a relentless pursuit of the scattered bodies of Confederate cavalry. Thus the latter had time to recover its nerve after the stunning blow of Stuart's death, and the new commander, Hampton, was able to draw

---

* In accordance with the Army order, only those wagons were taken which happened to be full at the moment of starting. The difficulties of rationing and foraging independent cavalry masses has received a good deal of attention in Europe. It is recognized that for cavalry to search the countryside for food and forage is often, if not almost always, a waste of precious time, and that fast-moving supply trains should accompany the troops. Bernhardi's *Cavalry in Future Wars* (English translation, p. 170) says: "The cavalry trains must be organized in such a manner that they will be able to march at least as fast as the cavalry itself, and be adequate in number to carry from five to six days' corn. Only when this demand has been complied with will it be possible to count on the attainment of strategical independence".

together his whole corps and to fit it once again to challenge the superiority of the Union cavalry, with results that presently appeared in the hard-fought actions of Hawes's Shop and Trevilian's Station.

CHAPTER XV

THE MANŒUVRE OF MAY 21

ONE tactical lesson of all these battles was that attacking entrenchments was a matter not of principles but of particular cases, that, in fact, light works could be stormed and heavy ones could not. Lee's shortened lines from Spindler's, by Harrison's to the lower Po, were of the latter class and had, in addition, excellent interior communications.

Critics have suggested both here and in the Wilderness that Grant should have merely prolonged the line leftwards on the basis of the existing situation, but this fails to take account of the moral of the army. On new ground and under new conditions it would respond to resolute leading, but another display of useless devotion on the ground fought over for so long was not to be expected. Every enlisted man in the army knew the strength of Lee's works round the Court House. The antidote for unprofitable assaults on entrenchments was a further movement southward, and this Grant, in spite of bad news from the Valley and the James (see Chap. XVII.), was prepared to undertake.

The stride forward was necessarily somewhat long. There was nothing to be expected from fighting in the marshy confluences of the Mattapony branches; the open country required to give full scope for the material superiority of the Union army would have to be sought beyond that river. Nor was this a disadvantage; the more time Lee had to spend in marching to the battle-ground the less time he would have to entrench. It will be remembered that the march to Spottsylvania on the 7th/8th was made chiefly for the purpose of assembling the army preparatory to moving towards Chilesburg (Chap. XI.). The Confederate centre of gravity having thereafter shifted eastward, the new line of operations towards the North Anna was correspondingly brought east of the line at first intended.

As regards direction, Lee's right flank is still the point aimed at. But as regards the employment of force, a new idea emerges. Meade's famous instructions, "Wherever Lee goes, there will you go too", are now modified, and the Army of the Potomac is to act so that wherever it goes, Lee is compelled to follow. There was even a hope of Lee's taking the offensive of his own free will, revived by his aggressive movement on the 19th, which, though partial, affected not less than two-thirds of his army.

Grant hoped to strengthen this idea in his opponent's mind, and thus to bring about a battle of quite another character to the passive defence of heavy earthworks to which Lee seemed to have resigned himself. by offering him a substantial

MANŒUVRE OF MAY 21

and attractive target. On the 18th he had written a directive to the following effect—

"Before daylight to-morrow morning I propose to draw Hancock and Burnside from the positions they now hold, and put Burnside on the left of Wright. Wright and Burnside should then force their way up as close to the enemy as they can get without a general engagement, or with a general engagement if the enemy will come out of the works, and entrench. Hancock should take up a position as if in support of the two left corps. To-morrow night at twelve or one o'clock he will be moved south-east with all his force and as much cavalry as can be given him, to get as far towards Richmond on the line of the Fredericksburg railroad as he can make, fighting the enemy in whatever force he may find him. If the enemy make a general move to meet this, they will be followed by the other three corps . . . and attacked if possible before time is given to entrench. Suitable directions will be given at once for all trains and surplus artillery * to conform to this movement."

A brief circular was issued to the various corps the same night, dealing with the immediate movements, and the trains were ordered to " this side of the Fredericksburg Road ". They were in park about the Harris house, having moved down from the vicinity of Tabernacle Church, when attacked by Ewell as narrated above. For Halleck's information the project—very summarily described as a flank movement to Bowling Green and Milford Station—was wired to Washington, coupled with a request to " stir up the navy " to secure Port Royal as a depôt (centre of operations). On the 20th, therefore, gunboats examined and took charge of the river as far up as Fredericksburg.

* The moribund Reserve Artillery of the army.

330 CAMPAIGNS OF 1864 AND 1865

Hancock was warned a little after midday on the 20th that the move interrupted by Ewell's attack would be resumed that night.*

This plan, even more than that of crushing Lee against Burnside on the 9th (see p. 241), is conceived in the Napoleonic spirit. The latter was an improvisation, and its designer had to work from a not very favourable situation already existing. This time, however, the Union commander was able to begin from zero with a prearranged scheme.

Hancock would have twenty miles to march in addition to the space occupied by his marching column, say twelve miles. By dawn on the 21st he would almost have reached Guinea's station, and towards the end of the afternoon his whole corps would have reached Milford (four hours' march *plus* four hours' time-length of the column, with four hours more in hand for halts and emergencies). It was presumed that Lee, if he intended to fall upon Hancock, would move promptly on missing the II. Corps from the Spottsylvania lines, and hearing of its position on the Richmond and Fredericksburg railroad from his cavalry. Six hours' marching, allowing for the time necessary for the issue of orders, and that for his columns to defile (one column on each of the two available

* Hancock informed headquarters that he should destroy Guinea's and Downer's bridges as he passed, and was at once informed that they would be needed for Warren's corps. The commander of the II. Corps then answered, " When I sent my despatch I was under the impression that my right flank would be uncovered. I did not know of General Warren's movement ". This would seem to indicate that he was not sufficiently made acquainted with the *rôle* his corps was to play.

MANŒUVRE OF MAY 21

roads), would bring him into action with the heads of one or two corps at or near Milford by 3 P.M.

There, or wherever he was met, Hancock was to attack him. The intelligent private, as represented by Wilkeson, said of this move to the North Anna, "Once behind entrenchments the II. Corps can whip Lee's army", but he was at fault. Nothing was further from Grant's and Meade's minds than that Hancock should halt and entrench. If the II. Corps passively went into camp, and Lee chose to ignore its existence, the result would have been merely that the Union army was reduced in strength by over twenty thousand bayonets.

The rest of the Union army, which was to follow up the enemy if he turned against Hancock and to act as hammer to the II. Corps' anvil, would be able to start about 10 A.M., Lee's intention having declared itself, and the heads of its columns, passing over the bridges that Hancock had wished to destroy, would strike the flank or rear of Lee's marching column as it crossed the Telegraph Road. The V. Corps, which was to be the head of the main body, would have four to five hours' marching, *plus* its own time-length of about four hours to make good, and would reach Mitchell's Store at three, the last regiment closing up on the head not later than seven. Burnside was to follow Warren, and Wright was to act as rearguard, holding a new short line of works on the Ny (Sketch Map 15), and then to join Hancock by a night march. If this programme were fulfilled, there was no need to fear that Lee would build impregnable entrenchments in time. The early morning of the 22nd would witness the opening of the encounter battle of which Grant had so often dreamed.

Supposing, however, that Lee acted otherwise, and merely extended his right to meet the new situation, the manœuvre would be a repetition of that of May 4/5, and Warren and Hancock would be swung round his right flank, followed by Burnside. The Union manœuvre would take the same character should Lee attack Wright and Burnside on the Ny. Orders in this sense, based on observation of affairs at Spottsylvania and on reports received from Hancock and Warren, could be issued in the early part of the evening of the 21st.

The least favourable supposition was that Lee would fall back at once to the North Anna, at the mere threat of Hancock's advance. In this case the only chance of an encounter battle was dependent upon whether Warren could catch up with the rear of one of Lee's columns and bring it to action. Hancock would be too far away to assist, but Wright could probably take the direct route through the Court House and over Snell's Bridge to join Warren and Burnside on the Telegraph Road.

At best, then, the manœuvre promised a battle in the open field on the 22nd, at worst a long forward stride to the North Anna, and "On to Richmond" was, short of a great victory, the best way of heartening the much-tried soldiers of the Army of the Potomac.

Hancock asked for and obtained permission to start at 11 P.M. in order to pass the enemy's signal station in the dark. But the time thus gained was lost by the cavalry, which was much scattered, and took a long time to collect. Torbert preceded the infantry, reconnoitring the front and watching the side roads, and the column arrived at Guinea's Station about daylight, pushing out thence on the Bowling Green road.

A slight cavalry skirmish took place at Guinea's, and Lee was at once informed. At 8.40 A.M., 21st, the Confederate general telegraphed to the Government—

"The enemy is apparently again changing his base. Three gunboats came up to Port Royal two days since. This morning an infantry force appeared at Guinea's. His cavalry advance at Downer's Bridge. . . . He is apparently placing the Mattapony between us and will probably open communication with Port Royal. I am extending on the Telegraph Road and will regulate my movements by the information . . . of his route. I fear [it] will secure him from attack till he crosses Pamunkey."

If Lee carried out these intentions, the operations would obviously not take the form that Grant most desired, and in view of the aggressive intention Lee is known to have possessed at this phase of the campaign, we can discuss Grant's scheme for taking advantage of them at once, and without reference to what actually happened.

The essential feature was that Lee should be offered a favourable target, upon which he would move during the 21st, as soon as he was satisfied that the Union army had no intention of fighting again at Spottsylvania. When Lee turned upon Hancock, the latter was to become an anvil for the blow of the other three corps.

Now, an anvil must be so placed as to be underneath, not to one side of the object to be hammered. To place himself underneath the enemy, Hancock had a night and a morning of liberty. In this time he could without difficulty reach the level of Mitchell's Store by way of Stannard's Mill or Guinea's Bridge, preferably the latter. Here he would indeed have been "twenty miles on the road to Richmond", and in all probability Lee would have turned upon him in order to clear that road. If Lee instead of doing so stood still, and the manœuvre became simply a turning movement, the evening of May 21 would have found it well advanced instead of scarcely begun. The least favourable case, that of Lee's direct and unmolested retirement, would have been wholly out of the question.

On the other hand, the risk to the II. Corps would of course have been greater, as it would come much closer within striking radius of the army at Spottsylvania, and make a mere temptation to attack it a military necessity. General Humphreys, therefore, in suggesting this movement on Mitchell's Store as the solution of the problem, suggests also that Warren should go with Hancock (*Virginia Campaign*, p. 127).

Why then did Grant, resolute as he was, choose a course that had less risks and less chance of success—a half-measure?

It would seem as if his first care was to clear

the ground around Bowling Green and Milford. As we know, he had already decided to make Port Royal his new centre of operations, a step rendered necessary by the mere fact that the army was moving to its left, but up to the 21st, except that gunboats had ascended the Rappahannock, there were no preparations for the change of line, and the enemy's cavalry were in possession of the new *route de l'armée*, as Napoleon called it, the Port Royal-Bowling Green road. Assume this to be cleared, and Hancock boldly advancing west or south-west to find the enemy's infantry. If checked he could safely fall back along the new line of operations and perhaps draw Lee, once contact had been gained, some miles to the eastward, thereby facilitating the hammer blow of the other three corps on his flank and rear.

The first of these advantages belonged rather to the general, the latter to the special, problem before the Union generals. The general problem was concerned chiefly with the direction in which the Union army was to attack the enemy, the special problem with the manner in which that attack was to be conducted. Rightly or wrongly, the *certainty* of solving the special problem is surrendered in the interests of the general. Instead of compelling Lee to attack Hancock and taking the risks of a cross-country movement, they invited or tempted him to do so and secured a new line of operations in the meantime.

So much for Hancock's move. The action of the other three corps is summarized in an order to Warren (7.30 A.M., May 21) to be ready to "follow Hancock or to follow the enemy if he turn upon Hancock".

The Telegraph Road from Fredericksburg to Richmond crossed the Po at Stannard's Mill, a very few miles below the Union left. The next important crossing was that of Guinea's Bridge, after which came Downer's, Haw's, and Milford Road Bridge, all on the single polysyllabic river formed by the junction of the Mat, the Ta, the Po, and the Ny. These were likely to be available in proportion as the military situation altered at Spottsylvania. Stannard's or Guinea's would be the point of passage for the vanguard of the main body. The choice between them, as both ultimately led to the same point (Madison's Store), would depend upon the situation in the forenoon of the 21st.

Lee would know that Hancock was unsupported as soon as he heard that the rear of the Union column was clear of Guinea's, or about 9 A.M. The corresponding movement of the Army of Northern Virginia (whatever this might be) could be begun about ten, and accordingly the V. Corps ought not to start earlier than that hour. This held good whatever the route adopted for the corps and whether or not the evening of the 21st or the early morning of the 22nd saw the first shots fired in Hancock's battle.

If it became obvious that Lee was not following up Hancock, Warren would take the route of the II. Corps and the others would be directed, according to circumstances, to take any convenient roads. The movement would thus become simply an extension to full manœuvre interval.

Early in the morning there were indications that Lee was massing troops on his right wing. Reports from Hancock up to 9 o'clock indicated that the enemy's cavalry was active at Guinea's Bridge, and that progress was being made towards Milford. But thereafter no messages came through to headquarters, in spite of the large force of cavalry assigned to Hancock and the warning that had been given him before starting as to the necessity of frequent reports. Thus Grant and Meade had to move the other three corps on the 21st, without having that definite information as to the state of things in front of Hancock that the scheme required.

At 7.30 Warren was ordered to be in readiness to move at 10, viâ Massaponax Church (where he was to pick up a cavalry detachment) to Stannard's Mill, and to cross the Po there. It was intended that he should not proceed more to the southward than was necessary to gain room for the whole corps to mass on the other side of the river.

At 9.45, in the absence of news from Hancock and of any definitive indications of Lee's being on the move, Warren's route was slightly modified so as to be on the safe side. He was to cross at Guinea's, not at Stannard's Mill. Warren therefore started, a little after his assigned hour, for Guinea's. Wright (VI. Corps) was warned to be ready to move on the night of the 21st by Guinea's and Bowling Green to follow Hancock.

Burnside (IX. Corps) was to move simultaneously with Wright—that is, at night—to cross at Stannard's Mill, and to follow Warren on the Telegraph Road; at 9.30, however, Burnside was informed that Warren's route had been changed, but that his own remained as before, and that Wright was to follow him.

The first strategic deployment of the Union army (10 A.M.), then, was based on feeble indications of intended movement on Lee's part and on the absence of news from Hancock's detachment. At three in the afternoon, or thereabouts, the V. Corps would be massed south of the Po at Guinea's Bridge, the VI. and IX. still confronting the old Spottsylvania lines but ready to move at nightfall, and early on the 22nd both these corps would be behind Warren on the Telegraph Road. Thus, so far from the plan being abandoned, the moving wing is to be strengthened at the expense of the retaining wing, as soon as it became certain from Lee's presence in the old lines that Hancock could not be seriously interfered with on the 21st. To clear up the situation towards Bowling Green at once, without prejudice to the strength or future movements of the moving wing, Warren was brought several miles nearer Hancock before crossing the river.

In the course of the day, as the withdrawal of Warren was not followed by any aggressive action of Lee against the VI. and IX. Corps, the orders to Burnside were again modified. He was to move at once, "as soon as practicable on receipt of this order", by Stannard's to Thornburg, where his march was to end. But it was left to his discretion to proceed *viâ* Guinea's if he found Stannard's seriously held by the enemy, and as a reconnaissance by part of Potter's division in the afternoon proved this to be the case, he took the alternative and marched to Guinea's Station. It was about 2 A.M. when the rear of the corps cleared Guinea's and the corps halted to rest and to cook.

Warren's movement was conducted with accuracy and success. Being notified from headquarters that his corps was not to advance beyond the Ta, but was to secure the passage of that river on the Madison's Store road, Warren contented himself with posting an advanced guard beyond the Ta, a flank guard towards Mud Tavern, and the main body about Catlett's.

Wright withdrew to the new short line of entrenchments on Burnside's moving off, and about 6 P.M. had a brisk skirmish with two brigades of Wilcox's division (Hill) that had been sent forward to ascertain what force of the Union army was still remaining in its Spottsylvania lines. In spite of this, the VI. Corps was able to follow Burnside closely, and arrived at Guinea's some hours after daylight on the 22nd.

The general trains and Ferrero's division with them were ordered early in the day (21st) to Guinea's Station.

All these movements were strictly in accordance with the original plan, as shown by Warren's instructions to halt his corps short of the Ta and the order to Burnside to stop at Thornburg.

The evening orders of the Army of the

Potomac indicate no change of plan.* As soon as Wright came up to Guinea's (this would presumably be as soon as Burnside's column had cleared that place), Warren was to move forward to Harris's Store, Wright following. Torbert, with the cavalry now with Hancock, was to come in to headquarters, which would move to Bethel Church. Burnside at Guinea's would then become the rear of the moving wing and the general reserve at Grant's immediate disposal. But shortly after the IX. Corps was formed up at Guinea's, information had at last come in from Hancock's detachment, the fortunes of which must now be briefly told.

Somewhat after 9 A.M. Torbert's cavalry had driven the enemy across the Mattapony at Milford. These were not cavalry, but infantry of Pickett's division from Petersburg—a new factor in the struggle in central Virginia and the first-fruits of Butler's ill-success on the James. More infantry was visible beyond the river, and Barlow was ordered up. The rapidity of his advance surprised the Confederates, and the bridge was secured, along with many prisoners. The rest of the II. Corps passed over and entrenched for the night, throwing out a flank guard of cavalry on the left bank towards Pole Cat Station and Burke's Bridge. Torbert with the balance of the cavalry moved back to watch the upper bridges.

* It is true that in the earlier order Burnside was told that fresh orders would be sent him if he chose the Guinea's route, but these were required in any case, owing to the presence of the V. Corps a little distance in front of him towards Madison's Store.

Additional information came in along with this, to the effect that Hoke's division (or brigade), also from the James, had arrived at Pole Cat Station.

This meant that on the 22nd two divisions, *plus* whatever force Lee had moved against Hancock, might attack the II. Corps in its entrenched position at Milford. Under these conditions all further extension of the Union forces towards Chilesburg was futile. The anvil had been definitively set up near Milford, and if the enemy, as perhaps Grant still hoped, went thither, the blow of the hammer must be delivered by roads not further west than the Telegraph or even than the Harris Store Road. Moreover, Hancock would have to deal, no longer with the heads of Lee's columns only, but with a force of 10,000 men already on the ground as well. For this reason, and also because the road to Harris's Store would be fully taken up by the two corps of the moving wing, it was necessary to put Burnside upon the Downer's Bridge–Bethel Church road, whence he could reinforce either wing as required. The Union general was able to do so the more readily because Torbert's cavalry would be available to bridge the gap between Hancock and Warren, and Burnside need not be brought up to the front at once.

At 6 A.M. on the 22nd, the V. Corps reported that a rebel wagon train had been passing down the Telegraph Road near Nancy Wright's since daylight. According to General Humphreys, also, Warren's cavalry had heard troops moving south on that line all night, and the detachment out towards Mud Tavern * sent in word that Ewell and Longstreet passed down in the night. Several hours earlier, headquarters had been informed that Hill's corps was in front of Wright (reconnaissance of Wilcox's two brigades) as late as 6 P.M.

On this information there was no need of further delay, and accordingly Warren was ordered at 6.45 to move towards Harris's Store. At first, owing presumably to the possibility of Hill's corps coming on to the Telegraph Road between them, he was told to wait until Wright was in a condition to follow him closely; but this part of the order was soon modified so as to allow Warren to move off at once. Burnside, on the other hand, was held back until 9 A.M., and then he was to march only to New Bethel Church *via* Downer's Bridge. Hancock was to stand fast; Wright to go forward, after resting his men, until he closed upon the rear of the V. Corps at Madison's Store.

Warren and Hancock were to gain touch directly with one another, the order for the latter to send Torbert's cavalry to headquarters being in due course rescinded. Headquarters were to be at New Bethel Church. The trains were ordered to Bowling Green.

The movements of the various corps were duly carried out on these lines. That they failed to strike the desired blow at Lee's army was due

* Herein Humphreys seems to have mistaken the 3.45 P.M. dispatch of Warren's Mud Tavern outpost for one of 3.45 A.M. Warren reported in the morning "no news" from Mud Tavern. He warned Griffin, however, that "it is quite certain that the enemy has fallen back", and the mistake, if it is one, does not affect the question seriously.

MANŒUVRE OF MAY 21

to the fact of the anvil, upon which they were to crush Lee, being in an out-of-the-way corner instead of full in Lee's path. The opportunity was offered, but Lee was at the same time permitted to take it or leave it as he chose.

As matters turned out, so far from taking the bait, Lee merely conformed to a supposed "change of base" of the Federal army, and, after the preliminary extension above referred to on the Telegraph Road, hurried his army back to Hanover Junction. Ewell left Spottsylvania at midday or one o'clock on the 21st, Anderson at night. Hill remained behind for a few hours, and then retired to Hanover Junction *viâ* Chilesburg and Beaver Dam. The head of Ewell's column reached the Junction at 9.30 on the morning of the 22nd; Anderson, coming up behind him, about midday. Hill duly came in during the afternoon. The detachments of Pickett's and Hoke's commands in front of Hancock fell back also. The Junction had been held since the 20th by Breckinridge's command, transferred thither (by the Virginia Central Railroad) from the Valley after the victory of New Market on the 15th (see Chap. XVII.). Thus early, less than three weeks after the opening of the campaign, Lee had been reinforced from the Valley (Breckinridge) and the James (Pickett and Hoke). The co-operation of the two minor Union armies had completely broken down.

All this, even the presence of the Valley contingent, became evident to the disappointed Union commanders during the course of the day. Warren captured some stragglers and wagons of Anderson's command, and gave many accurate details of the enemy's movements, including A. P. Hill's.* Hancock reported that he thought there was little or no infantry force in his front at Milford. Wright, in rear of Warren, had " nothing of interest to report ".

The corps halted for the night at and around Harris's Store (V.), Madison's and Nancy Wright's (VI.), New Bethel Church (IX.), and Milford Bridge (II.).

On this day the last convoy came in from Belle Plain. The centre of operations was now definitively Port Royal, to which point the stores at Belle Plain were promptly and successfully transferred.

At 8 p.m. on the 22nd, Grant telegraphed to Washington that the enemy had fallen back behind the North Anna, that Pickett's division and other troops had been sent from Richmond, and that Breckinridge was said to have arrived.

The army was now in a region where it had never yet manœuvred or fought. Sheridan's cavalry had just passed through, and in 1862 parts of the I. Corps had marched from Fredericksburg to Hanover Junction in connection with the Peninsular Campaign of McClellan. But that was all, and as the topographical engineers with the army had had no opportunity of mapping this region,

* Hill had now resumed command of his corps. Early went back to his division in Ewell's corps, and Gordon was given a new division in the same corps, formed chiefly of his own brigade and the remnants of Edward Johnson's division, destroyed on the 12th.

the maps, never above reproach, were here unusually inaccurate. However, Humphreys says this led to but little delay, as the general sense of the orders was apparent.

The North Anna country was open and well under cultivation, though there were many woods and swampy bottoms. Next to the Valley it was the most fertile part of Virginia, and on that account it had always been a region of considerable importance to the Confederates. The loss of it affected not so much Lee's present fighting efficiency as his power to continue the war indefinitely. To Grant, however, with his intention of destroying the enemy "by mere attrition *if by nothing else*", the conquest of a granary can only have been a *pis aller* compared with the scheme for a decisive battle on the 22nd. Moreover each successive manœuvre by the left brought him nearer and nearer to the edge of the Richmond fortifications, and when the Chickahominy was reached, there would be an end of manœuvring to fight Lee outside entrenchments.

Even Hanover Junction is not more than a good day's march from Richmond, and the appearance of Breckinridge and Pickett warns us that the duel of the Army of the Potomac and the Army of Northern Virginia is almost at an end.

CHAPTER XVI

NORTH ANNA (MAY 23–25)

May 23.—On the evening of the 22nd, General Grant issued the following directive:—

"MAJOR-GENERAL MEADE,
    Commanding A.P.

Hqrs. Armies of the U.S.
New Bethel, Va., May 22, 1864.

GENERAL,—Direct corps commanders to hold their troops in readiness to march at 5 A.M. to-morrow. At that hour each command will send out cavalry and infantry on all roads to their front leading South, and ascertain if possible where the enemy is. If beyond the North Anna the V. and VI. Corps will march to the forks of the road where one branch leads to Black Dam Station, the other to Jericho Bridge, then South by roads reaching the Anna as near to and east of Hawkins Creek as they can be found. The II. Corps will move to Chesterfield Ford. The IX. Corps will be directed to move at the same time to Jericho Bridge. The map shows only two roads for the four corps to march on, but no doubt by the use of plantation roads and pressing in guides, others can be found to give one for each corps. The troops will follow their respective reconnoitring parties. The trains . . . to Milford Station. Headquarters will follow the IX. Corps.

               U. S. GRANT,
                     Lieut.-General."

NORTH ANNA

At the same time he called upon Butler to send up all forces that were not required to maintain a foothold on the James (see Chap. XVII.). He had already (21st) ordered the despatch of a competent general officer from Washington to report as to the state of affairs within Butler's command. " Either those forces ", he said, " should be so occupied as to detain a force nearly equal to their own, or the garrison in the intrenchments at City Point should be reduced to a minimum and the remainder ordered here ".

The events of the 21st and 22nd showed that Beauregard was detaching forces to Lee, *i.e.* that the Army of the James was not holding the enemy in front of it, and Grant thereupon gave the order without waiting for the report of the mission to Butler. The reinforcements, under W. F. Smith, were to be embarked to join the Army of the Potomac *viâ* Tappahannock or West Point, or to march overland to West Point. In the last case, cavalry and artillery were to be sent with the column, for Lee might hear of Smith's approach and, falling back to the South Anna, turn upon him before he reached West Point. Otherwise the lieutenant-general desired that the column should consist of infantry only. He had already reduced the number of guns with the Army of the Potomac, and was contemplating a further reduction. As for the small force of cavalry that the Army of the James could supply, it would be well employed where it was in breaking up railways south of Richmond.

The directive implied that advanced guards of all arms were to find the enemy, no more. If

Warren and Hancock moved at 5 A.M., their infantry advanced guards would reach the North Anna in the ordinary course at 10.30 or thereabouts (twelve to fifteen miles), the heads of their main bodies, after allowing a full half-hour's start for the advanced guards, about noon. Burnside was kept back,* and only at 3 P.M. was his corps moved off to follow Hancock. The six or more hours of daylight remaining when the enemy had been located by the advanced guards would be utilized in accordance with the information obtained. There was no preconceived manœuvre.

No hostile force was encountered on the march except Rosser's cavalry brigade opposite the V. Corps; this fell back with but slight skirmishing. Practically all the places mentioned in army orders proved to be non-existent.

The II. Corps moved off from its lines near the Milford Road Bridge, Torbert's cavalry leading, at 5 or 5.30 A.M. On arriving at Chesterfield Station, Torbert took a wrong turning that brought him to Mount Carmel Church, and thus into the Telegraph Road, already occupied by Warren's men. Torbert's men assisted in driving in Rosser, and Warren, understanding that the II. Corps was following Torbert, drew off the rear of his column somewhat westward towards Jericho Mills, leaving those troops which had passed down the Telegraph Road to follow when Hancock arrived. The II. Corps, however, was heading a little west of South,

* There was some trouble in the IX. Corps owing to excessive straggling on the 22nd.

close to the railway, and reached the North Anna close to the railway bridge and the Telegraph Road Bridge (marked on the maps apparently as "Jericho Bridge" and "Chesterfield Ford" respectively). The V. Corps meanwhile arrived at Jericho Mills.

It will have been observed that there was nothing in the orders to Hancock and Warren indicating that they were to cross the river. But opportunities for securing the passage presented themselves to both corps, and in the free spirit of the offensive were instantly seized. At 1.30 Warren asked Hancock to inform Meade that the enemy made no show of resistance at Jericho Mills, and that the V. Corps infantry were wading across the river. "I do not believe they mean to hold the North Anna", added Warren, and Hancock's dispatch of 2.35, forwarded to headquarters with Warren's, reported the same as to the indications on the II. Corps front. Meade, with Grant's approval, at once ordered the whole V. Corps to cross and to entrench, and not long afterwards the lieutenant-general wrote, "If Hancock can secure a crossing he should do so". Infantry of both corps were already fording the river on the authorization of the respective corps commanders.

On the front of the V. Corps, Bartlett's brigade of Griffin's division waded across, and advanced in line on the other side. A pontoon bridge was begun at once, and the others passed rapidly, Crawford's men by wading the ford, Cutler's dry-shod over the bridge. All the infantry were over by 4.30, and, though the river banks were steep and the approaches and ramps bad, some field artillery was got across directly afterwards. The line of battle was formed right and left of Bartlett as the other brigades arrived.*

At this awkward moment the enemy appeared in force. About six, Hill's corps came forward to the attack from the Virginia Central Railroad.† Cutler's division (Warren's right), which had not yet formed up, was caught *en flagrant délit* and its outer flank was rolled up in confusion. But Griffin beat off his assailants, the artillery checked the pursuers, and Crawford, on the left nearest the river, sent up a brigade to aid Cutler. About nightfall, after a very sharp contest, the enemy fell back to the railroad, leaving a brigadier and many scores of prisoners in Warren's hands. The losses in killed and wounded were about equal on both sides, well over one thousand.‡

The VI. Corps had by now appeared. The head of the column was at Mount Carmel Church on the Telegraph Road when Warren was attacked, and

---

* There were no entrenching tools at the front, for the V. Corps train was far behind in rear of the VI. Corps combatant troops. For once the troops fought unprotected by anything more than (here and there) the very slightest log-works.

† It had marched in from Chilesburg *via* Beaver Dam.

‡ On the morning of the 24th when Lee came over to his left wing and realized the extent of Warren's success, he asked Hill in intense, though restrained wrath, "General Hill, why did you let these people cross the river? Why did you not drive them back as General Jackson would have done?" Lee's health was already greatly impaired by three years' campaigning and three years of responsibility, and during all these days, anxious as he was to strike a blow at the Union army, he was too ill to enforce his wishes. In his tent at night he was heard by his staff to say repeatedly, "We must never let them pass us again! We must strike them!"

moved to Jericho Mills to support him. It did not become necessary to cross. Warren's handsome success well deserved the congratulations that Meade hastened to bestow upon him and his corps.

On the other side Hancock also was engaged in a sharp and successful fight. The report that his men were fording the river, referred to above, was soon found to refer, not to the river, but to a creek about one and a quarter miles north of it—Hancock calls this a branch of the river and the ground beyond an island—and on the Telegraph Road beyond there appeared an enemy's redoubt covering the real bridge over the North Anna. The II. Corps deployed early in the afternoon. The right brigade of the right division was sent out towards Ox Ford to hold a place for Burnside, who was still halted at Bethel Church. The rest of Birney's division faced south, with its left on the road. Barlow prolonged the line to the left, and Gibbon formed the extreme left, beyond the Richmond and Fredericksburg Railroad. Tyler's heavy artillery division was in reserve.

Hancock, on Birney's report that the redoubt was not impregnable, prepared an attack *en règle*. His guns, much too slowly for their ardent commander, bombarded the redoubt and were bombarded in reply from the redoubt itself and its supporting works south of the Anna (held by Kershaw's division, Anderson's corps). A section of a Rhode Island battery, commanded by a gallant subaltern,* got up under the thin cover of a belt of woods to within case-shot range of the redoubt and remained in action, regardless of losses, to cover the formation and advance of the infantry.

The ground, except for this slight patch of woods, was open and sloped upward from the creek to the high brow overlooking the North Anna. Towards 7 P.M., Pierce's and Egan's brigades formed up under artillery fire and dashed forward over five hundred yards of open ground. In full sight of their comrades and of the enemy on the other side of the river, Pierce and Egan overran the works and swept out the garrison within twenty minutes of the word to charge. Hancock says: "I have seldom witnessed such gallantry and spirit as the brigades of Pierce and Egan displayed". The Union troops instantly followed up and secured the road bridge.

Further to the left, Gibbon gained possession of most of the railroad bridge, but the enemy held the extreme southern bay all night and then destroyed it.

Assuredly there was nothing on this day to show that Grant's army was not capable of great deeds. The generalship of the corps commanders, the bravery of their subordinate leaders, and the steadiness of the men, were beyond praise.†

---

* Lieut. Peter T. Hunt. He was mortally wounded in the action.

† The critical private, as represented by Wilkeson, held that Pierce's and Egan's assault on the redoubt was more of a spectacle than a real fight, and that the V. Corps was nearly ruined through Warren's negligence in remaining in a house north of the river and disregarding Griffin's reports of the enemy's proximity. A fairly close study of the official records shows nothing to support either of these stories.

NORTH ANNA

The IX. Corps left New Bethel Church about 3 p.m. and arrived on the North Anna, finding its way thither by plantation roads. Its leading division filled the gap between Warren and Hancock, on the general alignment Ox Ford–Quarles's Mill. The other two bivouacked south and southwest of the Hargreave house, where Burnside established his headquarters.

General headquarters did not leave New Bethel until afternoon. Headquarters Army of the Potomac went forward to Carmel Church in the morning, and remained there for the rest of the day. Grant joined Meade early on the 24th.

May 24.—The army was now formed roughly in a semicircle, in order from right to left— V. (Warren), VI. (Wright), IX. (Burnside), II. (Hancock). The right was entrenched beyond the river, the left held one of the lower bridges and part of another.

Warren, in the same order which congratulated him on his success was told that Wright's corps would be sent over to join him, and that Hancock and Burnside were to force a passage at daylight.

Warren was at Jericho Mills, less than three-quarters of a mile from his firing line, which was over a mile long. Hancock's attack was made under fire from the artillery beyond the river, not merely under that of a handful of men and two old howitzers in the bridge-head. The fire was heavy enough to make the line check for a moment. The Union volunteer's critical observations are subjectively accurate, and, in consequence, of intense interest to the student. But the "news gatherers" who spread the camp news from corps to corps are not more reliable than eye-witnesses of superior rank. In general, it may be well to remark that the American volunteer was too reckless in accusing his generals of cowardice and neglect of duty.

"If you have an opportunity with your own corps and Wright's to attack to advantage, do so".

Hancock was ordered (11 P.M., 23rd) to cross the river, if in his opinion the operation was practicable, and Burnside was similarly instructed with regard to Ox Ford. If either of these corps commanders attempted to cross, the other was to hold his position with the minimum force and to keep the rest of his corps ready to go to the point of passage. These dispositions were made in view of Lee's standing his ground and were preparatory to a battle, but ere long fresh information from the front seemed to justify a new hypothesis.

At 6.30, negroes came over the river from the enemy's lines, and were questioned by Hancock and afterwards by Meade. The conclusion arrived at was that Lee's Hanover Junction lines had been held on the 23rd only to gain time for the withdrawal of the trains to Richmond, and that the Confederates were now falling back behind the South Anna.

At 8 A.M. Grant sent his usual daily message to Halleck at Washington—

"The enemy have fallen back from North Anna; we are in pursuit. Negroes . . . state Lee is falling back to Richmond. If this is the case, Butler's forces will all be wanted where they are. Notify him to hold Smith in readiness to move, but to await further orders. I will probably know to-day if the enemy intends standing behind South Anna."

The idea of a battle has given way to that of a pursuit. Events at the front did not at first belie the supposition.

At 6 A.M. Warren reported that two of the VI. Corps divisions were across the river, and that the V. Corps skirmishers, moving down-stream, had met nothing but stragglers from Hill's corps. He reported unfavourably on the cavalry with him, which, he says, owing to their reluctance to go far out, had exposed his right to the surprise attack on the evening of the 23rd. In reply he was told that some cavalry, reported as trustworthy by Torbert, would be sent him (8 A.M.).

At 7.30 he announced the further advance of his skirmishers in all directions, still gathering in stragglers from the enemy.

At eight he was informed by General Meade of the news of Lee's retreat, and that " they still show a force opposite Hancock and Burnside, but impossible to tell whether cavalry or not ". Warren was to push out as far as he could, and to send in all information promptly. Before the receipt of this order Warren had ordered Crawford, nearest the river, to send out a force along the bank to get touch with Burnside and Hancock. At 9.30 he ordered Crawford to follow up his detachments and to clear Hancock's (or Burnside's) front of the enemy's force—" cavalry at least "—mentioned by General Meade. Torbert's " reliable " cavalry detachment had been sent promptly, and was now coming up under the command of Lieutenant-Colonel Hammond.

On the other flank, the indications were still that the works on the south side of the Anna were held by a skeleton force. By 9.15 Hancock was able to report that he had occupied the enemy's first line of works without much opposition. On his right, opposite Burnside, four hostile guns (possibly horse artillery) annoyed him somewhat by their fire, and he detached a brigade (Miles's) to go up-stream and attack those guns. On hearing that a division of the V. Corps was proceeding down-stream to clear the front of the IX. Corps, Hancock recalled Miles at once, lest he should be fired into by friendly troops. Extra bridges were laid near the railroad bridge, and Gibbon pressed forward (south-westward) without difficulty until he met the enemy one and a half miles beyond the (Virginia Central) railroad. Opposite the road bridge skirmishing was rather heavy, but Hancock did not attach much importance to it (11 A.M.).

Burnside in the centre lay quiet. Having agreed with Hancock that a demonstration was the best course for the IX. Corps, he placed Potter's division at the disposal of the II. Corps, and himself reconnoitred the river about Ox Ford. This, and the arrangement of the two remaining divisions for the attack at Ox Ford, took up most of the forenoon.

On the results of this morning's work, which, be it said, were quite negative, operation orders for the next advance were issued. It seems almost as if Grant and Meade were convinced by the evidence of the two negroes alone that Lee had retired, and gladly accepted the slightest confirmation, such as that afforded by Hancock's and Warren's reports.

These orders amounted to a continuance of the "pursuit". Burnside was ordered to pass over his

NORTH ANNA

entire corps with its trains, if possible by Ox Ford (which is presumed to have been opened by Crawford and Miles), otherwise by Quarles's Mill. The order concluded, "You must get over and camp to-night on the south side. To-night these headquarters will be on the south side of the river on the Telegraph Road". The route marked out for the IX. Corps was to lead it to the South Anna, just west of the Fredericksburg Railroad bridge.

Hancock was ordered to cross his trains and to move early in the morning through Hanover Junction to the road bridge near the Virginia Central Railroad bridge, or alternatively to a point just east of the Fredericksburg Railroad bridge.

The V. Corps was to be arranged in a marching column so as to move to the South Anna by any road, east of Burnside's allotted route, which the corps commander could find for himself during the afternoon. General Wright was to cross his trains and to follow the V. Corps as before.

It was not long after the issue of these orders (1 to 1.30) that it became evident that they would never be executed.

At 2.45 P.M. Warren reported that Crawford's division had opened the ford to Burnside's position (apparently Fall Mill, just above Ox Ford), but that there were hostile breastworks on Crawford's right, also that away towards the railway the cavalry attached to the corps (Hammond's) had met hostile cavalry and drawn artillery fire. Crittenden's division of the IX. Corps was at this time crossing to join Crawford, *viâ* Fall Mill, in pursuance of the general order of 1 P.M., and Crawford and Crittenden skirmished heavily with the enemy. Soon the two divisions, which were of course isolated from the main body of Warren's command, developed a Confederate entrenched line running from Ox Ford towards the Virginia Central Railroad (see Sketch Map XVII.).

On the other flank, Gibbon's advance down the Richmond and Fredericksburg line met serious resistance before 3 P.M. Some hours later the presence of parts at least of Ewell's and Longstreet's corps was ascertained from prisoners, and towards evening the enemy came out along the Richmond and Fredericksburg Railroad and assailed Gibbon.

Lee was, in fact, in position with his whole army. His earthworks had been constructed at leisure, during the previous winter, and extended from the Little River through Anderson's Station to Ox Ford. Thence for three-quarters of a mile down stream they ran along the high bluffs of the river bank, after which they trended away to the south-east, encircling Hanover Junction. Thence the line extended southward and again south-eastward. We are concerned, however, only with the section of this long line which was actually occupied, viz. the line, Little River, Ox Ford, Junction. Beyond this the convergence of the two Annas, and the existence of Sexton's Swamp in the tongue between them, precluded attack, and the extreme right of the line therefore plays no part in the history of these operations.

By 6.30 Hancock had come to the conclusion that he had in front of him a second Spottsylvania position, and sent word to that effect to headquarters. In reply he was ordered to envelop as much as he could of the enemy's right, and to watch his left flank carefully. Later (11.15 P.M.) he was informed that he was not expected to do more than entrench his present position and to hold it. Torbert was ordered to send him some cavalry, and Potter's division of the IX. Corps was also under his orders.

At 11 P.M. Warren was ordered to move forward at four in the morning, and to take position enveloping the enemy's left flank. The VI. Corps was to follow on the right rear of the V. The engineers attached to army headquarters were to throw a pontoon bridge at a point in rear of Warren's left—Crawford and Crittenden were, be it observed, isolated—and to make good approaches. It was apparently understood that the V. Corps was only to advance in a general line towards Hanover Junction, and not to attack if the enemy were found in force and behind entrenchments.

Burnside was left with one division only (Willcox's) opposite the strongest portion of the Confederate position. The inconveniences attaching to the treatment of the IX. Corps as a separate army had now become flagrant, and Grant issued an order this evening assigning the corps to the Army of the Potomac. Burnside and his chief-of-staff, Parke, were both senior to Meade, but they cheerfully waived their seniority in the interests of the service. On the morning of the 25th, Burnside said to Grant, in the presence of a number of officers: "The order assigning my corps to the

Army of the Potomac is excellent. I am glad it has been made". *

Sheridan and the Cavalry Corps, returning exultant and tired from the raid to Richmond, were now only a few miles away to the south-east.

May 25.—The details of the reconnaissance executed by the Army of the Potomac on the following morning are of no particular interest.† The intention was to pick up the alignment of Lee's army and to examine the character of its works. The information gained led Grant as early as 10.45 A.M. to suspend the advance of the V. Corps and to veto a suggestion that the VI. Corps should pass the Little River and work round towards Lee's extreme left. On Hancock's front, the Union line was already so close to the enemy that any advance would have brought on a heavy fight.

On s'engage partout et puis l'on voit, says Napoleon. The Union troops had effectually put into practice the first part of the maxim, and their commanders then "saw" that there was nothing to be effected.

If it were decided to fight a battle on this ground, a flank movement of the VI. Corps beyond the Little River, or a repetition of the hammer and

---

* Next day, one of his division commanders, Crittenden, an ex-corps commander of the Army of the Cumberland, found himself under the orders of Warren, his junior. Burnside answered Crittenden's complaints with true dignity in the words, " I fully appreciate your feelings . . . but I would as a friend advise you to remain where you are ".

† The losses of the Union army from the 21st to the 26th of May were little more than 2500. Lee's losses are unknown, but can hardly have been less than 1500.

anvil tactics attempted on the 10th and the 21st, were the only alternatives to a frontal attack all along the line. As to the former, Wright reported that the enemy's entrenchments were being prolonged from New Market westward, with the Little River as a wet ditch in front of them; the latter depended on whether Lee chose to move out of the lines to attack Hancock.

Discussion of the controversy that has raged over Lee's omission to do so would be outside the scope of this work. He had a strong, well-prepared position between the two halves of the Union army, neither portion of which could reinforce the other except by crossing the North Anna twice. On the other hand he was himself almost incapacitated by illness, and his army, inferior in numbers as it was, would have had to attack entrenchments* instead of defending them. It is proper to say, however, that the unfortunate position of the Union army was accidental, and that Grant and Meade lost no time and spared no effort in remedying it.

"Stalemate" is a Federal historian's name for the result of the operations on the North Anna. Lee could not move, but he was not obliged to move.

Grant promptly admitted the game drawn and began another—this time a manœuvre involving, directly and indirectly, every soldier in Virginia.

* For a discussion of this problem, see Humphreys, p. 132.

CHAPTER XVII

THE MINOR ARMIES IN THE EAST

THE main contending armies were now within one long day's march of Richmond, and the return of Sheridan's cavalry to the Army of the Potomac, and the appearance of Breckinridge's command from the Valley of Virginia, suggests that minor operations and detachments were for the present at an end.

Their independent existence had been of short duration, little more than three weeks, but we must consider what they had been required to do, summarize their marches and battles, and gain some idea of the results obtained or missed, before proceeding to study the next operations of the Army of the Potomac and the Army of Northern Virginia, which were closely affected by the sum total of these minor events.

Operations of the Army of the James

The Union Army of the James consisted of the X. Corps (Major-General Gillmore), made up of the forces lately employed on the South Carolina and Georgia coast; the XVIII. Corps (Major-General

Smith), consisting of the available troops of the Southern Virginia and North Carolina coast line; a cavalry division (Brigadier-General Kautz), and various details, under Major-General B. F. Butler.

General Butler was a civilian of considerable political influence. He had displayed great energy in reorganizing the local military forces of Massachusetts before the war, and unquestionably had a liking for the control of armies. He had begun with one or two minor successes, due purely to promptitude of action, and had earned a military reputation which his natural gifts did not enable him to sustain.

He had a sense of his own importance, strong opinions, and a violent temper, added to which, even after four years of continuous war employment as a general officer, he had, as it chanced, no real experience in front of an enemy in the field. But he was a man of commanding personality in politics, and carried with him thousands of waverers in his unquestioned devotion to the cause of the Union. As a general, however strongly he protested against an order, he invariably executed it to the best of his ability once it was made. He was fertile in expedients. It was he who foreshadowed the abolition of slavery by confiscating negroes who came within his lines as "contraband of war", to be confiscated to the United States. He designed the Dutch Gap Canal on the James,* with the idea of enabling the Federal

* This cut off the bend of Farrar's Island (see Map III.), and though not used during the war, it afterwards became the main waterway for vessels going up to Richmond.

monitors to ascend the river. He organized an impromptu coastal flotilla under one of his brigadiers, so as to be independent of naval co-operation. His last scheme was the famous powder vessel designed to blow up Fort Fisher.

As an administrator he had few equals amongst the Union generals. New Orleans, it was said, was never healthier or better governed than under the Butler *régime* of 1862. The occupation of this turbulent city showed Butler at his best and at his worst. He was a born provost-marshal, with a violent tongue. Insults offered by the ladies of New Orleans to Union soldiers provoked the celebrated order in which he directed that women so doing were to be considered for police purposes as women of the town. The outcry in the South led to his being " outlawed " by Mr. Davis's cabinet. The sentence recoiled on the heads of those who had passed it, for when the Union government decided to exchange no more prisoners, they made Butler " Commissioner for the exchange of prisoners ", and when the Southern government swallowed its pride and approached the general, it had the additional mortification of being refused.*

Not many days after the landing at Bermuda Hundred we find Butler intriguing for the removal of Gillmore, the next senior officer to himself with the army. His other major-general, W. F. Smith, commanding the XVIII. Corps, was an old West Pointer of finished skill and known intractable temper. He had served in the Army of the

---

* Even so impartial a Confederate as General Alexander cannot quite forgive Grant for putting this humiliation on the South.

Potomac, and at one time commanded the VI. Corps. He was one of the officers of that army whom Burnside proposed to dismiss from the service for "insubordination and wrongful criticism of his superiors" after Fredericksburg. His name had more than once been sent up to the Senate for promotion to the rank of major-general, and it was only at the express wish of General Grant that he was at last confirmed in that rank. Grant had formed a high opinion of Smith during the Chattanooga operations, in which that general had rendered exceptionally distinguished service as chief engineer of the Army of the Cumberland. General Grant desired to retain Butler as commander of the department, and to place Smith in command of the troops actually in the field. But Butler naturally intended to lead his army himself, and it was considered better to allow him to do so than to overstrain his patriotism in striking at his self-esteem, more especially on the verge of an important presidential election. At this juncture a reverse sustained by a subsidiary army was of far less importance than the victory of the peace party at the polls.

These preliminary remarks will, in a great measure, help to elucidate the haphazard and resultless operations which we must now set forth.

Butler's total force numbered about 38,000 officers and men for duty. One division of the XVIII. Corps was comprised of coloured troops, as was also West's independent cavalry brigade.

To oppose this force, the Confederates had

available, on May 1, little more than the garrisons of Richmond and Petersburg and the coast artillery in the batteries on the James.

The defences of Richmond, Lee's centre of operations and Butler's objective, consisted of a complete ring of detached forts (not shown on Map III.) at an average distance of over one mile from it, and an outer envelope of field and provisional works, chiefly for infantry, about one mile in advance of the forts. In addition on the west front there was a long line of works from the Chickahominy to Chapin's Bluff, partly a relic and partly an extension of the engineering work of the Fair Oaks campaign. At Chapin's Bluff, as at Drury's Bluff, coast batteries armed with heavy ordnance overlooked the James. These, with a small gunboat and torpedo-boat flotilla, the shoals of the river itself, and various lines of "torpedoes" (submarine mines) were supposed to be sufficient guarantee against the advance of the Federal navy.

From Drury's Bluff westward there was a line of field works—and not merely of field works, for the Federal engineer general Gillmore speaks of deep ditches—facing south, and barring the approaches to Richmond from Petersburg; there was in addition an advanced line facing south-east between the Bluff and Wooldridge's house, near the Richmond and Petersburg Railway. Petersburg had been fortified in 1862 with a ring of works (redans for artillery alternating with lengths of deep revetted infantry trenches) on a radius of about two miles from the city.

The defensive force available on May 1 was, as we have said, small. Of mobile troops there appear to have been 6000 only, not counting government clerks, militia, etc., who were organized in companies for local defence, nor the men for the heavy guns or the movable armament.

Pickett's division of Longstreet's corps, Army of Northern Virginia, had been serving for some months in scattered garrisons in West Carolina. These were veteran soldiers.*

In addition there were eight weak brigades on their way from North Carolina, inner Virginia, South Carolina, and Georgia, the whole being commanded by General P. G. T. Beauregard, who disposed also of two cavalry brigades. But little of this motley army of 30,000 or so was available when Butler's expedition made its appearance.

Grant's instructions to Butler were couched in the general terms of a directive. He suspected Butler's ability, but having decided to retain him in command, allowed him the same liberty of action as other army commanders, assigning him only his objective and his force, and informing him of the part he was to play in the general scheme.

After stating that concentration of effort is the first essential, the lieutenant-general proceeded—

"It will not be possible to unite our armies into two or three large ones . . . owing to the absolute necessity of

---

* Survivors, in the main, of the great assault on Meade's centre at Gettysburg, when Pickett had been wounded, all his brigadiers and colonels killed or disabled, and the regimental officers and rank and file had cost at least sixty per cent. of their total strength.

holding on to the territory already taken from the enemy. But generally speaking, concentration can be practically effected by armies moving to the interior . . . from the territory they have to guard. By such movement they interpose themselves between the enemy and the country to be guarded, thereby reducing the number necessary to guard important points, or at least occupy the attention of a part of the enemy's force, if no greater object is gained. Lee's army and Richmond being the greater objects towards which our attention must be directed . . . it is desirable to unite all the force we can against them. The necessity of covering Washington with the Army of the Potomac, and of covering your department with your army, makes it impossible to unite these forces at the beginning. I propose, therefore, what comes nearest this of anything that seems practicable. The Army of the Potomac will act from its present base, Lee's army being its objective point. You will collect all the forces from your command that can be spared from garrison duty to operate on the south side of the James river, Richmond being your objective point. . . .

"When you are notified to move, take City Point with as much force as possible. Fortify, or rather entrench, at once, and concentrate all your troops for the field there as rapidly as you can. . . . Directions cannot be given at this time for your further movements. The fact . . . that Richmond is to be your objective point, and that there is to be co-operation between your force and the Army of the Potomac, must be your guide. This indicates the necessity of your holding close to the south bank of the James as you advance. Then, should the enemy be forced into . . . Richmond, the Army of the Potomac would follow, and by means of transports the two armies would become a unit. All the details are left entirely to your direction. If, however, you think it practicable to use your cavalry south of you, so as to cut the railroad about Hicksford about the time of the general advance, it would be of immense advantage."

Butler had before this had a personal interview with Grant, in which the latter had pointed out

MINOR ARMIES IN THE EAST

the apparent importance of getting possession of Petersburg and of destroying the railroads southward, but had made Richmond the objective point, because there was a chance of capturing that city if Lee were prevented from sending reinforcements. There were no other Confederate forces north of the James that could arrive in time to meet a rapid movement.* Reinforcements from the South could be held off by breaking up the railroads towards Hicksford.

On the 18th of April, these instructions were developed in one or two points. Grant announced his intention of fighting Lee between Culpeper and Richmond if he would stand, but that if he fell back on Richmond the Army of the Potomac would follow up. In this case, "could I be certain you will be able to invest Richmond on the south side with your left resting on the James above Richmond, I would form the junction there. Circumstances may make this course advisable anyhow . . . use every exertion to secure footing as far up the south side of the river as you can, and as soon as possible after the receipt of orders to move . . . if you cannot carry the city, you should at least detain as large a force there as possible".

These directives appeal to a higher degree of strategical ability than Butler possessed. It is true that Grant gave Butler the same independence in matters of detail as he gave Sherman, but such a course was hardly justified by Butler's record.

* This I conceive, rightly or wrongly, to be the meaning of an involved sentence in Grant's report.

The one outstanding fact that amounted to a direct order was that Richmond was to be the objective, and was to be approached by the right bank of the James. That part of his instructions Butler obeyed to the letter.

The direct order to move at once on being notified of the general advance, and to seize City Point (which Grant believed to be on the north side of the Appomattox), to entrench, and to collect a field army there as rapidly as possible, the army commander carried out with accuracy and speed.

The suggestion that the cavalry might be used to break up the railroads to the south was taken *au pied de la lettre* by Butler and his cavalry commander, and, as a matter of fact, this scheme proved very successful in interfering with the enemy's concentration.

But beyond this his administrative skill and energy could not carry him. Not only the details were left to his discretion, but also the actual conduct of operations, and this under the terms of a directive that only a trained staff officer could be expected to develop into an " appreciation " of the situation.

A more experienced general would have realized that the damage to lines of communication effected by a fleeting cavalry raid was far from permanent. Grant guaranteed his subordinate against interference from the north, and showed him the way to guarantee himself from it on the south side, but he did not sufficiently impress upon him the fact that the latter only gave him a limited time in which to act irrespective of the enemy. Demands for rapidity of movement, though they appear in Butler's instructions, are not given any particular prominence, and can easily be read to mean that it would suffice if Butler appeared before Richmond before the Army of the Potomac and Lee arrived. As Butler was only two or three marches from his objective and *ex hypothesi* had no considerable force of the enemy to deal with, while the Army of the Potomac was at least six days from Richmond, without counting in the time required for fighting Lee, the necessity for haste was not obvious. It should have been made so, and the true reason for insisting upon it not only stated but also underlined.

Grant, it will be noted, directed Butler, as he directed other commanders, to hold as large a force of the enemy as possible.*

If Grant himself accounted for all forces north of the James, what was there left for Butler to hold in front of him? Obviously, only the army that the Confederates might bring up from the South, and these Butler presumed to be held off for a considerable time by the results of the cavalry raid towards Hicksford. The holding action of Butler's force could only begin when Beauregard showed a target. To Grant's mind the operation was one of containing Beauregard's army when it appeared, and utilizing any time that could be gained beforehand in the enterprise against the weakly held defences of Richmond. If at the end

* He said "*at least* hold as large a force". This again was liable to be gravely misunderstood.

of its time of immunity the Army of the James was on the south side of Richmond, perhaps inside the works of that city (which Grant thought to be within the bounds of possibility), Butler would have no difficulty at all in drawing upon himself very considerable forces of the enemy. The best answer to the first problem, in fact, would be the rapid solution of the second. It seems clear that Butler understood, and followed, with fierce and almost pathetic tenacity, the two objects of his army's existence. But he failed to correlate them, and in particular miscalculated the time of immunity his cavalry could give him.

To sum up, the text of the directive affords a fairly clear explanation both of Grant's intentions and of the causes of Butler's misapprehension of them. Had W. F. Smith been in command in the field * as Grant wished, the directive might possibly have sufficed to ensure good results, but, in Butler's case, a definite order to be on the south side of Richmond not later than May 9, prepared either to capture the city or to hold off Beauregard, would have been more suitable.

* Smith, however, was "obstinate and likely to condemn any course not suggested by himself", and his view was that Petersburg should be captured as a preliminary to any advance on Richmond. Gillmore concurred with him in this distinctively engineer view, but Butler, having firmly grasped his instructions to move on Richmond, refused to consider the suggestions of his two subordinates, and told them that he was not going to build a bridge on the Appomattox for West Point men to retreat over. In truth, and apart from the insulting words in which it was conveyed, the decision was subjectively right. For the present operation the "line of the Appomattox" that Smith adduced as an objective mattered nothing. Petersburg was nothing more than a point on two lines of railway, both of which ought to be broken, but it did not seriously matter whether they were broken there or elsewhere.

MINOR ARMIES IN THE EAST 373

The X. and XVIII. Corps were meanwhile concentrated not on the James but on the York, so as to mislead the enemy. On the night of the 4th of May, in response to Grant's message, "We have crossed the Rapidan", Butler's men swiftly and quietly embarked on their transports and proceeded up the James river with Admiral Lee's squadron and Butler's own gunboat flotilla as escort.

One brigade of the coloured division was landed on the morning of the 5th at Fort Powhatan, the rest at City Point. The main body of the army passed up and landed at Bermuda Hundred.* The coloured cavalry brigade moved from Yorktown across country and joined the army without mishap. Kautz's cavalry division, starting from Suffolk, successfully raided the Weldon railroad south of Petersburg, in pursuance of Grant's desire to interfere with the enemy's concentration. He came in to City Point on the 10th.

The main army (three divisions of the X. Corps, and two of the XVIII., all white troops) moved forward on the 6th, and entrenched across the narrow neck of land between Trent's Reach on the James and Port Walthall on the Appomattox. This gave the army a secure footing, the defensive line being only three miles in length, and the troops available to defend it being 30,000 strong. The same afternoon a reconnaissance towards the Richmond and Petersburg railroad developed hostile infantry.

* Grant seems to have thought that City Point was north of the Appomattox river instead of south of it.

The Confederate concentration was already in progress. On the 5th of May there were about one and a half brigades at Petersburg. On the morning of the 6th a force was sent out to Port Walthall Junction and encountered General Butler's reconnoitring detachment. But owing to the scattered condition of his army, and the success of the Union cavalry in breaking up his lines of transportation, Beauregard did not succeed in assembling his army, now about 25,000 strong, before the 15th.

Butler's operations in the meanwhile, from whatever cause, had been dilatory. He did not move out in force save for reconnaissances right and left until the 12th of May, six days after he had constructed his entrenched camp.

This advance was strictly in accordance with Butler's reading of the situation. He proceeded carefully and leisurely up the Richmond Turnpike with the greater part of two corps in line of battle, and as soon as the front of the Bermuda Hundred entrenchments was cleared, Kautz started on a second raid to break up the Richmond and Danville railroad. Forces were left behind near Port Walthall Junction and in the lines themselves to deal with a possible irruption from the side of Petersburg, and the positions of the black troops at City Point and Fort Powhatan were not altered.

Half a day's march, or less, from his objective point, Butler came upon the enemy's entrenchments on the morning of the 13th. At Wooldridge Hill, half a mile west of the railroad, Gillmore pressed up to the front of the enemy, turned their

MINOR ARMIES IN THE EAST 375

right and carried a mile or more of their outer entrenchments. The XVIII. Corps, moving on Gillmore's right flank, encountered works of great strength, and did not assault.

On the 14th, Smith's left carried the remainder of the outer line and connected with Gillmore's right. The enemy's second line of works was bent backward from the strong position that Smith's right division had encountered the day before, and extended to the railroad. Thence it was refused for a considerable distance and again bent back to the turnpike above Drury's Bluff. Beauregard thus held what was almost an enclosed position, with works facing in all directions.*

On the 15th there was skirmishing along the whole line, but, so far from being able to continue his advance, Butler was brought to a standstill for want of the necessary force to form a column of assault.

Beauregard's concentration being now more or less complete, he took the offensive in turn and fought the battle of Drury's Bluff (16th). The results of his attack and of the advance of his division at Petersburg to Port Walthall fell far short of what he expected, but Butler was none the less forced back into the lines of Bermuda Hundred, with the loss probably of 3500 officers and men. The Confederate casualties numbered 2184.†

---

* The Federal armoured ships were unable to ascend beyond Trent's Reach and the gunboats could not run under the Confederate batteries on the bluffs on each side of the James, which could fire on to their decks.

† On this occasion the use of a wire entanglement by the Union

Thus the Richmond enterprise ended in a tactical reverse. It is not too much to claim for Butler, however, that though he failed to capture Richmond he held a large force of the enemy—not less than 20,000—in front of him.

It was after his retirement to the lines of Bermuda Hundred that the Union commander failed to perform his share of the general scheme of Grant's operations. Beauregard followed him up and there was severe fighting on the 20th, but substantially Butler was "bottled up" in the great bend of the James river, and the short line across the neck, so thoroughly fortified by the Union army in the precious days preceding the advance, was equally advantageous to the Confederates, who entrenched themselves front to front. Soon afterwards the government at Richmond recovered from its fright and, disregarding Beauregard's somewhat ill-timed protests, ordered Pickett's division and Hoke's (Lewis's) brigade of Early's division to rejoin the Army of Northern Virginia. These were followed in a few days by Hoke's new division. The appearance at Hanover Junction of troops from the James, at the critical moment of Hancock's "decoy" manœuvre, told Grant that Butler had failed to hold the enemy in front of him. The order went forth at once for Smith, with all forces of Butler's command that were not required to hold the Bermuda Hundred entrenchments, to join the Army of the Potomac. On the erroneous supposition of Lee's retreat to the South

general created a great stir, and was so much of a novelty that the Richmond papers spoke of it as "a devilish contrivance"!

MINOR ARMIES IN THE EAST

Anna on the 24th, the order was countermanded, but next day, when Lee's true position was located, it was repeated, and on the 28th it was executed.

Kautz's second cavalry raid did considerable damage to the Danville, and even to the south side (Richmond and Lynchburg) railroads, but it was too late to be of material assistance. It was, in fact, locking the stable door after the horse had been stolen.

A study of these unsatisfactory operations leads us to suppose that if reliance had been placed on Butler's subordination rather than on his military judgment, the result would have been very different.

The Valley Campaign

On the other flank of the Army of the Potomac were the Union troops, mobile and immobile, in occupation of the widespread "Department of West Virginia", which stretched from the Ohio to the Blue Ridge.

Major-General Franz Sigel, the commander of the Department, was a political refugee from Baden, who had fought with energy in the insurrection there in 1848-9, and had then emigrated. He had earned a good, though not a great, reputation as a division and corps commander, under Lyon in his early days in Missouri, and then under Pope in Virginia. Major-General George Crook, commanding in the Kanawha region, which had just become a State of the Union under the name of West Virginia, was a hardy Indian fighter. Brigadier-General Averell, Crook's cavalry leader, had already distinguished himself by a far-ranging raid against the Virginia and Tennessee in December, 1863, and had been specially selected by General Grant for the command he now held in view of similar operations. The forces of the Department, owing to the necessities of garrison duty and the difficulties of supply, were very much scattered, and the early months of the year were fully occupied in redistributing them in accordance with strategical requirements, in remounting the cavalry, and in collecting transports.

The area of Sigel's intended operations, which may be designated by the general title of "The Valley", included the Valley of Virginia properly so-called (viz. the basins of the Shenandoah and the upper Potomac), the upland country at the head waters of the James and New rivers, and the mountains of eastern Kentucky and south-western Virginia.

Most of this area—that part of it lying within the limits defined by Lynchburg, Lewisburg, Saltville, and Buchanan—had been, so far as serious operations went, almost untouched in the whole three years of war. Fertile as it was in places, it was too sparsely populated to maintain armies. Situated moreover in the heart of the Alleghanies —the great natural barrier between west and east—it presented almost insuperable physical difficulties to the movements of troops in large bodies. Every invasion was in the nature of a raid—generally a more or less irregular cavalry raid—and a raid, too, strictly limited as to duration by the available supply of food and forage.*

The great routes of the armies lay on either side of it, and in the press of greater events on wider fields the quietude of this eyrie was rarely disturbed. Yet it had its importance. Hard pressed as they were for men, the Confederates yet found it necessary to maintain there a corps of occupation, in order to protect important industries and a still more important railway. The salt works at Saltville, the lead works at Wytheville, and every bridge and depôt of the Virginia and Tennessee Railroad were eminently suitable objectives for small offensive operations. For the destruction of these, many Union expeditions had been launched from time to time, sometimes from Kentucky, sometimes from the Knoxville region of Tennessee, sometimes from West Virginia, and even, more rarely, from the Shenandoah, and the Confederate leaders were accustomed to face in turn to every point of the compass.

This corner, as apart from the true Valley of Virginia into which it merged about Buchanan, formed roughly the Confederate "District of Southwestern Virginia" under Major-General J. C. Breckinridge, a leader of the old Democratic party, who had been vice-president of the United

---

* It was in this region chiefly that the celebrated partisan, General John Morgan, operated during his short and eventful career. His most celebrated raid was that of into Indiana and Ohio, where Confederate battle flags had never before been seen. But he was more usually occupied in smaller raids, and in repelling similar small raids from all the Union districts lying around him.

States before he turned general, and had served with credit at Shiloh and Chickamauga.

We have spoken of the Virginia and Tennessee Railroad as "important". This line led to Lynchburg, which is just east of the mountains that define the Valley theatre of war and just west of Lee's own battlefield. Lynchburg, with Charlottesville and Gordonsville north of it, was of the highest importance to the Confederates, not only as connecting the defensive or Richmond line of operations with the Valley, the great highway for Confederate counter-strokes, but also as the place which, with the sole exception of Richmond itself, was the most natural and the most suitable centre of operations for Lee. To the very end of the war Lee constantly meditated changing his line of operations so as to pivot on Lynchburg, "that (to the enemy) important point", as Grant called it, and he actually surrendered the wreck of his army on April 9, 1865, when in full march for that place, and less than a score of miles from it. A glance at the map will suffice to show the importance, from the point of view of railway communication, of these three places. At Lynchburg the Virginia and Tennessee Railroad turns north-east to join the Orange and Alexandria, the main route to the North through Washington, and from it the South-side Railroad runs to the Atlantic coast, meeting at Burksville and Petersburg other North and South lines to Richmond and Fredericksburg. At Charlottesville the Virginia Central Railroad comes in from Covington and Staunton in the Valley, and at

Gordonsville the Orange and Alexandria passes through the battlefields of central Virginia, while the Virginia Central goes East to Richmond *viâ* Hanover Junction on the North Anna. All these lines are "important" as lines of communication between the base (*i.e.* all friendly territory effectively occupied and producing for the needs of the army) and the centre of operations (*i.e.* the fortified depôt immediately in touch with the fighting troops).

With regard to operations on this side, Grant desired, in accordance with his general military policy, to destroy whatever accumulations of stores, supplies, and *matériel* his raiders could reach, and, whenever and wherever possible, to interrupt the flow of men and material to the enemy's actual or potential centre of operations. This could be effected either by breaking the line of communication or by threatening it so seriously that the reinforcements had to halt and to provide for their own safety.

The "Valley District" proper, that is, the basin of the Shenandoah between the James and the Potomac, was under the command of an enterprising cavalry leader, Brigadier-General Imboden. Breckinridge, however, commanded in person the field forces of both districts when they were united.

The Valley was at once the best offensive line of operations for the Confederates in Virginia and the most important granary of which they disposed. From the point of view of the Federals there was no "positive" object[*] in a Valley

[*] Clausewitz.

campaign unless the main hostile field army were there, which was rarely the case; but there were important negative (that is, literally, denying) objects to be obtained, viz. to prevent the enemy from interfering with the great east and west line, the Baltimore and Ohio, and to prevent his gathering the crops. The first is a defensive proposition, the second involves no more than a partial application of force for a limited time and a limited object only. Little or nothing was to be gained by the Federals from a deliberate conquest of the Valley, and, in fact, the only example of such a campaign is the "trapping Jackson" episode of June, 1862, for which there was the very good excuse that there was for the time being a serious field army of the enemy in the Valley. A normal hostile occupation of the Shenandoah region was defensive in the first instance, and partially and guardedly offensive in the second.

The topography of the Valley was, as regards obstacles and communications, that of Eastern Virginia turned through a quarter circle, that is, the roads and rivers were perpendicular, not parallel, to the fronts of the contending forces. There were a few short lateral roads, sometimes even turnpikes, connecting adjacent strips of the Valley, and the long ridges separating these strips were pierced at intervals by gaps, through which the lateral roads ran. It is easy to see that an enterprising commander possesses in the configuration and artificial development of the district many more opportunities for the display of strategical *fioritura*—of stratagems, surprises, and dainty technique—than he can expect in more normal theatres of war, where the ultimate test of good strategy is, not the occupation or maintenance of a strategic point or the mystification of the hostile general, but the tenacity of the last closed battalion under fire. In the Valley neither side seeks a decision by main force of armies, but each seeks to reap secondary advantages from the temporary possession of road-junctions and good positions. Add to this the fact that if the enemy abstained from counter-attacks of his own free will, or was forced to do so by the action of the main Federal army in Virginia, the Valley was no longer a strategical asset of any particular value, and it is easy to condone the tendency of the Union Government to consider it as the proper field for semi-police work carried out by small garrisons, fatal as that policy so often was when Lee, through no fault of the Valley commanders, was allowed to shift the centre of gravity of his army to that quarter.

The new feature introduced by Grant into the operations here was the idea of using the offensive for defensive objects. His own words give an interesting exposition of the situation as he conceived it.

"It was necessary to leave a great number of troops to guard and hold the country we had captured and to prevent incursions into the Northern States. These troops could perform this service just as well by advancing as by remaining still; and by advancing they would compel the enemy to keep detachments to hold them back or else lay his own territory open to invasion."

The details of execution proved more difficult, however, than the establishment of the general principles. The Kanawha and Shenandoah forces were to go forward, like other Union troops, but whither? The first course suggested by Grant was that one column should march from Beverly, on Covington and Staunton, and another from Charleston against New River Bridge. Both columns, according to this, were directly aimed at the enemy's railways, Ord's from Beverly against the Virginia Central, Crook's from Charleston against the Virginia and Tennessee. Sigel, however, represented that the time required for the available forces to concentrate in West Virginia—their assembly being slow and laborious owing to the state of the weather and the roads—would be utilized by the Confederates in raiding the depleted Union garrisons at the mouth of the Valley. These representations were emphasized by Ord's voluntary resignation of the command he was to have held in the proposed expedition, and Grant then sent Colonel Babcock of his staff to Sigel's headquarters to discuss alternative measures. On Sigel's suggestion the Beverly route was abandoned, and the available forces, with Grant's approval, were collected in two mobile columns, one under Crook in the Kanawha region, the other under Sigel himself in the neighbourhood of Martinsburg (see Sketch Map XVIII. and Map I.).

Crook was " to cut New River Bridge and the (rail) road ten or twenty miles east ", in Grant's words. But he was ordered to destroy the salt works at Saltville as well, and out of this extension of Crook's original programme some misunderstandings and mistakes undoubtedly proceeded.

General Crook proposed to meet these two requirements by dividing his forces, the cavalry to proceed into the heart of the mountains against Saltville, the infantry to undertake the New River enterprise.

On receiving this project from his subordinate, Sigel formulated several objections to the course proposed. The chief of these was that as the cavalry was placed so far to the west, co-operation between the Kanawha and the Valley forces was impossible with the enemy concentrated between them in the Staunton district. This was undeniably true, as also was his other objection, viz. that Crook's cavalry would be ineffective for some days after so hard a ride. What Sigel failed to see was that the mere fact of his own column assembling at Martinsburg, instead of at Beverly, made co-operation impossible under any circumstances unless the intervening enemy were beaten. His view was that Crook should operate between the New and James rivers, and that the operations should end with a grand demonstration on Staunton, and so firmly had he grasped this idea of co-operation that on his advance from Cedar Creek to Mount Jackson he hauled with him a special convoy—a legacy of the defunct Beverly scheme—so as to replenish Crook's supplies when the columns should unite. In Sigel's mind Staunton still remained the objective of the expedition, and it was merely the route to that place, not the whole plan of operations, that had been changed in the interests of the Baltimore and Ohio line.

No such considerations, however, entered into Grant's reading of this undeniably difficult problem. He abandoned the idea of co-operation as chimerical, and so far from assigning Staunton as the objective of a "grand combined demonstration", he limited the advance of the Valley column to the line of Cedar Creek. Sigel's own words define the task allotted to this column. It had the "double object of protecting the eastern part of the department from Harper's Ferry to Cumberland, and at the same time facilitating the operations of General Crook by inducing his opponents to detach a part of his forces in South-west Virginia against the Valley column". This arrangement was arrived at by Sigel in consultation with Colonel Babcock, but, judging by the course operations actually took, we may doubt if Sigel ever fully disabused his mind of the idea of a co-operative and concentric movement on Staunton.

However, Sigel and Grant were at one in commending the boldness of Crook's scheme and in giving him a free hand to carry it out.

The actual operations in the Shenandoah Valley and in South-west Virginia during May comprised three or four episodes, which we shall now describe in general terms and without reference to details of local significance.

Brigadier-General Crook, in West Virginia, disposed of somewhat less than 6000 infantry and 2500 cavalry for field operations. The latter, with the exception of a few hundred men whom he kept

MINOR ARMIES IN THE EAST

at his own disposal, were sent under Brigadier-General W. W. Averell into the Saltville-Wytheville region that we have referred to above as the eyrie of the Confederates. Crook himself, with perhaps 6000 men of all arms, set out towards the region of New Bern. Both Crook and Averell met with almost insurmountable difficulties in hauling their supplies over the high, bleak, and roadless mountains of the Alleghany mass.

Averell started from Charleston, West Virginia, on the 1st of May. He marched along valleys and crests by way of Logan and Wyoming County into Tazewell County. On May 9 he arrived in front of the enemy's outposts at Saltville, but finding the salt mines strongly guarded by Morgan and being destitute of artillery, he vanished in the night and arrived near the lead mines of Wytheville on the evening of the 10th. But Morgan promptly appeared with a force from Saltville and made a bold and active defence, driving Averell eastward with a loss of 123 men. The Union general then, moving at his best speed and actually gaining on Morgan (who followed him up from Wytheville), entered New Bern on the 11th. Here he expected to find Crook and the main body. Crook, however, had already started on his return march, and Averell, after destroying the railway around Christiansburg and the repair shops at that place,* followed him.

Crook meanwhile had achieved his object, and

---

* Averell found here some field guns destined for the Confederate army, which he destroyed.

in addition had fought and won a well-contested action. His command left Fayette on May 3, drove away a small Confederate force at Princeton on the 6th, and headed for its objective point, the New River bridge. On the morning of the 9th, he found a large force of the enemy under Generals W. E. Jones and A. G. Jenkins in position barring his advance on Dublin. Crook's attack (action of Cloyd's Mountain) was made vigorously and skilfully, and was an entire success. General Jenkins was killed, and the Confederates driven in disorder to Dublin, pursued by the handful of cavalry which Crook had kept with him when he despatched Averell on the raid towards Saltville. At Dublin, Crook met and defeated a party of Morgan's men which had come up by rail from Wytheville (Averell on this day was before Saltville), and destroyed various military stores. Passing on, on the morning of the 10th he destroyed the New River bridge with but little difficulty.

Having thus accomplished the object of his expedition he turned homeward. He had lost 600 men in the action of Cloyd's Mountain, but he had killed and wounded perhaps 500 of the enemy, and in addition had captured 230 unwounded prisoners and two guns. He had, however, to leave behind some 200 of his own men, who were too seriously wounded to face the hardships of the return march over the Alleghanies. The column started, late on the 10th, for Union. Averell came up with it in due course, and on the 19th, having suffered severely, not only from the ordinary and foreseen difficulties of a roadless and

MINOR ARMIES IN THE EAST

barren country, but even more from an almost continuous rain-storm, Crook and Averell went into camp at Meadow Bluff.

For the remainder of the month Crook was employed in resting his command, in replacing its broken-down transport, in remounting its cavalry, and in drawing together fresh supplies.

Crook and Averell had fought in the main against the troops of the district of South-western Virginia. Those of the Valley district, temporarily under Brigadier-General J. D. Imboden, were opposed to Sigel on the middle Shenandoah. Imboden was a native of the Valley and familiar with the country and its inhabitants from Staunton to Martinsburg. He utilized this knowledge with remarkable skill. By trapping successively each of Sigel's two cavalry flank guards, he gained four days' respite, and thus enabled Breckinridge to bring up all the forces that could be spared from the James and New River region, and gave time for the militia to assemble.

Sigel's advance to Cedar Creek had been made, as we know, with the object of tempting a part of Breckinridge's forces away from the region in which Crook and Averell were operating. He now formed the soldierly resolution to advance further still, and to threaten Imboden so effectually as to *compel* Breckinridge to come to the rescue.

The Union column, therefore, advanced to Woodstock (May 10), but, delayed by the mishaps to its cavalry, it only resumed the advance on the

13th, by which time Sigel had become aware that his purpose of drawing Breckinridge to the Shenandoah was accomplished. It was at this point that the Union commander made his single, but decisive, error. Instead of manœuvring to contain the united forces of Breckinridge and Imboden, he allowed himself to be prevailed upon by enthusiastic reports from the advanced guard * to fight a battle. "Believing", he says, "that a retreat would have a bad effect on our troops, and well aware of *the strategical value of New Market* † (as a road centre), I resolved to hold the enemy in check (with the advanced guard) until the arrival of our main forces from Mount Jackson, and then accept battle".

The action of New Market (May 15) was closely contested between almost equal forces. It was decided against the Union troops by what Sigel himself called "a timely and skilful manœuvre" of Imboden's mounted troops against the Federal rear. Sigel fell back in good order ‡ and unmolested to the line of Cedar Creek whence he had come, and, on reporting his reverse to General Grant, was superseded.

Grant was "dissatisfied" with the conduct of operations on Sigel's part. Only an hour or two

---

* Probably, also, by the still attractive idea of co-operating with Crook towards Staunton, to which new life had perhaps been given by the fact of his having been allowed to go forward from Cedar Creek.

† The italics are ours.

‡ Halleck's report to Grant, " Sigel will do nothing but run ; never did anything else", was more epigrammatic than it was true of the present case or just in general.

before he received news of the defeat he had written to Halleck in these terms: "Cannot Sigel go up Shenandoah Valley to Staunton? The enemy is evidently drawing supplies largely from that source,* and if Sigel can destroy the road there it will be of vast importance to us". It is evident, then, that he no longer objected to Sigel's advancing beyond Cedar Creek, of which, as also of Breckinridge's counter-move, he had been informed on the 14th. It was in fighting a battle that Sigel disobeyed the spirit of his instructions.†

His task, to paraphrase Grant's report, was "to threaten the enemy in the Shenandoah Valley and to advance as far as possible. By so doing he would compel the enemy to detach largely for the protection of his supplies and lines of communication, on pain of losing them. The troops in the department of West Virginia were held there for the defence of the North against raids, and for the occupation of conquered ground. They could act directly to their front and give better protection than if lying idle in garrison". The forces charged with this work were encouraged and ordered to do what they could so far as the limitations of their principal duty permitted. They were to contain

---

* *Viâ* the Virginia Central and Hanover Junction.

† When Grant explained Sigel's part in the general programme to Lincoln, the President replied with one of his Western aphorisms, "I see, if Sigel can't skin he must hold a leg while some one else does". It is to be regretted that Grant did not make matters as clear to Sigel as he did to Lincoln. This is often the case, as students of Napoleon are aware; a soldier speaking to soldiers often fails to impress them with his precise meaning, because he thinks it must be obvious to the trained mind, and does not wish to insult their experience and ability by the appearance of "talking down" to them.

the forces, or in their absence to destroy the communications, of the enemy, and at the same time to maintain their own territorial defence intact. A lost battle might easily involve failure in all three objects. The Confederates at Cloyd's Mountain were quite as severely defeated as the Federals at New Market, yet the effects of Sigel's reverse far outweighed those of Crook's victory.

Nothing, in short, could be gained by fighting that could not be gained by manœuvring,* and a general engagement would imperil not merely the secondary and negative object of binding and impeding the enemy, but also the primary and positive object of defending the mouth of the Valley. While Crook, whose positive object was the destruction of New River bridge, necessarily attacked the enemy who barred his way thither, Sigel, whose positive object was to hold his own, risked it in pursuit of a negative object which could equally well have been obtained without heroic measures.

The later operations in the Shenandoah Valley under General Hunter, who succeeded Sigel on May 21, do not fall within the scope of the present volume. It is interesting to observe, however, that so far as concerned the operations immediately in hand, Grant's instructions to Hunter were an

* Not, be it observed, by merely demonstrating, but by manœuvring to keep the enemy in play. Up to the 14th Sigel's conduct was a model in this respect, and was as successful as it deserved to be. The whole episode reminds us forcibly of the operations of Eugène Beauharnais in Italy in 1809, for which, and for an account of the principles of strategy in relation to secondary operations, see the third of Major-General Douglas Haig's *Cavalry Studies*. (London: Hugh Rees, 1907.)

emphasized repetition of those to Sigel. All movements, whether on Staunton, Gordonsville, Charlottesville, or Lynchburg, were to have for their object the breaking up of lines of communication and the occupation or control of supply areas. The execution of the movements ordered was definitely subjected to the condition that "too much opposition" was not encountered. Lastly, Hunter was informed that he would be doing good service if he could hold a force of the enemy equal to his own.

As in Butler's case, so in Sigel's, failure is distinctly traceable to the fact that a "directive" was misapplied by a commander who should have had an "order".

CHAPTER XVIII

THE PASSAGE OF THE PAMUNKEY, MAY 26-27

GENERAL GRANT'S decision not to fight a battle on the North Anna was based on the facts revealed by a close reconnaissance of Lee's lines on the 25th. It was found that the position and the works of the enemy were stronger than ever before. It was already known that he had been reinforced by Breckinridge's command from the Valley, and by part, at any rate, of Beauregard's from the James. Moreover, the Army of the Potomac had, however accidentally, placed itself in a very awkward position, both for attack and for defence.

There was another factor to be taken into account. Butler's field troops under W. F. Smith, being evidently useless where they were, had been called up to join the Army of the Potomac by way of West Point or White House.

The extrication of the Army of the Potomac from its false position, and its safe junction with Smith's command, were the immediate and obvious tasks of the superior leading, and most generals would probably have been content to manœuvre behind the Pamunkey until this was achieved. Grant, however, looking always to a battle, and unwilling to forego the least chance of forcing Lee

PASSAGE OF THE PAMUNKEY

to fight in the open, proposed the crossing of the Pamunkey as his next object, and after that either the utilization of a favourable opportunity to fight, or, when Smith arrived, the creation of such an opportunity.

His dispositions for the immediate operation—that of crossing the river—are of the greatest interest, reflecting as they do some lessons learned from earlier manœuvres.

On the afternoon of the 25th he issued the following directive (see Map III. and Sketch Map XIX.):—

"Direct Generals Warren and Wright to withdraw all their teams and artillery not in position to the north side of the river to-morrow (26th). Send that belonging to General Wright's corps as far on the road to Hanover Town as it can go without attracting attention. Send with it Wright's best division, or division under his ablest commander. Have its place filled up in the line, so if possible the enemy will not notice their withdrawal. Send the cavalry to-morrow afternoon, or as much of it as you may deem necessary, to watch and seize if they can Littlepage's Bridge and Taylor's Ford, and to remain on one or other side of the river at these points until the infantry and artillery all pass. As soon as it is dark to-morrow night start the division you withdraw first from Wright's corps to make a forced march to Hanover Town, taking with them no trains to impede their march. At the same time this division starts commence withdrawing all of the V. and VI. Corps from the south side of the river and march them for the same place. The two divisions of the IX. Corps not now with Hancock may be moved down the north bank of the river, where they will be handy to support Hancock if necessary, or will be that much on their road to follow the V. and VI. Corps. Hancock should hold his command in readiness to follow as soon as the way is clear for him to-morrow.

It will leave nothing for him to do, but as soon as he can he should get all his teams and spare artillery on the road or roads he will have to take. As soon as the troops reach Hanover Town they should get possession of all the crossings they can in that neighbourhood.

"U. S. GRANT,
"Lieut.-General.

"I think it would be well to make a heavy cavalry demonstration on the enemy's left to-morrow afternoon also.

"U. S. G."

Wright selected Russell's division, which he had formerly himself commanded, for this important service. The postscript was obeyed by the despatch of Wilson's cavalry division to join Hammond's force on the right of the VI. Corps.

The first point to be observed is that for once there is not a word of attacking the enemy or of a battle. The entire available effort was to be concentrated on the attainment of the *immediate* object in view—to gain and to maintain deploying space on the south side of the Pamunkey.*

Now, to seize a point, what is required above all is mobility, and to maintain it, resisting power. Hence, for the first time in the campaign, we meet with the independent advanced guard of all arms —a formation to-day almost stereotyped. Three weeks before this (May 5) Grant had moved his

* An order sent to Washington on the 26th, to have the reserve engineer troops and all bridging material available sent to Fortress Monroe so as to be ready to move up the James, foreshadows the immediate co-operation of Meade, Smith, and Butler in certain contingencies. These did not, however, arise during the manœuvre now under consideration.

army into an area gained for it by the cavalry, and had allowed the cavalry to move on elsewhere before the army was in the desired position; eighteen days ago (May 8) the cavalry again secured an area of ground for their comrades of the main body, but had been unable by themselves to maintain it. Since then there had been no cavalry mass available with the Army of the Potomac, and all the cavalry that could be got together had barely sufficed to provide for the needs of protective reconnaissance.

Now that Sheridan had returned, and the Union commander had resumed control of his "strategical cavalry", these lessons were to bear fruit. They may be summarized as follows: Local or tactical protection enables a marching column to turn and fight if the enemy unexpectedly advances upon it, general or strategic protection enables it to continue in the execution of its original orders, and by implication enables a commander to issue these orders with the certainty that they will be executed. The principle holds good whether it is applied in order to prepare a decisive battle or to place the army on a new line of operations as in the present case, or to any other operation. The situation upon which the manœuvre in each case is based must be at the end what it was at the beginning of the movement. If a great battle is looked for, the advanced guard has to use its last efforts to hold fast what it has gripped; the same formula defines its action if the occupation of an area of ground, for whatever purpose, is intended.

Such schemes depend for their success on the

soldierly qualities and tenacity of the advanced guard troops, the resolution of their leader, and other moral and material factors, the appreciation of which by the supreme command gives the all-important data as to how long the detachment can hold its ground against a superior force, and therefore how far it can be detached from the main body with safety.

Hanover Town, the selected point of passage,* was a little more than twenty miles distant from Lee at Hanover Junction, and thirty-four or thirty-five miles from the outer flank of the Army of the Potomac. Lee was twelve miles distant from Littlepage's Bridge, to Grant's twenty-seven or twenty-eight.

Sheridan's cavalry, being in rear of the army towards Pole Cat Station, could be moved suddenly and swiftly, without attracting attention. The same may be said of Russell's division, which was withdrawn from the line of the VI. Corps with all possible secrecy. There was little or no reason, then, to fear that Sheridan and Russell would find themselves forestalled at the crossing by any troops sent thither by Lee for the purpose. Now, at Littlepage's Bridge or thereabouts, it was to be expected that the enemy would already have a strong detachment for the protection of the Central Railroad, while at a little country place like Hanover Town there was no likelihood of finding any important post of troops.

* The existence or practicability of Nelson's Ferry was apparently not known at the Union headquarters until Sheridan had passed over the ground. As has been said above, the maps were at their worst in the neighbourhood of the Annas.

PASSAGE OF THE PAMUNKEY

But when Lee's cavalry had given definite information of Sheridan's presence at Hanover Town, the Army of Northern Virginia might be set on foot at once. It would, geographically, be ten or fifteen miles to the good in a race for position, as compared with the Union army, and the wider the area seized by the Union advanced guard the sooner Lee's heads of columns would take contact. Thus Sheridan's command, at whatever time it arrived and of whatever arms it consisted, would have to act as a living *tête-de-pont* for perhaps as much as twelve hours before matters were equalized by the arrival of a considerable portion of its main body. Hence the inclusion of a specially selected infantry division, the feint upon Lee's left ordered on Grant's postscript, and the provision that the withdrawal of the main army shall synchronize with Russell's departure for Hanover Town—all measures intended to facilitate, not Sheridan's actual movements, but the subsequent defence of the crossings he was to seize.

Meade's orders were as follows:—

Headquarters Army of the Potomac,
May 26, 1864, 10 A.M.

1. The VI. Corps will be withdrawn at dark by Jericho Bridge and follow the route of Russell's division . . . to Hanovertown, taking the road nearest the Pamunkey. The train of the corps will join it at Chesterfield station.

2. The V. Corps will be withdrawn at dark by Quarles's Ford Bridge and pass *via* Old Chesterfield to New Castle Ferry . . . by roads to be examined to-day, and respecting which further instructions will be given. The route of the V. Corps will be to the N. and E. of the route of the VI. Corps. The wooden pontoons forming Jericho Bridge

and as many others as are available will accompany the V. Corps. . . . Any surplus canvas pontoons with the cavalry at Hanovertown may be obtained if required for the bridge at New Castle.

3. Crittenden's division (IX. Corps) will be withdrawn at dark. The IX. Corps will hold the fords and crossings from Ox Ford to Jericho Mills.

4. The II. Corps and Willcox's division (IX. Corps) will be withdrawn at an hour to be hereafter indicated. The II. Corps will hold the fords and crossings below Ox Ford.

5. When the roads taken by the V. and VI. Corps are clear the IX. Corps will follow the V. to New Castle Ferry, the II. will follow the VI. to Hanovertown. The withdrawal of these two corps from the river and their movements by the route indicated will be simultaneous.

The corps commanders will act in concert. As soon as it can be done without interfering with the trains and movements of the V. and VI. Corps, the trains and surplus artillery of the IX. and II. Corps will be moved to the roads these corps will take. All bridges will be removed when the troops recross to the North Anna.

6. The division of cavalry on the right will hold the various fords and bridges as they are successively abandoned . . . and cover the rear of the army.

7. Headquarters will be on the route of the VI. and II. Corps.

8. The supply and other main trains . . . will be moved to-night . . . along the N. or E. bank of the Mattapony to Dunkirk or that vicinity . . . and thence to Hanovertown. A pontoon train will accompany them.

By command of Major-General Meade,

S. WILLIAMS, A.A.G.

It will be noticed that there are no orders for the main body of the cavalry corps. This may have been, in part, a precaution. In case a copy of the orders went astray, there was nothing in the text to show that Sheridan's entire command

PASSAGE OF THE PAMUNKEY 401

had returned to the army, and the division of cavalry mentioned in (6) is not named. But whether this be so or not, the strategic advanced guard, as we may justly term it, must certainly have acted under special, if not verbal, instructions from Grant, for army orders refer to Russell's division as distantly as if it were an independent army.

According to these orders, the V. Corps, instead of following the VI. to Hanover Town, was to proceed by a separate route to New Castle Ferry, some miles further down the river. Grant's directive had contemplated a march of the whole army—in order, Sheridan, Wright, Warren, Burnside, Hancock—along the river road, but Meade now disposed the army in two marching columns on two roads at wide intervals. Thus the rear corps were enabled to be clear of the now dangerous vicinity of the North Anna on the morning instead of the afternoon of the 27th. Another consideration seems to have weighed with Meade in making this decision—the desirability of opening up communication with White House as soon as possible. It was at Meade's suggestion that Smith was ordered on disembarkation to make White House a garrisoned centre of operations and to hold intact the railway bridge at that place, and Warren and Burnside, pointing towards New Castle instead of Hanover Town, would be by so much closer to the new line.

The simplicity of that part of the order which deals with the problem of recrossing the North Anna is very remarkable. The divided halves of the army were ordered, without comment or minute instructions, to retire over their bridges at night, in the presence of a vigilant enemy, to pack up their pontoons and their telegraph wire, and, extending a screen along the northern bank, to form up in two long marching columns with artillery and train complete, in one night. This ambitious programme was fulfilled to the letter.

At 9.55 P.M. on May 25, not "to-morrow" as Grant had originally ordered, Meade had sent instructions to Warren and Wright to withdraw their trains and surplus artillery over the Jericho and Quarles pontoon bridges, and to have everything packed in readiness for moving *via* Mount Carmel Church. This was done in the course of the night, as was the withdrawal of the selected division— Russell's (formerly Wright's own) division of the VI. Corps. The line vacated by Russell was filled up without a hitch.

At 8.45 A.M., 26th, Hancock was asked whether he could safely withdraw by daylight, but he replied that in general the corps was too close to the enemy to do so. He was then ordered to make every arrangement for recrossing the river at nightfall of this day (26th).* Burnside was to hold the upper fords, Hancock the lower, when everything had recrossed on both wings and the pontoons had been taken up. Meanwhile the II., V., and VI. Corps were employed in breaking up the railroads on either flank. Even the line about

* The general order evidently summarizes the results of a day's careful consideration and pre-arrangement with individual corps commanders.

Pole Cat Station was interrupted, preparatory to the change of the line of supply from Port Royal to White House. Hancock placed himself in communication with Burnside, and the two generals closely co-operated in the delicate work of retiring and extending along the north bank.

The withdrawal of the main army was accomplished during the night with complete success, the only hitch, and that a slight one,[*] being that a brigade of the IX. Corps cut through the marching column of the V. Corps. On the morning of the 27th, Lee's pickets found the whole of the south side clear of the enemy. If, as has been always so often maintained, this was the finest opportunity Lee ever had of destroying the Army of the Potomac, it was now gone, thanks to an exactitude of staff work with which the Union volunteer armies are not always credited on this side of the Atlantic.

Hancock and Burnside picketed the north bank and massed their main bodies in rear, ready to follow the V. and VI. Corps, which were making good speed in the track of the advanced guard.

The manœuvre was executed as ordered. Sheridan's two divisions (1st again under Torbert, and 2nd under Gregg) moved off on the afternoon of the 26th, and after detaching small bodies to hold Taylor's Ford and Littlepage's Bridge (as ordered by General Grant), marched by the river road to Hanover Town. Russell followed at nightfall, and moved with such celerity as

[*] It led, however, to some acrimonious correspondence between Meade and his senior and subordinate, Burnside.

to arrive only two or three hours behind the cavalry.

Only a strong picket of the enemy's cavalry opposed the crossing, and, the canvas pontoon train being well up to the front of the column, two bridges were in use and the whole of Torbert's division across by 9 A.M. on the 27th. At Hanover Town a Confederate cavalry brigade (Barringer's) was charged and driven away, and the Union cavalry gained ground northwards as far as Crump's Creek. The horses were somewhat overworked, and it is probable that there was a shortage of forage. Sheridan therefore halted Torbert at the south side of the creek. Gregg's division moved out a short distance on the Hawes's Shop Road and went into bivouac. Russell followed Gregg across about eleven. Soon afterwards Russell reported, through his corps commander,* that 10,000 hostile infantry under Breckinridge, and a cavalry brigade under Rosser, were at Hanover Court House, and between that place and Sheridan's outposts. Later advices were that the whole of Fitz Lee's cavalry division was on the Court House road.

Warren and Wright recrossed the North Anna, Wright having the lead through Mount Carmel. Thence the VI. Corps took the road nearest the Pamunkey, the V. a road to the northward. The roads about North Anna were not clear for the II. and IX. Corps to withdraw until about 10.30, as the VI. and V. Corps in the early stage of the

* It is open to question whether Russell should not have been assigned to Sheridan's command for the day.

march practically formed one column with a time-length of about eight hours. Burnside followed Warren, and Hancock Wright, and thus there was no further crossing of columns.

In the course of the day the route of Wright and Hancock was changed so as to bring them over Nelson's or Hundley's Ferry on the morning of the 28th, and the destination of Warren and Burnside was altered from New Castle Ferry to Hanover Town. The presence of a heavy mass of the enemy at Hanover Court House made it advisable to give immediate support to the cavalry at Crump's Creek, while at the same time it argued that Lee had not yet fallen back any considerable distance, and *ipso facto* offered some hope of a fairly large manœuvre area—*i.e.* of keeping away from the proximity of Richmond.

All eye-witnesses speak of the excellent spirits of the army as it marched away from the North Anna. They had left no vain sacrifice of men before the strong works at Hanover Junction, and the enlisted men knew well enough that the withdrawal had been a complete success. The present movement was understood as a "flank movement", and therefore satisfied their simple strategical canon.

The four corps of the main body halted for the night of the 27th/28th at a considerable distance from Hanover Town and Nelson's Ferry. The II. and IX. Corps, in particular, had a severe march owing to their late start and the heat of the day. The advanced guard (two cavalry divisions and one infantry division) was, as we know, beyond the

Pamunkey, and four to six miles out from Hanover Town, on the roads towards Hanover Court House and Richmond. Wilson's cavalry division took over the picket line along the North Anna, and brought up the rear of the whole army. The trains moved from Bowling Green to Dunkirk.

CHAPTER XIX

TOTOPOTOMOY CREEK, MAY 28–30

May 28.—On the evening of the 27th, orders were issued individually to the corps commanders to the following effect (see Sketch Map XIX.):—

Wright was to cross at daylight on the 28th at Hundley's (or Nelson's) Ferry, where a bridge was to be laid. He was then to deploy so as to hold the crossings of Crump's Creek with his right, and to extend towards the Totopotomoy with his left. Warren was to cross at Hanover Town, to send back Russell's division, which he would find there, to Wright, and to move forward until his left rested on the Totopotomoy and his right extended towards Crump's Creek. Hancock was ordered to cross at Hundley's Bridge and to take position on Wright's left. Last of all, Burnside was to cross at Hanover Town and to form on Warren's right. After the completion of these movements, which were expected to occupy the whole of the 28th, the order of the corps from right (Crump's Creek) to left (Mrs. Via's on the Totopotomoy) would be Wright, Hancock, Burnside, Warren. Meantime, Sheridan was to reconnoitre towards Mechanicsville on the upper Chickahominy (that is, practically, towards the north side of Richmond) in order to gain information of the enemy's movements.

At the time these orders were issued the Confederate cavalry and Breckinridge's infantry were reported to be at Hanover Court House. As to Lee's main army there was no information, but it might be presumed that whatever counter-move Lee designed would already be in progress. In these circumstances Grant's chief preoccupation was to keep the area of manœuvre as far from Richmond as possible, even north of the Totopotomoy. In assembling his army on the south bank of the river, then, he prepared to receive any attack that might come from Hanover Court House on the 28th, and to improve whatever tactical gain such an event might bring him, while at the same time he ordered Sheridan to make an extended reconnaissance to discover whether Lee had fallen back into or towards Richmond. Short of an attack on the VI. Corps, operations on the 29th would depend upon the reports of the cavalry. If, as was actually the case, these reports were not sufficiently full, the army would have to advance to reconnoitre for itself, and it would be time to devise and to execute the next actively offensive manœuvre after meeting the enemy and taking contact along his front. Meanwhile, space had to be economized and time wasted, if the Union army was still to have room to act on the 30th or 31st.

Sheridan's forward move on the Richmond Road was undertaken with Gregg's division only, Torbert's being still at Crump's Creek and Wilson's far away on the North Anna. He had advanced only a few miles when serious opposition was met. About a mile beyond Hawes's Shop on the road towards Atlee's Station, Gregg's leading troops found Fitz Lee's division behind log-works. A long and closely contested fire fight ensued, neither side giving way until late in the evening, when the arrival of Custer's brigade gave Gregg the necessary forward impetus. The log-works were then carried in the most gallant manner. The other two brigades of Torbert's division (Devin and Merritt) were called up from Crump's Creek, but did not arrive in time to take an active part.*

The Cavalry Corps lost 350 men. This severe engagement was the result of the bitter quarrel between Meade and Sheridan on the 8th, which had led to the latter's being detached without sufficient forage to pursue the enemy *à outrance*. It was, moreover, the prelude of the still fiercer action of Trevilian's Station in June.

The lives of Sheridan's troopers, however,† bought positive information of high importance, viz. that Ewell's and Longstreet's (Anderson's) corps were four miles west of Hawes's Shop, marching to keep pace with, or to head off, the Army of the Potomac. Infantry and trains were also reported at or near Shady Grove Church.

---

* General Sheridan bears tribute to the bravery of a strong brigade of South Carolinians under Colonel M. C. Butler, that formed part of Fitz Lee's forces, and were here engaged for the first time. Butler was soon afterwards promoted to command Hampton's division when Hampton received the command of the Cavalry Corps.

† Sheridan, at any rate, was proud of his casualties as a triumphant refutation of the infantry sneer, "Whoever saw a dead cavalryman?"

Further to the rear, a deserter from a South Carolina regiment informed Wilson that there were now no Confederates north of the South Anna, all having left Hanover Junction last night (27th) for Ashland. This latter report was most circumstantial, and it was easy for a sanguine temperament such as Grant's to argue, from the fact that Lee was advancing *beyond* Ashland eastward, an intention on the part of the Confederate general to attack, or at worst to try conclusions once more before falling back over the Chickahominy. The actual direction of Lee's forward movement seemed to be towards Wright's front and left flank. Breckinridge was still supposed to be at Hanover Court House, and Fitz Lee at Hawes's Shop was naturally thought to mark the right flank of the Southern army's movement.

At 10.30 on the evening of the 28th, then, Wright was told that the enemy was in strong force about a mile in his front, and would probably assume the offensive on the 29th. He was ordered to be on the look-out. At the same hour Hancock, who had spent the day, after crossing the Pamunkey, in endeavouring to bridge the gap between Warren and himself that Burnside was to fill on arrival, was given the same information and ordered to take up a good line of resistance.

Warren and Burnside were ordered to prolong the line through Hawes's Shop to the Totopotomoy, but to keep their lines as short as possible so as to have a force available for movement.

It is clear from this distribution that, should Lee advance, he would be met by well-covered defenders on the Union right, and by a mass of manœuvre on the Union left. It is the almost invariable manœuvre by the left applied to the "defensive-offensive". The offensive manœuvre of the left wing would open only when the enemy's attack had become pronounced all along the defensive front. If nothing happened on the 29th and the Army of the Potomac advanced on the 30th, its interior distribution in density and its extent of front might, and probably would, be materially altered. But the present problem was, how to take full advantage of Lee's possible offensive "outside works" on the 29th, and the solution of it by the Union headquarters was to form up the four corps in a connected line from Crump's Creek to the Totopotomoy, and to give this line the minimum density on the defensive front and the maximum at the point predestined for the counter-stroke.

Wright's corps covered one and a half miles of ground, Hancock's two miles, Burnside's and Warren's little more than one mile together.

Meanwhile, Smith (XVIII. Corps) was ordered to White House, and thence by the south side of the Pamunkey to New Castle Ferry, leaving a garrison with some artillery to constitute a depôt at White House, pending the arrival (already ordered) of General Abercrombie and the line of communication troops from Port Royal. Butler was not a great general, but he was a great administrator and a loyal subordinate. Once the order was made which deprived him of Smith and two-thirds of his army, he acquiesced without a murmur and did everything in his power to make the movement a success.

May 29.—Lee did not attack, after all, and eventually the Army of the Potomac moved forward to find out his positions. The Cavalry Corps (except Wilson's division, which was still on the other bank of the Pamunkey) had now been drawn off to the Old Church Road on the left of the general line and beyond the Totopotomoy.

At 8.45 A.M. reconnaissances of all arms were ordered, to begin at noon, by General Meade. Wright was to examine the road towards Hanover Court House, Hancock to send a division with artillery on the Hawes's Shop–Enon Church Road. Warren was to do likewise on the Shady Grove Church Road. Burnside was to reconnoitre with a smaller force between the II. and V. Corps columns. Engineers and topographers were to be sent with each expedition. The main bodies of the II., V., and VI. Corps were to be held ready to support their respective divisions, and that of the IX. Corps formed the general reserve.

Wright reconnoitred towards Hanover Court House, starting at midday, and at 4.45 reported that there was no hostile force in that direction except a few cavalry.

Hancock moved off Barlow's division at twelve as ordered. At two, a hostile skirmish line of cavalry was met at Polly Hundley's Corner and driven in. It was reported that the enemy had a line of battle on a small stream a mile ahead, but Barlow, keeping to the general north-westerly direction of his advance, left a small force at this point and went off to the right to meet Brooke's brigade, which had gone north-west from Enon Church. Brooke reported that he had met only some cavalry and a section of horse artillery, and Barlow thereupon promptly returned to Polly Hundley's with his main body. At 5.15, Meade, who was at the headquarters of the II. Corps, informed Grant that Barlow had met the enemy in force " about four miles from here (Hawes's Shop). He reports artillery in position and infantry in rifle pits ".

Warren's movement of Griffin's division by Armstrong's towards Sydnor's Mill produced similar information. Half a mile beyond Armstrong's the Union advance drove in cavalry skirmishers, and at 3 P.M. Griffin reported a line of battle towards his right " on the side of the stream (Totopotomoy) opposite you ".

The report of Burnside's reconnaissance is not preserved, and probably it was never made, as the corps was occupied all day in coming into position between Hancock and Warren. The last division of the corps had not crossed the Pamunkey until 1 A.M. that morning, and the head of the corps became entangled with the V. Corps in moving to its position at Hawes's Shop. All the roads towards the enemy were accounted for, as a matter of fact, by the II. and V. Corps, for Warren moved Cutler down to the Totopotomoy opposite Via's so as to be ready to support Griffin if required.

" It was apparent that we were close upon Lee's whole army ", says Humphreys. The Army of Northern Virginia had become aware of the withdrawal of its old opponent from the North Anna lines at daylight on the 27th. At 6.45 that morning Lee telegraphed to Richmond that portions of the Federal army were still visible on the north side of the Anna, but that cavalry and infantry * had crossed at Hanover Town. "I have sent the cavalry in that direction", he continued, "and will move the army to Ashland".

Ewell's corps (now under Early, Ewell having retired on account of illness) moved by the Virginia Central to Merry Oaks, and thence to Hughes Cross Roads, four miles north-west of Atlee's Station (distance about twenty miles). Anderson moved by the Telegraph Road to Half Sink, a spot a mile or two west of Early. Hill and Breckinridge followed. "The object of the general", wrote a staff officer in orders, "is to get possession of the ridge between Totopotomoy and Beaver Dam Creek", and in accordance with that object, the Army of Northern Virginia filed into position along the Totopotomoy early on the 28th. The construction of entrenchments was at once undertaken, though, both here and at Cold Harbor later, the entrenchments were, according to a Confederate general, "the worst we ever fought in". The two cavalry divisions were strung out on the right and left front of the line of works, Hampton on the left and Fitz Lee on the right. The small detachments in front of the line cleared away to the flanks on the advance of the Union army.

* No Federal infantry began to cross the Pamunkey until 11 A.M. on the 27th.

At 7 P.M. Meade's orders were issued for the 30th. They amounted to a deployment of the whole army opposite the Confederate line of defence that had been discovered in the afternoon's reconnaissances. No battle was intended for the 30th, pending the arrival of Smith's corps, but exact information as to the details of Lee's front and flanks was necessary for planning a battle for the 31st or June 1, and the maintenance of the existing situation (as ascertained on the 30th) until it could be exploited, would probably call for resolute skirmishing and, locally and at times, for brigade and divisional attacks in earnest. Meade is reported to have said, "In this country I must fight a battle to make a reconnaissance" —a truth which, however, is not special to the American Civil War, as Napoleon's practice shows. A few years before this, Marshal Bugeaud had expressed the same sentiment when he said, "On reconnaît une armée avec une armée".

The II. Corps was to move at dawn and to take up a position in front of the enemy. The IX. Corps was to form on the left of the II., and the V. was to continue the line. "As the enemy apparently was close to you this P.M. it is presumed that your left will not be greatly advanced".

On the extreme right, the uneventful reconnaissance of the VI. Corps had led to its becoming extended well out beyond Crump's Creek on the two roads leading to Hanover Court House. Wright's orders were to form on Hancock's right —which was now, of course, advanced to Polly Hundley's Corner—and it was hoped that the general left wheel of the VI. Corps towards the west might be prolonged southward until it placed itself square across Lee's left flank. This was in the nature of a manœuvre, and if successful would give definite form and purpose to a subsequent attack along the whole line.

On the other flank, Warren was not expected to do more than to feel his way outwards. Moreover, the Cavalry Corps, which might have reconnoitred towards Mechanicsville, was kept back, idle, at and near Old Church, where Wilson's division, the army rearguard, was ordered to join it. The left flank was, in fact, carefully refused, for fear that Lee should suspect another turning movement and fall back behind the Chickahominy. Sheridan at and near Old Church was merely directed to open and to keep open communication with Warren's left.

May 30.—Meade's orders to the VI. Corps were, to move at daylight, to close up on the leading division (Russell's), and then to form on Hancock's right and if possible across Lee's left, as mentioned. Wright, therefore, swung round *via* Cash Corner and the road junction one mile east of Peake's Turnout, and about three miles south of the latter encountered the pickets of Hill (Confederate left wing). The swampy heads of Crump's Creek made movement very difficult, and connection with Hancock's right almost impossible. Meade seems to have been greatly irritated by the delay of the VI. Corps, for at 1.30 Wright answers a (now missing) dispatch from headquarters in

TOTOPOTOMOY CREEK

very spirited terms. The result of the advance was, moreover, to develop fresh Confederate entrenchments east of the railroad near Atlee's.

On Hancock's front the day's skirmishing was opened by the Confederate artillery, which sought by occasional shots to drive off the Union working parties. Birney had taken up the line on Barlow's right overnight, and Gibbon now came up on the left. Before nine o'clock the enemy's rifle pits (north of the Totopotomoy) had been carried on Barlow's front. Thence Barlow felt his way slowly forward towards the bare crest on the other side of the swamp. A vigorous artillery duel went on during the morning and afternoon, and the Union signallers on the roof of Colonel Shelton's house * were under heavy fire. On Gibbon's front it proved more difficult to locate the enemy's line of battle, and on Birney's the chief preoccupation of the Union commanders was to watch for Wright's arrival, and to prevent a move of the enemy to interpose between the two corps. When Wright, later in the day, reported that he was waiting for the establishment of Birney's right, Meade naturally asked the meaning of this. Birney

---

* Hancock's dispatch records an incident at the Shelton house in terms that for quaint soldierly simplicity cannot be surpassed. "The house was struck by fifty-one artillery shots . . . A large family of ladies were in the cellar of the house . . . but I had last night advised them to leave and did so repeatedly to-day, offering them facilities for so doing, which they refused, trusting in God, as they were members of the church. I have sent my report of operations this evening by an orderly". The negress attending on those pious ladies was not so calm. When the firing was at its hottest, she ran out of the house in a frenzy of terror, and emptied a pan of red-hot coals into the open limber-chest of a neighbouring gun. Several gunners were killed and terribly mutilated.

thereupon replied that the VI. Corps had wasted time, and Hancock endorsed Birney's answer. However, Wright had come up with two out of the three divisions and formed on Birney's right, and this, after all, was the chief thing.

Turning now to Burnside's front, we find the IX. Corps slowly worked its way beyond the Totopotomoy until its right rested at Whitlock's and its left was in touch with Griffin's division of the V. Corps.

On the front of Warren's command there was more serious fighting.

The whole corps had taken up the line of march to follow Griffin's advanced division, which was on the Shady Grove Road, about a mile east of Hundley's Corner.* As Burnside moved into position with the front of about a division, Griffin's line, not without several times losing connection with Burnside's left, gradually worked away a little to the south, and the other three † divisions of the corps conformed, keeping towards Griffin's left rear.

Prisoners were taken from Rodes's division, Ewell's (Early's) corps, on the Shady Grove Road. The skirmishers of the V. Corps now extended on

---

* At eight a deserter came in from the enemy, whose story affords a good example of the result of mixing a true and a false rumour to produce important intelligence. He said that Lee was sick and Ewell in command of the army. The truth was that Lee was more or less sick and that Ewell was not in command of his corps. What would have been the result, however, of basing any plan of action on the change in the enemy's commanders?

† The old 2nd Division, which had been broken up after Robinson was wounded on May 8, was re-established this day under General Lockwood. Its renewed existence was, however, short, as we shall see.

TOTOPOTOMOY CREEK 419

to the Old Church Road, where the firing became so heavy, shortly after 2 p.m., that Crawford sent one of his Pennsylvanian brigades towards Bethesda Church * to " clear away the enemy's cavalry ".

It was not cavalry, but a whole division of Early's infantry, that this brigade encountered. At eleven that morning Lee had written to Early and Anderson that a leftward movement of the Union line was in progress as usual, and that it could only be stopped by striking at once against such forces as had already crossed the Totopotomoy. Anderson was then extended to hold Early's lines at Hundley's Corner, and Early, free to move, marched out to Bethesda Church and placed Rodes's division square across the left flank of the V. Corps.

When Crawford's brigade appeared, it was greeted with the " Rebel yell ", overlapped on both flanks and driven back rapidly to the Shady Grove Road. But for once there was a clear front, and a field battery stopped the Confederate advance with rapid fire. Crawford's other brigade and parts of Cutler's division were brought hastily into line, Burnside's rear divisions were placed at Warren's disposal, and headquarters ordered an attack along the whole line of the army to relieve the V. Corps.

The V. Corps, however, held its own, and the enemy was repulsed with heavy losses, leaving a

* The Union cavalry had been withdrawn to Linney's house and Old Church, and was, besides, engaged with Fitz Lee on the Matadequin (see below). Thus it only groped for Warren's corps along the Shady Grove Church road, not towards Bethesda.

brigadier and two colonels dead on the field. Early withdrew and entrenched himself across the Old Church Road.

This was the last fight of the "Pennsylvania Reserves" of Crawford's division. Next day they were mustered out as time-expired. On the 26th of June, 1862, at Mechanicsville, a few miles up this same Old Church Road, they had been engaged in their first battle, since when they had fought in Northern Virginia, in Maryland, and in Pennsylvania. The Army of the Potomac, after a three years' Odyssey, was now almost on the ground of its first battles.

About 7 P.M. Hancock received the order for the general attack. He was to assault "wherever he could find a suitable place", and, under stress of the emergency, like the true soldier that he was, did so from the front of each division, wherever the troops happened to be. Mott's brigade of Birney's division contented itself with pushing forward a skirmish line, but Barlow in the centre moved forward Brooke's brigade in a few minutes. Colonel Brooke had all the ardour of youth on his side, and by force of leadership got his brigade through the swamp and up to the crest beyond, driving in a strong skirmish line of the enemy and passing over its works. The order to attack was suspended half an hour after it was received, but the "cease fire" found Brooke in possession of a foothold beyond the Totopotomoy, and Mott's brigade of Birney, on the right, and Owen's of Gibbon, on the left, had advanced into line with him.

TOTOPOTOMOY CREEK

No attack was delivered on Burnside's and Wright's fronts.

The XVIII. Corps was now disembarking at White House, apparently unknown to Lee. How the Confederate cavalry on this side, well forward as it was and under so energetic a leader as Fitzhugh Lee, was prevented from giving this important information to the commanding general may be told briefly in Sheridan's own words.

> "The enemy collected on my front on the Cold Harbor Road not far from Old Church (crossing by Matadequin Creek). I directed General Torbert to attack them at one o'clock to-day. We defeated them and drove them down to Cold Harbor. It was a very handsome affair and very creditable to General Torbert and his division . . ."

The cavalry corps bivouacked about a mile and a half from Cold Harbor. Their move was destined to have important consequences.

CHAPTER XX

EXTENDING TO COLD HARBOR, MAY 31–JUNE 2

HITHERTO, it will have been observed, operations had been limited to the area north of the Shady Grove Church Road. But Warren's reconnaissance and the sharp counter-stroke that it provoked, as well as Sheridan's fight at the Matadequin crossing, necessarily shifted the centre of gravity somewhat, and Grant's anxiety to avoid further extension was reflected in his instructions to Smith. From White House, the XVIII. Corps could advance either towards New Castle Ferry or towards Cold Harbor—that is, either to the left rear of the existing Union line and north of the Matadequin, or against the right flank of the Confederate position and south of that stream. In Grant's eyes, it is evident, the importance of having adequate space was paramount, and Smith was drawn in to the main position. Thus on May 28, while the Army of the Potomac was still closely hugging the Pamunkey, he had been ordered to proceed by the south side of that river to New Castle Ferry, and on May 30, at 7.30 P.M., when Warren had just repulsed Rodes, and Hancock had cleared the enemy's rifle-pits beyond the

EXTENDING TO COLD HARBOR 423

Totopotomoy, the same place was indicated as the destination of the troops from the James.

But Grant's new order to Smith had in view something more than a mere route march. Sheridan was ordered to send a cavalry brigade to White House with the following letter:—

"Triplicated orders have been sent you to march up to New Castle, then to await further orders. I send with this a brigade of cavalry to accompany you. As yet no further directions can be given than are contained in your orders (of the 28th). The movements of the enemy on our left down the Mechanicsville (Old Church) Road would indicate the possibility of a design on his part to get between you and the Army of the Potomac. This will be so closely watched that nothing could suit me better than such a move. Sheridan is on our left flank . . . to watch as far out as he can go on the Mechanicsville and Cold Harbor roads. This, with the care you can give your flank with the cavalry you have, and a knowledge of the fact that any movement of the enemy toward you cannot fail to be noticed and followed up from here, will make your advance secure. The position of the Army of the Potomac this evening is (from the Shady Grove Road to the road from Hanover C.H. to Richmond).

"U. S. GRANT,
"Lieut.-General."

At the same time Wright on the extreme right flank was ordered to suspend his attack (*i.e.* that ordered to relieve the pressure on Warren) and to mass his command in readiness to move elsewhere. Later in the evening Warren was informed that in case the enemy turned on Smith, the VI. Corps would be brought over to the V., and the enemy would be attacked from the position of the latter corps.

Here, for the third time in the month, a hammer and anvil battle, as we have called it, is projected. So far from merely utilizing the opportunity, that would be afforded by Lee's movement against Smith, to storm the depleted entrenchments round Pole Green Church, the Union leader proposed to bring over the bulk of his forces to the side of Bethesda Church, and thence, in a great encounter battle in the open, to press Lee eastward and south-eastward.

Grant, however, as on the 21st, undoubtedly sacrificed the certainty of bringing about such a battle to other considerations—then, the seizure of a new line of supply, and now the maintenance of the manœuvre area. Had Smith been ordered to take the Cold Harbor road instead of that towards New Castle, the success of the projected manœuvre would have been far more likely. At the same time, of course, Smith's command was considerably weaker than that employed on May 21 to invite Lee's attack, and only one quarter the strength of the force that would have been used on that day to compel Lee's attentions (see p. 334). This important consideration doubtless turned the scale in Grant's mind and led to his being content to give Lee the refusal of the seeming opportunity.

At 7.30 A.M. on the 31st corps commanders all along the line were ordered to press their skirmishers up against the enemy's works and to report any change in Lee's dispositions. This was executed by the various corps, and Burnside and Gibbon gained ground to the front towards Pole Green Church during the morning. Warren once

EXTENDING TO COLD HARBOR 425

more extended towards the Old Church Road. But towards afternoon it became clear from the reports of Smith and the cavalry that the enemy was not advancing towards Old Church, and Grant reluctantly abandoned his plan and his hopes.

His second scheme was formed less from data afforded by cool reasoning than under the pressure of the fighting instinct. It was to utilize the foothold gained by Brooke on the 30th as a breach through which to pour the II. Corps, the VI. Corps, already massed in accordance with the previous scheme, giving direct and decisive support, and the IX. Corps helping by a vigorous attack on its own front. However, this too was given up, the corps commanders concerned reporting unfavourably on the prospects of success.

"Baldy" Smith's command * had arrived in its transports at White House after midday on the 30th and begun to disembark. General Ames's brigade, the advanced guard, was detailed to create a depôt at that place, and to maintain it and the railway bridge until relieved by the line of communication troops under Abercrombie. The conditions were, however, far from favourable to a quick disembarkation, and Smith was occupied till about midday on the 31st in assembling 10,000 field troops out of about 16,000 that he was to bring up to the front. The movement of his column towards New Castle Ferry was uneventful, but exhausting. When Smith went into camp,

* Called the XVIII. Corps because the general and staff of that corps were in charge of it. It was as a matter of fact drawn largely from the X. Corps.

just east of Old Church, his men were greatly fatigued by the heat and the unaccustomed strain of a march under service conditions.

The next manœuvre took shape from Sheridan's action.

Torbert's division had, on the evening of the 30th, driven Fitz Lee from the Matadequin towards Cold Harbor* and had halted for the night a mile and a half from that place. Next morning (31st), all the indications being that Fitz Lee was about to take the offensive, Torbert, by Sheridan's orders, anticipated him by attacking him, and after a sharp engagement drove him out of Cold Harbor. Gregg followed Torbert's movement.

But it became apparent that Hoke's division of infantry † was in support of Fitz Lee, and after Torbert had repulsed — and astonished — Hoke's leading brigade of Confederates by the rapid fire of his magazine carbines, Sheridan decided to withdraw. He had scarcely done so when General Meade ‡ ordered him to resume possession of Cold Harbor and to hold that place at all hazards.

Lee was, as a matter of fact, about to take

---

* Cold Harbour is a common place-name in England. It is understood to signify a roadside shelter without a fireplace.

† Hoke's division — not to be confounded with Hoke's old brigade (Early's division, Ewell's Corps) that had joined Lee at Hanover Junction on May 21—had arrived two days before from Beauregard's army.

‡ The original of the order is not preserved. Sheridan replied by acknowledging receipt at 1 A.M., June 1. The other corps commanders were notified of the movements intended between 9.30 and 10.30 P.M. on May 31.

EXTENDING TO COLD HARBOR

the offensive, and Anderson's corps was in full march to join Hoke and Fitz Lee on the side of Cold Harbor. The Confederate general hoped to repeat Early's manœuvre on a larger scale, and to roll up Grant's left * with Anderson's corps, while Hill and Breckinridge occupied the long thin line on the left, and Early assailed the Union centre on the Shady Grove and Old Church roads. Indications of this move being intended or in progress had not been wanting all day, and the report of Hoke's division being near Cold Harbor set all doubts at rest. The Union superior leading made its decision promptly. Not only was Sheridan † to stand fast at Cold Harbor, but two army corps were to march thither.

The transference of the decision to Cold Harbor implied the abandonment of the attempt to give Richmond a wide berth. Grant did not readily accept this disquieting contraction of his manœuvre area; on the contrary, when it became clear that Smith would not be attacked, he made an attempt to bring off a direct frontal attack of two corps on the entrenchments of the enemy's left centre. But on the Totopotomoy no battle was to be had "outside works", and to the south of that obstacle a deliberate turning manœuvre could not be hazarded, for fear that Lee would use the respite to extend the dreaded "works" to the Chickahominy. Should he succeed in doing so, the only

---

* He was not yet aware of the arrival of Smith's corps.

† With two divisions. Wilson had been sent out to look after the right rear of the army towards Hanover Court House, and on this day had a spirited fight there with Hampton's division.

battle obtainable would be a plain, undisguised frontal attack on entrenchments, and such an attack Grant, for all that his critics have maintained to the contrary, was doing his utmost to avoid. No wonder, therefore, that Grant eagerly grasped at the opportunity that Lee's movements seemed to promise, and hurried to Sheridan's help all the forces that were in a condition to move at once. Near Cold Harbor there was more than a little hope of bringing on an engagement before the usual long entrenched lines could be thrown up, for it was not to be supposed that a force of two or three divisions of infantry and one of cavalry, such as Lee might well have on that side before the morning of June 1, would tamely deploy and entrench in front of three or four cavalry brigades.

The total effective force under Grant's hand on this day (June 1) was not less than 100,000. Inclusive of his reinforcements (Breckinridge, Pickett, and Hoke), and such reinforcements as could in case of necessity be brought up from Richmond, Lee had perhaps 70,000. But unaware of Smith's presence, and therefore reckoning Grant at 85,000, he might boldly take the offensive against one wing of the Army of the Potomac in equal and even superior force. The details of such an offensive scheme, supposing that it existed, could not of course be known definitely at the Union headquarters, but there was no doubt, as to fact, that there was a threatening accumulation of force opposite Sheridan, and no doubt, in Grant's mind, of the measures to be taken to turn it to account.

EXTENDING TO COLD HARBOR

These were, in the first place, defensive. Sheridan was to be reinforced as soon as possible by the VI. Corps, the commander of which was even advised to send off one division at once.

Wright had massed his corps on the night of the 30th; Russell's division had skirmished a little on the 31st; but the main body of the corps had been held ready to move to support Hancock or Burnside if either of these officers should attack. At 9.45 P.M. the VI. Corps was ordered to move at once to Cold Harbor viâ Hawes's Shop and Old Church. "The cavalry are directed to hold on until your arrival, and it is of the utmost importance that you should reach that point as soon after daylight as possible".

Smith was to come into line between Warren and Wright.*

Hancock was charged with the defence of the right wing of the army. For this purpose Birney was ordered to throw back his extreme right. However, the advanced line captured on the evening of May 30, which Hancock desired to abandon —considering it of value only if an assault were intended—was maintained, by order of General Meade. No special task was assigned to Burnside. Warren was ordered to throw the left of his line

---

* Dana (Assistant Secretary of War, at Grant's headquarters), quoted by Badeau, says that Grant's and Meade's intention was for Wright to be on the ground at daylight and to attack. Wright's orders contain no word of attacking, and as for the other point, by no conceivable effort could the VI. Corps have massed for action near Cold Harbor much before eleven (eight hours' marching (10.30 to 6.30) for the head of the columns), and Smith would be even later, as the line of march of the VI. Corps necessarily crossed his. Warren's dispatch to Griffin (see below) is also very clear and explicit.

forward so as to attack at once from Bethesda Church, and promptly set about drawing off troops from his entrenchments so as to form a mobile column. "Baldy Smith is coming up to take position between Wright and me, but it will take all day to do it", Warren told Griffin that evening. "My attack is to be a diversion in favour of Wright and [to] prevent their accumulating against him".*

In the event, defensive precautions proved superfluous. Lee moved towards Cold Harbor in the first instance with the distinct intention of taking the offensive, but he was not present in the early morning of June 1 (before the arrival of the VI. Corps) to enforce his wishes, and the plan collapsed owing to the want of concert between Anderson and Hoke. It is not within the purview of this work to examine the causes of Confederate failures, but it is hard to resist the conclusion that the simple idea of resisting to the last—the passive defensive—dominated Lee's principal subordinates at this time so far that nothing short of Lee's own presence could ensure a vigorous forward movement.

Sheridan was not attacked, and Hoke's infantry spent the morning in going into position on the extreme right of Lee's army (see Sketch Map 20). Kershaw's division (Anderson's corps), however, as it moved down towards Hoke, sharply attacked the Union cavalry and was as brusquely repulsed by the Spencer carbines as Hoke had been the evening

* This dispatch is misdated 9.45 A.M. in the official records.

EXTENDING TO COLD HARBOR 431

before. A second attack met with the same fate All this took place before the arrival of the VI. Corps.

Wright's corps had an exhausting march over sandy roads, and so far from being able to reach Cold Harbor soon after dawn, he only arrived with his staff, ahead of the troops, at 9 A.M. Sheridan was still there, and had not been attacked, but was of opinion that something more than a division of infantry was in front of him. The morning was spent in arraying the troops, as they came up, in a semicircle around Cold Harbor covering the roads to Bethesda Church, Gaines's Mill, and Despatch Station. It was after 2 P.M. when the last division came in.

Smith's corps had been the victim of a staff blunder in General Grant's headquarters. He was ordered to report to General Meade for orders, and to take position at New Castle Ferry between the V. and VI. Corps. On arrival at New Castle Ferry he naturally saw nothing of the Army of the Potomac there, and Grant meantime, learning of the mistake, had sent Colonel Babcock to correct it, and to bring the XVIII. Corps to Cold Harbor. The consequent delay was of little importance, as even with the extra distance to march, the head of Smith's column (about 10,000 strong) arrived at Cold Harbor soon after the last of Wright's divisions had come in, and, as the two lines of march crossed at Old Church, the XVIII. Corps had to let the VI. pass in any case. Much more serious, however, was the fact that the young troops of Smith's command were overtaxed.

Unaccustomed as they were to covering long distances, they had had a march of 25 miles without food or a long halt.*

On the march he received orders from Meade to take position on Wright's right, "endeavouring to hold the road from Cold Harbor to Bethesda Church. General Wright is ordered to attack as soon as his troops are up, and I desire you should co-operate with him and join in the attack. The enemy have not long been in position about Cold Harbor, and it is of great importance to dislodge and if possible to rout him before he can entrench himself".

It was now not the defence of Cold Harbor, but the attack of the enemy's position in front of that village that Grant and Meade contemplated. The logical outcome of concentrating a large mass of troops at Cold Harbor was a battle there, and as Lee did not attack, his opponents arranged to do so as early as possible lest the Confederates should be found heavily entrenched. Moreover, the almost unavoidable deduction from the lame ending of the Confederate offensive was that, from whatever cause, the moral of the Southern troops or their leaders was impaired, and that therefore an attack had good chances of success, more especially as the log-works that could be constructed in a few hours of miscellaneous skirmishing were hardly to be classed as " entrenchments "

---

* Judging from the tenor of his orders that a battle was imminent, Smith had not waited, before moving off, to allow the men to get their morning coffee.

EXTENDING TO COLD HARBOR

as veterans of May 10 and May 12 understood that term. Neither of these hypotheses were far short of the truth, as the events of this evening were to prove, and the advisability of fighting at once, if at all, was self-evident.

The decision to attack was arrived at, or rather promulgated, about midday.* It could not be executed for some hours, and in the meantime we turn to events on the front of the II., IX., and V. Corps.

The II. Corps had now become the extreme and more or less exposed right of the Union army, except for parts of Wilson's widespread cavalry line. There was more or less skirmishing all day along the front of the corps, and the Union skirmishers almost uniformly reported that the enemy was still in force in his entrenchments. The same may be said of events on Burnside's front.

On Warren's front there was naturally more activity. At 10.30 he reported that his skirmishers had passed through the wood south of Bethesda Church, and that the enemy was beyond the open field on the other side of this wood. Being compelled to hold close with his right to Burnside's left, he felt his way out towards the left very cautiously, and, like Smith later in the day, made no attempt to bridge the four-mile gap between the Church and Cold Harbor. But movements of the enemy towards the south or south-east having

* The order to Wright has not been preserved. Smith's order is headed "12 midday".

been observed, Warren decided, in pursuance of his orders to prevent a concentration against Wright, to attack. This was more easily said than done, for in extending to the left the V. Corps encountered a many-branched swamp that formed one of the heads of Matadequin Creek.

Consequently Warren had to report failure in the following terms: "The rear of the enemy's column passed at 10.15. A wagon train is following it. General Lockwood is getting his men into line". Warren then, seeing no object to be gained by attacking on his own front to assist Wright, extended as fast as possible over the rough and intersected ground between, so as to connect with him. The result was naturally that all closed masses of troops were frittered away in finding garrisons for the over-extended line of works (1.30). Later in the day when Warren desired to collect a movable mass of troops on his outer flank, his best exertions only enabled him to form up one and a half out of his four divisions.

To return to the troops at Cold Harbor. By 3 P.M. the VI. Corps had formed up, and the XVIII. was coming in on its right.

Wright was ordered to attack as soon as his corps was in hand, Smith to join in on the right and to connect with Warren. But Smith, having only a small force available, took the soldierly resolution of using every man to help Wright's attack, and made no attempt to carry out the latter part of his orders.

Warren's co-operation was intended and ordered,

EXTENDING TO COLD HARBOR

and with great difficulty he drew out two brigades to support Lockwood in attacking on Smith's right. Lockwood, however, "in some unaccountable way took the whole division away from the line of battle, and turned up at dark two miles in my rear". He was deprived of his command the same night, but the mischief was done. The fortune of war had willed it that the least competent general officer in the Army of the Potomac was at the very point at which he could do the most harm.

By 6 P.M. Smith and Wright were ready.
The forces were equal or nearly so—Anderson's corps and Hoke's division against the VI. and the weak XVIII. Corps. The Confederates had the advantage of position, but their entrenchments were nothing more than hasty log-works. There were veterans and relatively raw troops on each side. The Confederates had an unusually favourable field of fire, as much as 1400 yards deep on Wright's front, measured from the main line of resistance. There was as usual a strong line of rifle-pits well in front of the main line, and a portion of this advanced line, in a pine wood due west of Cold Harbor, was only 300 yards from Smith's front.

At six, in full view of the enemy, the two corps moved forward to the attack. Smith's force, weak as it was, had to find a division to protect the right flank, which was in the air, but his two available divisions swept over the enemy's rifle-pits in the pine wood. This, however, was the limit of the effort that could be expected of seven thousand tired men. The passage of the wood broke their ranks, and the fire of the main line beyond beat down all attempts to rush across the last stretch of open ground, but they gathered in 250 prisoners, and entrenched themselves on the ground gained. One of Smith's brigadiers was killed, and about 1000 men were killed and wounded.

Wright attacked south of the Old and New Cold Harbor road with his right and part of his centre division. Ricketts, on the right, swiftly drove in the enemy's skirmishers, and then stormed their main line at a small salient on Anderson's extreme right. Part of the Union troops which entered the enemy's works turned the right flank of this salient by passing down the wooded bottom, three-quarters of a mile east of New Cold Harbor, where a gap had, carelessly enough, been left open between Anderson's right and Hoke's left.*

Though a counter-attack regained the lost works, 500 prisoners were taken, and the Confederate picket line made into a connected breastwork for the Union line of battle. The VI. Corps lost 1200 men in the charge.

Such a success, analogous to that of Upton on the 10th of May, seemed to call for similar measures on the part of the superior leading to

---

* The gap was retrenched, the same night, by General Law of Anderson's corps, who levelled the salient and, instead, built a new line across the base. This, and the details of the ground, are shown on Sketch Map 21.

EXTENDING TO COLD HARBOR

improve it. The accident of position once again assigned the principal *rôle* to the II. Corps.

Hancock had already (3 P.M.) been ordered to prepare to move, at nightfall, to a point at or near Bethesda Church, presumably in order that he should fill the gap between Warren and Smith, and thus free the latter from the necessity of making large detachments to provide for its own security. At 9 P.M. the destination of the corps was changed to Cold Harbor. The reports of the evening attack and of the positions gained therein seemed to indicate that there was still room for an army corps between Wright's left and the swamps bordering on the Chickahominy, and still some opportunity of finding unentrenched ground on the extreme right of the new Confederate position. Hancock was therefore ordered to prolong Wright's line to the left. But at 11, when the corps was already on the move, he received further instructions.

About nightfall the enemy had again shown signs of forward movement. The sound of artillery fire at Cold Harbor reached Grant and Meade. Wright's reports, cheerful though they were, indicated that Anderson was preparing to recapture the ground he had lost. Smith was despondent as to the chances of maintaining his conquests. On Warren's front a sudden attack fell upon Griffin's division towards nightfall, but it was repulsed.

These alarms—Lee's usual "last word"—were not without effect, and Meade thought it advisable to give Wright and Smith the direct support that they asked for. Hancock was now ordered to get into position as early as possible on the left of Wright to attack the enemy at once, and to interpose between him and the Chickahominy. If possible he was to detach a force to secure a passage on that river. But should he prefer, after consulting Wright, to support the VI. Corps in its attack instead of extending to the left he was at liberty to do so, on notifying headquarters by the field telegraph.

Hancock, eager to leave the refused flank of the army to take a place of honour on the offensive wing, moved off so rapidly that by eleven two-thirds of his corps was on its way, in spite of the difficulties of drawing out troops from a complicated line of trenches close to the enemy. For greater promptitude he assigned Hawes's Shop as the initial point, sending Barlow and Gibbon* thither by different routes. Birney was to take over the breastworks covering both routes, and to follow when the roads were clear (see Sketch Map 20).

The last order to Warren on the night of June 1 was to join in the attack of Wright, Smith, and Hancock.

Wright was ordered to renew the attack as soon as Hancock came up, which would probably be at six or seven in the morning. Smith's orders were to the same effect. Burnside, on receiving news of Hancock's movement, decided to withdraw

* Burnside was made a little uneasy by Gibbon's prompt withdrawal. Both he and Meade thought that Gibbon should have been withdrawn last.

EXTENDING TO COLD HARBOR

to his original line and prepared to bring his vehicles south of the Totopotomoy, after which there would be nothing north of the creek but cavalry.* An advance of the enemy, half attack, half reconnaissance, was easily repulsed. At 11 P.M. the *rôle* of the IX. Corps was defined in a brief order to be ready to attack to its front or to support Warren as required.

This was indeed to be a general offensive. Four out of five army corps were to assault, and the fifth to be ready to support.† Three of these were to deliver a deep massed attack on one-third of the enemy's front—Smith and Wright frontally, while Hancock was either to envelop the enemy's right, or to give additional impetus to Wright's blow, according to circumstances. To provide for the utilization of any fleeting opportunity of striking a blow on the secondary front, and to ensure that Lee should be kept occupied along his whole line,

---

* Wilson's cavalry, which had been busily engaged on the 1st in breaking up the Fredericksburg railroad at Ashland, was, on the 2nd, attacked and severely handled by Hampton, the successor of Stuart in command of the Confederate cavalry. This was now organized in three divisions, Fitz Lee's, Butler's, and W. H. F. (Rooney) Lee's. The last was General Robert E. Lee's second son. His eldest was Major-General Custis Lee, in command of the mobile troops in Richmond. Fitz Lee's division remained on the right of the Confederate army near the Chickahominy. Sheridan had withdrawn to camp, after the arrival of Wright's corps at Cold Harbor had released him.

† Meade wrote to Grant at 10.15 P.M., 1st June: "What are your views about to-morrow? I think the attack should be renewed as soon as Hancock is within supporting distance, and should be made by Wright, Smith, and Hancock. . . . Warren should be ordered to attack in conjunction with the others . . . Burnside to reinforce Warren if necessary". The reply was: "The attack should be renewed to-morrow by all means, but not till Hancock is within supporting distance".

Warren was directed to attack and Burnside to mass his corps in readiness to move.

Such was the plan, but trouble promptly arose in attempting to carry it out.

The march of Hancock's corps through the close, hot woods and over the sandy roads, like that of Wright's corps on the previous evening, and those of Warren's on the 8th and the 14th, set at defiance all calculations of time. The head of the column arrived at Cold Harbor about six, but the rest was strung out all along the road from Hawes's Shop. One of his divisions was taken to strengthen Smith's weak and now considerably shaken line of battle. The ardour even of the born fighting general was quenched, for on reaching Cold Harbor he reports that it will be several hours before the corps is ready to attack, and that he is forming on Wright's left so as to "control the ground" to the Chickahominy.

Smith, meantime, had replied to the order to attack with Jeremiads. His command was tired, had lost ten per cent. of its strength in the brief evening battle, and had been on the alert all night. He had come from White House without trains, and he had to replenish ammunition and supplies by begging them from other corps commanders. These difficulties, and an irate and unjustified remark of Meade's, "What the h—— did he come here for without his supplies?", roused the sleeping spirit of insubordination. His first dispatch was merely to the effect that the line was "perfectly indefensible", but this was followed by another

EXTENDING TO COLD HARBOR

which began, "Your order for an attack received. I have endeavoured to represent to you my condition. In the present condition of my line an attack by me would be *simply preposterous*".

There is no complaint, however, on record from the VI. Corps. It had had a fair measure of success, and its veterans, according to McMahon, the chief-of-staff of the corps, felt that "this was the final struggle, and that Richmond was dead in front".

Warren laboriously advanced his left to connect with Smith. At 5 A.M. he reported that his lines were nearly five miles long and that, though he was not yet aligned on the XVIII. Corps, there was a good road to Cold Harbor which his new position guaranteed against interruption by the enemy. It will have been remarked that the circuitous route *viâ* Hawes's Shop and Old Church had hitherto been used in each attempt to forestall Lee on the side of Cold Harbor, and that the Confederate general had been first in the field in each case.

Burnside was ordered, early in the morning (7.45), to withdraw and to mass on Warren's right rear. So much was a repetition or confirmation of the 11 P.M. order of the night before, but the new instructions contained a phrase which could only be understood by assuming that the first and provisional order was not to be acted upon—"The defence of the right of the line is intrusted to yourself and General Warren". There was no word of Warren's attacking or of Burnside's supporting Warren in an attack. Burnside therefore, thinking only of the defence of the right, naturally failed to see how he was to hold on to his line and yet to find a large local reserve for the V. Corps. He was anxious, moreover, on account of the general trains, which he supposed were near Hawes's Shop. Only on a repetition of the order to mass his whole corps, and an assurance that the trains were well on their way to New Castle Ferry and White House, did he at last begin to withdraw.

In the circumstances, Hancock's urgent request for the attack to be put off to a later hour was granted, and the hour was changed to 5 P.M. The interval was occupied by brisk skirmishing, and several changes were made in the distribution of the Union forces at Cold Harbor.

On the other side Lee moved down Hill, with Wilcox's and Mahone's divisions, and Breckinridge's command, to beyond New Cold Harbor. Breckinridge was next to Hoke, Hill on Breckinridge's right. Fitz Lee's horsemen, crowded out of the line of battle, passed over the Chickahominy and picketed the roads towards the James, while his opponents rested their wearied horses or moved off to camp wherever report said that there was forage still unconsumed. Early, with his own (Ewell's) corps and Heth's division of Hill, remained on the left of the Confederate line along the Totopotomoy.

CHAPTER XXI

COLD HARBOR, JUNE 3

THE net result of all this close skirmishing, and of the various local attacks and counter-attacks that had so fully occupied the six days since Sheridan's battle at Hawes's Shop, had been to narrow the problem before the Union leaders to one simple issue. We have attempted to follow, in the two previous chapters, Grant's successive attempts to fight with the balance of chances in his favour. He had sought first to define Lee's flanks and to manœuvre round them, next to entrap his opponent into a "hammer and anvil" engagement, and lastly, to bring on a front-to-front battle outside works. All expedients had failed—from one reason and another, but above all because the country and the season set at defiance all ordinary calculations of time and space—and Lee was now in position, his front entrenched and his flanks unattainable. About midday on June 2, then, Grant had to make his decision in the plain problem whether to attack these entrenchments or not. He has been generally and unsparingly criticized, after the event, for this decision, and he himself said that he regretted having made it. But the question, "Ought I to fight a battle?" has to be answered beforehand, and answered after a careful review of all the data then available.

General Humphreys, a cerebral of the Moltke type, to whom, as to Moltke, duty was a creed and calm reasoning a habit, thus summarizes the outward and objective considerations prompting Grant's decision:—

"Lee's position was about six miles from the main line of the Richmond defences. . . . The Chickahominy was at its lowest stage of water and could be crossed anywhere by infantry above Lee's right. . . . This appeared to bring turning movements to an end. . . . Lee's left being among the wooded swamps of the Totopotomoy and Matadequin, made it difficult of attack. The front was the assailable part, though it had not been reported that it was practicable to carry it by assault, and the question was whether to take the chances of an assault there, which if successful would give the opportunity of inflicting severe loss upon Lee when falling back. . . ."

What then were the chances of success? Lee's line was six miles in length and could not be shortened in the face of the V. and IX. Corps. On little more than one-third of that line nearly three-fifths of the Union army was already massed —60,000 men for somewhat over two miles, or thirteen men to the running yard of front.

Upton's depth at Spottsylvania—though there the ground was more favourable—had been seven or eight men per yard, and this had sufficed, not only to carry the first line of works but to hold them against counter-attack for some hours. The other great attack on "works"—Hancock's on May 12—had succeeded only too well.* There

* In this connection, it is interesting to observe what an American

COLD HARBOR

had been nothing to show that one line of works was sufficient to stop a determined rush, and it was fair to suppose that on the present occasion, with but six men per yard of front, Lee could not have any important bodies of troops in reserve. Nor, in fact, had he. The Army of Northern Virginia fought at Cold Harbor, it is said, without a regiment in reserve at the disposal of its commander.

The moral of the Union army had, of course, undergone the unavoidable depression consequent upon a month of practically incessant marching and fighting. Moreover, the influx of reinforcements in great numbers had lowered the general average of the army's soldierly qualities, and the veterans, inured to war and therefore capable of forming judgments, right or wrong, of things that they knew, had become imbued with the feeling that attacks on "works" were foredoomed to failure. Yet, in the six days that had passed since the unopposed crossing of the Pamunkey, the results of the fighting, wherever locally it had been pushed to extremes, had been on the whole in favour of the Union army. Each corps had

officer, who lectured at the Royal United Service Institution shortly after the war, said of entrenchments. "To provide for this (the fall of the first line of works) a second line is arranged in the same manner, and the men are made to lie down. The moment the fugitives have run over them the second line should rise and open fire. . . . More lines should be in position to the rear if there be troops enough. . . *Three lines are ordinarily enough, but in some cases a single line may be sufficient if the works are well made*". This quotation, the reference to which I owe to Major-General C. W. Robinson, C.B., seems to demonstrate not so much the formidable nature of the works, strong as they unquestionably were, but the almost irresistible force of a really resolute attack on them.

something to record as a success; in the II. Corps the dashing advance of Barlow on the night of the 30th, in the V. the severe repulse inflicted on Early on the same evening, in the VI. and XVIII. the capture of a strong line of advanced rifle-pits on June 1, and in the IX. the gradual advance of the skirmish line without a reverse on the 30th and 31st. On the other hand, after these night marches in the heat of a swampy district, the troops came on to the field of battle in a jaded and weary condition, and this was particularly true of the newly joined men, who by this time constituted one-third of the army. They could stand in line and endure a Confederate rush, even when new to the work, for they had been well drilled. They could be "electrized" into making a determined rush, but their capacity for one day was limited to one concentrated effort.

The veterans, however, useless though they might think an assault, made it—with little dash, perhaps, but with splendid earnestness—and on the whole the balance of moral factors might seem, to a fighting temperament like Grant's, favourable to making the attempt. For Lee's men, too, had a moral, and the vague and disconnected offensive moves of the last few days might easily and honestly be understood, or misunderstood, as implying that that moral was impaired.

There was less doubt possible as to the results of victory, should a victory be achieved.

Supposing the lines carried, would the sacrifice of fifteen or twenty per cent. of the Army of the Potomac be rewarded by "having the execution"

COLD HARBOR

—in Cromwell's expressive phrase—of a routed army falling back in many independent bodies, without a strong intact rearguard? This was possible, though, to judge by Gettysburg and similar experiences, it was more probable that the cheerful veterans of the Army of Northern Virginia would rally promptly enough on a new line. Nevertheless, part of the retreating army would undoubtedly be most severely handled, and this, with the capture of the lines by pure force, would give the Union soldiers and—what was at this moment of political crisis * of still more importance—the Union people the moral strength of a victory. If the Army of the Potomac could show the world that it had expelled its opponents from their selected position by sheer fighting, the end of the war was surely at hand.

Such were the doubtful, though not definitely unfavourable chances, and the important, almost decisive, results that might be expected from success.

Grant's resolution to attack was announced in a very brief directive to Meade. This has been criticized as severely as the decision to fight the battle,† but it does not seem that detailed orders by headquarters were in any way necessary. The

* The pending Presidential election. The war expenses of the North at this time averaged $4,000,000 a day.

† According to W. F. Smith, Meade himself, like Grant, was amongst the critics—after the event. Meade's criticism took the form, natural to him, of ill-tempered remarks which he was himself, later, the first to regret. He said—in the heat of the moment, and perhaps lashed by Smith's equally intemperate criticism of his superior—that he had let Grant plan his own battle for once.

troops were on the ground and the enemy in front of them. No troops were now free to manœuvre, except Burnside's distant corps, and, in fact, the superior leading, when it ordered a general assault, had said its last word.

The battle was once more postponed in the afternoon of the 2nd. The attack was now to be made at 4.30 A.M. on the following day, June 3, by the II., VI., and XVIII. Corps, and secondarily, but with equal energy, by the IX. and V.

The afternoon of the 2nd was not uneventful, however.

Burnside's withdrawal and forming up in rear of Warren was delayed in execution, as already mentioned, through the somewhat misleading wording of the orders from headquarters. The idea was that Warren should close on Smith's right, and at the same time shorten his line so as to have one and a half divisions free to move. Burnside's lines were to be abandoned and the IX. Corps to form in mass ready to move on Warren's right rear. This was expected by headquarters to save about three miles of infantry entrenchments, and to release over 30,000 men for general service. But this intention of the headquarters' staff was made known to neither Warren nor Burnside, and in addition the actual orders sent revealed so little of the purport of the manœuvre that Warren asked as late as 4.15 P.M., "Does the commanding general wish us to hold our right and front with General Burnside's corps massed behind my right, or for General Burnside to hold my right?" He had barely received a reply when heavy fighting began on the right flank.

Lee had directed Early to place himself across the Union right and to drive down the line. The scene was Bethesda Church where, on the 30th, a precisely similar order had been carried out by the same officer with respect to the Union left. Thus it is that the official maps show two sets of Federal entrenchments, near the Shady Grove road, literally facing one another.

As early as 10.30, before any movement of withdrawal had been made by the IX. Corps, General Potter reported great activity in the Confederate skirmish line near the Jones house.* But it was in the afternoon that Early's blow fell at last. It routed a strong skirmish line that was holding the old line of the IX. Corps while the main body moved back, and pressed on towards Bethesda Church. But the loss of some of its skirmishers warned the V. Corps, and Griffin's division, which had been formed up in answer to Meade's order to draw out half the corps from the lines, deployed, moved forward, and drove back Rodes's division with severe loss, including one of Rodes's best brigadiers, General Doles, killed. Heth's division, on Rodes's left, inflicted some loss on the rear division of the retiring IX. Corps. Gordon, still further out on the left, was not engaged.

This fight, showing as it did that Lee still had some considerable force on his extreme left,

* North of the Totopotomoy, where Gibbon's division (II. Corps) had been on May 30–June 1 (Sketch Map 19).

caused a last modification in the plan of battle for the 3rd.

It was clear that Lee could not be in really strong force on both flanks at the same moment. Warren and Burnside, therefore, were to become an offensive mass and not a support to the main body. They were in fact to attack on their own front at 4.30 A.M. on the 3rd. Whichever wing stormed the enemy's position would swing inwards towards the other. Meade even went so far as to suggest that Burnside should be placed under Warren's orders for the day, but this was naturally vetoed by the lieutenant-general, who, however, directed the two generals to act in close concert.

Grant, it is said, was much annoyed that Early was permitted to retire whence he had come—*i.e.* into his works—after the cessation of fighting on the night of the 2nd. While he was not generally in favour of night attacks,* he said, the enemy had here put himself in such a position as to render one justifiable. An order was soon afterwards issued reminding corps commanders of the necessity of promptly seizing opportunities to attack the enemy whenever and wherever he came out of his lines.

The fact that Warren had one division and Burnside three in a condition to move made this particular failure especially galling. The excuse of the corps commanders concerned, if it had been demanded by superior authority, would doubtless have been

* The action of Wauhatchie, immediately before the battle of Chattanooga, attained considerable celebrity simply as being a night attack, so rare were such operations in the war.

that night was coming on, and that their orders plainly defined their part in the general scheme as the defensive, the shortening of the line, and the gradual gathering up of their forces towards the storm centre of Cold Harbor. They were perfectly right in acting as they did, in accordance with their lights. It rested with the supreme command to modify the general scheme. But, unluckily for the Union army, the field telegraph station at Bethesda Church, communicating with Grant and Meade, who had now joined Wright at Cold Harbor, was destroyed in the first rush of the Confederate attack.

The men of the II., VI., and XVIII. Corps spent the afternoon and evening in preparing for the morrow. Wills were made and witnessed, and labels, bearing the name and regiment, sewn on their clothing by the soldiers who knew what work was before them. A close study of the Civil War fails to reveal a moment in the history of the Union volunteer at which his courage more nearly approaches the sublime.

The front of the main assault was from Hancock's left, a little south of the road to Despatch Station, to Smith's right at Woody's, a distance of a little more than two miles.

During the afternoon and evening of June 2, Hancock placed Barlow on the left on the outside of the Despatch Station road, and Gibbon on Barlow's left. The left division of the VI. Corps was thereupon transferred to the right of the New

Cold Harbor road, releasing Devens's division of the XVIII. Corps, which Smith then placed on his extreme right, with orders to string out as much as possible along the entrenchments of the whole corps when the other two divisions moved out to the assault. Behind Barlow and Gibbon, Birney was held in reserve; Wright and Smith made no provision, beyond the ordinary second line of battle, inherited from Frederick the Great, for controlling the fight by closed bodies of reserves in their own hands.

According to the Confederates, Grant had the rare merit of making his battles keep to the schedule time. The general assault was ordered for 4.30, and within five or ten minutes of that hour the battle was at full intensity, in spite of a blinding mist.

In front of Barlow the first thinly guarded and slightly salient line of the defenders was formed by the outer bank or hedge of the road to Despatch Station, which ran along the foot of a gentle slope. Gibbon, extending out towards the place vacated by the left of the VI. Corps, had before him a plain which, unknown to him, was intersected by the heads of the wooded swamp through which the Confederate line had been penetrated on the 1st, and which, unfortunately for the assailants, had now been carefully retrenched. Opposite Wright and Smith the ground was open, as these generals knew from their experience of the 1st.

On this ground, two years before this, the V. Corps had fought the battle of Gaines's Mill, and

Lee had gained his first victory by force of superior numbers. Meade, Warren, Griffin, Smith, and Martindale had all commanded brigades on that occasion.

Barlow's division was in two lines, two deployed brigades in each line; the right brigade of the first line, however, formed in two lines by order of Colonel Brooke, its commander. The force of resolute leading carried the troops over the first Confederate line along the road, and up the slope to the main line on Watts's Hill. Miles and Brooke entered the main line almost along with, close behind the retreating enemy.* Between two and three hundred prisoners, a colour, and three guns were taken. But Brooke was wounded, the second line advanced with less vigour than the first, and the inevitable counter-stroke threw the two victorious brigades back upon it. Yet so stubborn were the men and their leaders that they dug themselves into cover 50 to 75 yards from the hostile line which they had lost.

Gibbon was also in two lines, but had formed his second line into columns, with orders to pass over the first line when the latter had reached the entrenchments and, then and not before, to deploy to the front. The right brigade of the first line was commanded by Tyler (whose heavy artillery division had been broken up on May 25), the left by Smyth. The advance was made gallantly, but the broken ground bordering on the swamp delayed its development while both the first and

* The Confederate attack at Franklin, Tennessee, later in the year, may, in many respects, be compared to this of Cold Harbor.

the second lines were held under effective fire. Tyler was wounded and his advance checked. McKeen came up behind him, but lost heavily, McKeen being killed. Colonel Porter and Colonel Haskell, who succeeded to the command of their respective brigades, were also killed. A part of Smyth's brigade actually reached the works, and Colonel McMahon, of the 164th New York, which was on the south side of the swamp, was killed inside the Confederate lines with the regimental colour in his hand. Owen's brigade behind Smyth had been ordered on no account to deploy before advancing, but he disobeyed * and his brigade effected nothing. Gibbon was, in fact, even less successful than Barlow, but he, too, gained and entrenched a line close up to the enemy. The losses amongst the colonels and brigadiers were almost unprecedented and bear eloquent witness to the truth of Hancock's bitter words, " The men went as far as their officers could carry them ".

Birney's division, one-third of the corps, stood in reserve. Perhaps the mist and the difficulty of observing the state of things on the fighting line, added to the remembrance of the overcrowding of May 12, prevented this reserve being sent up in time to help Barlow. But it was not used even to renew the effort, and for this General Hancock must bear the responsibility. The troops already engaged made several brave attacks here and there, but these were profitless.

* He was " mustered out of the service " soon afterwards, as it was inconvenient to assemble a court-martial for the trial of a general officer in the field.

COLD HARBOR

On the front of the VI. Corps the assault was equally punctual and equally unsuccessful. Ricketts was in the centre, Russell on the left, and Neill on the right. They, too, carried an advanced line at the first rush. They were repulsed from the main entrenchments, and entrenched the ground gained.

Smith had determined to make use of the ravine in his centre to shelter his principal attacking mass, Martindale's fresh division, which was for the most part formed in several lines of battalion columns. Devens's was on the right, somewhat refused and under orders to spread out leftwards along the lines vacated by Brooks and Martindale. Brooks was on the left next to the VI. Corps. Here, too, the enemy's rifle-pits were carried, and Smith halted to readjust his lines under fire. But, ere long, Martindale, hearing the firing on the front of the VI. Corps and mistaking it for Brooks's battle, went up the ravine with Stannard's brigade, whereupon the corps commander sent Brooks forward also. Brooks's formation was quite dense —a line of battle followed by a line of battalions in columns of double companies—but he effected nothing under the frontal and cross fire of the Confederates, which swept the open upland from end to end. Martindale attacked three times with (presumably) three successive lines of his leading brigade, but met with no success, while the other faced to the right in a vain attempt to keep down the enfilading fire on the right flank.

Such were the principal events on the main front attacked. An attempt is made on Sketch Map 21 to show the *ensemble* of these fruitless assaults, and also the configuration of the Confederate lines, which admitted of the tremendous enfilade fire to which all the three corps commanders virtually attributed their repulse.*

At Cold Harbor, Grant and Meade were anxiously awaiting reports from the front.

Those of 6.30 and 6.45 spoke of "renewed attacks" and "entrenching on the ground gained", but conflicting as they were in details, they were agreed as to the fact of a general repulse. As early as seven, Grant foresaw the possibility of complete failure. But in authorizing Meade at that hour to suspend the offensive as soon as he thought fit, he said at the same time that should a foothold be gained at any point troops from every other point must be crowded into the gap. *La brèche faite, le reste ne fait rien*, as Napoleon says. There is no more talk of one corps attacking to its own front to "relieve the pressure" on another—the theory of Lee's over-extension had obviously broken down, and with it the simultaneous attack "all along the line". Corps commanders were ordered to assault without waiting for each other. It was not now a question of which

---

* Moreover, each thought that his own corps was in advance of the others, and complained of the enfilade to which he was subjected in consequence. Actually, the various lines of attack were not parallel, but divergent, and thus each assaulting body more or less laid open one of its flanks to the enfilade. It may be asked why artillery, thus potent in defence, was useless for attack. The answer is found in the technical condition of artillery in those days. The only thoroughly effective man-killing projectile was the short-range case-shot, and the attacking guns could not approach the defending rifles sufficiently close to use it.

COLD HARBOR

front of Lee's fortress to attack, but of utilizing a narrow breach to flood the interior. It must be borne in mind that this order was given at the critical moment of the battle, and of the campaign, when "under pressure of unusual circumstances unused brain-cells vibrate". Reason spoke its last word in sanctioning the abandonment of an attempt to achieve the impossible; but the instinct of the fighting general, the real tactician, comes to the front in the words "but when one does succeed, push it vigorously, and if necessary pile in troops at the successful point from wherever they can be taken".

The promptings of instinct are irrespective of consequences. The effect of a repulse on the moral of the army, the political results of the battle, weigh nothing at all. Grant's resolution was not in the least a calculated military policy, but the instinct of the supremely military character.

The same influence ruled his orders to the right wing.

Burnside, Warren, and a mixed force of veteran cavalry and raw infantry, in their minor theatre of operations north of Bethesda Church, had some considerable measure of success, driving Early off the Shady Grove road. The thin defensive line of the V. Corps also repelled a sharp assault from Gordon. But at 10 A.M. Warren was forbidden to draw up his line to the northward, and ordered to co-operate with Smith, for which purpose Birney's division of the II. Corps was sent over to Woody's house. The plan of sweeping down from left to right or from right to left had been abandoned, and every effort was to be concentrated on the sole aim of making a breach in the line of Lee's army somewhere. Warren manifesting some reluctance to give up his well-advanced attack on Early, Meade instantly sent word to Birney that he was to take his orders direct from army headquarters.

But the morning's work on the decisive front, from Woody's to the Magee house, brought no hope of a "successful point" being gained. We need not follow or detail the correspondence between Meade and his corps commanders. It will suffice to say that at 1.30 Meade suspended the offensive. The remainder of the day was marked by little serious fighting. Early attacked the IX. Corps without success in the afternoon, and near Cold Harbor the opposing forces were so close to one another that the ordinary movements of relieving a picket line were, in the superexcited state of the men's nerves, sufficient to produce a wild brush of firing and an official report from the local commander on each side of the narrow impassable zone that he "repulsed an attack".

Meade's order was in response to a direct order from General Grant—

"The opinion of corps commanders not being sanguine of success in case an assault is ordered, you may direct a suspension of further advance for the present. Hold our most advanced positions, and strengthen them. Whilst on the defensive, our line may be contracted from the right if practicable. Reconnaissances should be made in front of each corps, and advances made to advantageous positions by regular approaches. To aid the expedition under General Hunter, it is necessary that we should detain all the army now under Lee until the former gets well on the way to Lynchburg. To do this effectually, it will be better to keep the enemy out of the entrenchments of Richmond than to have them go back there. . . ."

These instructions are the first of the campaign in which the Army of the Potomac is told off to subserve the purposes of other armies controlled by the generalissimo. They, therefore, mark the close of the overland campaign against Lee's army. The sequel—Petersburg, the Valley Campaign, Atlanta, and the triumphal procession of Sherman's army to North Carolina—belongs to another and even greater chapter in the history of the American Civil War.

As to Cold Harbor as a battle, it was the only one of his battles that Grant expressed his regret at having fought. There is no need of laboured criticism. It was a direct frontal attack all along the line, based on a theory of Lee's over-extension, deduced, before the battle, from the partial evidence that could be obtained.

The later resolution to crowd the army through a breach, if a breach could be made, was never realized, owing to the completeness of the original failure.* The chances of such a failure were

* It is an oft-repeated story that the second order to assault—it is not clear what this means—was deliberately and tacitly disobeyed by the "thinking bayonets". Doubtless there was more firing and less ardour to advance after the first repulse; but the regimental officers, as well as the generals and staffs, have practically unanimously repudiated the idea of disobedience as an insult to the military honour of their

accepted beforehand, and the fortune of war had willed it that the Union army should lose what it had staked on these chances. Grant himself says in his report: "In this attempt our loss was heavy, while that of the enemy, I have every reason to believe, was comparatively light". Not even the policy of attrition made any progress at Cold Harbor.

Of the ten days of sniping, fever, and prostration that followed the battle, it is impossible to convey any impression by words. The dead lay unburied between the two lines. Many of the wounded were rescued by the gallant dash of a comrade or by the curious process of sapping up to where they lay, but the delays in arranging for their removal under a flag of truce were so serious that it was not until the 7th that the remainder were taken away. Most of them, after three days' exposure, were dead. Controversy, and bitter controversy, has raged round the question of whether Grant and Lee sacrificed the unfortunate men to a punctilio of military etiquette. Neither of these great captains can fairly be accused of deliberate and gross inhumanity, and it must be taken for granted that, in the exercise of what they conceived to be their duty, the one

men. The story is probably an excellent example of the effect produced by the subjective impressions of individual combatants. The army, as a whole, was beaten, but also disciplined. The individual, entirely under the control of the army's collective will, would therefore obey orders to advance again, but would account for the least delay in a regiment's moving into position or deploying by reference to his own subjective impressions of defeat. He would, in a word, sacrifice his own life if ordered, but the slowness of his comrades would be attributed by him to the feeling of defeat by which he himself was depressed.

refused to admit that he had been defeated by suing for permission to remove his dead and wounded, and the other sought to compel his opponent to do so. We cannot judge them, for we cannot know how necessary at that moment an acknowledged victory was for the South, or whether in the North another admitted defeat would have involved the death-blow to the war spirit and the ideals it represented.

The losses of the Union army at Totopotomoy and Cold Harbor were about 13,000 in all, of which some 8000 are assigned to the assaults of June 1 and 3 at Cold Harbor. Lee's losses are unknown, but may have amounted to 5000 for the whole period, May 28–June 12. His losses on June 3 were but slight.

The material and moral results of this tremendous campaign of but one month's duration form the starting-point of its sequel—the move on Petersburg. But the latter, at any rate, may be summarized without discussion, by way of an epilogue to this study.

Grant's campaign from the Rapidan to Richmond was undertaken with the expressed object of inflicting losses upon, and if possible decisively defeating, Lee's army. In the second of these he had clearly and undeniably failed. What progress then had he made towards ending the war by " mere attrition if by nothing else " ?

Lee's losses, according to an estimate which is considered on high authority to be " conservative ", totalled 31,800, or 46 per cent. of the original force of priceless veterans he had commanded in April. The other forces, set free to assist Lee by the failures of Butler and Sigel, may be considered as reducing the net loss to about 20,000 or 29 per cent., but a Confederate killed, wounded, or captured was a unit in the sum of losses, from wherever he came, inflicted by Grant as director of the whole war. A comparison of this percentage of losses in the Army of Northern Virginia shows that Grant's method produced material results in excess of those obtained by his many predecessors, and these material results were the more efficacious as the Confederates could no longer replace their fallen soldiers by others.

The Union army, on the other side, had lost about 50,000 men—an appalling aggregate that has passed into history as the classical example of a reckless interpretation of the phrase "at all costs". It represents, however, not more than 41 per cent. of the army that crossed the Rapidan on May 4. If we count in the reinforcements joining the army prior to June 12, the net losses shrink to the insignificant figure of 14,000—even this including 10,000 sick. After many more months of battles and losses, the Army of the Potomac (March 31, 1865) was only some 12,000 men weaker than it had been on April 31, 1864, and even then the resources of the North were not at an end.

But, to touch for the last time on a question of moral, although on the percentage of losses the South suffered more severely than her adversary, although, even without its reinforcements, the

Army of the Potomac was still, on June 12, stronger than the Army of Northern Virginia, both sides were spellbound by the idea of 50,000 men dead and wounded, and history has faithfully reflected current opinion.

Yet this idea, the moral and physical depression of the defeated army, and the political crisis after Cold Harbor—of which we know but little save that the Northern government was within an ace of making peace on what terms it could obtain— even these did not suffice to crush the personality of the truly great soldier. On the contrary, he imposed upon the worn-out army and the harassed government a new and brilliant effort.

Optimism, so-called, never justified itself more remarkably in the history of wars and armies. To Grant, the optimist of supreme moral strength and supreme "faith in success", Cold Harbor was not a death-blow but a mistake to be repaired.

APPENDIX

ARMY OF THE POTOMAC

Maj.-General G. G. Meade, Commanding; Maj.-General A. A. Humphreys, Chief of Staff; Brig.-General H. J. Hunt, Chief of Artillery; Brig.-General Rufus Ingalls, Chief Quartermaster; Brig.-General Seth Williams, Assistant Adjutant-General.

II. Corps:—Maj.-General W. S. Hancock.
- 1st Division, Brig.-General F. C. Barlow.
- 2nd Division, Brig.-General John Gibbon.
- 3rd Division, Maj.-General D. B. Birney.
- 4th Division, Brig.-General G. Mott (discontinued May 14).
- 4th (Heavy Artillery) Division, Brig.-General Tyler (from May 16, discontinued May 26).

V. Corps:—Maj.-General G. K. Warren.
- 1st Division, Brig.-General C. Griffin.
- 2nd Division, Brig.-General J. C. Robinson (broken up May 9, re-established under Brig.-General H. H. Lockwood May 30, and again broken up June 1).
- 3rd Division, Brig.-General S. W. Crawford.
- 4th Division, Brig.-General J. S. Wadsworth (May 6, Brig.-General L. Cutler.)

VI. Corps:—Maj.-General John Sedgwick (May 9, Maj.-General H. G. Wright).
- 1st Division, Brig.-General H. G. Wright (May 9, Brig.-General D. A. Russell).
- 2nd Division, Brig.-General G. W. Getty (May 6, Brig.-General F. Wheaton; May 11, Brig.-General T. H. Neill).

APPENDIX

3rd Division, Brig.-General J. B. Ricketts.
Cavalry Corps:—Maj.-General P. H. Sheridan.
    1st Division, Brig.-General A. T. A. Torbert (May 8, Brig.-General W. Merritt; May 25, Brig.-General A. T. A. Torbert).
    2nd Division, Brig.-General D. McM. Gregg.
    3rd Division, Brig.-General J. H. Wilson.
IX. Corps:—Maj.-General A. E. Burnside.
    Chief of Staff, Maj.-General J. G. Parke.
    1st Division, Brig.-General T. G. Stevenson (May 11, Col. D. Leasure; May 12, Maj.-General T. L. Crittenden).
    2nd Division, Brig.-General R. B. Potter.
    3rd Division, Brig.-General O. B. Willcox.
    4th (Coloured) Division, Brig.-General E. Ferrero.

ARMY OF NORTHERN VIRGINIA

General R. E. Lee, Commanding.
First or Longstreet's Corps:—Lieut.-General J. Longstreet (Maj.-General R. H. Anderson from May 7).
    Pickett's Division, Maj.-General G. E. Pickett (joined the army on May 20-21).
    Field's Division, Maj.-General C. W. Field.
    Kershaw's Division, Maj.-General J. B. Kershaw.
Second or Ewell's Corps:—Lieut.-General R. S. Ewell (May 25, Maj.-General J. A. Early).
    Early's Division, Maj.-General J. A. Early (May 8-21, Brig.-General J. B. Gordon; May 21-25, Maj.-General J. A. Early; from May 25, Maj.-General S. D. Ramseur).
    Rodes's Division, Maj.-General R. E. Rodes.
    Johnson's Division, Maj.-General Edward Johnson (destroyed in the battle of May 12, and reformed with other commands as
    Gordon's Division, Maj.-General J. B. Gordon).
Third or Hill's Corps:—Lieut.-General A. P. Hill (May 7-20, Maj.-General J. A. Early).

Anderson's Division, Maj.-General R. H. Anderson (May 7, Brig.-General W. Mahone).
Heth's Division, Maj.-General H. Heth.
Wilcox's Division, Maj.-General C. M. Wilcox.

Cavalry Corps : Maj.-General J. E. B. Stuart (succeeded by Maj.-General Wade Hampton).
Hampton's Division, Maj.-General Wade Hampton (succeeded by Maj.-General M. C. Butler).
Fitzhugh Lee's Division, Maj.-General Fitzhugh Lee.
(W. H. F. Lee's Division, Maj.-General W. H. F. Lee.)

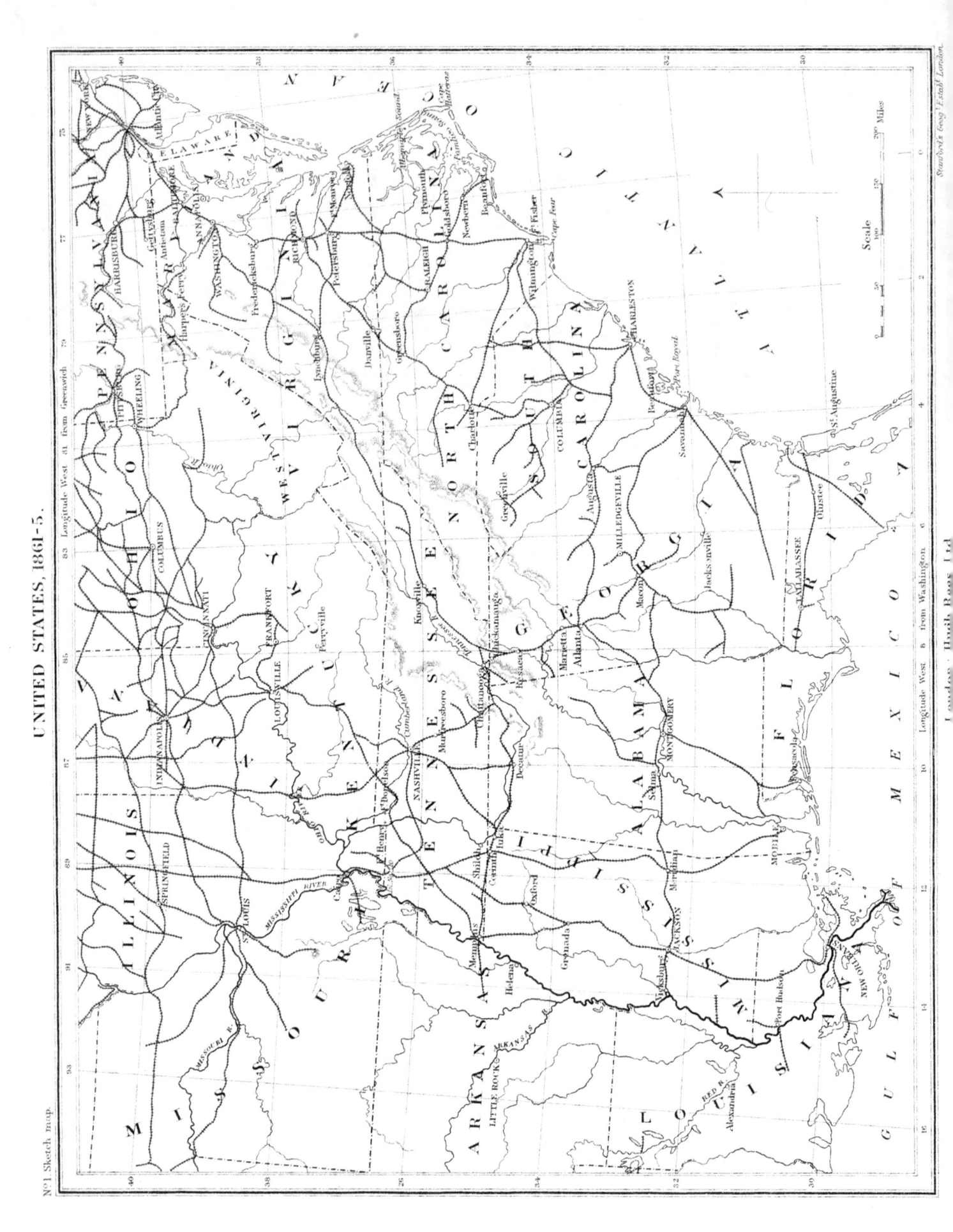

No. 1 Sketch map. UNITED STATES, 1861-5.

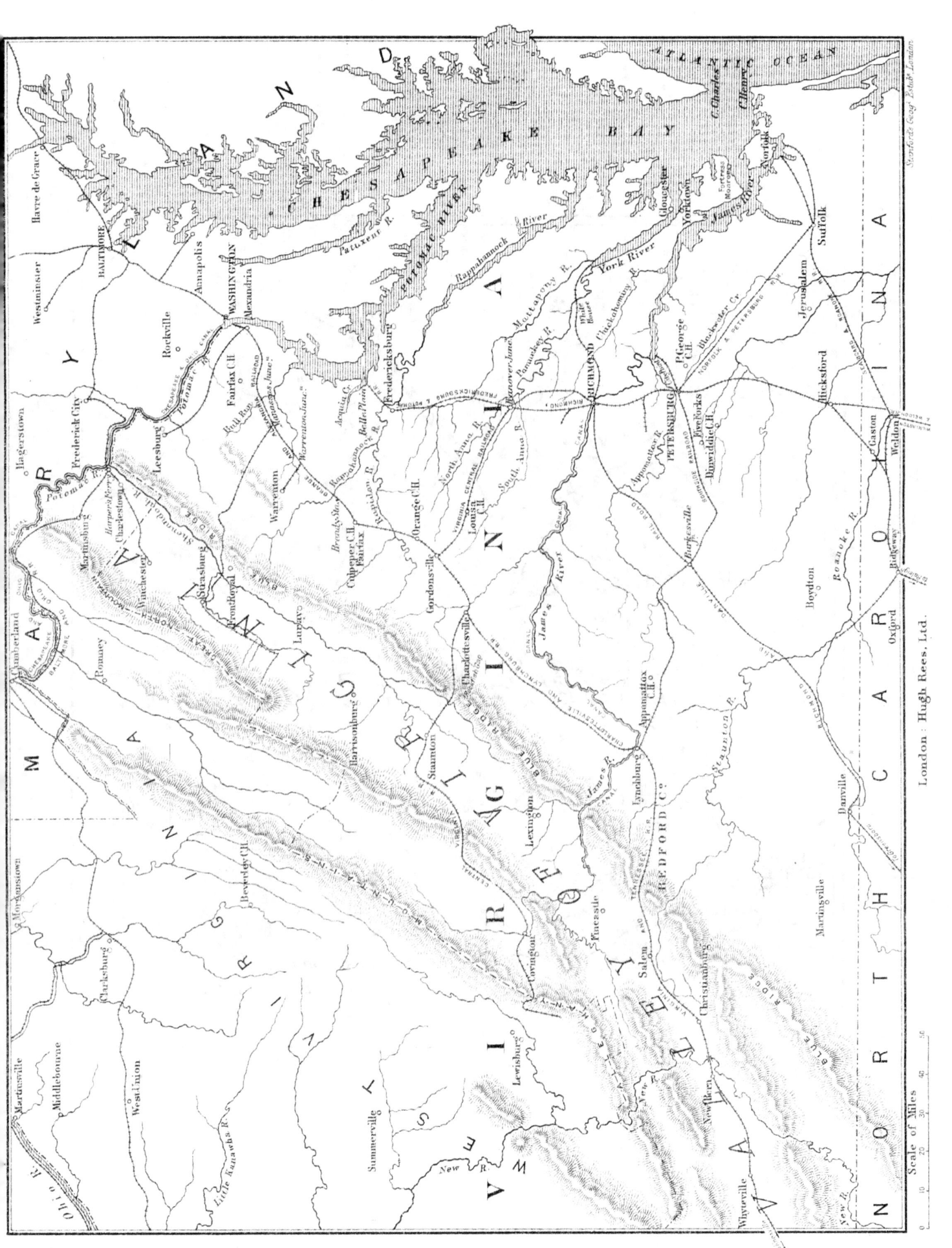

Sketch Map 3.

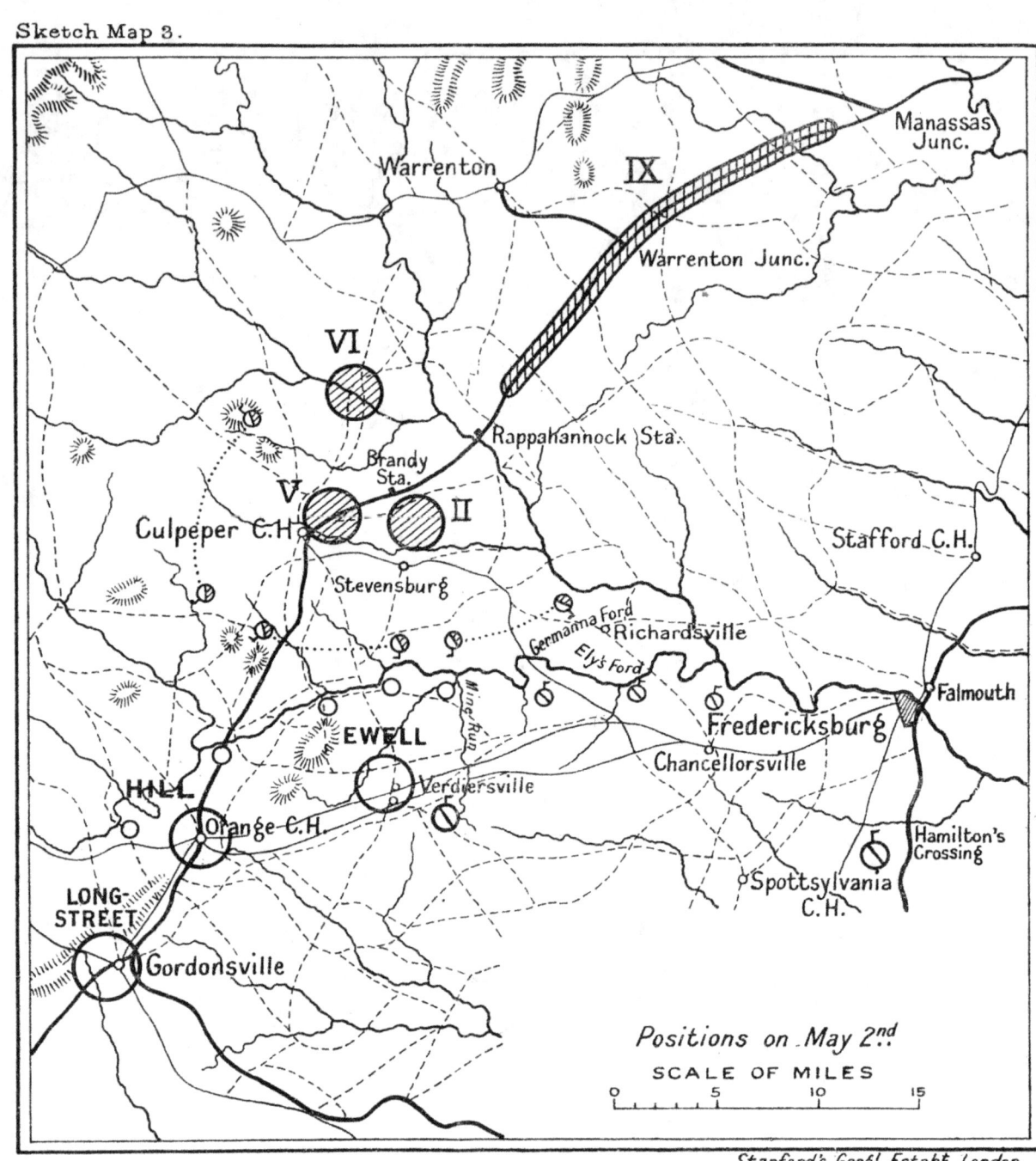

Positions on May 2nd

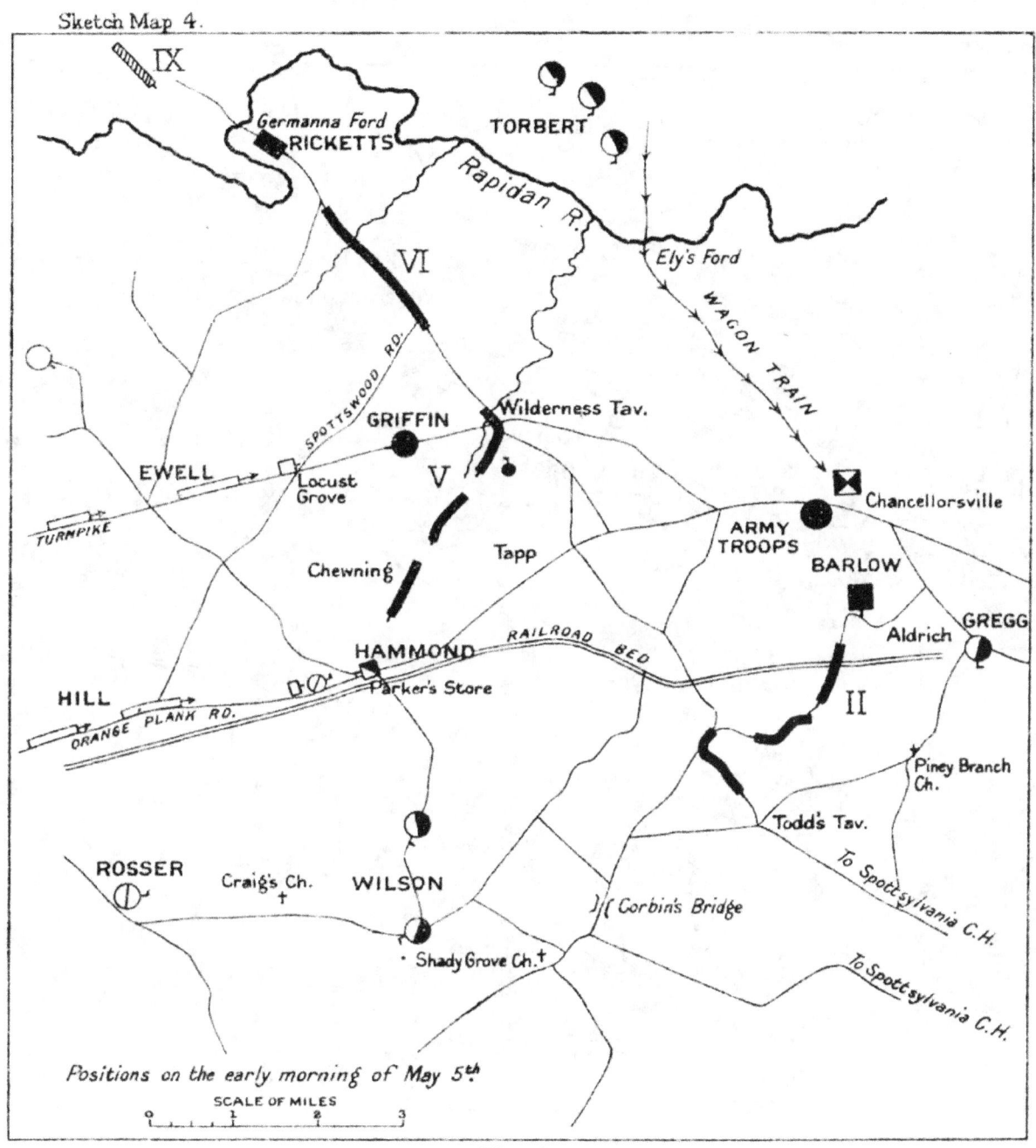

Sketch Map 5.

THE WILDERNESS
MAY 5TH
Approximate Union positions at 12 noon.

SCALE 0 — ½ — 1 MILE

- Union
- Confederate

London: Hugh Rees, Ltd. Stanford's Geogl Estabt, London.

Sketch Map 6.

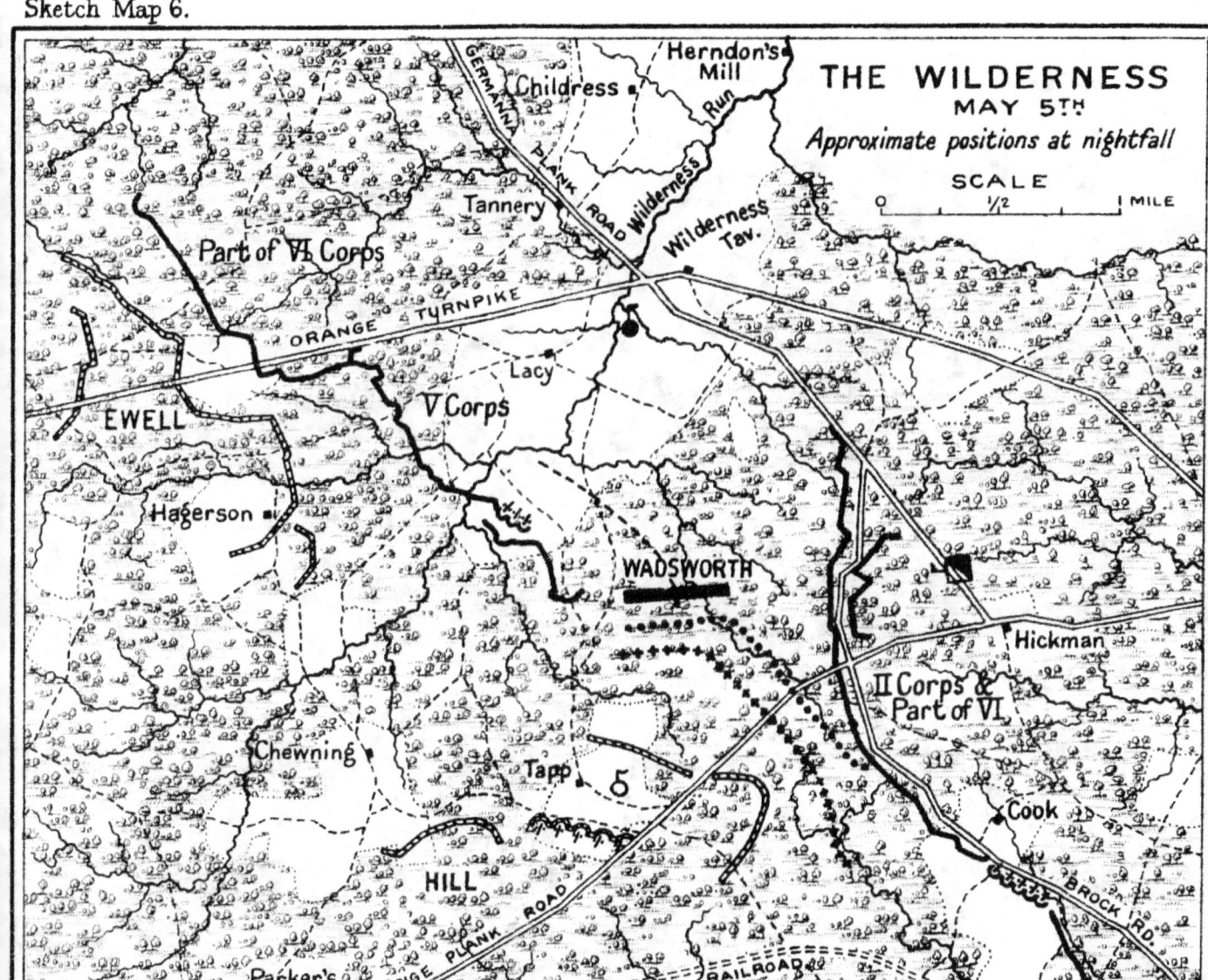

Sketch Map 7.

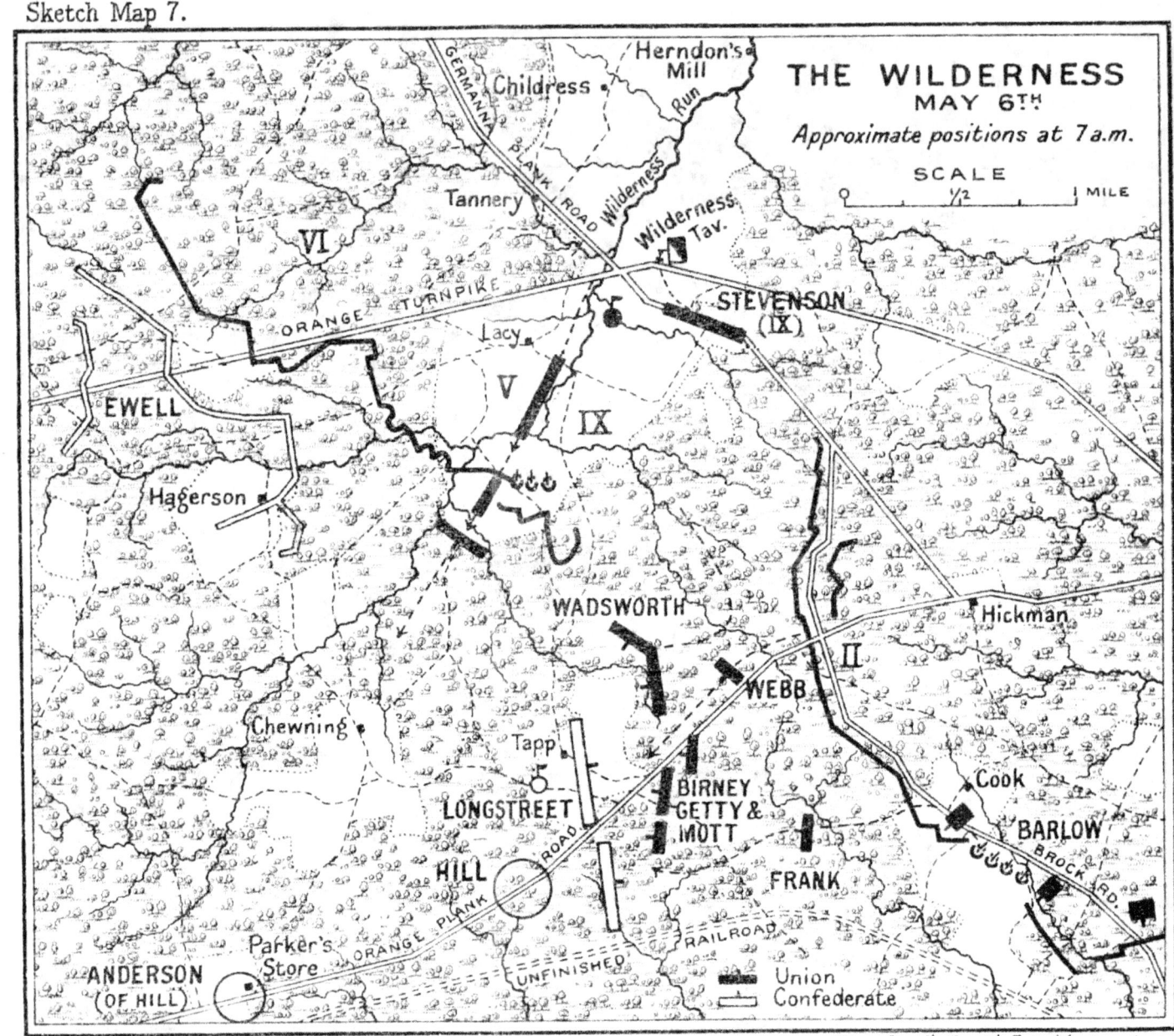

Sketch Map 8.

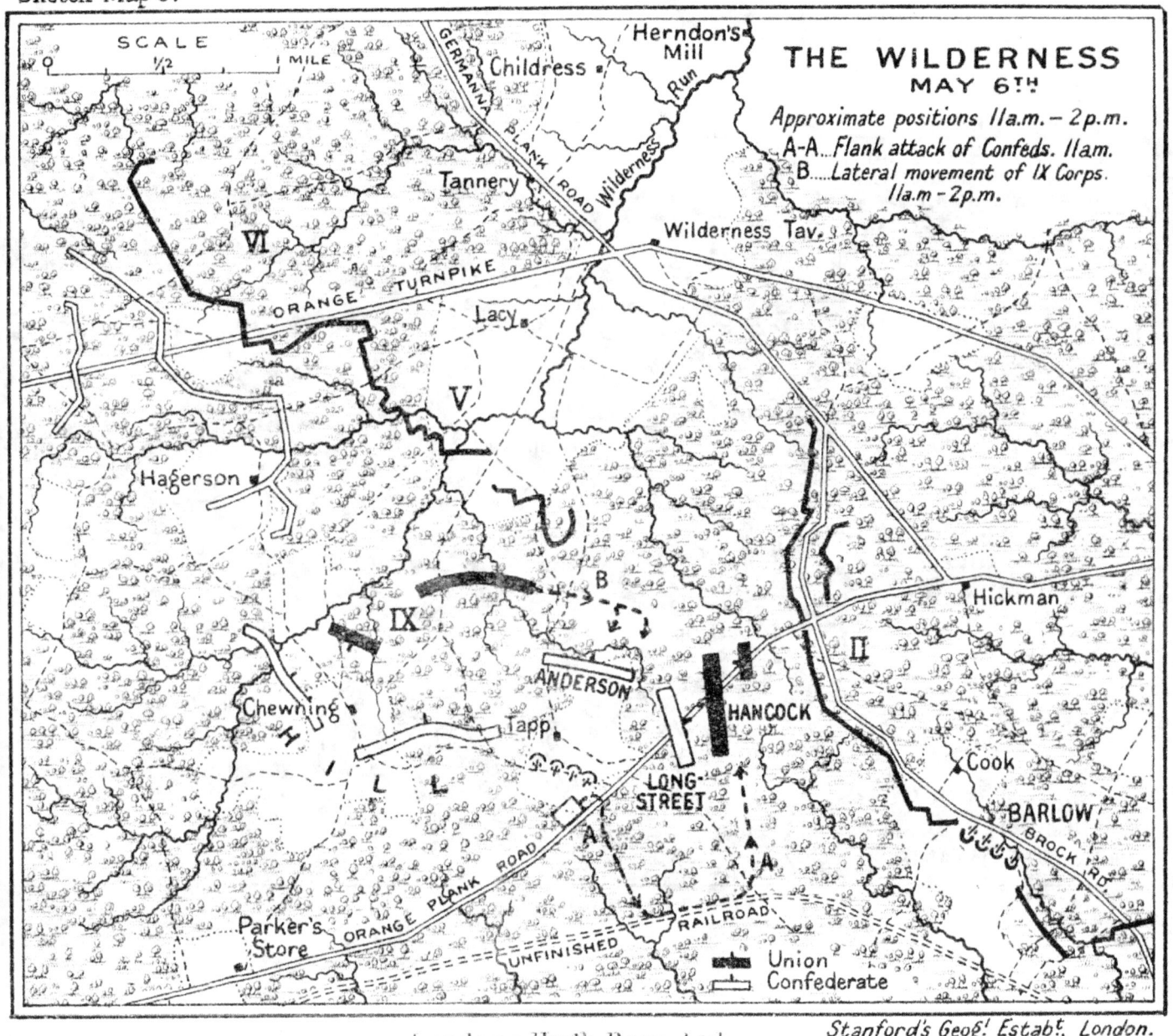

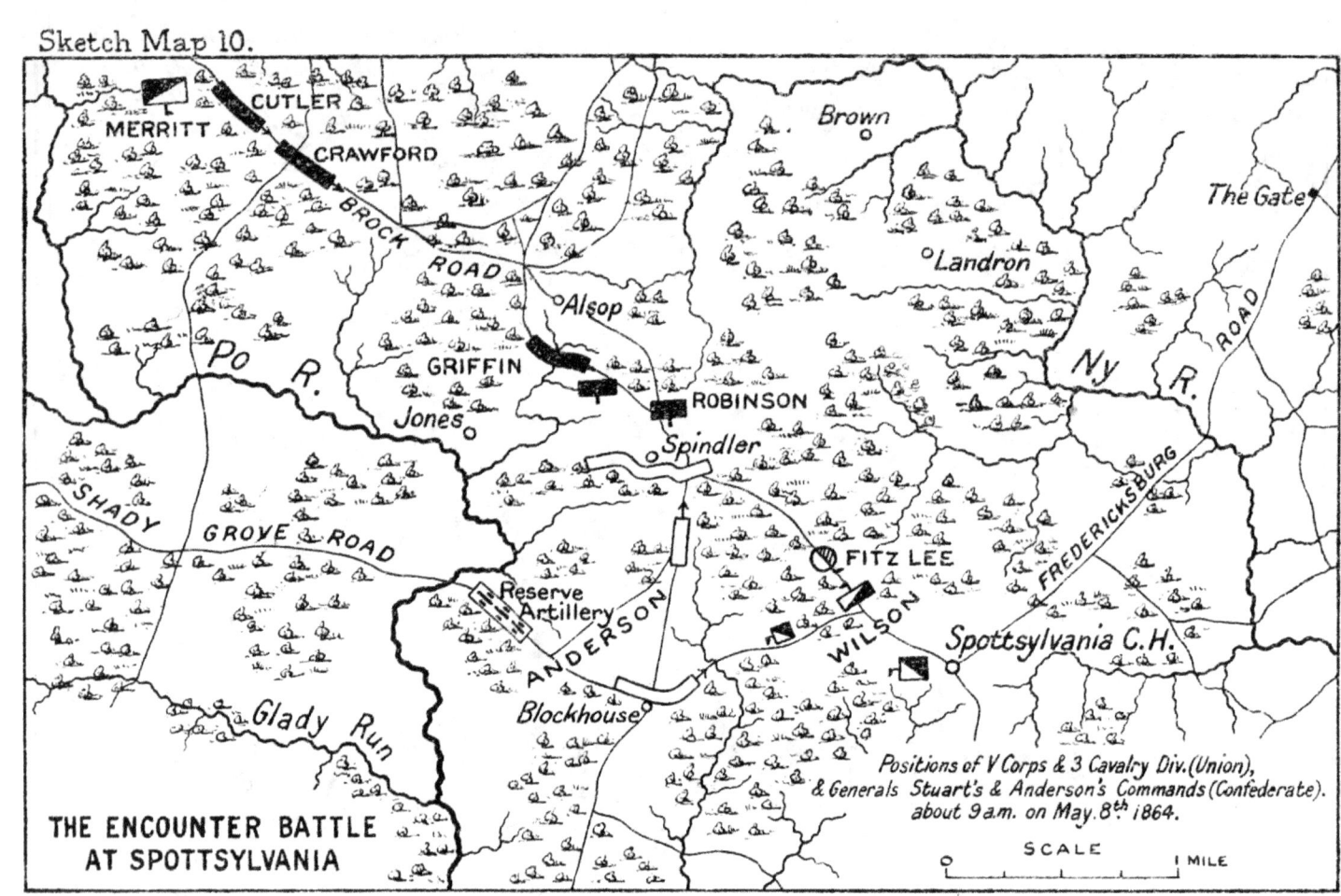

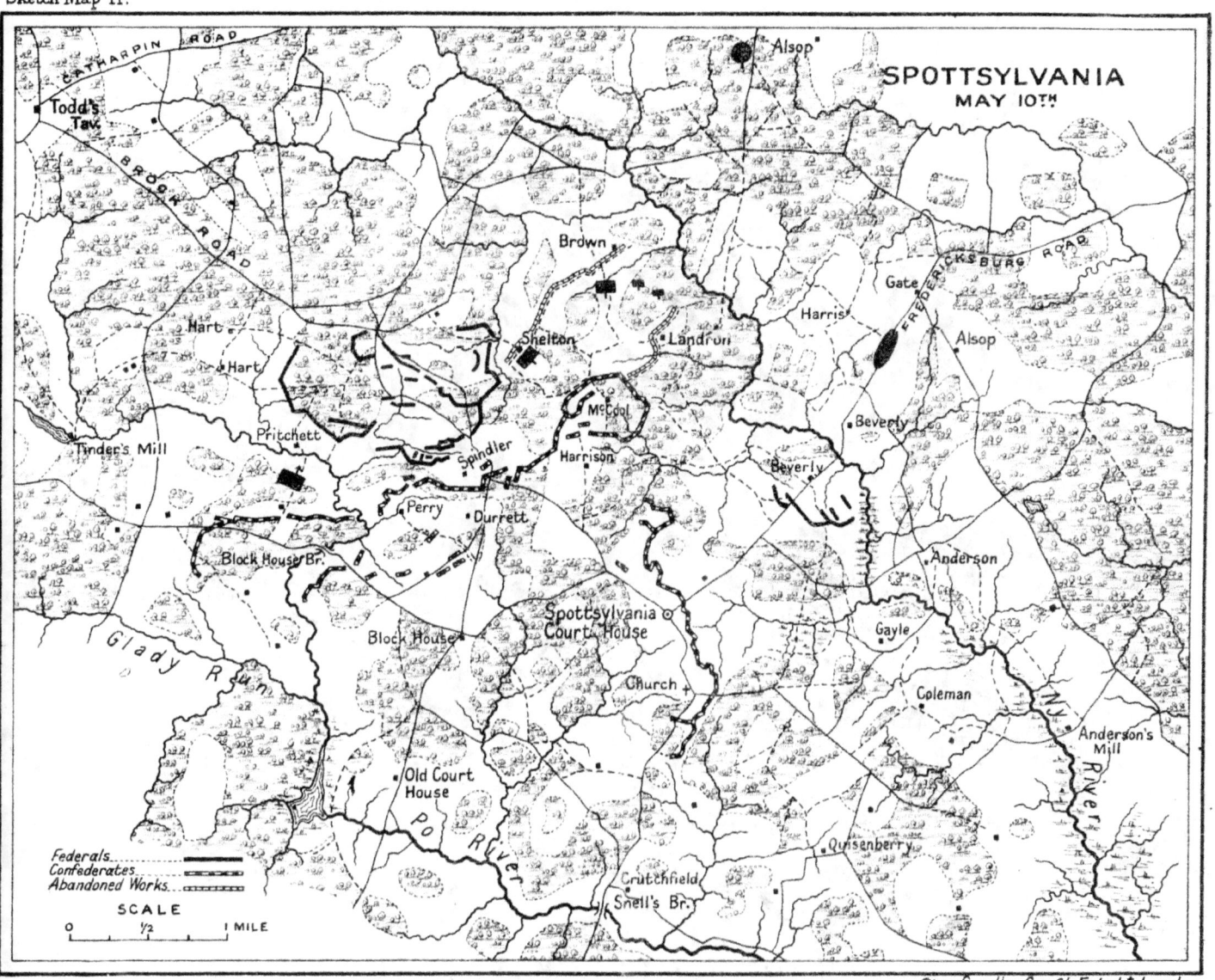

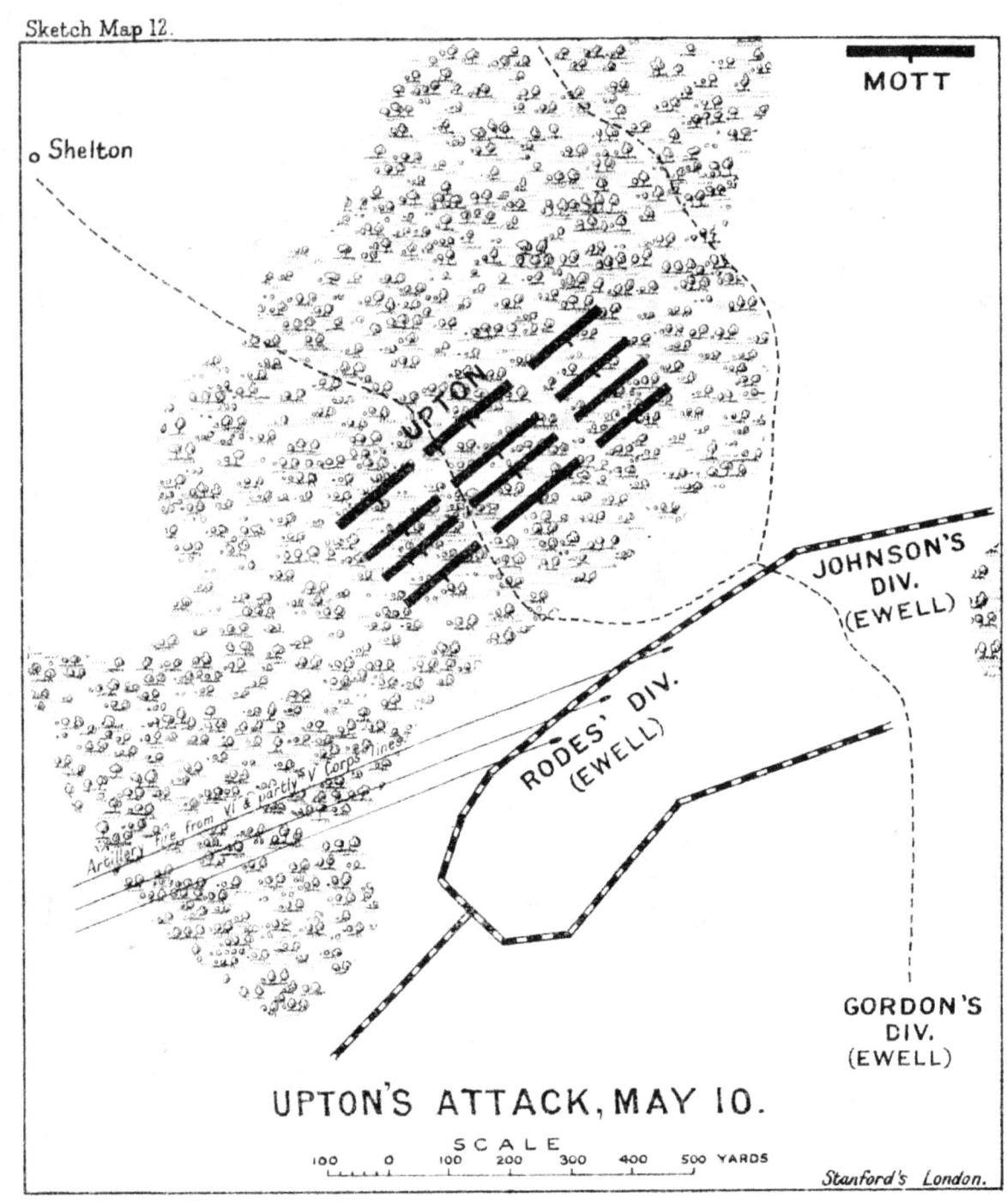

Sketch Map 14.

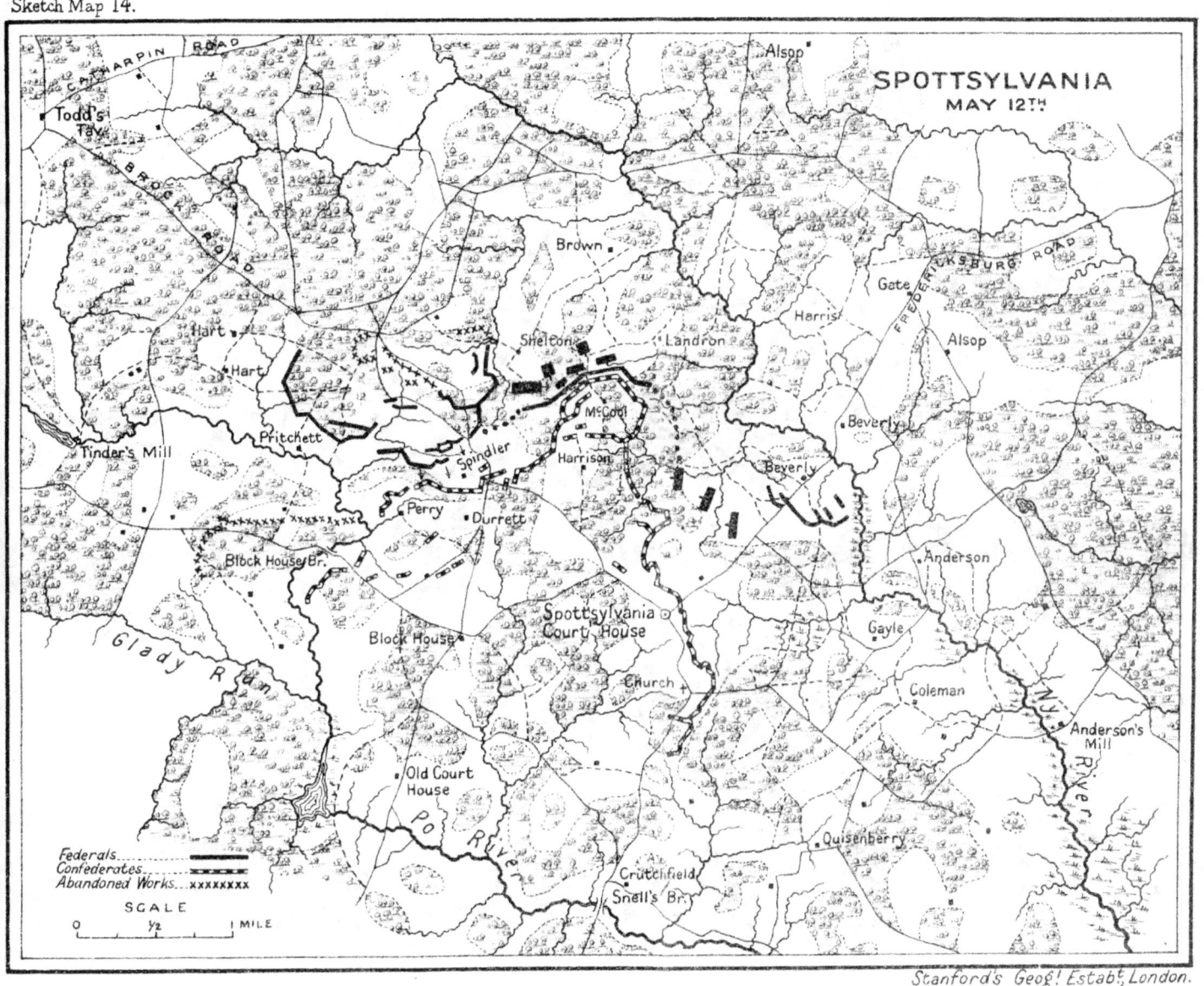

Sketch Map 15.

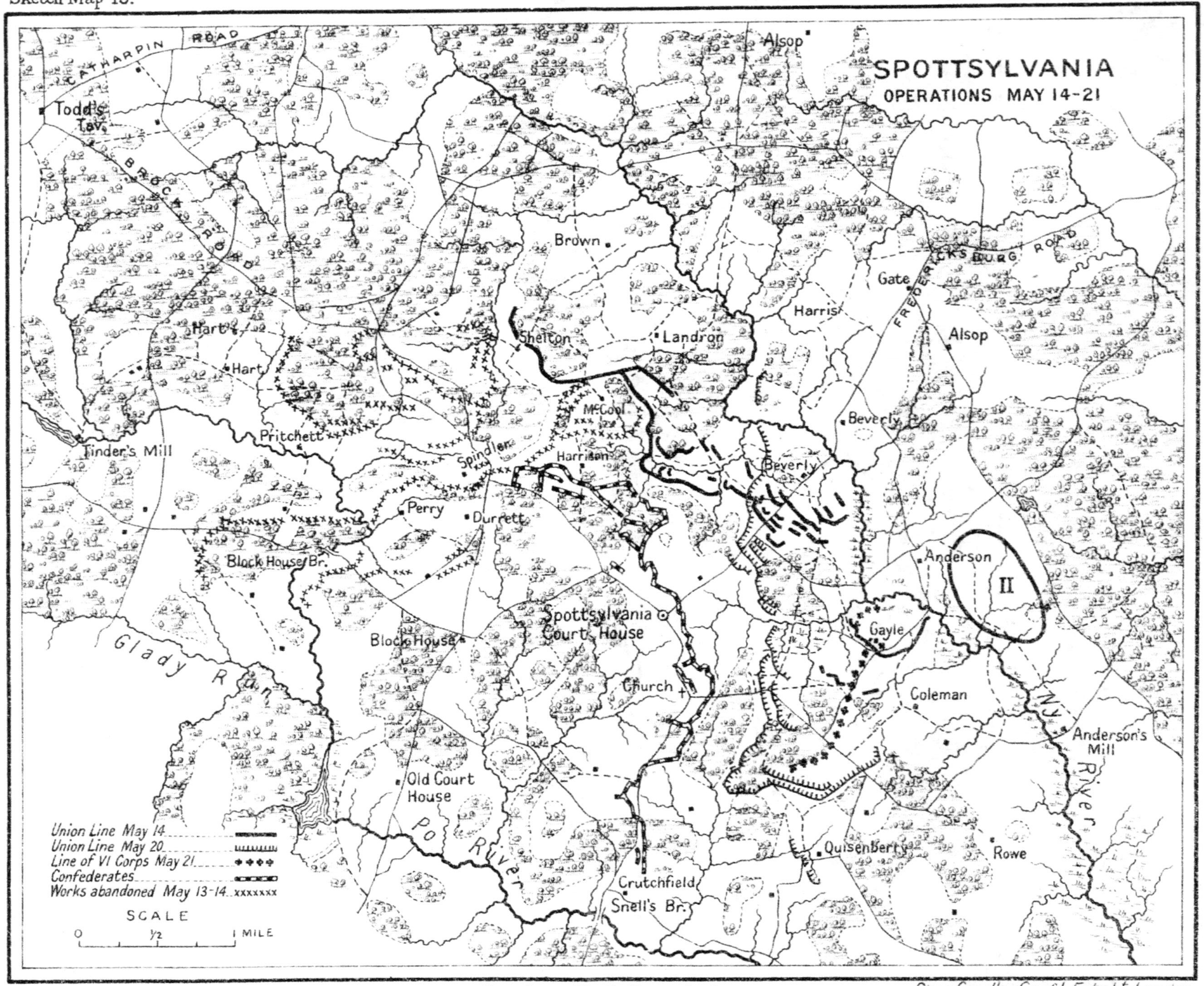

SPOTTSYLVANIA
OPERATIONS MAY 14–21

Union Line May 14
Union Line May 20
Line of VI Corps May 21
Confederates
Works abandoned May 13–14

SCALE
0   ½   1 MILE

London: Hugh Rees, Ltd.
Stanford's Geogl. Estabt., London.

Sketch Map 16.

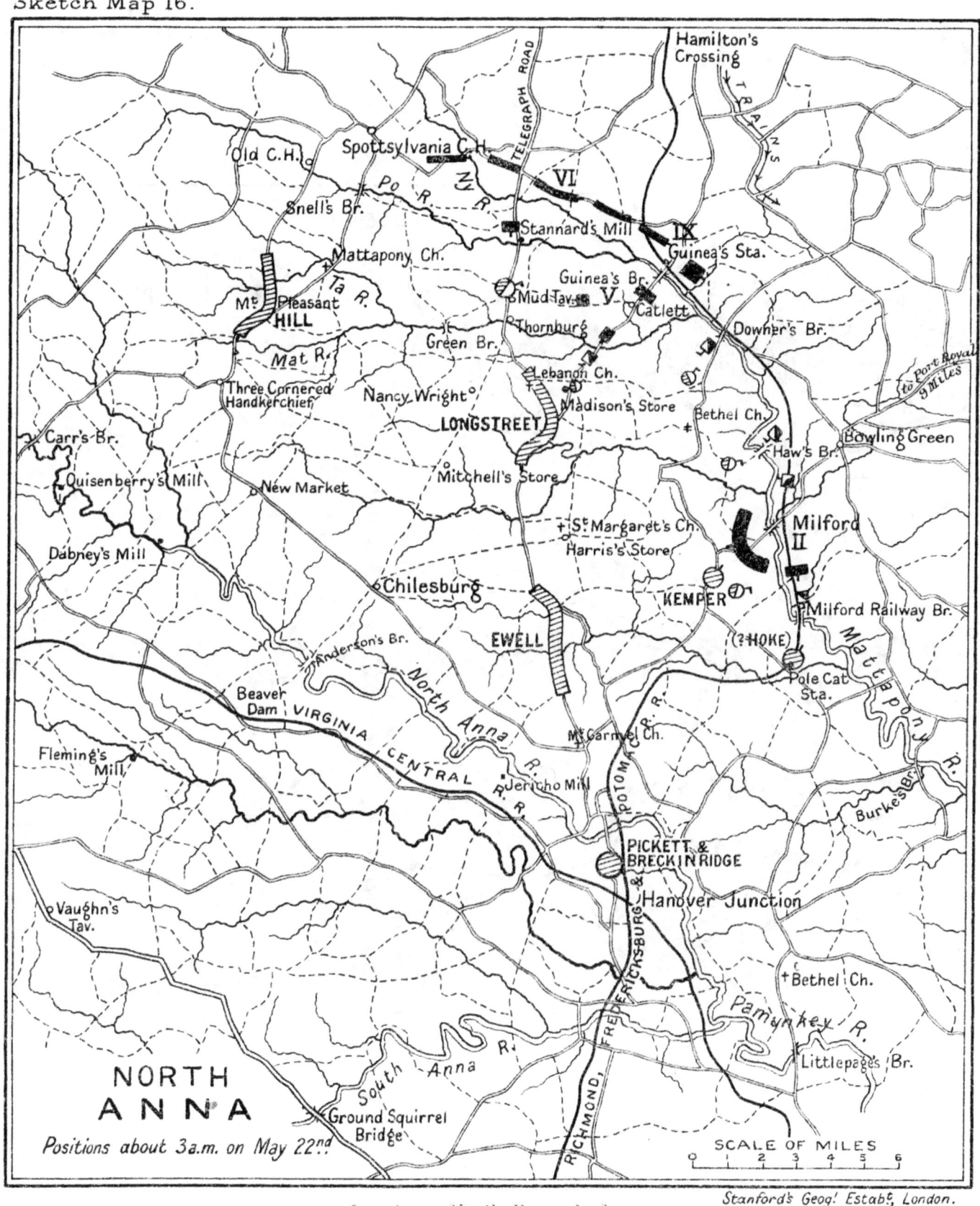

NORTH ANNA
Positions about 3 a.m. on May 22nd

London: Hugh Rees, Ltd.

Stanford's Geogl Establt, London.

Sketch Map 17.

NORTH ANNA

SCALE
0   1/4   1/2   3/4   1 MILE

⌒⌒⌒ *Union Works*
⌒⌒⌒ *Confederate Works*
x *Redoubt captured by II Corps*

Sketch Map 18.

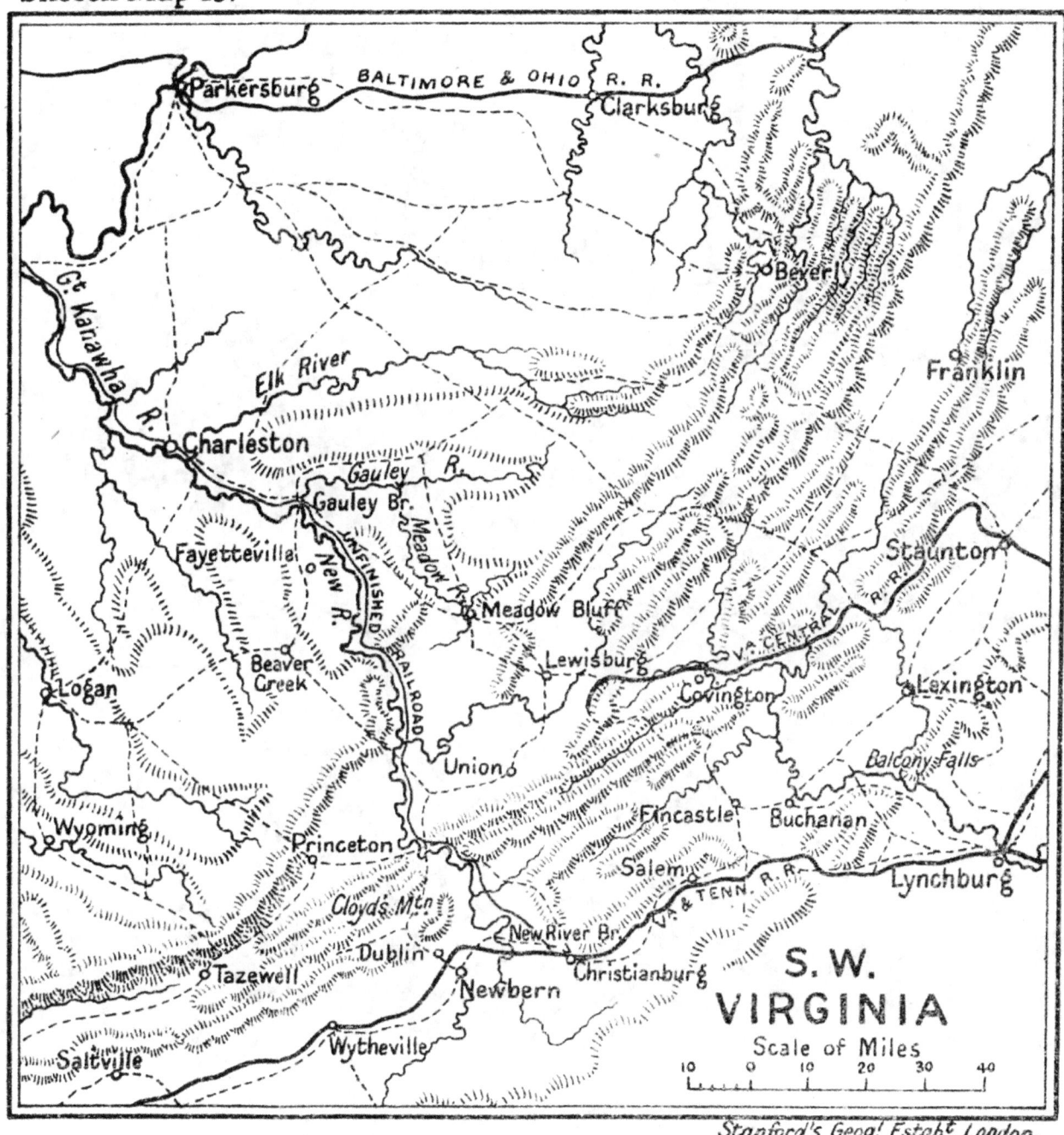

Sketch Map 19

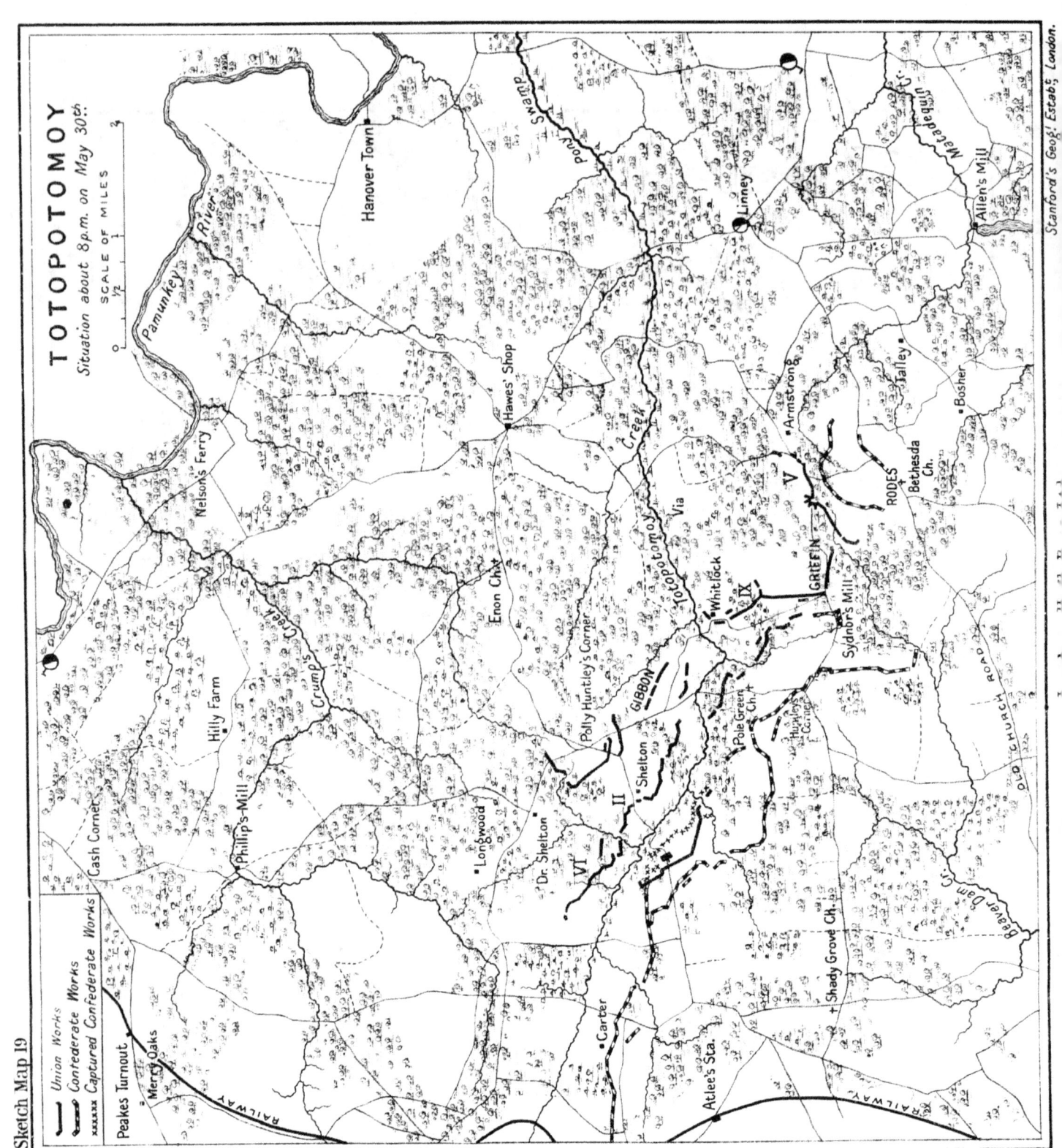

Sketch Map 20

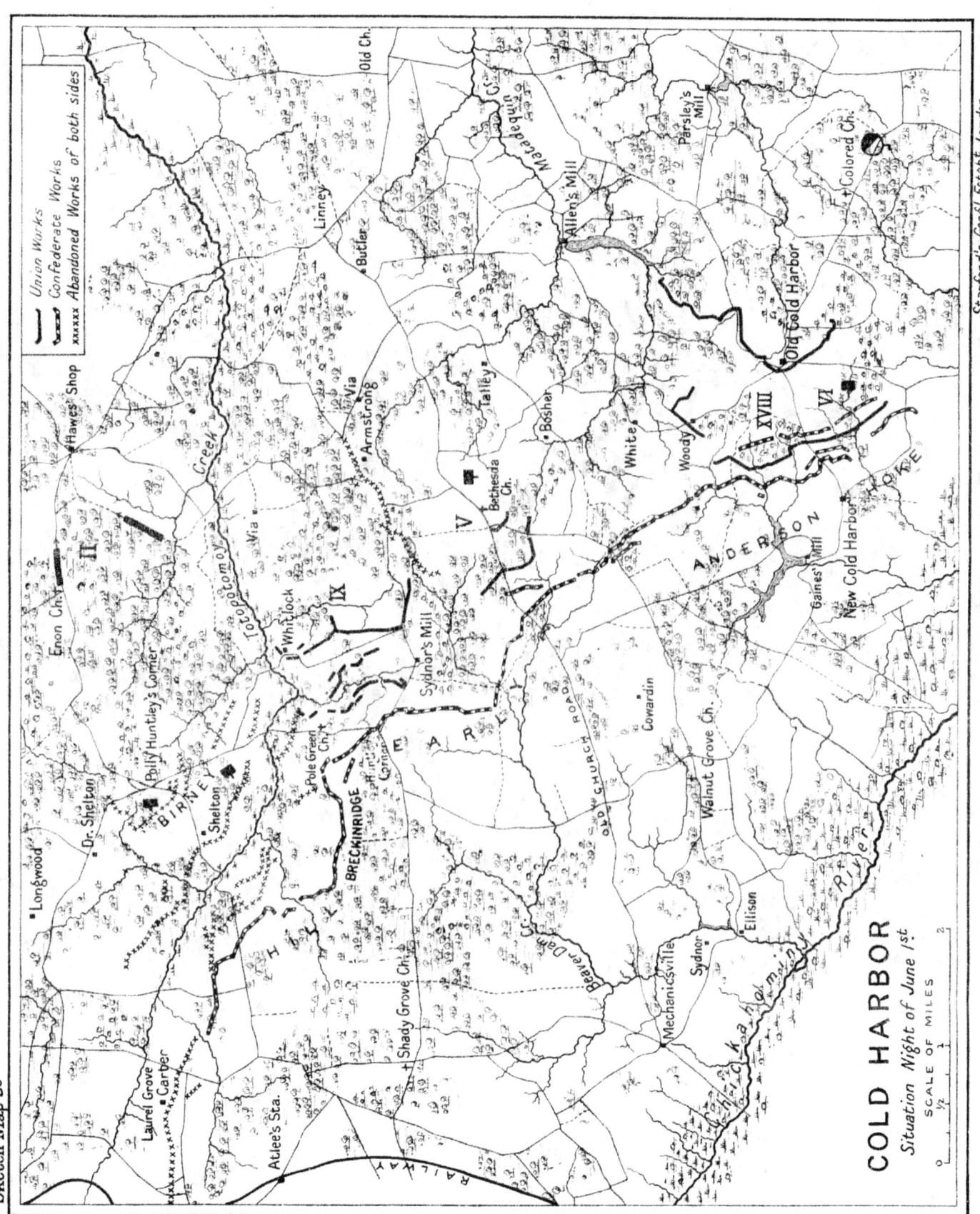

Sketch Map 21.

ATTACK OF THE
II, VI & XVIII CORPS
AT COLD HARBOR
JUNE 3RD 1864

AAA Confederate advanced works captured.
Union ....
Confed. Entrenchments ====

London: Hugh Rees, Ltd.   Stanford's Geogl. Establt, London.

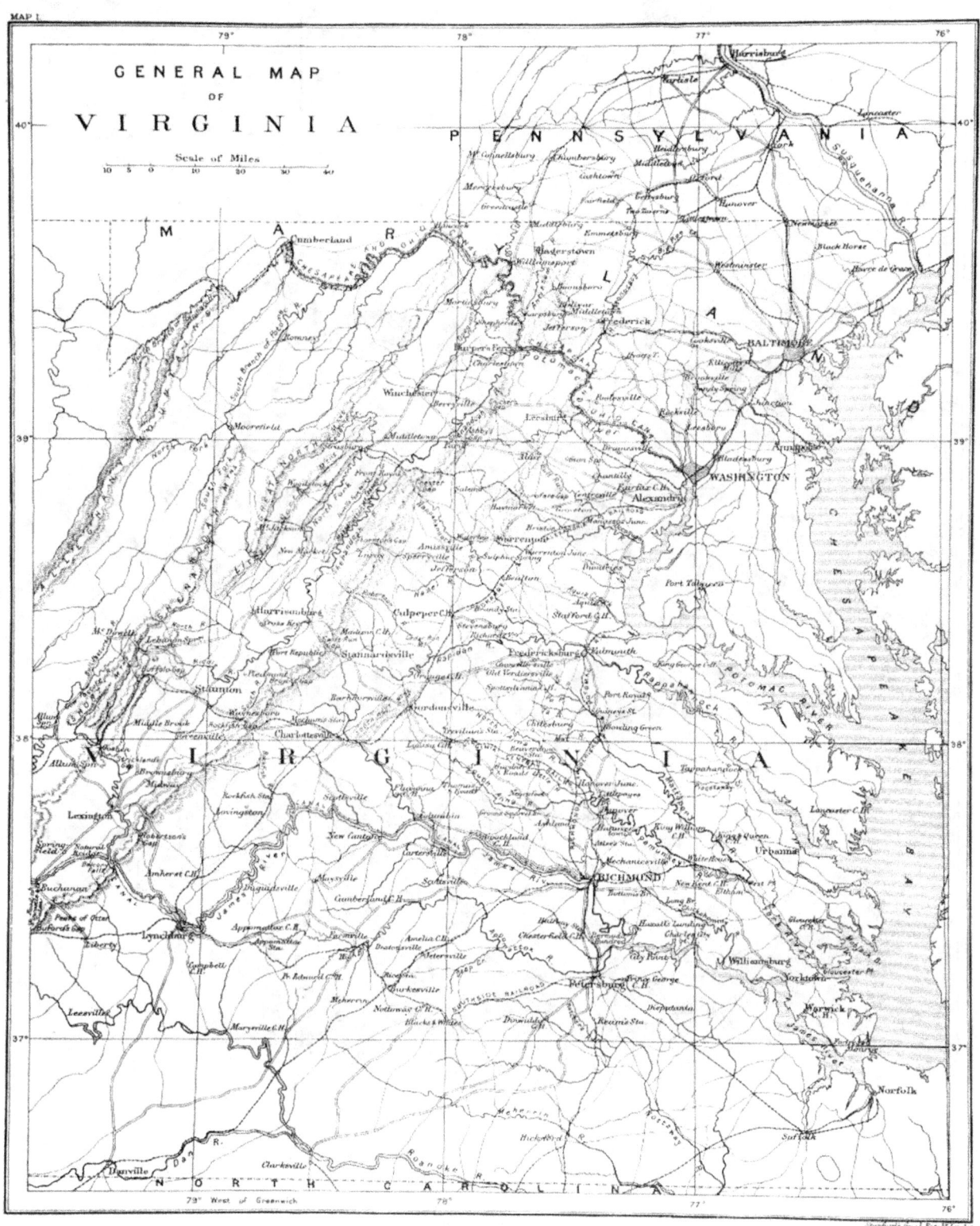

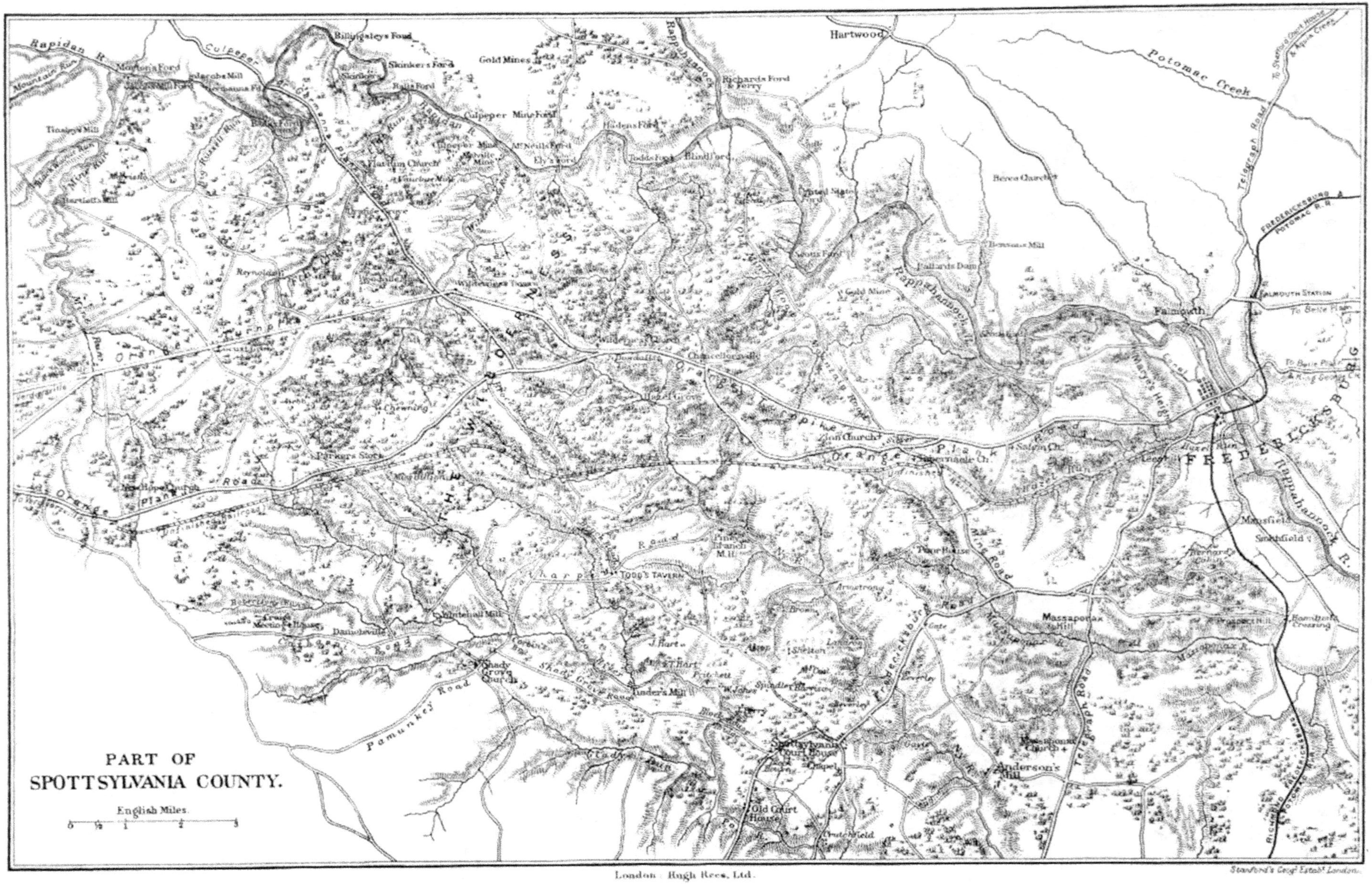

MAP II

PART OF SPOTTSYLVANIA COUNTY.

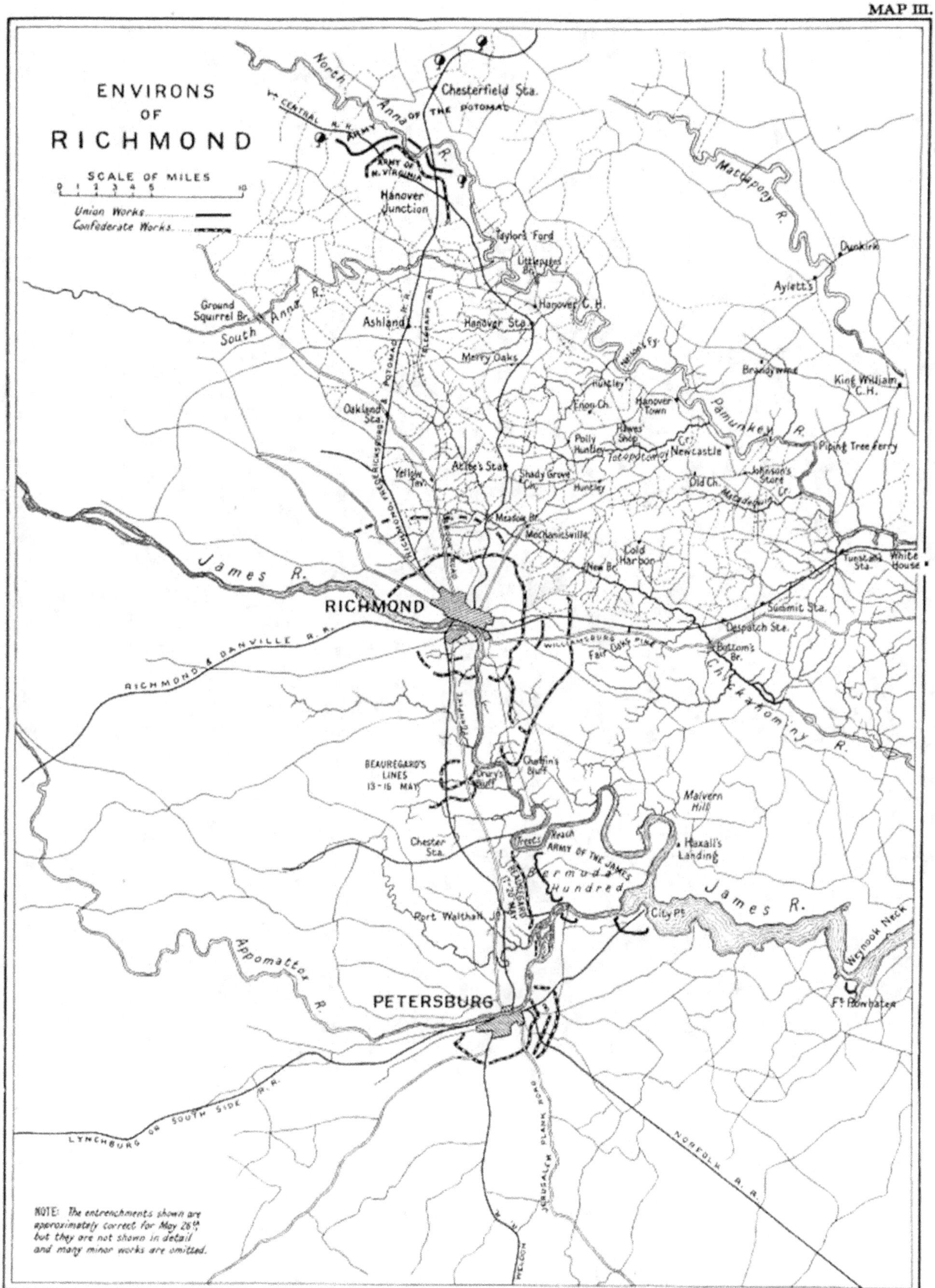

MAP III.

ENVIRONS OF RICHMOND

SCALE OF MILES
0 1 2 3 4 5 10

Union Works ————
Confederate Works - - - - -

NOTE: The entrenchments shown are approximately correct for May 28th but they are not shown in detail and many minor works are omitted.

London Hugh Rees, Ltd.   Stanford's Geogl. Estabt. London.

www.ingramcontent.com/pod-product-compliance
Lightning Source LLC
Chambersburg PA
CBHW080847010526
44114CB00018B/2390